TEMPORALITIES IN MESOAMERICAN RITUAL PRACTICES

TEMPORALITIES IN MESOAMERICAN RITUAL PRACTICES

EDITED BY

Valentina Vapnarsky, Dominique Michelet,
Aurore Monod Becquelin, and Philippe Nondédéo

UNIVERSITY PRESS OF COLORADO
Denver

Published by University Press of Colorado
1580 North Logan Street, Suite 660, PMB 39883
Denver, Colorado 80203-1942

The University Press of Colorado is a proud member of
Association of University Presses.

The University Press of Colorado is a cooperative publishing enterprise supported, in part, by Adams State University, Colorado School of Mines, Colorado State University, Fort Lewis College, Metropolitan State University of Denver, University of Alaska Fairbanks, University of Colorado, University of Denver, University of Northern Colorado, University of Wyoming, Utah State University, and Western Colorado University.

ISBN: 978-1-64642-680-5 (hardcover)
ISBN: 978-1-64642-681-2 (paperback)
ISBN: 978-1-64642-682-9 (ebook)
https://doi.org/10.5876/9781646426829

Library of Congress Cataloging-in-Publication Data

Names: Vapnarsky, Valentina, editor. | Michelet, Dominique, editor. | Monod-Becquelin, Aurore editor. | Nondédéo, Philippe, editor.
Title: Temporalities in Mesoamerican ritual practices / edited by Valentina Vapnarsky, Dominique Michelet, Aurore Monod Becquelin, and Philippe Nondédéo.
Description: Denver : University Press of Colorado, [2024] | Includes bibliographical references and index.
Identifiers: LCCN 2024056849 (print) | LCCN 2024056850 (ebook) | ISBN 9781646426805 (hardcover) | ISBN 9781646426812 (paperback) | ISBN 9781646426829 (ebook)
Subjects: LCSH: Indians of Mexico—Rites and ceremonies. | Indians of Central America—Rites and ceremonies. | Mayas—Rites and ceremonies. | Aztecs—Rites and ceremonies. | Time—Social aspects—Mexico. | Time—Social aspects—Central America.
Classification: LCC F1219.3.R56 T46 2024 (print) | LCC F1219.3.R56 (ebook) | DDC 299.7/92—dc23/eng/20250124
LC record available at https://lccn.loc.gov/2024056849
LC ebook record available at https://lccn.loc.gov/2024056850

This book will be made open access within three years of publication thanks to Path to Open, a program developed in partnership between JSTOR, the American Council of Learned Societies (ACLS), University of Michigan Press, and The University of North Carolina Press to bring about equitable access and impact for the entire scholarly community, including authors, researchers, libraries, and university presses around the world. Learn more at https://about.jstor.org/path-to-open/.

Published with the support of the Centre National de la Recherche Scientifique, Institut des Sciences Humaines et Sociales, France: International Research Network "Ritual Actions and Time: Creation, Destruction, Transformation in Past and Present Mesoamerica."

Cover photograph: Burning of copal resin in front of ancestor artifacts during a Q'eqchi' ritual in the Guatemalan lowlands, 2022. © Romain Denimal Labeguerie

Contents

Figures

Tables

Acknowledgments

This volume is a product of an International Research Network (IRN),[1] Ritual Actions and Time: Creation, Destruction, Transformation in Past and Present Mesoamerica, funded by the French Centre National de la Recherche Scientifique (CNRS), involving collaboration by the Université de Paris Nanterre; the Université de Paris Panthéon-Sorbonne; the Centro de Estudios Mayas, Instituto de Investigaciones Filológicas, Universidad Nacional Autónoma de México; the Centro de Investigaciones y Estudios Superiores en Antropología Social, Mexico; the University of California, Berkeley; the University of Texas, Austin; the Rheinische Friedrich-Wilhelms Universität, Bonn; the Università degli Studi di Napoli Lorientale; and la Sapienza, Università di Roma.

Preliminary versions of the chapters were presented at the international closing conference Ritual Temporalities in Mesoamerica—Interdisciplinary Approaches, organized in Paris, November 14–16, 2018, under the auspices of the Académie des Inscriptions et Belles-Lettres and with support of the Fondation Simone et Cino Del Duca, at the Hôtel Pereire of the Fondation and at the Palais de l'Institut de France. The editors and contributors gratefully acknowledge the support of the CNRS, the Académie des Inscriptions et Belles-Lettres, and the Fondation Simone et Cino Del Duca.

They are also grateful to the two anonymous reviewers of the manuscript for their stimulating suggestions.

---

1 Formerly known as Groupe de Recherche International (GDRI).

TEMPORALITIES IN MESOAMERICAN RITUAL PRACTICES

I

Temporalities in Mesoamerican Ritual Practices

An Introduction

VALENTINA VAPNARSKY, DOMINIQUE MICHELET,
AND AURORE MONOD BECQUELIN

Adopting a multidisciplinary approach (in archaeology, ethnohistory, anthropology, and linguistic anthropology), the present book examines the temporal dimensions of ritual activities in past and present Mesoamerican societies, including pre-Hispanic, colonial, and modern times. The chapters engage empirically and theoretically with the multiple temporalities of ritual, in relation both to the unfolding of ritual performance and to its external and symbolic anchors. Each chapter presents new analysis of fieldwork data relative to the meaning and pragmatics of artifactual, gestural, discursive, or scriptural temporal patterns, and addresses comparative and theoretical aspects of the diverse facets of ritual temporalities. Rather than following a diachronic or a disciplinary order, the organization of the book aims to encourage interdisciplinary dialogue by highlighting features, patterns, and questions across the disciplines. Chapters are organized in five sections: I. Rhythms in Rituals, II. Ritual Multitemporalities, III. Material and Sensorial Dimensions of Ritual Temporalities, IV. Ritual Temporalities in the Longue Durée, and V. Ritual Temporalities in Confrontation.

The chapters take rituals as a series of specific, formalized actions that, by introducing a scenario that differs from those of everyday life activities, are expected to produce changes—from transitory to definitive—within an initial context. The focus on ritual temporalities calls for processual and pragmatic approaches to the changes aimed at by the ritual and to its relation to the context. Such approaches also engage with the essential fact that the rituals concerned here work with and

https://doi.org/10.5876/9781646426829.c001

on the agencies of human and nonhuman entities, including spirits, deities, souls, ancestors, and (super)natural forces as well as objects and artifacts, and the relationships between them (see also Kreinath, Snoek, and Stausberf 2006 for critical views on ritual definitions and conceptualizations).

A variety of apparently dissimilar rituals are examined that reveal different ways and patterns of generating changes. The rituals are linked to artifact production, life cycles, agricultural work, healing, conflict resolution, crisis management, the enthronement of rulers, and the transfer of responsibilities, or practices related to the occupation, abandonment, reuse, or conversion of socialized spaces. Starting from fundamental actions such as creating, transforming, and destroying, the authors explore rituals as significant cognitive and cultural manifestations of the temporal dimensions of transition processes. This perspective has the advantage of being conducive to the joint exploration of a multiplicity of modes of action used in rites, in particular those stemming from interventions on matter and objects as well as from performativity in gestures and speech.

Numerous studies have concentrated on spatial, personal, social, political, and agentive dimensions of rituality, adopting a symbolic, pragmatic, or cognitive approach. The intention of this volume is to consider the temporal dimensions of rituals, which have been the object of much less thorough attention, leaving aside well-explored questions such as the use of ritual calendars. Building upon previous work carried out by the editors on spatiotemporal boundaries (Monod Becquelin 2012), the pragmatics of temporality (Vapnarsky 2022; Vapnarsky, Pierrebourg, and Michelet 2017; Vapnarsky et al. 2020), and the materialities of ritual (Dussol, Sion, and Nondédéo 2019; Johnson and Joyce 2022; Michelet et al. 2010), the path taken by the book aims at understanding how temporal categories and processes operate in rituals; how they are sociohistorically, culturally, and pragmatically elaborated; and how rituals and temporal categories fundamentally interact. To achieve this, two levels of analysis are favored, and their interconnections are developed: at the performance level, the authors elucidate the internal processual configuration of rituals (action sequences, periods, synchronies and asynchronies, limits, liminalities, etc.); at a sociohistorical level, rituals are examined as markers and driving forces of time and history, from the perspective of how they were and are conceived, organized, and projected by Mesoamerican past and present societies. As an area where time and rituality have been the object of considerable local elaboration, Mesoamerica appears to be a particularly fertile ground for the development of new methodological and theoretical perspectives on ritual temporalities. As a corollary, it is our hope that the reflections on ritual developed in the volume, the similarities but also disparities between cases analyzed here, can contribute to the debate concerning the specificities and the very relevance of Mesoamerica as a cultural

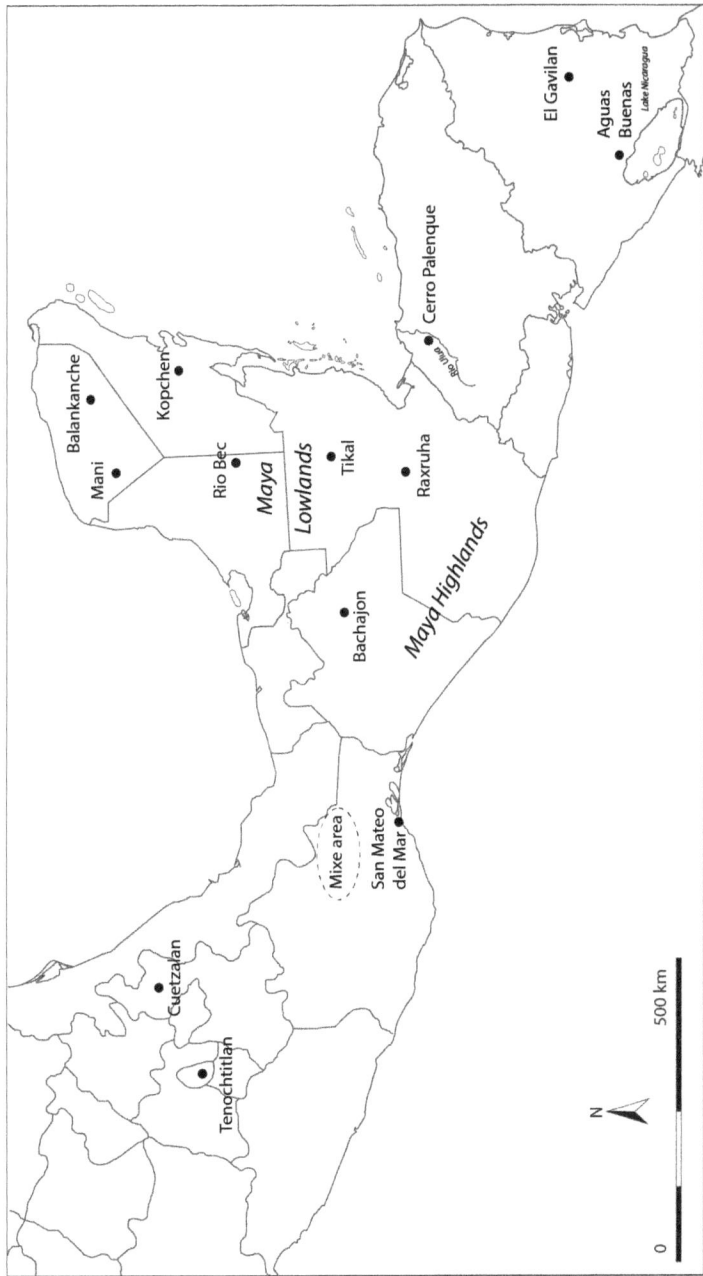

Figure 1.1. Location of places and regions covered in this volume

area, a discussion that cannot be developed in the context of this volume but for which the chapters—including those from Joyce and from Geurds on Central America—provide insightful material.

The authors of this volume are especially mindful of the risk of overdrawing analogies when comparing rituals from distinct and distant periods of time socio-historical contexts and through various phenomenological materialities and methodological disciplinary approaches. The thematic sections of the volume show that the value of multi- and interdisciplinary work lies elsewhere than in analogies.

The book is a result of long-term exchanges between the authors, carried out in particular within the international cross-disciplinary network RITMO (2015–2018), in continuity with the activities of the GERM group of research.[1] It presents the results of collective reflection developed during the project Ritual Actions and Time: Creation, Destruction, Transformation in Past and Present Mesoamerica, and the series of conferences organized in this context.[2] Preliminary versions of the chapters in this book were presented and discussed at the international closing conference organized in Paris in 2018 under the auspices of the Académie des Inscriptions et Belles-Lettres, at the Fondation Simone et Cino del Duca and at the Palais de l'Institut de France. While adopting a more encompassing view and exploring other facets of *temporalities in ritual practices*, the present book offers a further extension of the recent volume *Materializing Ritual Practices* (Johnson and Joyce 2022), which also brings together contributions by members of our network.

RITUAL TIME AND RITUAL TEMPORALITY: A BRIEF CROSS-DISCIPLINARY "STATE OF THE ART"

In archaeology, the analysis of temporalities in rituals is still emerging (see Barrett 1991; Fogelin 2007; Kyriakidis 2007; Rowan 2012; Swenson 2015). Even in a field that was more precocious than others in analyzing sequences of practices, that of funerary practices, it has been hardly forty years since the importance and potential of this research area were recognized, that effective study methods were implemented (Duday et al. 1990; Pereira 2013; Tiesler, Suzuki, and Pereira 2022), and that a social perspective was developed (Renfrew, Boyd, and Morley 2015). In fact, when archaeologists have ventured into the sphere, they have usually done so hoping to either get to the roots of the symbolic and cosmological systems that have a dialectical relationship with rites (see, for example, Rice 2009, 2019), or to explore relations between religions and social structures: for example, the control of religion by political authorities (Baudez 2002; Lucero 2003), or the question of levels of practice, particularly public rituals versus domestic or private ones (Ciudad et al. 2010; Gonlin and Lohse 2007; Plunket 2002). More recently, ritual archaeology has paid closer attention to the material traces left by these acts, contributing to theories on materiality (Geurds this volume; Joyce this volume; see also Howey and O'Shea 2009; Insoll 2009; Johnson and Joyce 2022). Other researchers explore the integration in a historical narrative of the remains of past and abandoned societies (Johnson 2019).

In the pre-Hispanic Mesoamerican world, as elsewhere, the archaeology of ritual has long concentrated on trying to identify sets of objects or assemblages and places that are used for rituals (Gheorghiu and Nash 2013), whether conceived specifically for this purpose or not. In this cultural area, the study of ancient rituals was highly influenced by the existence of rich ethnohistorical sources (López Luján this volume) and the reading of glyphic inscriptions, particularly those from the Classic period in the Maya region (300–900 CE) (Valencia Rivera and Lefort 2006). Some fundamental ritual practices have been subject to rich analyses, such as those relative to human sacrifice (López Luján and Olivier 2010), self-sacrifice (Baudez 2012), the dedication of monuments (Nondédéo et al. 2022; Stuart 1996), or the numerous terminal floor deposits associated with the Classic Maya collapse (Newman 2019; Clayton, Driver, and Kosakowsky 2005).

Yet the central, more specific problem of the relations between rituals and temporalities has itself hardly been touched except for some specific cases, such as rituals seen from an archaeobotanical perspective (Morehart 2017). Certainly, in Mesoamerica the important issues of timekeeping and of the ceremonial, political, and divinatory aspects of calendars have received close attention (see, for example, Alcina Franch 1993; Boone 2007; Edmonson 1988; Olivier 2012, 2022; Pharo 2013; Rice 2009). They are linked to such Mesoamerican fundaments as the cyclical vision of history (Navarrete Linares 2004; Stuart 2012) and the political reference to ancestry (Jansen and Pérez Jiménez 2017). However, due to the narrow definition of ritual practice in archaeology and ethnohistory, which is mostly restricted to the domain of religion, one aspect that has not been examined is the ritual and temporal dimension of production activities as transformation (see, however, Wells and Davis-Salazar 2006). Although the ritual interlinking of destruction and creation with transformation can be glimpsed in several studies (Mock 1998; Newman 2019; Stanton, Brown, and Pagliaro 2008; Walker and Lucero 2000), much work still remains to be done in this area. To address the issue of ritual practices and its temporal dimensions, archaeology could benefit from developing an approach that aims at an ordered reconstruction of gestures, that is, of temporal sequences, in line with the tradition of "behavioral archaeology" (Michelet this volume; Schiffer 1976; Skibo and Schiffer 2008) and of work on *chaînes opératoires*, the technical and cognitive processes involved in object making (Lemonnier 1976; Leroi-Gourhan 1965). This epistemic move enables a shift of focus away from (religious) meaning toward the structured organization of productive activity. Such an approach makes fairly general reference to Bourdieu's theory of practice (1977), but it more concretely gives rise to a whole range of research in dialogue with theories in sociology and anthropology (e.g., Giddens 1979; Sahlins 1981) dedicated to individual or collective action as an effect of social agents' creative capabilities as they organize their practices in such a way as to transform and produce new states (Dornan 2002; see also Andrieu et al. this volume and Arnauld and Andrieu this volume).

In anthropology, in the tradition of the first works by Hubert and Mauss (1897), building on Durkheim, or by Van Gennep (1981 [1909]), the relationship between time and rites has often been understood through rites of passage that show spatially and temporally marked chains of sequences, at the end of which either an initial situation or the state of a person is transformed. Elaborations of this view have discussed the temporal orientation of rituals, while specifying patterns of time manipulation depending on the type of rituals. One famous analysis is the statement by Lévi-Strauss that ritual has the function of overcoming and integrating three oppositions: those of diachrony/synchrony, periodicity/aperiodicity, and reversible/nonreversible time. Thus historical rites, which recreate the past so that it becomes the present, are inverse to death rituals, which convert present people into past beings, and distinct from control rites, which adjust the here-and-now to fixed schemes established in mythic times, equating the present with the past (Lévi-Strauss 1962, 283).[3] While time-reversal rituals—and the tension between irreversibility and repetitiveness they instantiate—have been the object of some discussion (e.g., Leach 1961; Gell 1975, 1992), authors have more often stressed that ritual actions should be viewed as repetitions of past "archetypal" actions (Humphrey and Laidlaw 1994), to which participants may connect through "deference" processes (Bloch 2004): for example, when they say they are following a tradition or acting as their ancestors did. Such reenactment rituals involve mythical, ancestral, or historical actions which are reperformed in the ritual present (Pitrou this volume; López Luján this volume). Other studies have focused on the inaugural dimension of rites, sacrifices in particular (Lambek 2007; see also Chosson, Begel, and Becquey this volume). Van Gennep's work, and especially its emphasis on process, was also developed by elaborating the perspective on liminality and stressing the intimacy of the ritual with social formation and transformation (Turner 1969 and subsequent work, such as Nahum-Claudel 2019; see also Monod Becquelin and Breton 2002; Breton, Chosson, and Monod Becquelin this volume, for Mesoamerica).

In contrast to views that treat rituals by means of dichotomies that are reintegrated by the ritual (Bell 1992, 21), practice-based and interactional approaches have emphasized the contingent and contextual nature of ritual. Ritualization is then seen as the key concept to address the strategic aspects of rituals, the fact they are performed as practical ways of dealing with specific circumstances and that they act with and on flexible categories. Being rooted in the body as much as it is sociohistorical, ritualization may maximize or minimize its differentiation from other forms of practices, in cultural specific ways (Bell 1992, 92–93; Joyce this volume). According to this view, features such as repetition are not intrinsic to rituals. Following a more cognitive approach, it has also been suggested that variations in ritual frequency and intensity give them distinct transmission capacities: for example, unrepeated initiation rites are characterized by a strong intensity (Whitehouse 2004). However, cognitive perspectives linking the experience and conceptualization of time to the specificities of rituals have been scarce (see, however, Bloch 2012; Gell 1992).

Discussions on the distinctiveness of ritual time with respect to other social times have thus grown more complex over the years, moving beyond simplistic oppositions such as cyclic versus linear (e.g., Bloch 1977) to encompass the intricacies of contrasting regimes of temporality (e.g., Gell 1992; Pitarch 2011; Schieffelin 2002), and the combination of multiple temporalities (see below). Some have even suggested that the specific rhythmicities of ritual (such as "an extraordinary union of the quick [internal tempos] and the changeless [of punctilious recurrence of rituals as wholes]" [Rappaport 1999, 225]) are nodal to a ritually generated state of the mind and society (Rappaport 1992, 1999) or that ritual operates as "a virtualizing wherein the chaotic formations of actuality are slowed down" (Kapferer 2006). It is now clear that expressions such as "atemporal" or "time out of time" used to describe ritual time conceal a great deal of complexity. Also, against the view that ritual should be defined essentially in relation with myth (Lévi-Strauss 1971), and ritual time be dependent on mythic time, it has been argued that rituals articulate an individual experience with a set of traces of collective memory. Ritual memory, constructed through the words, gestures, and objects of the ritual, appears to be key to the sociocultural elaboration of images of historical change (Severi 1993b, 1996).

The notion of "frame" (see Bateson 1972; Goffman 1974) has led to a consideration of the specificity of ritual interactions with a view to resolving two problems: how to describe the rite's internal organization and dynamics—particularly its temporal organization into oriented sequences of actions—and how to describe the effects that rites have on everyday life or in an ecological or social environment (Dehouve 2007; Handelman 1998; Handelman and Lindquist 2005; Kapferer 1983; Pitrou 2016a). Pragmatic theories such as that of ritual condensation (Houseman and Severi 1998 [1994]; Severi 2002)—which consider contradictory connotations to be combined in each sequence of ritual action, and multiple perspectives to coalesce in paradoxical identities—lead to treating ritual time as a heterogeneous texture made of parallel timelines that may unite and disunite according to a variety of dynamics. Fractality, reversibility, simultaneity, anachronicity, synchronicity, and asynchronicity may interact in a complex ritual scenario formed by a combination of semiotic and material elements and especially revealed by the textual and prosodic subtleties of ritual speech (see, for Mesoamerica, Becquey 2017; Hanks 2006; Lira 2017a, 2017b; Monod Becquelin and Breton 2002; Vapnarsky 2022, this volume).

Recent sensory approaches to ritual and the materialities they are made of—taken as entities with processual, relational, and agential properties that emerge in action (Barad 2007; Dupey 2013, 2019; Erikson and Vapnarsky 2022; Johnson and Joyce 2022; Pitarch 2022; see also Okoshi this volume) and affect the ritual experience as well as the formation of religious subjectivities (Cohen and Mottier 2016)—potentially multiply the temporal layers and textures at play in rituals (Lupo 2022, this volume). However, as with other aspects of rituality—in particular ritual speech and multimodal communication, to which we turn below—they have rarely been analyzed from the point of view of their specific temporalities.

The expression of time in language and speech has been amply studied in linguistics, including the study of temporal shifters (Jakobson 1957) and temporal frames of reference in enunciative approaches (Benveniste 1966; Fleischman 1982, 1990) and more recent cognitive and pragmatic perspectives (Desclés and Guentchéva 2012; Evans 2013; Le Guen 2017; Le Guen and Pool Balam 2012; Núñez and Sweetser 2006; Tenbrick 2011). It has received less attention in linguistic anthropology (but see Basso 1996; Faudree and Pharao Hansen 2014; Kockelman 2007; Vapnarsky 2017). Within this approach, the Bakhtinian concept of chronotope (Bakhtin 1978 [1975])—originally the matrix where the main temporal and spatial sequences of a narrative work intersect—has been extended to analyze situated verbal practices, in particular the discursive negotiation of multiple spatiotemporal frames (Lempert and Perrino 2007; Silverstein 2005).

However, temporal aspects of speech have been considered mainly from the point of view of the specificities of narration in comparison with ordinary discourse. The temporal dimension of ritual discourse, by contrast, has itself been subject to little analysis, as demonstrated by recent publications on ritual communication (e.g., Keane 2004; Senft and Basso 2009; Stasch 2011; Tavárez 2014). Yet it opens the door to very promising perspectives. The treatment of language as action, initiated by Malinowski (1935) and theorized especially by Austin (1962) and by subsequent pragmatic approaches, implies conceiving of words as agents of context transformation and modification that are therefore associated with a transition between the performance's before and after (Duranti and Goodwin 1992). A set of analyses has made it possible to elucidate some of the modalities by which linguistic forms of ritual discourse effect such transformations, particularly those concerning relations of authority (e.g., Bloch 1975; Duranti 1993; Lempert 2012; Merlan and Rumsey 1991) or the states of the person (e.g., Monod Becquelin 2000; Lupo 1995;

Pitarch 2013; Signorini and Lupo 1989). There has also been some elaboration of the role of ritual utterances in the establishment of specific systems of interpersonal relations and in the construction of frameworks of co-participation and co-activity (e.g., Hanks 1996, 2006, 2013; Haviland 2000; Pitrou 2012, 2016b).

These approaches have contributed to altering perspectives on rituals, causing a shift from a symbolic analysis often centered on cosmologies (Geertz 1957, 1973; Galinier 2004 [1994], among others) to a conception in terms of a situated, emerging, participatory experience (Hanks 2006; Senft and Basso 2009; Vapnarsky 2022). On the basis of local ethnotheories of communication, other authors have questioned the conception of action used in ethnological and pragmatic theories, in order to emphasize the notion of "event," introducing a more integrative view of verbal and nonverbal actions (Merlan and Rumsey 1991). The recent development of analyses and theories on multimodality—the fact that communication operates through multiple modes (verbal, vocal, gestural, postural, gaze, etc.)—has expanded this view to the level of microinteractions as well as to the spheres of invariants and cognition (Enfield 2009; Goodwin 2002; Haviland 2004).

Ritual speech has often been linked to a past temporality due to its more formal, stereotyped character, and to its possible references to mythical or foundational events as well as to the discursive and cognitive sedimentations to which it is subjected, which can turn it into a sociohistorical artifact (Cuturi, this volume; Hanks 1993, 2010; Romero this volume; Tavárez 2014). However, viewing rituals as emerging, creative situations has led this relationship with time to be reconsidered as a relational, indexical, dynamic construction between the past and the contemporaneity of the ritual performance's context (Keane 1997; Schieffelin 2002). Indications of this anchoring, configured by different scales of embedded contexts, from the sociohistorical to the microcontextual (Hanks 2006), can be found in linguistic forms and their variation (see Hanks 1984, 2017; Monod Becquelin et al. 2010 for Mayan; Severi 1993a), but also in gestures, music and dance, or artifacts. While some works have analyzed forms of effectiveness in prophetic speech (e.g., Csordas 1997; Vapnarsky 2009), a more recently recognized characteristic of ritual communication is the significant amount of speech anticipation in comparison with nonritual spoken forms (Senft and Basso 2009). This is an important element for understanding not just the specificities of temporal projections in rituals but also the forms of participant and chronotopic coordinations at play.

This volume focuses on Mesoamerica. In this area, anthropological studies have reflected on ritual time along three main lines: the elaboration of ritual and divinatory calendars (Tedlock 1992); the cosmological conflation of spaces and times and its structuring role in ritual actions and symbolism, such as in oriented ritual deposits or circuits (Dehouve 2007; Galinier 2004 [1990]; Geist 1996; Gossen

1974; Hanks 2017; López Austin 2001; Pitrou 2016a; Vapnarsky 2003); the analysis of death rituals and of reenactment rituals such as Indigenous carnavals (Monod Becquelin and Breton 2002; Neurath 2017; Rubio Jiménez and Neurath 2017; Ruz 2005). Historical anthropology but also philology and iconography have addressed the superposition and conflict of temporal regimes produced by colonization and its consequences for religious innovations (Gruzinski 2002; Navarrete Linares 2004; Ruz 2017; Tavárez 2022; see also in this volume the chapters by Cuturi, by Gaillemin, and by Romero). A few works in anthropology and linguistic anthropology have elaborated on the combination and dynamics between multiple temporalities in rituals, by considering the specifics of ritual speech, actions, and artifacts (Dehouve 2021; Hanks 2017; Lira 2017b; Martínez 2017; Martínez Ts'ujul 2021; Pitarch 2011; Vapnarsky 2022, this volume).

The lines of inquiry that emerge from this brief "state of the art" survey show that the understanding of ritual activity and its temporal dimensions can be considerably stimulated and enriched by being situated in a context of multi- and interdisciplinary dialogues such as those proposed in this volume.

SYNOPSIS OF THE BOOK
Rhythms in Rituals

Conceiving rituals as series of moments that succeed one another according to a clearly defined "before" and "after" does not account for the complexity of the temporal processes at work. It proves more productive to take a methodical inventory of the multiplicity of rhythms and synchronicities as well as asynchronicities at work in ritual dynamics. Central to this is the very precise reconstruction of sequences of gestures, occurrence of material elements, coordinated actions, and spoken words, as well as the consideration of the forms of transformation (changes and transitions)—internal or external, induced or performed—that lie at the heart of observed ritual actions. This offers new clues for the understanding of forms of reenactments, ritual reiterations and cyclicity, and their relation with human practices and nonhuman agencies.

In the first contribution to this section, "Night and Day in the Templo Mayor at Tenochtitlan: The Different Renderings of Huitzilopochtli's Creation Myth," Leonardo López Luján addresses the fundamental rhythm of the night/day cycle and, through it, the question of the reenactments of actions present in origin myths. The chapter shows how the miraculous birth of Huitzilopochtli and his triumph over his lunar sister and stellar brothers, a metaphor of the victory of the day over the night, opened the way in Tenochtitlan to multiple celebrations. With the Templo Mayor as a stage, these ceremonies reenacted the rebirth of the sun early every morning. The mythoastronomical periodicity functioned as a powerful mode of institution and ritualization of night/day temporality.

Not all the rites carried out in pre-Hispanic times, or later, have as their origin the commemoration of a myth with more or less fixed dates, nor are they always performed within the framework of calendar cycles. Strictly speaking, untimely events (such as a delay or insufficiency of rainfall over one or more years) or events inscribed in other temporalities (the life cycle, for example) also gave rise to retroactive and proactive rites, inscribing these events in specific temporalities. In the chapter "Probable Occasional Ceremonies at the End of the Maya Classic Period," Dominique Michelet explores how, away from religious calendar requirements, seemingly profane events or processes became temporal anchors and triggered new ritual chronologies.

In "Ritual Speech and the Transformation of Time: The Grammar and Voice of Temporalization in Yucatec Maya Rituals," Valentina Vapnarsky concentrates on the complexities and plurality of time in ritual performances and how they are configured through ritual speech. Based on the comparative analysis of performances of agricultural, land, and therapeutic rituals practiced by contemporary Yucatec Maya, she pays particular attention to how the main dimensions of linguistic temporality—indexical anchoring, aspectuality, textual and vocal rhythmicity—are mobilized depending upon the specific purposes and the agentive participation frames of rituals. It is argued that the rhythmic and chronotopic composition of the ritual speech induces specific causalities and a proper experiential texture of temporality that are both essential components of the ritual performative and transformative action.

Ritual Multitemporalities

As suggested in the previous section, rituals embed, conflate, condense, or unfold a plurality of temporalities. They elaborate time compression and expansion, rhythmic variations in and across the different temporalities, including during the performance. They produce chronological disruptions so as to create generative relations between distinct chronotopes and distinct ontological domains. Thus, rituals activate links between past, present, and future times; they connect and articulate different orders of time and action, such as those of life cycles, technical activities, lived rhythms, political organizations, and historical or cosmic orders. It is a matter of inquiry whether, within a ritual, multimodal and multisemiotic aspects can converge, structuring a unique robust temporal frame, or if they always present divergences, involving dialectically contrasted temporal anchorings and forces.

This section starts by exploring a specific temporal figure that articulates moments and events of different orders. This is "temporal compression," which

Danièle Dehouve, in her chapter "Time Compression in Aztec Ritual Artifacts and Gods," elaborates from the conceptual trope "metalepsis" and cognitive blending theory. Based on the analysis of artifacts that are part of Tlapanec and Mexica ritual deposits, as well as on the attire of the Aztec gods, the author shows how material and sensory expressions imply a temporal compression that condenses the time of the ritual, of the myth, and of future events that they are supposed to influence. The rhetorical device acts as a cognitive operator fundamental to temporal rituality.

In the following chapter, "*Witz* and *Tz'uultaq'a*: Ritual Temporality in Caves at Raxruha, Alta Verapaz, Guatemala," Chloé Andrieu, Carlos Efraín Tox, Divina Perla-Barrera, Julien Sion, and Fidel Tuyuc Nij explore a converse multitemporal ritual setting, that of temporal accumulation. The Alta Verapaz caves, where the authors conducted archaeological investigations, were important pilgrimage sites during the Classic period. Today, these same caves are the main locations for the Maya Q'eqchi' to interact with the *tz'uultaq'a* (the spirits of the mountain caves). Given the lack of any sedimentation process, the objects deposited over a long time have accumulated in continuous layers, remaining visible for ritual practitioners and participants of different ancient and recent times. Although the superimposed and intermingled layers of artifacts and sherds result from ritual acts produced by distant historical groups in distinct types of ceremonies, synchronically the accumulation creates an inclusive sensorial and temporal configuration that resignifies successive series of ritual gestures, their causal links, and the density of nonhuman and human agencies involved.

The two final chapters of this section address the relation between the temporal structuring of ritual practices, life processes, and social and cosmic orders. In "Myth and Ritual: Temporality through the Lens of Analogy," Perig Pitrou revisits the relation between myth and rites, from the perspective of their temporal properties. Reversing the temporal perspective of ritual actions as reenactments of past mythic ones, the author elaborates on how mythic actions also depend on a way of imagining the past from the present, and how this projection is grounded in analogical schemas that capture the power of entities capable of bringing life as technical actions. A dual temporal logic of succession and synchronization is illustrated with myths and rituals related to maize cultivation.

It is the ritual imbrication of the life process par excellence, pregnancy and birth, and mythohistoric orders and temporalities that are explored in the chapter "Male Pregnancy and the Rebirth of the Year: Actors and Temporalities in a Tseltal Instauration Ritual (Bachajon, Chiapas)" by Alain Breton, Marie Chosson, and Aurore Monod Becquelin. In a unique ritual that precedes the Maya Carnival of Bachajon, the parodic impregnation and pregnancy of a male-authority-to-be-substituted acts both as an image of the renewal and succession of annual civil office (*cargo* system) and as the prelude to the rebirth of the solar cycle, the day-and-night alternation restored from darkness and the renewal of the social order. The analysis of the different sequences of actions and of the accompanying ritual dialogues and prayers reveals the multitemporal and multispatial transformative dynamics that underlie what can be considered as a ritual of instauration.

MATERIAL AND SENSORIAL DIMENSIONS OF RITUAL TEMPORALITIES

The third section furthers the multidisciplinary reflection on materialities in ritual practices, initiated in Johnson and Joyce (2022). A broad view on the range of materialities that are agential in rituals is adopted: aspects as diverse and as durable or ephemeral as substances and artifacts present in ritual deposits; pits or niches where deposits are made; written signs; and breath and voice, odors or colors, and bodily engagements with them. Materialities are seen here as entities with processual, agential, and relational properties that emerge through diverse relationships created and unfolding during and around ritual practices—which echoes the view in linguistic anthropology that words take their meaning and efficacy from emerging speech, performances, and situations. Materialities, together with the complex sensorium of (in)visibility, textures, odors, tastes, and thermic feelings they stimulate, generate and transform in different ways the temporalities of the ritual performance. They act as phases and sequence markers, function as transition operators, and may index parallel times. They are also essential for memorability and thus strongly involved in the sense of repetition, sometimes deviation, attached to ritual practices. Considering sensations—such as the perception of duration—as biocultural constructs calls for detailed and meticulous ethnographies and opens to the study of the cultural affordances involved (Canna 2019). The chapters explore all these different aspects.

In "The Materialities of Ritual Practices: An Archaeology of Traces of Stylized Events," Rosemary Joyce's analysis of marks, residues, and other traces left by ritual acts challenges previous definitions of events, while highlighting the implication of materialities in the making of ritual temporalities. Based on a sustained investigation of deposits excavated in western Honduras sites dating to the Formative Period (1500–500 BCE) and Late to Terminal Classic Period (500–1000 CE), her approach calls into question the way archaeologists and ethnographers are accustomed to think about time, as an unfolding, unidirectional flow along which moments can be placed and separated from each other. Ritual events, seen following Deleuze and Guattari (1980) as emergent, "visible striations in otherwise smooth matter," appear to be heightened moments, as much future-oriented as they are past-oriented (see also the chapters by Pitrou and by Gaillemin).

With "Recreating the Memory of the Origins: Sociocultural Meanings of 'Graphic Symbols' in Land Titles," Tsubasa Okoshi invites us to consider a very different dimension of materiality, that of paper and the voice, of the graphic trace, as embodying the acts of writing and reading and so contributing to ritual practices intended to maintain and reaffirm the social order in territories during Mayan colonial times. The analysis concentrates on a neglected aspect of colonial Maya land titles: its graphic, maybe punctuation marks. Their presence and rhythmic distribution in the manuscripts, interpreted as a translation of breath and prosodic aspects, tend to show that the titles were read out loud in ritualized performances, which reproduced in audio form the scene of the foundation of the territory. The sociocultural functions of these documents appear to depend on the internal and external temporal dimensions of their oralization, intimately attached to fixed as well as evanescent materialities.

In "Substances, Subjects, and Senses: Temporality of Perception in Nahua Rituals," Alessandro Lupo analyzes the sensory dimensions attached to objects, substances, words, and gestures in "soul illnesses" and ritual offerings to the dead among the Nahuas of the Sierra del Norte of Puebla. The author shows that the sensory properties not only vary depending on the contrasted perspectives and perceptive capacities of the various ritual human and nonhuman protagonists, but that they also change according to different temporal phases of the ritual that they contribute to establish. Playing a major part in the appropriation of the goods and essences that circulate during the performances, the ritual sensorium appears to be a complex and composite agential medium, with its own transformative dynamics.

RITUAL TEMPORALITIES IN THE LONGUE DURÉE

In Mesoamerica, rituals are not situated in a time that is more or less external to them: they constantly found, re-found, and model time. This holds true for rituals that reenact origin myths or the birth and death of ancestral or supernatural entities, as seen in the first chapter of the volume, and for ceremonial offerings of foundation (or abandonment) or enthronement ceremonies. This is also constitutive of so-called calendrical rituals, which have a very strong presence, especially in Mayan archaeology and epigraphy, since rituals of this kind are literally the processes that drive the celebrated cycles. The instituting and sociohistorical power of such rituals rests on their ability to connect individual actions with collective phenomena. But the fact that rituals mark time, and can hence function as cognitive, experiential, and material structures of social and historical memories, certainly does not mean that these markings are set in stone. On the contrary, if we step back and look at the long term, we discover that these traces, whether material or memorial, are continually subject to a process of re-elaboration by human groups. It therefore proves necessary to consider the transformation of temporal patterns—temporality in and through rites—in the course of the history of Mesoamerican societies. The comparison with societies of Central America with less clear traces of practices of timekeeping is of particular interest in this respect.

In the cross-disciplinary chapter "Rituals of Inauguration: Temporalities and Spatialities in the Maya Area and Mesoamerica," by Marie Chosson, Johann Begel, and Cédric Becquey, the authors bring together archaeology and ethnology to analyze rituals of founding houses or other buildings and specific spaces (milpas, household enclosures, etc.), both in pre-Hispanic and modern times, eventually questioning the very notion of foundation rituals. Their comparative study reveals that, in many cases, such rituals do not constitute single initial events but are rather part of series of recurrent rites necessary for occupying and using spaces of various types. What is at stake is not so much the creation—or the ensoulment, as commonly assumed in the literature—of a new inhabited or cultivated space but the continuous renegotiation between humans and the masters of the terrestrial spaces that any anthropic land use requires in Maya practices.

In "Monuments and Mounds as Time: A Brief Argument for the Isthmo-Colombian Area," Alexander Geurds critically argues for a historical and temporal view of ritual. His proposal is all the more stimulating in that it unfolds in a cultural context for which, contrary to neighboring Mesoamerica, the question of Indigenous practices of timekeeping is unclear and has hardly been discussed. Considering public ceremonial places marked by a high number of stone sculptures and regularly arranged and multiplied mounds in Nicaragua, the author highlights how repeating practices of ritual action may have generated a sense of history, due to the long-lasting character of monumental spaces of earth and stone but also to processes such as the weathering of the igneous rock, which provided sensorial clues for the aging of stones and the passage of time. These ritual practices may have developed a sense of momentum, resulting in—and perceivable from—increasing numbers of sculptures being crafted as responses to collective disruptions provoked by such predictable and unpredictable events as volcanic eruptions and political tensions.

How ritual practices and the ordering of temporalities are affected by major disruptions is precisely the focus of the chapter "The End of the Long Dynastic Time in the Southern Maya Lowlands (750–810 CE)," by M. Charlotte Arnauld and Chloé Andrieu. The authors reconsider the so-called Maya collapse of the end of the Classic period (ninth and tenth centuries CE), especially its initial phase, an era of increased warfare and dynastic endings, which preceded the dramatic times to come and introduced significant political and sociocultural changes. The political powers that were then shaken and eventually destroyed rested on the rulers' mastery of the rhythmic repetition of public ceremonies, guarantors of the world's continuity through the renewal of calendrical cycles. What can be commonly taken as a chronological series of disconnected events would in fact represent the loss by the elites of their ritual hold on time (past, present, and future), in particular their knowledge and control of the longest-practiced calendar cycle, the *baktun*, with the emergence of new temporalities in political action and its ritual foundation.

RITUAL TEMPORALITIES IN CONFRONTATION

The previous section introduces the question of how, in various moments of their history, Mesoamerican populations and their neighbors have arranged their temporalities—or invented new ones—in reaction to situations in which several conceptions of space-time have come into contact and, usually, into conflict. Part V further develops this topic with the highly disruptive case of Spanish colonization and evangelization. The chapters inquire into various semiotic and discursive modes through which traditional Indigenous conceptions of time and Catholic missionary teaching were confronted.

The first chapter investigates the semiotic properties of evangelical texts and their implication in the reconfiguration of Indigenous temporalities, with a focus on pictorial representation. In "To Figure, to Condense, and to Stretch: Temporalities and Gestures in the Colonial Catechisms of Mexico," Bérénice Gaillemin explores the visual strategies invented to convert the colonial catechisms into images to penetrate the Indigenous mind. The author deciphers the visual figurative means and the temporal recourses and manipulations used by the missionaries to transfer Christian time markers, Catholic liturgical sequences of gestures, and complex ritual actions. All these were intended to replace the Nahua ritual universe—as imagined by the missionaries in a fraught dialogue with their Indigenous interlocutors—with the Christian logic of mnemonics, time marking, and religious temporalities.

In the following chapter, "The Liturgical Challenge to Historical Temporality: From St. Dominic's Ways of Prayer to the Contemporary Ikoots *Mipoch Dios* (God's Words) of San Mateo del Mar (Oaxaca, Mexico)," Flavia Cuturi analyzes some theological and semantic principles that characterize the liturgy of the Huave of San Mateo del Mar and that of their Dominican evangelizers. It focuses in particular on "monosemic intentions," a principle which prescripts the association of ritual words and gestures with a unique and constant meaning. Based on a meticulous study of Huave ritual discourse, the author questions the way these principles affect the macro and micro temporalities constitutive of the liturgies, arguing that they counter the potential effects of history (change, oblivion, individual creativity).

The last chapter reverses the perspective. In "Biblical Landscapes and Migration Histories: The 'Ten Lost Tribes of Israel' in Colonial Highland Guatemala," Sergio Romero reveals how, as early as the mid-sixteenth century, the K'iche' Maya incorporated the Old Testament for their own benefit in order to capture exogenous historicity and traditions and to legitimize their power and continuity, subtly relying on the colonizers' history. The analysis makes explicit the tense confrontation between Maya lords and Dominicans that resulted in the dialectical articulation of Maya and Christian temporalities found in these texts, and the solutions Maya scribes developed to make Christian timescales and cycles compatible with Maya conceptions of time and elite political agendas.

At the end of this journey in the intricacies of temporalities and ritualities in Mesoamerica, we hope that, beyond the richness of the cases presented in each chapter, and their diversity in terms of historical periods, disciplines, and analysis, the reader will also perceive the convergent threads that the whole reflects. This is seen in particular in the many echoes between the texts, within and between sections, such as the temporal dialectics between the primacy of performance versus the primacy of the model (for example, in the chapters by López Lujan; Breton, Chosson, and Monod Becquelin; and Geurds), the foreground on ritual as a creative emerging process (for example, in the chapters by Vapnarsky, Lupo, Andrieu et al., and Michelet), and the view of rituals as confrontations and strategies (for example, in the chapters by Joyce, Cuturi, and Romero), to name but a few examples. As a result of the multifaceted approach to temporality and the comparative perspective adopted in the volume, which were made possible thanks to the reasoned confrontation of a variety of Mesoamerican fields, new research topics and questions emerge. We hope they might contribute to further our understanding of temporality in ritual practices, in and beyond Mesomerica.

NOTES

1. The GERM (Groupe d'Enseignement et de Recherche sur les Mayas et sur la Mésoamérique), based in Paris, has developed cross-disciplinary conferences, teachings, and publications on several related topics such as *Espacios mayas: Usos, representaciones, creencias* (Breton, Monod Becquelin, and Ruz 2003), "Decir y contar la diversidad" (Monod Becquelin et al. 2010), "Thick Boundaries: Alterity and Continuity in Mesoamerica" (Monod Becquelin 2012), and "Measures and Textures of Time among the Mayas: The Spoken, the Written and the Lived" (Vapnarsky, de Pierrebourg, and Michelet 2017).

2. The four main conferences were Ritual Temporalities: Action Sequences, Processes and Coordination, Abbaye de Royaumont, October 22–24, 2015; *Time in Recomposition*, Rome, Università Sapienza, November 3–5, 2016; Materializing Temporalities, University of California at Berkeley, September 20–22, 2017; Temporalities in Mesoamerican Rituals: Interdisciplinary Approaches, Paris, November 14–16, 2018. A book stemming from one of

these conferences was edited by Lisa Johnson and Rosemary Joyce under the title *Temporalities in Mesoamerican Rituals: Interdisciplinary Approaches* (Louisville: University Press of Colorado, 2022).

The RITMO project was funded by the Centre National de la Recherche Scientifique, France (GDRI 2015–2018), with complementary fundings by partner institutions. The RITMO network concerned with this project included the Centre National de la Recherche Scientifique (CNRS); the Université Paris Nanterre; the Université Paris 1, Panthéon-Sorbonne; the Mesoamerica Center of the University of Texas at Austin; the University of California, Berkeley; the Universidad Nacional Autónoma de México (UNAM); the Centro de Investigaciones y Estudios Superiores en Antropología Social (Ciesas); Kyoto University of Foreign Studies; the Abteilung für Altamerikanistik und Ethnologie at the University of Bonn; the Sapienza, Università di Roma; and the Università degli Studi di Napoli l'Orientale.

3. Lévi-Strauss comments on the classification of Australian rituals from the Cape York peninsula, proposed by R. Lauriston Sharp.

REFERENCES

Alcina Franch, José. 1993. *Calendario y religión entre los zapotecos*. Mexico City: IIH / UNAM.

Austin, William J. 1962. *How to Do Things with Words: The William James Lectures Delivered at Harvard University in 1955*. Oxford: J. O. Urmson and M. Sbisà.

Bakhtin, Mikhaïl. 1978. *Esthétique et théorie du roman*. Paris: Gallimard.

Barad, Karen. 2007. *Meeting the Universe Halfway: Quantum Physics and the Entanglement of Matter and Meaning*. Durham, NC: Duke University Press.

Barrett, John C. 1991. "Toward an Archaeology of Ritual." In *The Sacred and Profane: Proceedings of a Conference on Archaeology, Ritual, and Religion*, edited by Paul Garwood, David Jennings, Robin Skeates, and Judith Toms, 1–9. Oxford: Oxford University Committee for Archaeology.

Basso, Keith. 1996. *Wisdom Sits in Places: Landscape and Language among the Western Apaches*. Albuquerque: University of New Mexico Press.

Bateson, Gregory. 1972. *Steps to an Ecology of Mind: Collected Essays in Anthropology, Psychiatry, Evolution, and Epistemology*. Chicago: University of Chicago Press.

Baudez, Claude François. 2002. *Une histoire de la religion des Mayas: Du panthéisme au panthéon*. Paris: Albin Michel.

Baudez, Claude François. 2012. *La douleur rédemptrice: L'autosacrifice précolombien*. Paris: Riveneuve Éditions.

Becquey, Cédric. 2017. "Rituel d'inauguration de maison chez les Chols: Une étude ethnolinguistique." In *(Re)Fonder: Les modalités du (re)commencement dans le temps et dans l'espace*, edited by Philippe Gervais-Lambony, Frédéric Hurlet, and Isabelle Rivoal, 243–58. Nanterre: Editions de Boccard.

Bell, Catherine. 1992. *Ritual Theory, Ritual Practice*. New York: Oxford University Press.

Benveniste, Émile. 1966. *Problèmes de linguistique générale I, section V*. Paris: Gallimard.

Bloch, Maurice. 1975. *Political Language and Oratory in Traditional Society*. New York: Academic Press.

Bloch, Maurice. 1977. "The Past and the Present in the Present." *Man* 12: 278–92.

Bloch, Maurice. 2004. "Ritual and Deference." In *Ritual and Memory: Toward a Comparative Anthropology of Religion*, edited by Harvey Whitehouse and James Laidlaw, 5–78. Lanham: AltaMira Press.

Bloch, Maurice. 2012. *Anthropology and the Cognitive Challenge*. Cambridge: Cambridge University Press.

Boone, Elizabeth Hill. 2007. *Cycles of Time and Meaning in the Mexican Books of Fate*. Austin: University of Texas Press.

Bourdieu, Pierre. 1977. *Outline of a Theory of Practice*. Cambridge: Cambridge University Press.

Breton, Alain, Aurore Monod Becquelin, and Mario Humberto Ruz, eds. 2003. *Espacios mayas: Usos, representaciones, creencias*. Mexico City: IIFL / Centro de Estudios Mayas, UNAM.

Canna, Magdalena. 2019. "Mapping Bodily Empires." *Annales de la Fondation Fyssen* 34: 30–43.

Ciudad Ruiz, Andrés, María Josefa Iglesias Ponce de León, and Miguel Ángel Sorroche Cuerva, eds. 2010. *El ritual en el mundo maya: De lo privado a lo público*. Madrid: Sociedad Española de Estudios Mayas.

Clayton, Sarah C., David W. Driver, and Lisa J. Kosakowsky. 2005. "Rubbish or Ritual? Contextualizing a Terminal Classic Problematical Deposit at Blue Creek, Belize." *Ancient Mesoamerica* 16 (1): 119–30.

Cohen, Anouk, and Damien Mottier. 2016. "Pour une anthropologie des matérialités religieuses." *Archives de sciences sociales des religions* 174 (2): 349–68.

Csordas, Thomas J. 1997. "Prophecy and the Performance of Metaphor." *American Anthropologist* 99 (2): 321–32.

Dehouve, Danièle. 2007. *Offrandes et sacrifice en Mésoamérique*. Paris: Riveneuve éditions.

Dehouve, Danièle. 2021. "Epilogue." In *Mesoamerican Rituals and the Solar Cycle: New Perspectives on the Veintena Festivals*, edited by Élodie Dupey García and Elena Mazzetto, 299–311. New York: Peter Lang Publishing.

Deleuze, Gilles, and Félix Guattari. 1980. *Mille plateaux*. Paris: Les Éditions de Minuit.

Desclés, Jean-Pierre, and Zlatka Guentchéva. 2012. "Universals and Typology." In *The Oxford Handbook of Tense and Aspect*, edited by Robert I. Binnick, 123–54. Oxford: Oxford University Press.

Dornan, Jennifer, L. 2002. "Agency and Archaeology: Past, Present, and Future Directions." *Journal of Archaeological Method and Theory* 9 (4): 303–29.

Duday, Henri, Patrice Courtaud, Éric Crubézy, Pascal Sellier, and Anne-Marie Tillier. 1990. "L'anthropologie 'de terrain': Reconnaissance et interprétation des gestes funéraires." *Bulletin et Mémoires de la Société d'Anthropologie de Paris* 2 (3/4): 29–50.

Dupey García, Elodie. 2013. "De pieles hediondas y perfumes florales: La reactualización del mito de creación de las flores en las fiestas de las veintenas de los antiguos nahuas." *Estudios de Cultura Náhuatl* 45: 7–36.

Dupey García, Elodie. 2019. "Lo que el viento se lleva: Ofrendas odoríferas y sonoras en la ritualidad náhuatl prehispánica." In *De olfato: Aproximaciones a los olores en la historia de México*, edited by Elodie Dupey García and Guadalupe Pinzón Ríos, 83–131. Mexico City: Secretaría de Cultura / Fondo de Cultura Económica.

Duranti, Alessandro. 1993. *From Grammar to Politics: Linguistic Anthropology in Western Samoan Village*. Berkeley: University of California Press.

Duranti, Alessandro, and Charles Goodwin. 1992. *Rethinking Context: Language as an Interactive Phenomenon*. Cambridge: Cambridge University Press.

Dussol, Lydie, Julien Sion, and Philippe Nondédéo. 2019. "Late Fire Ceremonies and Abandonment Behaviors at the Classic Maya City of Naachtun, Guatemala." *Journal of Anthropological Archaeology* 56: article 101099.

Edmonson, Munro S. 1988. *The Book of the Year: Middle American Calendrical Systems*. Salt Lake City: University of Utah Press.

Enfield, Nick. 2009. *The Anatomy of Meaning: Speech, Gesture, and Composite Utterances*. Cambridge: Cambridge University Press.

Erikson, Philippe, and Valentina Vapnarsky, eds. 2022. *Living Ruins: Native Engagements with Past Materialities in Contemporary Mesoamerica, Amazonia, and the Andes*. Louisville: University Press of Colorado.

Evans, Vyvian. 2013. *Language and Time: A Cognitive Linguistics Approach*. Cambridge: Cambridge University Press.

Faudree, Paja, and Magnus Pharao Hansen. 2014. "Language, Society and History: Towards a Unified Approach." *The Cambridge Handbook of Linguistic Anthropology*, edited by Nick J. Enfield, Paul Kockelman, and Jack Sidnell, 227–49. Cambridge: Cambridge University Press.

Fleischman, Suzanne. 1982. *The Future in Thought and Language: Diachronic Evidence from Romance*. Cambridge: Cambridge University Press.

Fleischman, Suzanne. 1990. *Tense and Narrativity*. Austin: Texas University Press.

Fogelin, Lars. 2007. "The Archaeology of Religious Ritual." *Annual Review of Anthropology* 36: 55–71.

Galinier, Jacques. (1990) 2004. *The World Below: Body and Cosmos in Otomí Indian Ritual*. Louisville: University Press of Colorado.

Geertz, Clifford. 1957. "Ritual and Social Change: A Javanese Example." *American Anthropologist* 59 (1): 32–54.

Geertz, Clifford. 1973. *The Interpretation of Cultures: Selected Essays*. New York: Basic Books.

Geist, Ingrid. 1996. " 'Espacialización del tiempo' como categoría de análisis en el estudio de contextos rituales." *Cuicuilco* 2 (6): 87–101.

Gell, Alfred. 1975. *Metamorphosis of the Cassowaries: Umeda Society, Language and Ritual*. London: Athlone.

Gell, Alfred. 1992. *The Anthropology of Time*. Oxford: Berg Publishers.

Gheorghiu, Dragos, and George Nash, eds. 2013. *Place as Material Culture: Objects, Geographies, and the Construction of Time*. Newcastle-upon-Tyne: Cambridge Scholars Publishing.

Giddens, Antony. 1979. *Central Problems in Social Theory: Action, Structure, and Contradiction in Social Analysis*. Berkeley: University of California Press.

Goffman, Erving. 1974. *Frame Analysis: An Essay on the Organization of Experience*. New York: Harper and Row.

Gonlin, Nancy, and Jon C. Lohse, eds. 2007. *Commoner Ritual and Ideology in Ancient Mesoamerica*. Boulder: University Press of Colorado.

Goodwin, Charles. 2002. "Time in Action." *Current Anthropology* 43 (supplement): S19–S35.

Gossen, Gary H. 1974. *Chamulas in the World of the Sun: Time and Space in a Maya Oral Tradition*. Cambridge: Harvard University Press.

Gruzinski, Serge. 2002. *The Mestizo Mind: The Intellectual Dynamics of Colonization and Globalization*. New York: Routledge.

Handelman, Don. 1998. *Models and Mirrors: Towards an Anthropology of Public Events*. Oxford, New York: Berghahn.

Handelman, Don, and Galina Lindquist. 2005. *Ritual in Its Own Right: Exploring the Dynamics of Transformation*. Oxfor: Berghahn.

Hanks, William F. 1984. "Sanctification, Structure and Experience in a Yucatec Maya Ritual Event." *Journal of American Folklore* 97 (384): 131–66.

Hanks, William F. 1993. "The Five Gourds of Memory." In *Mémoire de la tradition*, edited by Aurore Becquelin Monod and Antoinette Molinié, 319–45. Nanterre: Société d'ethnologie.

Hanks, William F. 1996. "Exorcism and the Description of Participant Roles." In *Natural Histories of Discourse*, edited by Michael Silverstein and Greg Urban, 160–200. Chicago: University of Chicago Press.

Hanks, William F. 2006. "Conviction and Common Ground in a Ritual Event." In *Roots of Human Sociality: Cognition, Culture and Interaction*, edited by Nick J. Enfield and Stephen C. Levinson, 299–328. Oxford: Berg Publishers.

Hanks, William F. 2010. *Converting Words: Maya in the Age of the Cross*. Berkeley: University of California Press.

Hanks, William F. 2013. "Counterparts: Co-presence and Ritual Inter-subjectivity." *Language and Communication* 33: 263–77.

Hanks, William F. 2017. "The Plurality of Temporal Reckoning among the Maya." *Journal de la Société des Américanistes*, online special issue, *Maya Times*. https://doi.org/10.4000/jsa.15294.

Haviland, John B. 2000. "Warding Off Witches: Voicing and Dialogue in Zinacantec Prayer." In *Les rituels du dialogue: Promenades ethnolinguistiques en terres amérindiennes*, edited by Aurore Monod Becquelin and Philippe Erikson, 367–400. Nanterre: Société d'ethnologie.

Haviland, John B. 2004. "Gestures." In *A Companion to Linguistic Anthropology*, edited by Alessandro Duranti, 97–221. Malden: Blackwell Publishing.

Houseman, Michael, and Carlo Severi. (1994) 1998. *Naven, or, The Other Self: A Relational Approach to Ritual Action*. Leiden: J. Brill.

Howey, Meghan C. L., and John O'Shea. 2009. "On Archaeology and the Study of Ritual: Considering Inadequacies in the Culture-History Approach and Quests for Internal 'Meaning.'" *American Antiquity* 74 (1): 193–201.

Hubert, Henri, and Marcel Mauss. 1897. "Essai sur la nature et la fonction du sacrifice." L'Année sociologique 2: 29–138.

Humphrey, Caroline, and James Laidlaw. 1994. *The Archetypal Actions of Ritual: A Theory of Ritual Illustrated by the Jain Rite of Worship*. Oxford: Clarendon Press.

Insoll, Timothy. 2009. "Materiality, Belief, Ritual—Archaeology and Material Religion: An Introduction." *Material Religion. The Journal of Objects Art and Belief* 5 (3): 260–64.

Jakobson, Roman. 1957. *Shifters, Verbal Categories and the Russian Verb*. Harvard: Russian Language Project, Department of Slavic Languages and Literatures, Harvard University.

Jansen, Maarten, and Aurora Pérez Jiménez. 2017. *Aztec and Mixtec Ritual Art*. Leiden, Boston: Brill.

Johnson, Erlend. 2019. "Considering Memory and Processes of Abandonment and Reorganization in the Past with Case Studies from Southeastern Mesoamerica." *Journal of Anthropological Archaeology* 56: article 101086.

Johnson, Lisa M., and Rosemary A. Joyce, eds. 2022. *Materializing Ritual Practices.* Boulder: University Press of Colorado.

Kapferer, Bruce. 1983. *A Celebration of Demons: Exorcism and the Aesthetics of Healing in Sri Lanka.* Bloomington: Indiana University Press.

Kapferer, Bruce. 2006. "Virtuality." In *Theorizing Rituals: Issues, Topics, Approaches, Concepts,* edited by Jens Kreinath, Jan Snoek, and Michael Stausberf, 671–84. Leiden, Boston: Brill.

Keane, Web. 1997. "Religious Language." *Annual Review of Anthropology* 26: 47–71.

Keane, Web. 2004. "Language and Religion." In *A Companion to Linguistic Anthropology,* edited by Alessandro Duranti, 429–48. Malden: Blackwell Publishing.

Kockelman, Paul. 2007. "Meaning and Time: Translation and Exegesis of a Mayan Myth." *Anthropological Linguistics* 49: 308–87.

Kreinath, Jens, Jan Snoek, and Michael Stausberf. 2006. *Theorizing Rituals: Issues, Topics, Approaches, Concepts.* Leiden: Brill.

Kyriakidis, Evangelos, ed. 2007. *The Archaeology of Ritual.* Los Angeles: Cotsen Institute of Archaeology at UCLA Publications.

Lambek, Michael. 2007. "Sacrifice and the Problem of Beginning: Meditations from Sakalava Mythopraxis." *Journal of the Royal Anthropological Institute* 13: 19–38.

Leach, Edmund R. 1961. *Rethinking Anthropology.* New York: Humanities Press.

Le Guen, Olivier. 2017. "Una concepción del tiempo no-lineal en dos lenguas: El maya yucateco colonial y actual y la lengua de señas maya yucateca." *Journal de la Société des Américanistes,* online special issue, *Maya Times.* https://doi.org/10.4000/jsa.15327.

Le Guen, Olivier, and Lorena Pool Balam. 2012. "No Metaphorical Timeline in Gesture and Cognition among Yucatec Mayas." *Frontiers in Cultural Psychology* 3. https://doi.org/10.3389/fpsyg.2012.00271.

Lemonnier, Pierre. 1976. "La description des chaînes opératoires: Contribution à l'analyse des systèmes techniques." *Techniques et culture* 1: 100–151.

Lempert, Michael. 2012. *Discipline and Debate: The Language of Violence in a Tibetan Bouddhist Monasery.* Berkeley: University of California Press.

Lempert, Michael, and Sabina Perrino. 2007. "Temporalities in Text." *Language and Communication* 27 (3): 205–11.

Leroi-Gourhan, André. 1965. *Le Geste et la Parole,* Vol. 2: *La Mémoire et les Rythmes.* Paris: Albin Michel.

Lévi-Strauss, Claude. 1962. *La pensée sauvage.* Paris: Plon.

Lévi-Strauss, Claude. 1971. *Mythologiques,* Vol. 4: *L'homme nu.* Paris: Plon.

Lira, Regina. 2017a. "Nuestra Madre Milpa Joven: Una imagen de la totalidad efímera en un ritual wixárika." *Journal de la Société des Américanistes* 103 (1): 151–78. https://doi.org/10.4000/jsa.14874.

Lira, Regina. 2017b. "Caminando en el lugar del día (tukari), caminando en el lugar de la noche (tikari): Primer acercamiento al cronotopo en el canto ritual wixárika (huichol)." In *Mostrar y ocultar en el arte y los rituales: Perspectivas comparativas*, edited by Guilhem Olivier and Johannes Neurath, 537–62. Mexico City: UNAM.

López Austin, Alfredo. 2001. "El núcleo duro, la cosmovisión y la tradición mesoamericana." In *Cosmovisión, ritual e identidad de los pueblos indígenas de México*, edited by Johanna Broda and Félix Báez-Jorge, 47–65. Mexico City: Fondo de Cultura Económica / Consejo Nacional para la Cultura y las Artes.

López Luján, Leonardo, and Guilhem Olivier, eds. 2010. *El sacrificio humano en la tradición religiosa mesoamericana*. Mexico City: INAH / UNAM.

Lucero, Lisa J. 2003. "The Politics of Ritual: The Emergence of Classic Maya Rulers." *Current Anthropology* 44 (4): 523–58.

Lupo, Alessandro. 1995. *La tierra nos escucha: La cosmología de los nahuas a través de las súplicas rituales*. Mexico City: Consejo Nacional para la Cultura y las Artes-Instituto Nacional Indigenista / Instituto Nacional Indígena, Mexico.

Lupo, Alessandro. 2022. "Heaps of Prayers: The Materiality of Catholic Prayers, Their Temporal Dimension and Ritual Effectiveness within Nahua Ritual Discourse." In *Materializing Ritual Practices*, edited by Lisa M. Johnson and Rosemary A. Joyce, 162–91. Louisville: University Press of Colorado.

Malinowski, Bronislaw. 1935. *Coral Gardens and Their Magic: A Study of the Methods of Tilling the Soil and of Agricultural Rites in the Trobriand Islands*. London: G. Allen and Unwin.

Martínez G., Rocío Noemí. 2017. "*Ts'akiel*: Vestidos rituales, prácticas de transfiguración y temporalidades superpuestas en la fiesta del *k'in tajimol* (Chenalhó y Polhó, Chiapas)." *Journal de la Société des Américanistes*, online special issue, *Maya Times*. https://doi.org /10.4000/jsa.15491.

Martínez Ts'ujul, Rocío Noemi. 2021. *Fiesta, memoria y autonomía: El k'in Tajimol (los juegos del sol)*. Batsilk'op, San Cristobal de Las Casas: El Rebozo Palapa Editores.

Merlan, Francesca, and Alan Rumsey. 1991. *Ku Waru: Language and Segmentary Politics in the Western Nebilyer Valley, Papua New Guinea*. Cambridge: Cambridge University Press.

Michelet, Dominique, Philippe Nondédéo, Grégory Pereira, Julie Patrois, Alfonso Lacadena, and M. Charlotte Arnauld. 2010. "Rituales en una sociedad 'sin reyes': El caso de Río Bec y del Edificio A (5N2) en particular." In *El ritual en el mundo maya: De la privado a lo público*, edited by Andrés Ciudad Ruiz, María Josefa Iglesias Ponce de León, and Miguel Ángel Sorroche Cuerva, 153–80. Madrid: Sociedad Española de Estudios Mayas.

Mock, Shirley, ed. 1998. *The Sowing and the Dawning: Termination, Dedication and Transformation in the Archaeological and Ethnographic Record of Mesoamerica*. Albuquerque: University of New Mexico Press.

Monod Bequelin, Aurore. 2000. "Polyphonie thérapeutique: Une confrontation pour la guérison en Tzeltal." In *Les rituels du dialogue*, edited by Aurore Monod Becquelin and Philippe Erikson, 511–54. Nanterre: Société d'ethnologie.

Monod Becquelin, Aurore, ed. 2012. "Thick Boundaries: Alterity and Continuity in Mesoamerica." *Ateliers d'anthropologie* 37. https://doi.org/10.4000/ateliers.9169.

Monod Becquelin, Aurore, and Alain Breton. 2002. *La "guerre rouge," ou, Une politique maya du sacré: Un carnaval tzeltal au Chiapas, Mexique*. Paris: CNRS Éditions.

Monod Becquelin, Aurore, Valentina Vapnarsky, Cédric Becquey, and Alain Breton. 2010. "Decir y contar la diversidad: Paralelismo, variantes y variaciones en las tradiciones mayas." In *Figuras mayas de la diversidad*, edited by Alain Breton, Aurore Monod Becquelin, and Mario Humberto Ruz, 101–55. Mérida: UNAM.

Morehart, Christopher T. 2017. "Ritual Time: The Struggle to Pinpoint the Temporality of Ritual Practice Using Archaeobotanical Data." In *Social Perspectives on Ancient Lives from Paleoethnobotanical Data*, edited by Matthew P. Sayre and Maria C. Bruno, 145–58. Cham: Springer.

Nahum-Claudel, Chloé. 2019. "In Permanent Transition: Multiple Temporalities of Communitas in the Enawenê-nawê Ritual Everyday." *Anthropology Today* 35 (3): 11–15.

Navarrete Linares, Federico. 2004. "¿Dónde queda el pasado? Reflexiones sobre los cronotopos históricos." In *El historiador frente a la historia: El tiempo en Mesoamérica*, edited by Virginia Guedea, 29–52. Mexico City: IIH / UNAM.

Neurath, Johannes. 2017. "Tiempo, ritual y biopoder: De la poliontología a la transgresión carnavalesca." In *Tiempo, transgresión y ruptura: El carnaval indígena*, edited by Miguel Ángel Rubio Jiménez and Johannes Neurath, 105–43. Mexico City: UNAM.

Newman, Sarah E. 2019. "Rubbish, Reuse, and Ritual at the Ancient Maya Site of El Zotz, Guatemala." *Journal of Archaeological Method and Theory* 26 (2): 806–46.

Nondédéo, Philippe, Johann Begel, Julien Hiquet, Julie Patrois, Isaac Barrientos, and Ma. Luisa Vázquez de Ágredos Pascual. 2022. "The Role of Altars in Maya Public Rituals of the Early Classic Period: Analysis and Contexts of the Associated Deposits." In *Materializing Ritual Practices*, edited by Lisa Johnson and Rosemary Joyce, 117–43. Boulder: University Press of Colorado.

Núñez, Rafael E., and Eve Sweetser. 2006. "With the Future behind Them: Convergent Evidence from Aymara Language and Gesture in the Crosslinguistic Comparison of Spatial Construals of Time." *Cognitive Science* 30 (3): 401–50.

Olivier, Guilhem. 2012. "Divination, manipulation du destin et mythe d'origine chez les anciens Mexicains." In *Deviner pour agir: Regards comparatifs sur des pratiques divinatoires anciennes et contemporaines*, edited by Jean-Luc Lambert and Guilhem Olivier, 145–72. Paris: Centre d'études mongoles et sibériennes, École Pratique des Hautes Études.

Olivier, Guilhem. 2022. "¿Descubrir, aceptar o manipular los destinos? Las prácticas adivi-natorias relacionadas con el calendario de 260 días en Mesoamérica." Paper presented at the RITMO Colloquium Imitación, Adopción e Innovación en Mesoamerica, Colegio Nacional, Mexico City.

Pereira, Grégory, ed. 2013. "Une archéologie des temps funéraires? Hommage à Jean Leclerc." Special issue, *Les Nouvelles de l'Archéologie* 132.

Pharo, Lars Kirkhusmo. 2013. *The Ritual Practice of Time: Philosophy and Sociopolitics of Mesoamerican Calendars*. Leyden: Brill.

Pitarch, Pedro. (1996) 2011. *The Jaguar and the Priest. An Ethnography of Tzeltal Souls*. Austin: University of Texas Press.

Pitarch, Pedro. 2013. *La palabra fragante: Cantos chamánicos tzeltales*. Mexico City: Artes de México.

Pitarch, Pedro. 2022. "Sinestesia ontológica: Fragmentos de una etnografía de la comu-nicación sensorial en el chamanismo tseltal." In *Volver al chamanismo: La oscuridad, el silencio y la ausencia*, edited by Laura Romero, 57–83. Mexico City: Universidad Iberoamericana.

Pitrou, Perig. 2012. "Figuration des processus vitaux et co-activité dans la Sierra Mixe de Oaxaca (Mexique)." *L'Homme* 202: 77–112.

Pitrou, Perig. 2016a. *Le chemin et le champ: Parcours rituel et sacrifice chez les Mixe de Oaxaca (Mexique)*. Nanterre: Société d'ethnologie.

Pitrou, Perig. 2016b. "Co-activity in Mesoamerica and in the Andes." *Journal of Anthropological Research* 72 (4): 465–82.

Plunket, Patricia, ed. 2002. *Domestic Ritual in Ancient Mesoamerica*. Los Angeles: Cotsen Institute of Archaeology Press.

Rappaport, Roy. 1992. "Ritual, Time, and Eternity." *Zygon* 27: 5–30.

Rappaport, Roy. 1999. *Ritual and Religion in the Making of Humanity*. Cambridge: Cambridge University Press.

Renfrew, Colin, Michael J. Boyd, and Iain Morley, eds. 2015. *Death Rituals, Social Order and the Archaeology of Immortality in the Ancient World: "Death Shall Have No Dominion."* Cambridge: Cambridge University Press.

Rice, Prudence M. 2009. *Maya Calendar Origins: Monuments, Mythistory, and the Materialization of Time*. Austin: University of Texas Press.

Rice, Prudence M. 2019. *Anthropomorphizing the Cosmos: Middle Preclassic Lowland Maya Figurines, Ritual, and Time*. Boulder: University Press of Colorado.

Rowan, Yorke M. 2012. "Beyond Belief: The Archaeology of Religion and Ritual." *Archeological Papers of the American Anthropological Association* 21 (1): 1–10.

Rubio Jiménez, Miguel Angel, and Johannes Neurath, eds. 2017. *Tiempo, transgresión y ruptura: El carnaval indígena.* Mexico City: UNAM.

Ruz, Mario Humberto. 2005. "'Cada uno con su costumbre': Olvido y memoria en los cultos funerarios contemporáneos." In *Antropología de la Eternidad: La muerte en la cultura maya,* edited by Andrés Ciudad Ruiz, Mario Humberto Ruz, and Ma. Josefa Iglesias Ponce de León, 531–48. Mexico City: UNAM.

Ruz, Mario Humberto. 2017. "'Linajes de embustes': Cargas de centurias y tiempos universales en el mundo maya colonial." *Journal de la Société des Américanistes,* online special issue, *Maya Times.* https://doi.org/10.4000/jsa.15379.

Sahlins, Marshall D. 1981. *Historical Metaphors and Mythical Realities: Structure in the Early History of the Sandwich Islands Kingdom.* Ann Arbor: University of Michigan Press.

Schieffelin, Bambi. 2002. "Marking Time: The Dichotomizing Discourse of Multiple Temporalities." *Current Anthropology* 43 (supplement): S5–S17.

Schiffer, Michael B. 1976. *Behavioral Archeology.* New York: Academic Press.

Senft, Gunter, and Ellen B. Basso, eds. 2009. *Ritual Communication.* Oxford: Berg Publishers.

Severi, Carlo. 1993a. "Talking about Souls: On the Pragmatic Construction of Meaning in Cuna Chants." In *Cognitive Aspects of Religious Symbolism,* edited by Pascal Boyer, 165–81. Cambridge: Cambridge University Press.

Severi, Carlo. 1993b. "La mémoire rituelle: Expérience, tradition, historicité." In *Mémoire de la tradition,* edited by Aurore Monod Becquelin and Antoinette Molinié, 347–64. Nanterre: Société d'ethnologie.

Severi, Carlo. 1996. *La memoria ritual.* Quito: Abya Yala Ediciones.

Severi, Carlo. 2002. "Memory, Reflexivity and Belief: Reflections on the Ritual Use of Language." *Social Anthropology* 10 (1): 23–40.

Signorini, Italo, and Alessandro Lupo. 1989. *Los tres ejes de la vida.* Xalapa: Universidad Veracruzana.

Silverstein, Michael. 2005. "Axes of Evals: Token versus Type Interdiscursivity." *Journal of Linguistic Anthropology* 15 (1): 6–22.

Skibo, James M., and Michael B. Schiffer. 2008. *People and Things: A Behavioral Approach to Material Culture.* New York: Springer.

Stanton, Travis, M. Kathryn Brown, and Jonathan B. Pagliaro. 2008. "Garbage of the Gods? Squatters, Refuse Disposal, and Termination Rituals among the Ancient Maya." *Latin American Antiquity* 19 (3): 227–47.

Stasch, Rupert. 2011. "Ritual and Oratory Revisited: The Semiotics of Effective Action." *Annual Review of Anthropology* 40: 159–74.

Stuart, David. 1996. "Kings of Stone: A Consideration of Stelae in Ancient Maya Ritual and Representation." *RES: Anthropology and Aesthetics*, nos. 29/30: 148–71.

Stuart, David. 2012. *The Order of Days: Unlocking the Secrets of the Ancient Maya*. New York: Three Rivers Press.

Swenson, Edward. 2015. "The Archaeology of Ritual." *Annual Review of Anthropology* 44: 329–45.

Tavárez, David. 2014. "Ritual Language." In *The Cambridge Handbook of Linguistic Anthropology*, edited by Nick J. Enfield, Paul Kockelman, and Jack Sidnell, 516–26. Cambridge: Cambridge University Press.

Tavárez, David. 2022. *Rethinking Zapotec Time: Cosmology, Ritual, and Resistance in Colonial Mexico*. Austin: University of Texas Press.

Tedlock, Barbara. 1992. *Time and the Highland Maya*. Albuquerque: University of New Mexico Press.

Tenbrick, Thora. 2011. "Reference Frames of Space and Time in Language." *Journal of Pragmatics* 43: 704–22.

Tiesler, Vera, Shintaro Suzuki, and Grégory Pereira, eds. 2022. *Tratamientos mortuorios del cuerpo humano: Perspectivas tafonómicas y arqueotanatológicas*. Mexico City: Centro de Estudios Mexicanos y Centroamericanos, Research Institute for the Dynamics of Civilizations / Okayama University.

Turner, Victor. 1969. *The Ritual Process: Structure and Anti-Structure*. New York: Aldine de Gruyter.

Valencia Rivera, Rogelio, and Geneviève LeFort, eds. 2006. "Sacred Books, Sacred Languages: Two Thousand Years of Ritual and Religious Maya Literature; 8th European Maya Conference, Madrid, November 2003." Special issue, *Acta Mesoamericana* 18. Munich: Verlag Anton Saurwein.

Van Gennep, Arnold. (1909) 1981. *Les rites de passage*. Paris: Picard.

Vapnarsky, Valentina. 2003. "Recorridos instauradores: Configuración y apropiación del espacio y del tiempo entre los mayas yucatecos." In *Espacios mayas: Usos, representaciones, creencias*, edited by Alain Breton, Aurore Monod Becquelin, and Mario Humberto Ruz, 363–81. Mexico City: IIFL / Centro de Estudios Mayas / UNAM.

Vapnarsky, Valentina. 2009. "Predicción y performatividad en la memoria histórica maya yucateca." In *Texto y contexto: La literatura Maya Yucateca en perspectiva diacrónica*, edited by Antje Gunsenheimer, Tsubasa Okoshi Harada, and John F. Chuchiak, 160–89. Frankfurt: Estudios de Americanistas de Bonn, Shaker Verlag.

Vapnarsky, Valentina. 2017. "Senses of Time: Exploring Temporality in Mayan Discourses, Experiences and Remembrances." Habilitation à Diriger des Recherches, École des Hautes Études en Sciences Sociales, Paris.

Vapnarsky, Valentina. 2022. "Voice Matters: The Vocal Creation and Manipulation of Ritual Temporalities." In *Materializing Ritual Practices*, edited by Lisa Johnson and Rosemary Joyce, 70–94. Boulder: University Press of Colorado.

Vapnarsky, Valentina, Fabienne de Pierrebourg, and Dominique Michelet, eds. 2017. "Tiempos Mayas: Compases y texturas del tiempo entre los mayas; Lo dicho, lo escrito y lo vivido." "Maya Times: Measures and Textures of Time among the Mayas: the Spoken, the Written and the Lived (s.l., s.n.)." *Journal de la Société des Américanistes*, online special issue. https://doi.org/10.4000/jsa.15521.

Vapnarsky Valentina, Fabienne de Pierrebourg, Dominique Michelet, Mario Humberto Ruz, and Aurore Monod Becquelin, eds. 2020. *Compases y texturas del tiempo entre los mayas*. Mexico City: UNAM.

Walker, William H., and Lisa J. Lucero. 2000. "The Depositional Histories of Ritual and Power." In *Agency in Archaeology*, edited by Marcia-Anne Dobres and John Robb, 130–47. London: Routledge.

Wells, Christian E., and Karla L. Davis-Salazar. 2007. *Mesoamerican Ritual Economy: Archaeological and Ethnological Perspectives*. Boulder: University Press of Colorado.

Whitehouse, Harvey. 2004. *Modes of Religiosity: A Cognitive Theory of Religious Transmission*. Walnut Creek, CA: AltaMira Press.

PART I

Rhythms in Rituals

2

Night and Day in the Templo Mayor at Tenochtitlan

The Different Renderings of Huitzilopochtli's Creation Myth

LEONARDO LÓPEZ LUJÁN

This research explores a paradigmatic case in the Mesoamerican religious tradition, where myth, architectural setting, and ritual are inextricably linked. My analysis is based on a rich and diverse array of fifteenth- and sixteenth-century evidence, including native pictography, colonial sources, and various archaeological artifacts and contexts excavated in the Historic Center of Mexico City by the Templo Mayor Project team under my direction. My objective here is to deepen the century-old proposition that the narrative account of the extraordinary birth of the Mexica patron deity Huitzilopochtli had its most lucid worldly manifestation in the Templo Mayor of Tenochtitlan, thus linking the ideal with the material, that is, the collective imaginary with tangible cultural creation. It is well-known that evocations of this myth permeated the 45-meter-high mass of earth, stone, wood, and stucco, in terms of both its structural plan and its iconographic program. In fact, in the Templo Mayor one could say that architecture, mural painting, and polychrome sculpture came together to make the Mexica empire's preeminent religious edifice the perfect theater for ritual remembrance. As we will see in this chapter, it was the religious scenarios where the cyclical battle between the sun and the moon was performed and, consequently, the triumph of the daylight over the night shadows was publicly celebrated in crowded festivals organized by the Mexica state. Let us examine, then, various aspects of the proposition, beginning with the ideal, imaginary realm of myth.

https://doi.org/10.5876/9781646426829.c002

MYTH

Fortunately, today, several poetic evocations and narrative versions of the myth recounting Huitzilopochtli's birth have survived (Garibay Kintana 1958, 78; 1965, 43). The fullest and best-known account is recorded in book 3 of the Florentine Codex, produced by the Franciscan friar Bernardino de Sahagún and his native colleagues and informants (Sahagún 1979, 3:1r–4r; Sahagún 2000, 300–302; López Austin and López Luján 2009, 238–44). Allow me to briefly summarize the basic elements of this myth:

It begins with a woman named Coatlicue performing her daily penance on top of Coatepetl, that is, "Serpent Mountain" in Nahuatl. One day, while sweeping, a ball of down fell from above, right before her eyes. Without hesitating, she snatched it up and placed it on her abdomen, which resulted in a miraculous pregnancy. A short time later, Coatlicue's children—Coyolxauhqui and the Centzonhuitznahuah—learned of this inexplicable transgression, and, feeling dishonored, they decided to go and kill the very woman who had given them life.

Setting out for Coatepetl, Coyolxauhqui and the Centzonhuitznahuah went through Tzompantitlan, Coaxalpan, Apetlac, and then up the mountainside to reach the summit. When they got to their mother, they witnessed the birth of their brother Huitzilopochtli, already a young man fully equipped for battle and prepared to fight them. With a magical *xiuhcoatl* fire serpent, he slashed his sister Coyolxauhqui's torso, beheaded her, and threw her down the mountain, where her limp body landed at the bottom in pieces. Huitzilopochtli then attacked his male siblings and chased them toward the sky.

This fascinating account, written in the Florentine Codex in alphabetic script, is also accompanied by two illustrations (López Austin and López Luján 2009, 244–45). In the first, we see Coatlicue, identified by her serpent skirt, giving birth to Huitzilopochtli, who is depicted as a fully grown adult holding a throwing stick, a spear, and a shield (figure 2.1a). In the second illustration, Huitzilopochtli wields an obsidian-blade-studded club and a shield against one of the Centzonhuitznahuah, while another below him prepares to fight their newborn brother (figure 2.1b). Between these combatants rises the glyphic image of a mountain with a serpent, which identifies the place as Coatepetl. Halfway down the slope, we see a severed human head and, at the bottom, a headless, dismembered corpse. One might suppose that these corporeal members belong to Coyolxauhqui, but the body is clearly male and wears a truss. In addition, it has a male hairstyle and lacks the goddess's characteristic facial insignia.

To these accounts and evocations of the great warrior Huitzilopochtli's exploits we should add a supposedly historical passage from the Crónica Mexicáyotl

Figure 2.1. (a) Coatlicue giving birth to Huitzilopochtli (Sahagún 1979, 3:3v).
(b) Huitzilopochtli attacks the Centzonhuitznahuah (Sahagún 1979, 3:3v).

(Alvarado Tezozómoc 1949, 34–36), which records an episode during the Mexica migration at a place significantly called Coatepec in which the protagonists receive the names of mythical characters. Huitzilopochtli, the main leader of the exodus, gets into a conflict with the Centzonhuitznahuah, a portion of the group led by Coyolxauhcihuatl. The reason for the disagreement was the Centzonhuitznahuah's refusal to leave the paradisiacal settlement of Serpent Mountain, in spite of the main leader's order to do so. The leader armed himself for war, confronted and defeated them in the divine ballgame (Teotlachco), and, finally, opened their chests and viciously devoured their hearts.

How should we interpret this passage from the Crónica Mexicáyotl? Some researchers, adopting a euhemerist position, think that a historical event during the migration gave rise to the cosmological myth (Matos Moctezuma 1991; 2003, 48–49). Alfredo López Austin and I, on the other hand, believe that an actual episode was subsequently adapted and resignified by augmenting historical memory with elements of an old mythic account (López Austin and López Luján 2009, 245). In our judgment, this was a way to sacralize lived events by joining them to ancient cosmic exploits long recognized by the community.

Whatever the case may be, the various versions of this account were analyzed more than a century ago by Eduard Seler (1993, 157–62; 1996, 96). The German Mesoamericanist insightfully identified Huitzilopochtli with the young rising sun, Coyolxauhqui with the moon, and the Centzonhuitznahuah with the stars and explained that the myth represented the astral struggle between diurnal and nocturnal forces (see also Caso 1953, 23–24; Milbrath 1997, 186–88; Read 1998, 74–76). López Austin and I agree with Seler's general interpretation and that this excerpt from the Florentine Codex is the classic expression of a canonic Mesoamerican myth, beginning with a stable situation of absence, followed by a destabilizing divine adventure, and then concluding with a creative act in the space-time of creatures (López Austin and López Luján 2009, 236–37).

In this specific case, the nodal sense of the myth focuses on the primordial existence of a nocturnal domain, the successive gradual development of a diurnal force, and the ultimate overcoming of the night by an impulse that produces the permanent dynamism of the daily dark/light cycle in the form of a divine contest. This account specifically refers to the daily rising of the sun out of darkness; thus it differs considerably from the well-known myth of Nanahuatzin at Teotihuacan, which posits the beginning of the world with the pristine appearance of the sun and the subjection of all creatures to its dominion (Sahagún 2000, 694–97).

MYTH AND ARCHITECTURAL SETTING

Inspired by Seler, the Mexican archaeologist Eduardo Matos Moctezuma (1982, 110; 1986, 74–75; cf. Seler 1992, 138; 1996, 96) argued that the Birth of Huitzilopochtli Myth was materially crystallized in the Templo Mayor of Tenochtitlan. The most striking proof of this proposition is the spectacular round Coyolxauhqui monolith from Phase IVb, found on February 21, 1978, which depicts the goddess decapitated and dismembered. Matos Moctezuma rightly observed that this massive stone was located precisely at the bottom of the stairway leading to the top of the pyramid, where the solar Huitzilopochtli's image stood triumphant in zenithal position.

Matos Moctezuma also noted that certain architectural elements of the Templo Mayor recorded the name Coatepetl. This was enunciated, in his judgment, by the four large serpent heads protruding from the rough-hewn stone bands flanking the stairway, at the respective bases of the two superimposed bodies of the pyramid. According to this logic, the serpents had the phonetic value of *coa*[*tl*], while the numerous rough stones set into the facades corresponded to the mountainous nature of the word *tepetl*.

Upon this firm basis, Matos Moctezuma (1982, 112) then formulated a series of hypotheses intending to provide coherent explanations for other elements in the

Figure 2.2. Anthropomorphic sculptures from Phase III (drawing by D. Matadamas and M. De Anda Rogel, courtesy of the Templo Mayor Project)

Templo Mayor's iconographic program. He suggested, for example, that the large anthropomorphic sculptures he discovered on the southern stairway of Phase III (figure 2.2) were effigies of the Centzonhuitznahuah mentioned by Alvarado Tezozómoc (2001, 291), who said that Huitzilopochtli's astral warrior siblings were depicted around the pyramid with shields. Matos Moctezuma also assumed that the human visage sculpted on the top step of Phase II represented the informant Cuahuitlicac and that the famous Coatlicue sculpture probably would have been situated at the top of the Templo Mayor (Matos Moctezuma 1986, 75), as many other authors have stated (Boone 1999, 201–2; Gurría Lacroix 1978, 23–34; López Austin and López Luján 2009, 454–62; López Luján 2012, 220–29; Seler 1992, 115).

To Matos Moctezuma's list of monuments, we could add, on the one hand, the mural paintings he discovered in 1979 inside the Huitzilopochtli shrine corresponding to Phase II, and, on the other, the three sculptures we fully exhumed in 1987 from Phase IVa-1 (López Austin and López Luján 2009, 401–3). Although severely damaged, the pictorial group depicts a motley collection of weapons and elite military items, including shields, arrows, banners, and devices, all associated with the solar war god Huitzilopochtli.

The sculptural group, however, consists of a rudimentary effigy of Coyolxauhqui, a serpent mat, and a stone slab with a shield, a banner, and four arrows carved in relief (López Austin and López Luján 2009, 298–303). Here the goddess—headless and dismembered—is represented as an archetypal victim lying at the bottom of the serpent mountain-pyramid. The weapons, in turn, commemorate the confrontation between the sun and the moon while also sanctifying war as the way to supply divine sustenance. Finally, the mat alludes to an augury mentioned in the Florentine Codex, that those who sat on this web of serpents were already dead, as would happen to Coyolxauhqui as in the case of Huitzilopochtli.

MYTH AND RITUAL PERFORMANCE

According to Seler (1992, 97–98), the moniker Coatepetl bestowed upon the Templo Mayor in the historical documents (Alvarado Tezozómoc 1949, 304–413; Sahagún 1979 2:108r; see also, León-Portilla 1987, 79–81; López Austin and López Luján 2009, 15–18; Schwaller 2019, 140–43) clearly identifies the structure as an arena for ritual performance, that is, the stage where a procession of the faithful, bearing Huitzilopochtli's image during the Panquetzaliztli festival, reenacted the mythic offensive against the Centzonhuitznahuah. The German scholar also noted that this connection was further reinforced by the names Tzompantlitlan, Coaxalpan, and Apetlac given to the places visited by Coyolxauhqui and the Centzonhuitznahuah in the myth, and to three of the structures in the sacred precinct, which include the trophy skull rack found in front of the Templo Mayor, the base of that pyramid, and its platform (López Austin and López Luján 2009, 247–52, 304–10; Paso y Troncoso 1979, 214; Seler 1992, 96).

Based on Seler, researchers such as Yólotl González Torres (1968, 182–90), Miguel León-Portilla (León-Portilla 1978, 58–65), H. B. Nicholson (1985, 83), Matos Moctezuma (1987, 200–201), Michel Graulich (1990, 380–86), Davíd Carrasco (1999, 64), and John F. Schwaller (2019, 144–45) have developed the idea that during Panquetzaliztli, the Templo Mayor was converted into the ritual axis of the annual reenactment of the myth. Their evidence includes a passage from Sahagún (1993, 252v), which states that during this festival period, "Huitzilopochtli was born." Moreover, this same writer, when enumerating the structures inside the sacred precinct, mentions that at the Huitznahuac Teucalli, "they killed the images of the gods they called *centzonhuitznahuah* in honor of Huitzilopuchtli, and they also killed many captives . . . each year, during the festival of Panquetzaliztli" (Sahagún 2000, 275; see also Garibay Kintana 1965, 43).

In addition, the description of the festival reveals the mythic origin of many of the ritual actors' names and accoutrements, as well as various songs, paintings, libations, and cult objects, as passages from the cosmic drama were evoked during its worldly reenactment (López Austin and López Luján 2009, 252–53). For example, in one of the most spectacular parts of the ceremony, a priest descended from the top of the Templo Mayor with a pine torch in the shape of a serpent, with paper head and tail, and red feathers between its jaws simulating fire (Sahagún 2000, 162–63, 247–53).

This fantastic being came down wiggling its tongue until it reached the foot of the pyramid. There it was lit to burn the sacrificial papers known as *tetehuitl*, which were material metaphoric representations of the Centzonhuitznahuah (Dehouve 2009, 19–33). This figure was significantly named *xiuhcoatl*, indicating that it was the weapon Huitzilopochtli used to kill his siblings.

RITUAL MATERIALIZATION

Our recent archaeological excavations at the foot of the Templo Mayor resulted in the discovery of another way of invoking the myth of Huitzilopochtli's birth that complemented the various oral and written accounts, its allusion in songs, its ritual dramatization, and its iconographic crystallization in the pyramid's architecture, mural painting, and sculpture (López Luján 2015, 296–313; 2017, 35–57). Although quite different, this particular form of expression, unknown to us up until now, is part of the same semantic complex. It follows a kind of general code or metalanguage that offers an alternative explanation for the same transcendental phenomenon of the daily rising of the sun in the east.

This form of expression is the sacrifice and offering of human beings, animals, plants, and cultural objects as gifts to the divinities (López Luján 2005). In very general terms, it consists of the delivery of these gifts to the gods to establish communication with them, pay homage and propitiate them, and, finally, obtain retribution. This ritual action is materialized in the sacrificial and oblatory deposits that were definitively buried by the faithful within the bowels of the Templo Mayor, only to be uncovered and analyzed by archaeologists five centuries later.

These discoveries occurred at the intersection of Guatemala and Argentina Streets, in the Historic Center of Mexico City (López Luján 2019). The explored area is located precisely on the central axis of the Huitzilopochtli shrine, that is, the southern half of the Templo Mayor. Unfortunately, this section of the pyramid has been severely damaged by the successive installations of a sewage collector in 1900, a cast iron pipe in the 1950s, an electric transformer by the Light and Power Company in the 1970s, a utility box by Telephones of Mexico in the 1990s, and a high-density pipe in 2011.

Nevertheless, we still were able to document a complex superimposition of modern, nineteenth-century, colonial, and pre-Hispanic architectural features, as well as three exceptional Mexica ritual deposits alluding to Huitzilopochtli, which I will now describe.

THE HUITZILOPOCHTLI IMPERSONATOR

The first deposit was discovered in June 2005 while excavating a pit in the platforms of Phases IVa and IVb, which correspond to the reigns of Motecuhzoma I (Ilhuicamina) and Axayacatl, that is, between 1440 and 1481 (López Luján et al. 2010). At a depth of just 50 centimeters, and totally unexpectedly, we found the complete skeleton of a very young individual who apparently had been sacrificed. We were quite bewildered by this, since the only child victims previously discovered by the project were found in 1980 at the opposite end of the building, that is, on the side associated with Tlaloc, the rain god.

This was the famous Offering 48, which contained the remains of forty-two children between the ages of 2 and 7, in addition to eleven vessels depicting this pluvial deity (López Luján 1982; 2005, 148–58; 2018). The presence of this offering in the northwest corner of the Templo Mayor (figure 2.3) fully concurs with the sixteenth-century documentary sources that say that the vast majority of child sacrifices were intended to propitiate aquatic and fertility deities. It is well known that the Mexica and their neighbors used this method to solicit rain and abundant harvests. During such ceremonies, whether subject to the calendar or performed during severe droughts, the children were symbolically associated with the rain god's dwarf assistants, and their profuse tears shed when they were being sacrificed served as a heartening augury of copious precipitation.

Thus we were able to grasp the exceptional nature of the deposit, which, twenty-five years later, we were about to exhume on the southern side of the pyramid and would call Offering 111 (figure 2.3). The cadaver of the child was found on the stairway of the platform in a seated position upon an irregular surface of sand with its back leaning on the riser of a step. The priests carefully oriented it toward the west, although the head and torso were turned slightly north (figures 2.4a and 2.4b). The skeleton was accompanied by the remains of a bird of prey, copal, and tomato seeds, along with a few artifacts, all of them quite modest. In a particularly interesting manner, the child's shoulders had two superimposed carpometacarpals and the first and second phalanges of the wings of a sharp-shinned hawk (*Accipiter striatus*). The bird's bone laterality suggested that both of the wings were originally extended with ventral feathers upward, exposing their characteristic horizontal ocher-colored stripes.

Associated with the bones were three pine objects. Two of them were found respectively on the left forearm and next to the right foot. They are arcs of a large circle, perhaps the miniature representation of a shield. The third and best preserved object is a wooden ring placed on the chest, which had collapsed northward as a result of the cadaver's decomposition. Each of the child's ankles were strung with two strands of pear-shaped copper bells that flanked a central strand

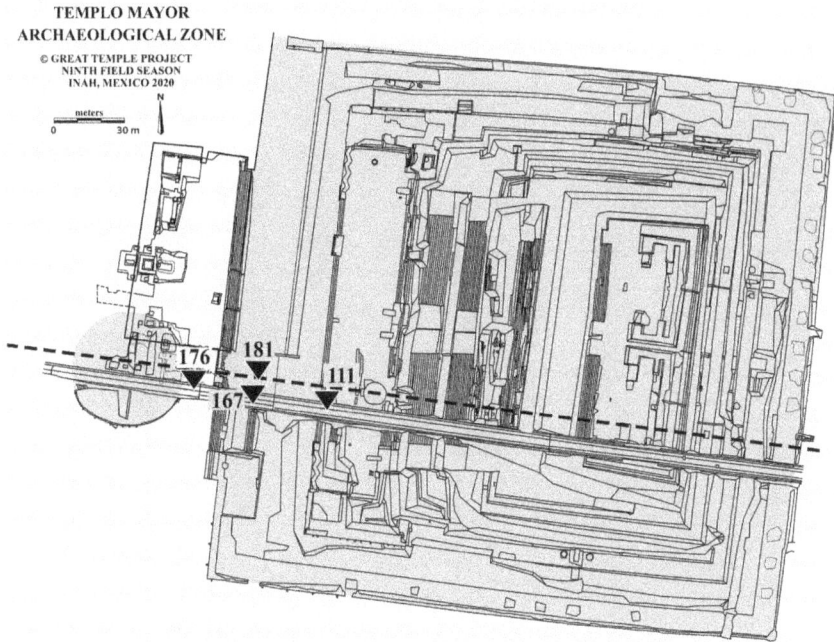

Figure 2.3. Location of Offerings 111, 167, 176, and 181 at the Templo Mayor (drawing by M. De Anda Rogel, courtesy of the Templo Mayor Project).

bearing four sea snails. These sea snails were white with a hole made in the ventral area and belonged to the *Polinices lacteus* species from the Atlantic Ocean. Next to the child's left elbow were three orange ceramic aerophones, including two transverse flutes with a single finger hole, and a dual instrument consisting of a transverse flute and a whistle. We also recovered two greenstone beads, along with a biface and an obsidian blade.

Based on dental examination, we ascertained that the individual was approximately five years of age at the moment of death. Unfortunately, it was impossible to determine the sex, as we were not able to extract enough DNA for polymerase chain reaction (PCR) analysis. We were, nevertheless, able to learn that this child lived in optimal conditions of health and nutrition, unlike the malnourished infants sacrificed to Tlaloc in Offering 48.

Taphonomic analysis revealed numerous traces of cutting on both sides of the rib cage, as well as perimortem fractures produced by this same action. These marks were concentrated on the inner sternal third of the third, fourth, and fifth ribs, where cuts were repeatedly made from inside the thorax with a very sharp obsidian

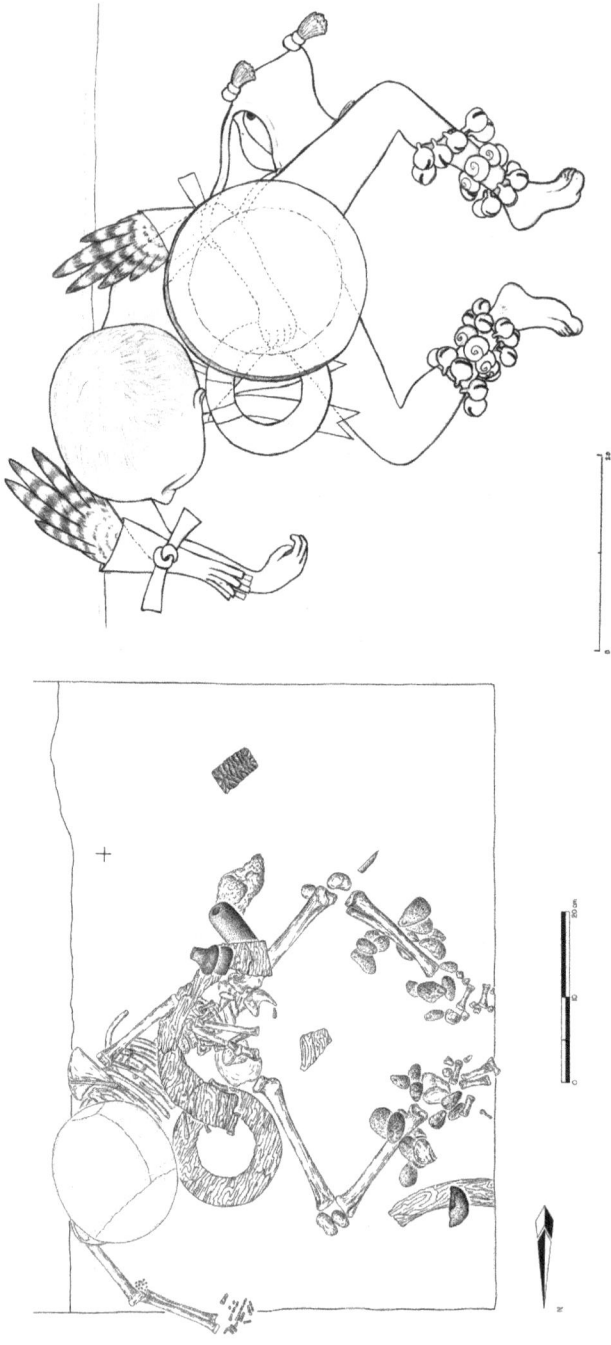

Figure 2.4. (a) Complete skeleton of the child found in Offering III (drawing by F. Carrizosa, courtesy of the Templo Mayor Project). (b) Hypothetical reconstruction of the child found in Offering III (drawing by G. Pereira, courtesy of the Templo Mayor Project).

instrument. This led us to conclude that the child was sacrificed by extracting his or her tiny heart. We are convinced that the sacrificers entered the thorax from the abdominal cavity, cutting the muscular tissues of the diaphragm.

Historical documents tell us that not all child sacrifices were associated with aquatic and fertility deities (Graulich 2005, 208–10). In some cases, the lives of children were offered in honor of Quetzalcoatl or Huitzilopochtli right before armed confrontations. Their hearts were extracted in order to learn the outcome of a battle in advance, as narrated, for instance, by chronicler Francisco López de Gómara (1954, 115) and in the *Relación de Coatepec y su partido* (Acuña 1985, 164).

The written sources also mention an interesting connection between the Mexica patron deity and his own image as a child. This is evident, for example, in Diego Durán's *Book of the Gods and Rites and The Ancient Calendar* where he describes the Pachtontli festival, in which the coming of Huitzilopochtli as a child was celebrated. According to the Dominican friar, the faithful awaited his arrival, which was indicated by a tiny footprint that miraculously appeared on a lump of corn dough (Durán 1984 1:277–78, 287–88):

> At seven o'clock in the evening the natives placed a gourd filled with dough in the upper part of the temple and watched over it. Carefully, vigilantly they visited it from time to time until they found a child's footprint . . . on the dough. Then the trumpets and conch shells sounded, and there was great rejoicing over the advent of the divine Huitzilopochtli.

Another child connection with Huitzilopochtli is found in the Nahuatl version of the myth of his birth in the Florentine Codex, where one of his attributes relates him with an infant (Sahagún 1979 4:3r; 2000, 300–302). The text literally says: "his face was painted with his child's excrement," undoubtedly alluding to the horizontal stripes on his face whose colors alternate between ocher and blue. Remember that unweaned, breastfeeding infants defecate a liquid that is light ocher in color, very similar to that of the patron deity's face in Mexica iconography.

Getting back to Offering 111, three indications in the archaeological context suggest that the sacrificed child was a Huitzilopochtli impersonator (figure 2.4b). The first is the wooden ring found on the child's chest. The Mexica called this pectoral *anahuatl* and it appears in their codices as one of Huitzilopochtli's attributes, as Nicholson (1988, 244–47) and Boone (1989, 6) have noted. The second indication involves the anklets strung with bells and sea snails—another attribute seen in several pictographic depictions of this deity. The third consists of the two sharp-shinned hawk wings associated with the child's shoulders. Huitzilopochtli appears wearing such wings in the Primeros memoriales (Sahagún 1993, 261r). This leads me to suspect that the youngster had been dressed as a bird whose plumage bore the colors of the solar god. In fact, the sharp-shinned hawk's dorsal feathers are bluish-gray, while its ventral feathers have horizontal ocher stripes.

In sum, we may conclude that the cadaver found in Offering 111 belongs to a healthy five-year-old who died at the Templo Mayor from an abdominal cardioectomy, sacrificed at the time of an enlargement of the massive structure, perhaps to predict the outcome of a battle, and was dressed as Huitzilopochtli.

ANOTHER HUITZILOPOCHTLI IMPERSONATOR

The second deposit was discovered in June 2017 while excavating at the bottom of the Phase VI platform, which dates to the time of Ahuitzotl, who reigned from 1486 to 1502. This deposit is named Offering 176 and was found aligned to the Huitzilopochtli shrine (López Luján et al. 2018).

Inside a cylindrical stone box, we found another child skeleton, also placed in a seated position, with its body facing west and the head northward (figure 2.3). Based on dental examination, it was determined that this individual was older, about nine years of age. But because this is a recent discovery, we do not have a DNA analysis to ascertain the sex, or strontium and oxygen isotopes to establish local origin, or taphonomy to determine the cause of death. What we do know is that this child also had been dressed as the solar deity, because the skeleton was associated with the bones from the wing of a roadside hawk (*Rupornis magnirostris*), a wooden ring pectoral, and anklets strung with sea snails and copper bells.

In addition, the child held an adult femur as a scepter with the date 2-Reed carved on one of its ends. In terms of meaning, the *Historia de los mexicanos por sus pinturas* (Garibay Kintana 1965, 43; Graulich 2002, 2–4), a fundamental document on Nahua cosmology and history, is particularly revealing. It specifically notes that Huitzilopochtli was born and fought his siblings to save his mother in a 2-Reed year. In other words, this femur, carried by a young Huitzilopochtli impersonator, directly alludes to the Coatepec Myth.

THE FIGURATION OF COYOLXAUHQUI

Let us turn now to the third ritual deposit, Offering 167, discovered in September 2015, 2 meters below the level of the street (López Luján 2020; Pedraza Rubio, López Luján, and Fuentes Hoyos 2017, 44–50). It was deposited in the constructive nucleus of the Phase VI platform, which also dates from Ahuitzotl's reign. It is a circular cavity, 80 centimeters in diameter and 36 centimeters deep (figure 2.3). Most of the offerings found in this confined space were aligned with the solar ecliptic, and their proximal extreme pointed toward the sunset. This suggests that the priest buried them while kneeling before the main facade of the pyramid, gazing up toward Huitzilopochtli's shrine.

The bottom of the cavity had a thin layer of apparently ocean sand, upon which were placed, one by one, 27 knives, 17 projectile points, 6 tiny *tzotzopaztli* (a weaver's flint machete or batten), 5 greenstone beads, 192 greenstone flakes, a small *atlatl* or throwing stick adorned with a *Turbinella angulata* sea snail from the Atlantic and a *Pinctada mazatlanica* shell from the Pacific, as well as 11 Pacific *Oliva julieta* sea snail earrings, 8 copper bells, 8 more made of gold, and 12 gold insignias. Topping off the deposit was a rattlesnake of the *Crotalus* genus, along with copal, carbon, and wood fragments. After the oblation was complete, the priest or his assistants poured a mortar of lime, sand, and *tezontle* gravel directly on the offerings, irremissibly imprisoning them when the mixture solidified.

Although we still have not managed to decipher the logic governing the spatial distribution of this set of offerings, we know that most of them were systematically arranged in the cavity and surrounded by copper bells and sea snails. The utter dominance of artifacts symbolically associated with sacrifice and war is quite striking. On the one hand, we have flint knives and, on the other, multiple miniature representations of an arrow, throwing stick, and *tzotzopaztli*. Remember that this weaver's machete or batten in Central Mexican iconography is the female weapon par excellence (McCafferty and McCafferty 2019). In fact, scenes abound in codices such as the Magliabechiano (*Codex Magliabechiano* 1996, 45r), Telleriano-Remensis (*Codex Telleriano-Remensis* 1995, 6r, 22v), and Primeros memoriales (Sahagún 1993, 253r, 264r), or on sculptures such as the neo-Toltec effigy from Pasaje Catedral (López Luján and López Austin 2009, 403–4) and the Tizoc Stone, where women warriors threateningly brandish the *tzotzopaztli*. In most of these cases, they can be identified with the war goddess Cihuacoatl.

But in addition to these beautiful stone and shell creations associated with sacrifice and war, there were artifacts made of gold that offer us the best clues for uncovering the mysterious meaning of Offering 167 (figure 2.5). The first clue is the presence of four pairs of *omicallo*, or crossed long bones, a pan-Mesoamerican symbol for death (Ruz 1968, 37–39; López Luján 2006, 1:126–27). The second involves the two pairs of beautiful earrings that incorporated a circle, two trapezoids, and a triangle (López Luján and González 2014, 33–34). These ornaments are characteristic of captives about to be sacrificed, the souls of dead warriors, the Cihuateteo (heroic women who perish during the battle of childbirth), Chantico (the warrior goddess of the hearth fire), and, especially, the belligerent Coyolxauhqui. Since they were exhumed from the bottom of a building also called Coatepetl, I am inclined to associate them with the lunar goddess, supported by the proximity of the four earrings with their pairs of gold bells, which, in my judgment, reiterate their connection to

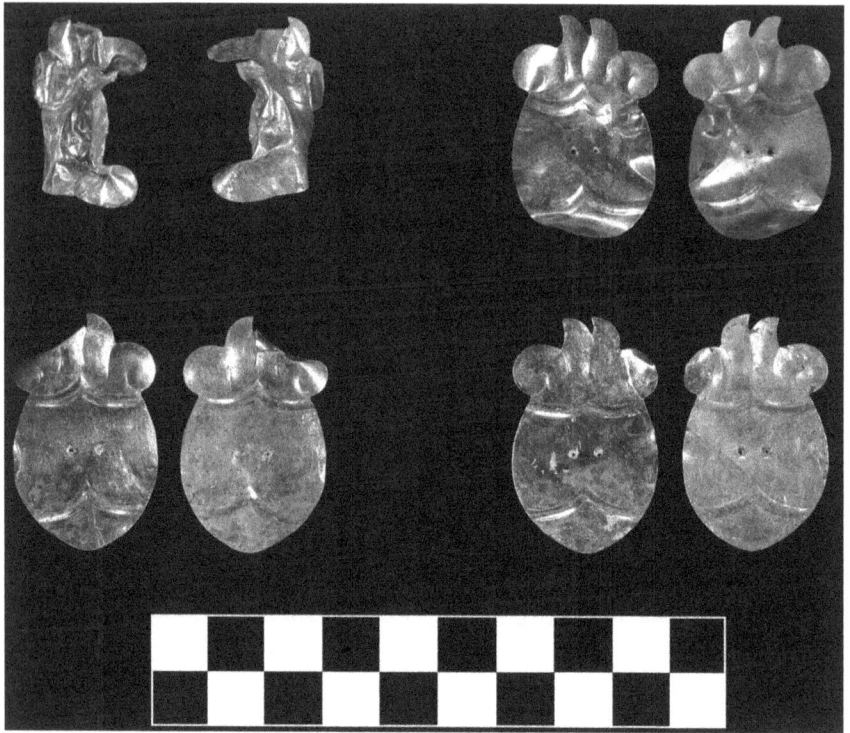

Figure 2.5. Four representations of human hearts made of gold sheet (photo by M. Islas, courtesy of the Templo Mayor Project)

Coyolxauhqui, a name that may be translated *ad litteram* as "she with bells painted on her face" (according to Alfredo López Austin).

The third and final clue highlighted here is the existence of four representations of human hearts. I still doubt that these exceptional pieces allude to the hearts of Coyolxauhqui and her astral brothers, which, according to the Crónica Mexicáyotl (Alvarado Tezozómoc 1949, 33–34) version of the myth, were devoured by Huitzilopochtli. This act has been interpreted by Miguel León-Portilla (1978, 22–23) as the appropriation of the vital energy of the nocturnal beings, the adversaries of the sun.

Significantly, one of the gold hearts clearly had been deformed in the hands of the priest who buried it. Perhaps this was meant to signify that Coyolxauhqui was "perverse," as might be inferred from the metamorphic meaning of the words *yollochico* and *yollonecuil*, which may literally be translated, respectively, as "crooked heart" and "bent heart," a coronary condition expressly alluding to perversity

(Burkhart 1989, 177; León-Portilla 2004, 93–103). Another possible explanation is that the priest tried to magically "offend" the lunar goddess, as evident from the metaphorical sense of the verb *teyolitlacoa*, whose literal translation is "to damage someone's heart," as Louise Burkhart (1989, 28–29; León-Portilla 2004, 93–103) has shown. In sum, this action may have symbolized either the perverse or malevolent character of the goddess who tried to kill her own mother, or the aggrieved or dishonored condition of that goddess after the confrontation with her brother. In this way, Coyolxauhqui appeared as a victimizer who became a victim.

A few days before submitting this manuscript to the editor, we discovered another ritual deposit 3 meters below Offering 167, which also belongs to Phase VI of the Templo Mayor and is now designated as Offering 181. Although its exploration and registration are still in progress, and the corresponding analysis has not begun, it is important to report that its principal element is the skull of a woman about thirty-five years of age, under which were found the jaw bone and first cervical vertebrae. Based on the preceding discussion, it is highly suggestive that, at the bottom of the pyramid, aligned with the Huitzilopochtli shrine, the head of a mature woman who was unquestionably beheaded has appeared.

CONCLUSIONS

I would like to conclude this chapter by venturing a "reading" of this last archaeological context as if it were a text. In order to make sense of each ritual element and the ceremony as a whole, imagine, for a moment, a hypothetical priest situated at the foot of so-called Coatepetl. More than five hundred years ago, as an enlargement of the empire's most important religious structure reaches completion, he kneels on the platform facing Huitzilopochtli's shrine. With aromatic copal smoke, he honors the deity who rules the world from the top of the Great Temple, while offering in Nahuatl a prayer, a song, and perhaps a solemn plea. Very close to the effigy of a vanquished Coyolxauhqui, he performs the oblation that through drama and offerings will evoke the mythic battle. He places the lunar goddess's bells and earrings along with the feminine weapons into the cavity. Then he envelops these insignias with symbols of war, sacrifice, and death, and viciously twists the hearts of the luminous nocturnal beings. Following a strict liturgy, he zealously repeats the cosmogonic actions of Huitzilopochtli himself, recalling that primordial moment when the moon and the stars disappeared to the west of the Sacred Mountain, as the sun assumed its throne at the highest reaches of the firmament.

REFERENCES

Acuña, René. 1985. "Relación de Coatepec y su Partido." In *Relaciones geográficas del siglo XVI: México*, vol. 1, edited by René Acuña, 125–78. Mexico City: Universidad Nacional Autónoma de México.

Alvarado Tezozómoc, Fernando. 1949. *Crónica Mexicáyotl*. Mexico City: Universidad Nacional Autónoma de México / Instituto Nacional de Antropología e Historia.

Alvarado Tezozómoc, Fernando. 2001. *Crónica Mexicana*. Madrid: Dastin.

Boone, Elizabeth H. 1989. *Incarnations of the Aztec Supernatural: The Image of Huitzilopochtli in Mexico and Europe*. Philadelphia: American Philosophical Society.

Boone, Elizabeth H. 1999. "The 'Coatlicues' at the Templo Mayor." *Ancient Mesoamerica* 10 (2): 189–202.

Burkhart, Louise M. 1989. *The Slippery Earth: Nahua-Christian Moral Dialogue in Sixteenth-Century Mexico*. Tucson: University of Arizona Press.

Carrasco, Davíd. 1999. *City of Sacrifice: The Aztec Empire and the Role of Violence in Civilization*. Boston: Beacon.

Caso, Alfonso. 1953. *El pueblo del Sol*. Mexico City: Fondo de Cultura Económica.

Codex Magliabechiano. 1996. Edited by Ferdinand Anders and Maarten Jansen. Mexico City: Fondo de Cultura Económica / Akademische Druck- und Verlagsanstalt.

Codex Telleriano-Remensis: Ritual, Divination, and History in a Pictorial Aztec Manuscript. 1995. Edited by Eloise Quiñones-Keber. Austin: University of Texas Press.

Dehouve, Danièle. 2009. "El lenguaje ritual de los mexicas: Hacia un método de análisis." In *Image and Ritual in the Aztec World*, edited by Silvye Peperstraete, 19–33. Oxford: British Archaeological Reports.

Durán, Fray Diego. 1984. *Historia de las Indias de Nueva España e islas de tierra firme*. 2 vols. Mexico City: Porrúa.

Garibay Kintana, Ángel María. 1958. *Veinte himnos sacros de los nahuas*. Mexico City: Universidad Nacional Autónoma de México.

Garibay Kintana, Ángel María. 1965. "Historia de los mexicanos por sus pinturas." In *Teogonía e historia de los mexicanos: Tres opúsculos del siglo XVI*, edited by Ángel María Garibay Kintana, 21–90. Mexico City: Porrúa.

González Torres de Lesur, Yólotl. 1968. "El dios Huitzilopochtli en la peregrinación mexica de Aztlan a Tula." *Anales del INAH* 19: 175–90.

Graulich, Michel. 1990. *Mitos y rituales del México antiguo*. Madrid: Istmo.

Graulich, Michel. 2002. "Tezcatlipoca-Omacatl, el comensal imprevisible." *Cuicuilco* 25: 1–9.

Graulich, Michel. 2005. *Le sacrifice humain chez les aztèques*. Paris: Fayard.

Gurría Lacroix, Jorge. 1978. "Andrés de Tapia y la Coatlicue." *Estudios de Cultura Náhuatl* 13: 23–34.

León-Portilla, Miguel. 1978. *México-Tenochtitlan: Su espacio y tiempo sagrados*. Mexico City: Instituto Nacional de Antropología e Historia.

León-Portilla, Miguel. 2004. "Significados del corazón en el México prehispánico." *Archivos de Cardiología de México* 74 (2): 93–103.

López Austin, Alfredo, and Leonardo López Luján. 2009. *Monte sagrado–Templo Mayor: El cerro y la pirámide en la tradición religiosa mesoamericana*. Mexico City: Universidad Nacional Autónoma de México / Instituto Nacional de Antropología e Historia.

López de Gómara, Francisco. 1954. *Historia general de las Indias*. Barcelona: Iberia.

López Luján, Leonardo. 1982. "Neues aus der alten Welt, Mexiko." *Das Altertum* 28: 126–27.

López Luján, Leonardo. 2005. *The Offerings of the Templo Mayor of Tenochtitlan*. Albuquerque: University of New Mexico Press.

López Luján, Leonardo. 2006. *La Casa de las Águilas: Un ejemplo de la arquitectura religiosa de Tenochtitlan*. 2 vols. Mexico City: Harvard University / Instituto Nacional de Antropología e Historia, Fondo de Cultura Económica.

López Luján, Leonardo. 2012. "Coatlicue." In *Escultura monumental mexica*, edited by Eduardo Matos Moctezuma and Leonardo López Luján, 115–229. Mexico City: Fundación Conmemoraciones 2010, Fondo de Cultura Económica.

López Luján, Leonardo. 2015. "The Great Temple Project: In Search of the Sacred Precinct of Mexico-Tenochtitlan." In *2015 Shanghai Archaeology Forum: Awarded Projects*, 296–313. Shanghai: Chinese Academy of Social Sciences.

López Luján, Leonardo. 2017. "El Proyecto Templo Mayor (1991–2017): Recuento de cinco lustros de actividades." In *Templo Mayor: Revolución y estabilidad*, edited by Eduardo Matos Moctezuma and Patricia Ledesma Bouchan, 35–57. Mexico City: Instituto Nacional de Antropología e Historia.

López Luján, Leonardo. 2018. "Cuando la gente 'se uno-aconejó': La gran sequía de 1454 en la Cuenca de México." *Arqueología Mexicana* 149: 36–45.

López Luján, Leonardo. 2019. "Al pie del Templo Mayor: Excavaciones arqueológicas en torno al monolito de la diosa Tlaltecuhtli y el Cuauhxicalco." In *Al pie del Templo Mayor de Tenochtitlan: Estudios en honor a Eduardo Matos Moctezuma*, edited by Leonardo López Luján and Ximena Chávez Balderas, vol. 2, 37–86. Mexico City: El Colegio Nacional.

López Luján, Leonardo. 2020. "Miguel León-Portilla and Archaeology." *Ancient Mesoamerica* 31 (1): 1–6.

López Luján, Leonardo, Ximena Chávez, Norma Valentín, and Aurora Montúfar. 2010. "*Huitzilopochtli* y el sacrificio de niños en el Templo Mayor de Tenochtitlan." In *El sacrificio en la tradición religiosa mesoamericana*, edited by Leonardo López Luján and Guilhem Olivier, 367–94. Mexico City: Instituto Nacional de Antropología e Historia / Universidad Nacional Autónoma de México.

López Luján, Leonardo, and Ángel González López. 2014. "Tierra, agua y fuego al pie del Templo Mayor de Tenochtitlan: Un conjunto de bajorrelieves de la época de Motecuhzoma Ilhuicamina." *Estudios de Cultura Náhuatl* 47: 7–51.

López Luján, Leonardo, and Alfredo López Austin. 2009. "The Mexica in Tula and Tula in Mexico-Tenochtitlan." In *The Art of Urbanism: How Mesoamerican Kingdoms Represented Themselves in Architecture and Imagery*, edited by William L. Fash and Leonardo López Luján, 384–422. Washington, DC: Dumbarton Oaks Research Library and Collections.

López Luján, Leonardo, et al. 2018. "Proyecto Templo Mayor: Informe de la Octava Temporada (fase 2017–2018)." Unpublished technical report. Mexico City: Instituto Nacional de Antropología e Historia.

Matos Moctezuma, Eduardo. 1982. "El Templo Mayor: Economía e ideología." In *El Templo Mayor: Excavaciones y estudios*, edited by Eduardo Matos Moctezuma, 109–18. Mexico City: Instituto Nacional de Antropología e Historia.

Matos Moctezuma, Eduardo. 1986. *Vida y muerte en el Templo Mayor*. Mexico City: Océano.

Matos Moctezuma, Eduardo. 1987. "Symbolism of the Templo Mayor." In *The Aztec Templo Mayor*, edited by Elizabeth H. Boone, 185–209. Washington, DC: Dumbarton Oaks Research Library and Collections.

Matos Moctezuma, Eduardo. 1991. "Las seis Coyolxauhqui: Variaciones sobre un mismo tema." *Estudios de Cultura Náhuatl* 21: 15–30.

Matos Moctezuma, Eduardo. 2003. "Templo Mayor: History and Interpretation." In *Moctezuma's Mexico: Visions of the Aztec World*, edited by Davíd Carrasco and Eduardo Matos Moctezuma, 3–98. Boulder: University Press of Colorado.

McCafferty, Geoffrey G., and Sharisse D. McCafferty. 2019. "Weapons of Resistance: The Material Symbolics of Postclassic Mexican Spinning and Weaving." *Latin American Antiquity* 30 (4): 707–23.

Milbrath, Susan. 1997. "Decapitated Lunar Goddesses in Aztec Art, Myth, and Ritual." *Ancient Mesoamerica* 8: 185–206.

Nicholson, Henry B. 1985. "The New Tenochtitlan Templo Mayor Coyolxauhqui-Chantico Monument." *Indiana* 10: 77–98.

Nicholson, Henry B. 1988. "The Iconography of the Deity Representations in Fray Bernardino de Sahagún's *Primeros Memoriales*: Huitzilopochtli and Chalchiuhtlicue." In *The Work of Bernardino de Sahagún, Pioneer Ethnographer of Sixteen-Century Aztec Mexico*, edited by Jorge Klor de Alva and Eloise Quiñones-Keber, 244–47. Albany: State University of New York.

Paso y Troncoso, Francisco. 1979. *Descripción, historia y exposición del Códice Borbónico.* Mexico City: Siglo veintiuno.

Pedraza Rubio, Gerardo, Leonardo López Luján, and Nicolás Fuentes Hoyos. 2017. "Huesos cruzados y corazones torcidos: Una ofrenda con insignias de oro al pie del Templo Mayor de Tenochtitlan." *Arqueología Mexicana* 144: 44–50.

Read, Kay. 1998. *Time and Sacrifice in the Aztec Cosmos.* Bloomington: Indiana University Press.

Ruz Lhuillier, Alberto. 1968. *Costumbres funerarias de los antiguos mayas.* Mexico City: Universidad Nacional Autónoma de México.

Sahagún, Bernardino de. 1979. *Códice Florentino: Manuscrito 218–20 de la Colección Palatina de la Biblioteca Medicea Laurenziana.* 3 vols. Mexico City: Archivo General de la Nación.

Sahagún, Bernardino de. 1993. *Primeros memoriales.* Norman: University of Oklahoma Press / Patrimonio Nacional / Real Academia de la Historia.

Sahagún, Bernardino de. 2000. *Historia general de las cosas de Nueva España.* 3 vols. Edited by Alfredo López Austin and Josefina García Quintana. Mexico City: Consejo Nacional para la Cultura y las Artes.

Schwaller, John F. 2019. *Aztec History in the Rituals of Panquetzaliztli.* Norman: University of Oklahoma Press.

Seler, Eduard. 1992. "Excavations at the Site of the Principal Temple in Mexico." In *Collected Works in Mesoamerican Linguistics and Archaeology*, vol. 3, 114–93. Culver City–Lancaster: Labyrinthos.

Seler, Eduard. 1993. "Some Remarks on the Natural Bases of Mexican Myths." In *Collected Works in Mesoamerican Linguistics and Archaeology*, vol. 4, 157–62. Culver City-Lancaster: Labyrinthos.

Seler, Eduard. 1996. "Uitzilopochtli, the Talking Hummingbird." In *Collected Works in Mesoamerican Linguistics and Archaeology*, vol. 5, 93–99. Culver City–Lancaster: Labyrinthos.

3

Probable Occasional Ceremonies at the End of the Maya Classic Period

DOMINIQUE MICHELET

> Les anthropologues se sont surtout intéressés aux régularités cérémonielles, aux aspects formalisés des religions, et ont accordé peu d'intérêt aux accidents de parcours, aux grains de sable dans la machine: ils ont privilégié les structures au détriment de l'événement [...] et c'est dommage.
>
> (Jacques Galinier, personal communication, 2018)

> ... a return to or increased ritual activity during the Terminal Classic period due to dry conditions is not an unreasonable notion.
>
> (Jobbová 2021, 162)

More than forty years ago, Pierre Smith, in a work on the organization of rites (Smith 1979), insisted that a distinction be made between those that should be considered "periodic," or governed by a cycle, and those that can be described as "occasional." This division is reminiscent of the dichotomy that Misha Titiev had attempted to put forward twenty years earlier (Titiev 1960) when he contrasted "calendrical" practices, which would be characteristic of strict religions, and "critical" rites—critical in that they are imposed by events of the crisis type—which would be more along the lines of magic. Whatever the reservations that may have been formulated with regard to Titiev's position, starting with the immediate one of Downs (1961), it is important, when we reflect on the temporalities of rituals, to take into account the distinction put forward by Smith (and perhaps prefigured

https://doi.org/10.5876/9781646426829.c003

by Titiev). We must take care, however, to avoid confusing *occasional* with *unique*, because rites responding to specific circumstances may well have to be repeated at times unrelated to any timetable, either when those circumstances actually recur, or when they simply may occur again, or when their effects necessitate a repetition of the ritual treatment.

In the Classic period Maya world, even outside the funerary domain, rites were numerous (see, for example, the second part of the book edited by S. B. Mock [1998], which presents seven examples). A priori, they are likely to fall into one or other of the two main categories mentioned. The importance of cyclical thinking about time among the ancient Maya has long been well known, and it is therefore not surprising to note that those rites that are evoked in a certain number of inscriptions appearing on stone monuments, and that are also commonly represented in the images accompanying the texts, are often associated with dates corresponding to the end of important cycles (the *katun* in particular) or even to subdivisions of these cycles (the *hotun* in particular).[1] But there must also have been rituals that were not necessarily aligned with the calendars: these may have taken place specifically in response to the appearance or anticipation of unusual phenomena and, as such, must have fallen outside what might be considered "ceremonial routine."

It seems possible to place within this category a series of ceremonies whose material traces—which obviously represent only part of these rites—have been brought to light by the excavations of the great palatial building 5N2 (formerly known as Structure A) at the Maya site of Río Bec. The very tone of the rituals discovered there suggests that they may have had the function of trying to restore or ensure a sufficient supply of rainwater in the area or to prevent eventual droughts and famine, possibly both at the same time.[2] This took place in the context of the ninth century, which is well known today, thanks to palaeoclimatological data, for having been marked by a general trend toward greater aridity and the repetition of multiannual episodes of drought, episodes that would have had serious consequences for the end of the Classic period apogee in the central lowlands (Douglas et al. 2016; Michelet forthcoming), although this is by no means to claim that drought was the sole cause of the Classic Maya "collapse."[3]

THE DATA AND THEIR CONTEXT

In what has been called the "nuclear zone" of Río Bec (159 hectares: figure 3.1), there is no real center that would have grouped mainly public buildings and plazas (these are actually very rare in this cultural region or "province") surrounded by a periphery of a more residential nature and where the density and importance of the structures would have been less (Nondédéo, Arnauld, and Michelet 2013). In fact,

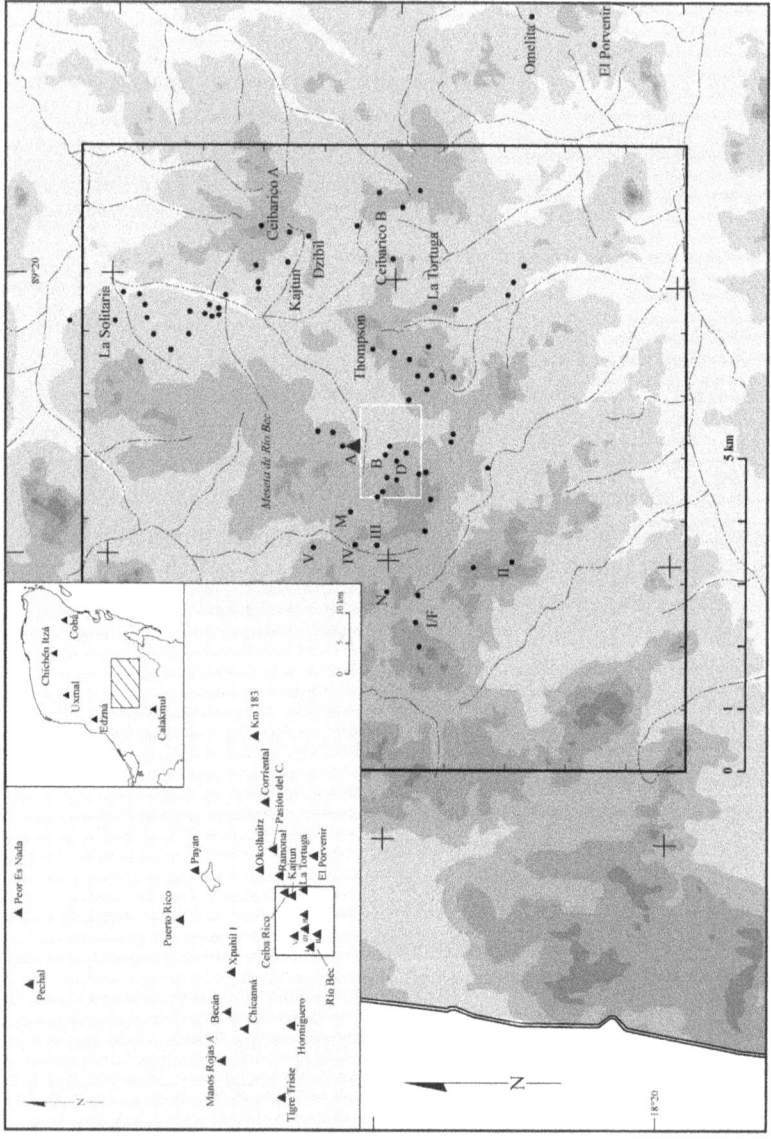

Figure 3.1. The working sector of the Río Bec Project (2002–2010): the central rectangle delimits the "nuclear zone," while the square surrounding is the microregion. Map by P. Nondédéo, modified by S. Éliès.

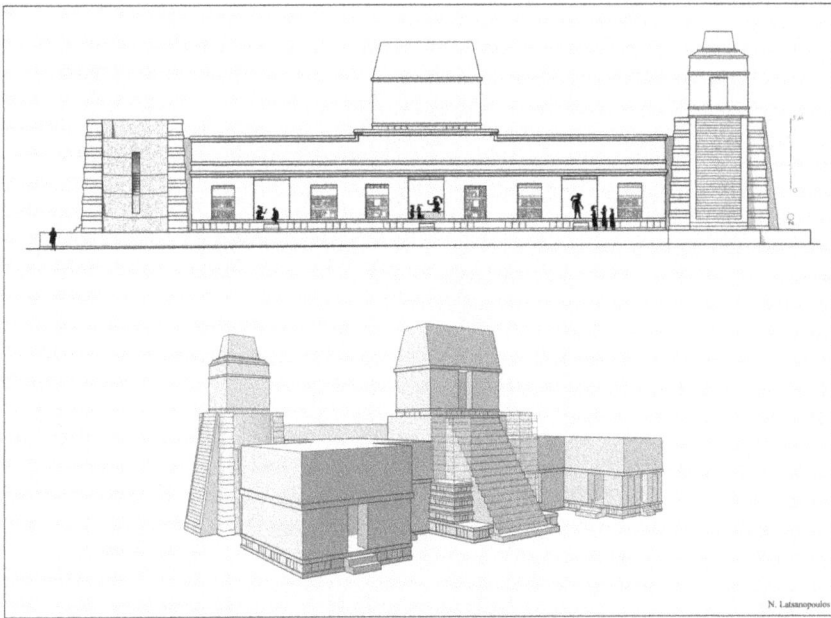

Figure 3.2. Reconstruction of the north facade of Structure 5N2 at Río Bec. Drawing by Nicolas Latsanopoulos after field sketches by Dominique Michelet. Below: 3D reconstruction of Structure 5N2 seen from the southwest. Drawing by Nicolas Latsanopoulos after field sketches by Dominique Michelet and Céline Gillot. Computer graphics assembly by Sylvie Éliès.

this area was termed "nuclear" because it has the highest concentration of monumental groups (a dozen): a type of settlement grouping that is present throughout the 100-square-kilometer study area (or microregion) and is characterized by the agglomeration of, on average, ten structures, sometimes fewer, one or more of which is of clearly monumental size and often distinguished by decorative elements on their facades.

In the microregion, Group A (Michelet et al. 2013) is dominated by the range-building 5N2 (about 50 m long W–E and 23 m wide N–S); it consists of twelve rooms that may be designed as dwellings. Its northern facade (figure 3.2 top) is flanked by towers (trompe l'oeil pyramids), while each of the three doorways of the main body of the building on this side is framed by panels decorated with low-relief carved motifs arranged in superimposed horizontal registers. Finally, at the level of the cornice at the top of the walls, still on this facade, there was originally a long bas-relief frieze. The southern facade of the building (figure 3.2 bottom) opens onto a small area bordered by quarries; this area gave access to four pairs of chambers, but in the center of these there is also a pyramidal basement which was surmounted by what was very probably a temple: its internal dimensions were about 8.60 m long and less than 1.50 m wide. As this pyramid temple did not open onto a proper plaza that would have been accessible to the general public, it must be considered a kind of private chapel or sanctuary, more or less strictly reserved for the occupants of the building or, at most, of neighborhood groups.

The building as it appears today, after clearing and consolidation, is in fact a structure that was built in stages and that was never completed. The study of the architectural sequence between its different parts (Michelet et al. 2013; Gillot 2018, appendix 5)—through what is sometimes referred to as horizontal stratigraphy—and the results of the multiple test pits carried out in and around them (31 in total; see their position in figure 3.3) make it possible to distinguish two major construction phases, encompassing six successive stages (figure 3.4), and to place this architectural sequence approximately in the real timescale (cf. Taladoire et al. 2013, figure 5 in particular).

The history of 5N2 began with the only two rooms in the southern section, called g and h. No dedication offerings were identified under the floors of these rooms, although it cannot be excluded that they once existed.[4] After a period of occupation equivalent to approximately four generations, the second major construction period began, based on the Makan 2 ceramics, around 830–850 CE. This new period was marked, first, by the construction of two rooms in tandem (e and f) laid out symmetrically in relation to the first building and located on the other side of a pyramid temple (m) that had been built at the same time. Two sets of ritual deposits are known from this stage (Michelet et al. 2010). In the corner formed by room f and the basement designated m (test pit S8, figure 3.3), we discovered a concentration of potsherds dating back to the Preclassic period, a period not represented by any occupation in the immediate vicinity. It can therefore be hypothesized that this act of deposit may have been in response to a desire to anchor the process of enlarging the structure in a deep history.

However, below the floor level of temple m (in test pits S25, S25W, and S25E), items placed as offerings attracted most of our attention (figure 3.5). This deposit consists of a series of at least six ceramic vessels distributed in the center and in the eastern and western portions of the room. Although they are diverse, particularly in their shape, they all fall into the category of incense burners (Rice 1999; Tobias 2011). None of them show clear burn marks.[5] But vessel 2 contained ash and a large amount of microcharcoal, mostly pine (Dussol et al. 2016); furthermore, just below the underlay of the floor and in the vicinity of each vessel, there was a pocket of ashes of varying size. Whether these were produced in situ or brought from a different burning site, they are clearly spatially and contextually related to the censers. The main characteristics of each deposit are summarized in the following table (table 3.1).

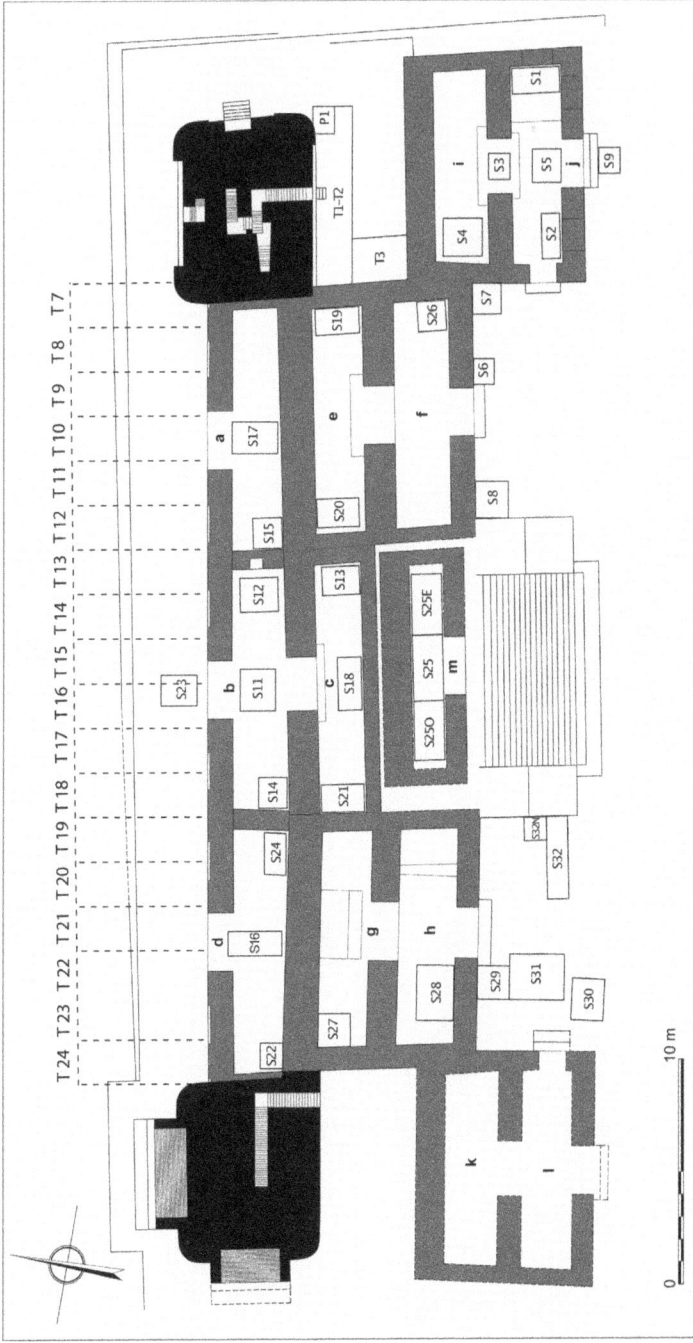

Figure 3.3. Test pits and excavations in Structure 5N2 and in the building's external areas.

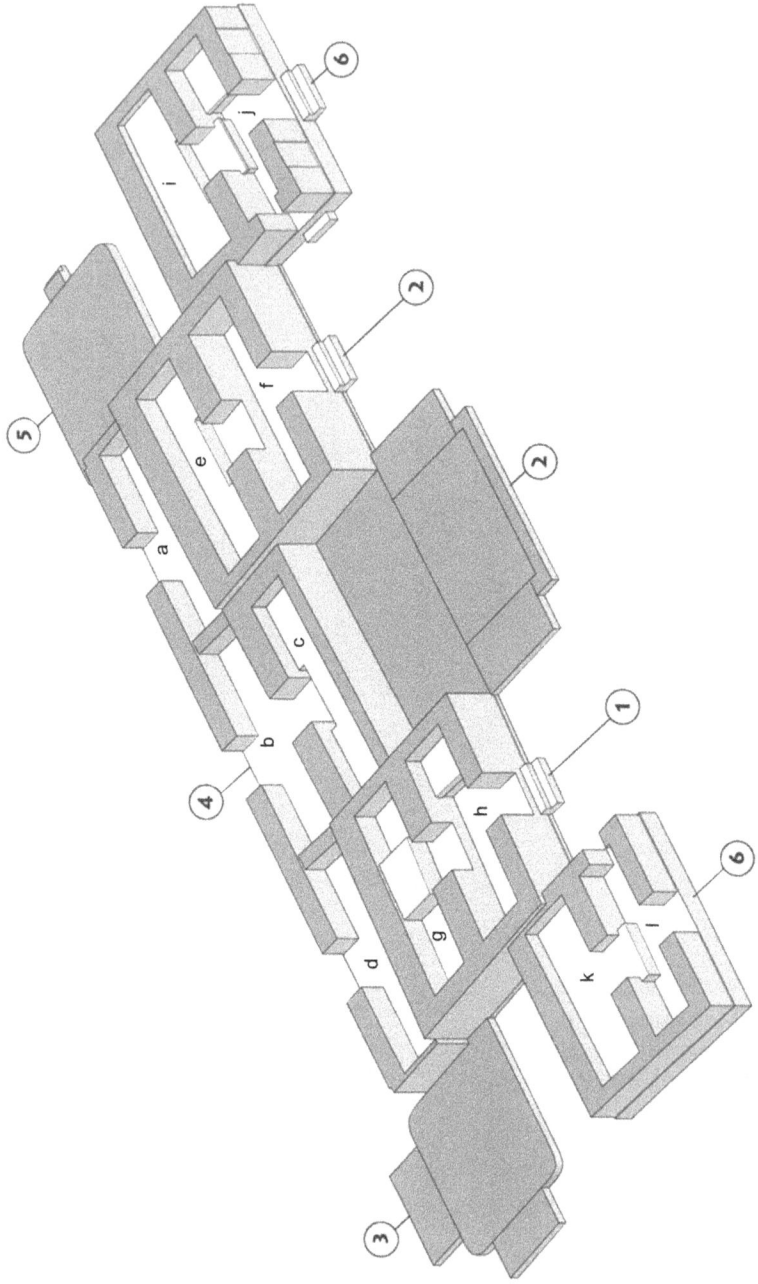

Figure 3.4. Axionometric view of the different construction stages of Structure 5N2, from 1 to 6. Drawing by Nicolas Latsanopoulos after field sketches by Dominique Michelet and Céline Gillot.

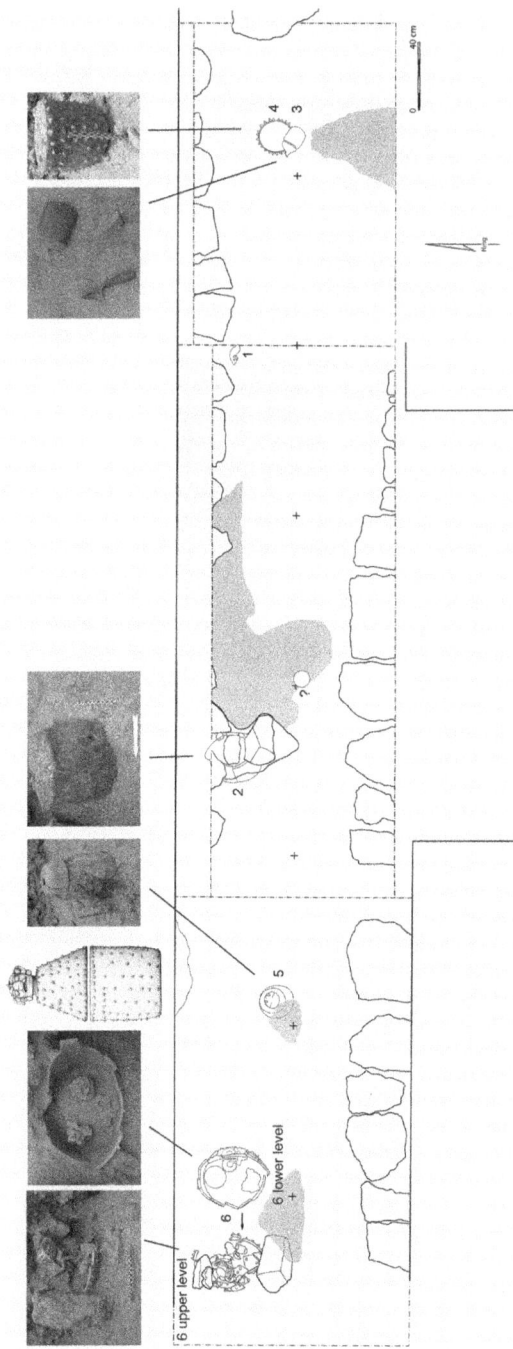

Figure 3.5. Floor plan of temple m (Structure 5N2), with location of censers found below floor level. Drawing by Grégory Pereira and Dominique Michelet. Computer graphics assembly by Sylvie Éliès.

In addition to the items listed in table 3.1, to the west of vessel 6 there were potsherds, particularly of incense burners, at the top of the fill. They could have belonged to other objects of this type used in the rite(s) and broken in the course of the ceremony or ceremonies. This treatment (that is, the breakage of containers) would be the same as the one observed with the objects assigned the number 1 and with the question mark in the table 3.1. In fact, if these are two fragments of the same small, lidded incense burner, we must conclude that it was broken and deposited in two incomplete parts almost 2 m apart.

Faced with the deposits that are present under temple m, the first question to be asked in order to try to reconstruct the ritual sequence(s) is whether the process was unique or was repeated multiple times. The state of the floor of the sanctuary may have been the main indicator in this respect, since repairs to its surface could have testified to the possible digging of pit(s). However, its surface has not really been preserved, except in the vicinity of the western door jamb and in a very narrow strip along the rear north wall. There are two possible explanations for this state of affairs: either the destruction of the floor surface may have been due simply to the collapse of walls and roof of the building on top of it well after the structure had been abandoned, or all or some of the deposits were completed at an equally late date but left without any subsequent repair of the stuccoed floor. The stratigraphic position of the various incense burners reveals that, unlike the others, the censers marked 1, ?, and 3 in figure 5 are located in a higher layer, above the fill itself. This makes it possible to imagine that they must have been placed after the others, although we cannot tell whether they were placed there jointly or separately. As for the spatial organization of the deposits, it does not seem to clearly conform to a single scheme, particularly a cosmologically inspired one, even though we can distinguish more or less three groups: one in the center and one on each side of the room (west and east). The question posed above cannot therefore be answered unambiguously.

In Mesoamerica it is usual to consider the deposits under the floors as relating to foundation, consecration, or inauguration rites, but it is nevertheless not possible to exclude that there were multiple offerings, some of which could have been made when the temple was still in use. In any case, whether they were placed there all in one go or during multiple events, they cannot predate the beginning of the monumental extension of the initial building, that is to say, around 830.

Chronologically speaking or, more precisely, based on the construction sequence of 5N2, a second under-floor deposit comes from the northeastern corner of room c and is part of architectural stage 4 (test pit S13). It consists of a large, intact water jar (traditionally interpreted in this way because of its characteristics, notably its size and the porosity of its unslipped walls); it was standing upright and was covered with a fragment of another jar acting as a lid (figure 3.6 above). This closure

TABLE 3.1. Main characteristics of the deposits from temple m, presented in the order in which they were uncovered and numbered

Deposit Number	Description	Position and Stratigraphic Context	Contents
1	Fragment of the lid of a small incense burner with owl effigy	NE of S25, toward the base of the floor's underlay	None
?	Fragment (circular base) of a small incense burner. Maybe from the same vessel as the fragment numbered 1	Center of S25, toward the base of the floor's underlay	None
2	Complete, piriform container with simple lid	Center of S25. Placed upright under stones and into the fill	Abundance of ash and charcoal in the interior. At the bottom, bones and teeth of a young child (less than three years old)
3	Small, cylindrical incense burner with lid with owl effigy	S25E. Laid on its side into the floor's underlay, above piece 4	None
4	Intact, vertically spiked container. Also, incised decoration on the wall (vertical panel with small crosses)	S25E. Placed upright beneath the floor's underlay	Fragments of coral, small shells, double-scroll ceramic element (cf. images of K'awiil): see vessel 6
5	Intact lidded container (lid with owl effigy)	S25O. Placed upright beneath the floor's underlay	Large number of bones and spines of one or more porcupinefish (*Diodon*). Fragment of foliate coral
6	Large, vertically spiked container with voluminous, also spiked, effigy lid (head of a bat)	S25O. Upright. Into the fill	Placed on the bottom, branching coral, foliate coral, shells, and a double-scroll ceramic element (cf. images of K'awiil): see vessel 4

obviously worked well, because the jar, the main object in the deposit, was totally empty. In room c, like in the other rooms on this north side of the building, no stucco coating was applied over the fill of the floor. But the presence of the deposit was noticed as soon as the floor surface of the room was cleared, because the support layer of the floor was missing over an area of about 70 cm in diameter. It was then assumed that a pit had been dug after the aforementioned preparatory layer had been put in place. However, the removal of the deposit revealed that the jar was originally surrounded, a little below its equator and between two distinct fills,

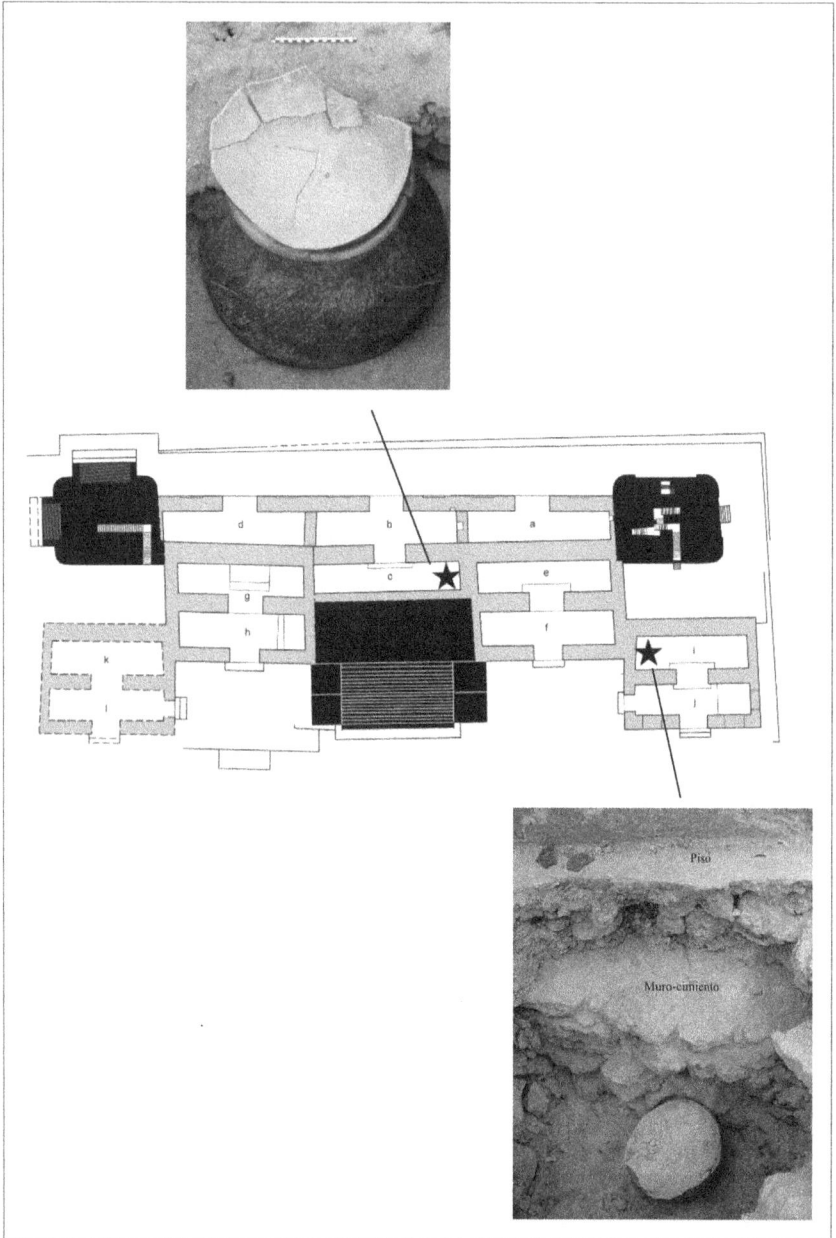

Figure 3.6. Location of ritual deposits under the floors of rooms c and i. Above: jar in room c. Below: half jar in room i. Computer graphics assembly by Sylvie Éliès.

by a thin layer of sediment. It seems unlikely that this very particular stratigraphy along the outside of the vessel would have existed if this were an ordinary pit fill. Rather, the context suggests that the jar was first deposited during the construction of the room and that the local population would subsequently have felt the (ritual?) obligation to regain access to the container and would then have been forced to perforate the subsoil layer to do so. We can therefore imagine that there would have been at least two separate events or ritual actions involving this vessel: at the time of the construction of the room and some years later.

The last deposit found was in test pit S4, at the southwestern corner of room i, in a lower level of the fill (at a depth of nearly 2.50 m) (figure 3.6). Room i belongs to the sixth stage of the building's construction, the last stage before its abandonment. Here the offering is typical of a foundation rite: it consists of the deposition of a flat-bottomed jar with a maximum diameter of 52 cm, deliberately truncated from its upper part (neck and rim) and left without any closure. Inside, there was, as expected, only fill, similar to the rubble fill of the room.

Building 5N2 thus yielded an entire series of remains in the form of under-floor deposits, which testify to the performance of rituals beginning after AD 830. It is now necessary to review the data relating to these remains more closely in order to better understand what they correspond to and what may have motivated the practices that gave rise to them.

DISCUSSION

Although all of the under-floor deposits recorded in building 5N2 at Río Bec definitely postdate the second decade of the ninth century, it is impossible to attribute precise or absolute dates to them. In the Classic Maya world, such dates appear mainly on monuments (above all the stelae) bearing inscriptions. In the microregion under study, of the eight stelae exhibiting dates that are still legible, none were found in Group A, and the only one with a date that corresponds to later than 830 is stela 2, in Group V. Its date is 10.[2].0.0.0 3[Ajaw 3 Kej], that is, 869, but it is unclear which event it celebrates, as the stone face with iconography lies against the ground surface, and the inscription is barely legible apart from the date (Lacadena García-Gallo, Alfonso, and Arnauld 2019). Two even later dates, from stelae 1 (889) and 2 (899) from Pasión de Cristo, are the only known examples from a place relatively close to Río Bec (Nondédéo et al. 2010). They could constitute a *terminus ante quem* for the performance of the rites that we are examining here, although the occupation of Structure 5N2 may have continued into the Xpuhuk 2 phase (900–950; Taladoire et al.).

What is clear, however, from the ritual remains excavated in and around the building is that, with the exception of the collection of Preclassic sherds buried under the northwest corner of the southeast patio, the other offerings are all, more or less, closely linked to water—and probably solely to water.[6] This is obviously true for the water jars found under rooms c and i, but the elements placed inside censers 2, 4, 5, and 6, which appeared under the floor of temple m, are strongly linked to the aquatic world (specifically the marine world), with their corals, shells, and fishes.[7] It can also be the case for the bones and teeth, present in censer 2, at the very center of the deposit, of a small child, whether or not he was sacrificed.[8] As for the almost identical double-scroll ceramic ornaments found in censers 4 and 6, they clearly refer to an attribute associated with the ax of K'awiil, but also often carried by Chaahk, which evokes lightning, storm, and, therefore, rain (Valencia 2022; see also what concerns the *tok* glyph "sparkle" in Stone and Zender 2011, 65).

We can therefore assume that the concern for water and for obtaining good rains, that is, good harvests, which is expressed in a more or less obsessive way through all the rites uncovered in 5N2—and which in fact was probably a permanent preoccupation of the ancient Maya and the object of multiple ceremonies (see in particular Lucero 2006)—must have been related to the environmental, and more particularly the climatic, conditions of this period.[9] Eva Jobbová and Christophe Helmke (Jobbová, Helmke, and Bevan 2018; Jobbová 2021) have studied, in the most detailed manner to date, Maya ritual reactions to climate change and drought, specifically from inscriptions. Although, according to their inventory, only one Classic text of a historical nature speaks about drought and famine,[10] the inscriptions referring to agrarian rituals offer copious material relating to this topic. Two type of rites are thus documented. The rite of scattering precious substances, or of symbolic sowing (found in the inscriptions as *chok*, "to scatter, sprinkle"), has been present for a very long time and is known even outside the Maya world in Mesoamerica. In fact it is not certain whether it was carried out to fix or to prevent a crisis, by imitating the initial act of the agricultural cycle in front of either the images of the gods or objects embodying their power, such as the censer on Altar 4 of El Cayo, dated from 731.[11] This rite may have served, rather, to place routinely agricultural activity under their protection. The rite of the bath of the Paddler gods (*at*: "to bathe") may have been more intended to attract rain. In any case, an examination of the chronological distribution of the two expressions (rites) shows, for both of them, a resumption of their performance precisely in the interval when the Macal Chasm speleothem data indicate major rainfall deficits, between 750 and 950. But the resumption is more clear-cut for the *chok* rite than for the *at* one (Jobbová 2021, figure 8.20).

On the other hand, the rituals performed in caves have long been the subject of research (see Helmke 2019 for recent work), without, however, integrating much about the diachronic dimension of the cults. However this is exactly the focus of the systematic study of Chechem Ha Cave (Moyes et al. 2009), a ceremonial place, apparently of pilgrimage, given that it is several kilometers away from the nearest settlement sites. The analysis by Moyes and colleagues of the rituals carried out in this place over time tends to demonstrate that before they ceased entirely, these rituals increased in the Late Classic, and not necessarily as a corollary of the demographic growth that took place then. What, in reality, is better highlighted is the change in the form of the rituals over time, and especially in the last period of use of the cave: the number of deposited ceramics, mostly whole jars, increases, while the concomitant disappearance of charcoal—most likely the result of the burning of torches—could indicate a reduction in the duration of the ceremonies (see Moyes et al., figure 7). Beyond demonstrating the transformation of the rites, this example shows the perhaps growing importance of the acts of water petition at the very moment when episodes of drought were worsening or at least becoming more frequent (see, for instance, Kennett and Hodell 2017).

Returning now to the rites represented under the floors of Structure 5N2 at Río Bec, even if the deposits found within temple m represented but a single, magisterial celebration—which is not certain—the repetition of a rite dedicated to the master entities of water and rain under room c, and then under room i, is well established. In the context of several multiyear droughts, attested at least during the ninth and early tenth centuries, the reproduction of rites—in an increasingly simplified form, perhaps reflecting a relative loss of means—may well have been apotropaic in nature, with the experience of a crisis prompting people to ritualistically (magically, as Titiev would probably have written) petition for no new natural calamities of this kind to occur. In this case, the actual timing of the rites would not have been regulated periodically but would have corresponded to the appearance, whether real or imagined and feared, of crises, or even to the simple agenda of the building's process of construction in the context of threats, in this case climatic.[12] The control of cyclical time was therefore not the only, or even the main, driving force of ritual life at Río Bec at that time.

NOTES

1. Also, we must not overlook the fact that the cyclical conception of time and, of course, of the events occurring in it may have been a source of fatalism (see, for example, Puleston 1979).

2. To repair and to prevent are in fact two sides of the same ritual action.

3. In another chapter of this volume, Arnauld and Andrieu focus on the "obsession" with history, calendars, and mythical schemes as a destabilizing factor for ruling elites as the end of Baktun 9 (AD 830) approached.

4. On the general subject of foundation deposits in the Maya area, see the chapter in this volume by Chosson, Begel, and Becquey.

5. Nevertheless, during the restoration process of the largest of the specimens (vessel 6), smoke stains were detected on both parts of it.

6. However, with regard to the exclusive use of incense burners in the under-floor deposits of temple m and the consistent presence of ash and charcoal, these are fully consistent with the analyses of Nikolai Grube, according to whom, on the basis of inscriptions, rites with cremation were essential in the Classic period: "fire was a vehicle for the transmutation of sacred offerings," and also "the energy and warmth of fire were considered the expression and manifestation of the presence of divine power" (Grube 2018).

7. The trade winds of the rainy season come fundamentally from the east. In the eyes of the ancient Maya, and especially of the inhabitants of Río Bec, who must have been aware of this sea only 100 km away, it was from the Caribbean Sea that the rains principally came, forming the basis of prosperity or of simple food security. On the relationship of the ancient Maya with the sea, see, among others, Finamore and Houston (2010). Nor should we forget that, according to the above-mentioned publication, in the Maya's horizontal vision of the universe, the terrestrial world rests on a primordial ocean, one of the access points to the underworld (and to life).

8. On the importance of child sacrifice as part of water petition rites in the classical Maya world and, more broadly, throughout Mesoamerica, see, among others, Arden 2011 or Chávez 2010.

9. P. Nondédéo was kind enough to remind me that in the study he and J. Patrois devoted to the roofcombs in the Río Bec microregion, wherever there were two successive decorations, the most recent concerns vegetation and water, as if this were a more worrying theme (Patrois and Nondédéo 2014).

10. It is engraved on a stingray spine found at the site of Comalcalco and refers to the years 783 or 763.

11. Actually, it is a ritual to petition for prosperity and abundance.

12. In the conclusion of the Geurds chapter in this volume we find a very similar consideration: "Societies [...] are continually shaped by, and to some degree always in friction with, the irregular or unpredicted consequences of being entangled with a wider world around. In other words, events invade societies, even those with a high degree of structure."

REFERENCES

Arden, Traci. 2011. "Empowered Children in Classic Maya Sacrificial Rites." *Childhood in the Past* 4: 133–45.

Chávez, Ximena. 2010. "Propiciadores de lluvia, agoreros en la guerra, representaciones de los dioses: El sacrificio de infantes en el Templo Mayor de Tenochtitlan." In *Los niños actores sociales ignorados: Levantando el velo, una mirada al pasado*, edited by Lourdes Márquez Morfín, 283–302. Mexico City: INAH.

Douglas, Peter M. J., Arthur A. Demarest, Mark Brenner, and Marcello A. Canuto. 2016. "Impacts of Climate Change on the Collapse of Lowland Maya Civilization." *Annual Review in Earth Planetary Science* 44 (1): 613–45. https://doi.org/10.1146/annurev -earth-060115-012512.

Downs, R. E. 1961. "On the Analysis of Ritual." *Southwestern Journal of Anthropology* 17 (1): 75–80.

Dussol, Lydie, Michelle Elliott, Grégory Pereira, and Dominique Michelet. 2016. "The Use of Firewood in Ancient Maya Funerary Rituals: A Case Study from Río Bec (Campeche, Mexico)." *Latin American Antiquity* 27 (1): 51–73.

Finamore, Daniel, and Stephen D. Houston, eds. 2010. *Fiery Pool: The Maya and the Mythic Sea*. Salem, MA: Peabody Essex Museum; New Haven, CT: Yale University Press.

Gillot, Céline. 2018. "L'art de bâtir à Río Bec." PhD diss., Université de Montréal.

Grube, Nikolai. 2018. "Fire Rituals in Maya Inscriptions." Paper presented at the colloquium Temporalités rituelles en Mésoamériqe. Approches interdisciplinaires, Paris, November 14–16.

Helmke, Christophe, ed. 2019. *The Realm Below: Speleoarchaeological Investigations in the Macal River Valley, Belize*. San Francisco: Precolumbian Mesoweb Press.

Jobbová, Eva. 2021. *The Maya and Environmental Stress from Past to Present: Human Responses and Adaptation to Climate Change in the Maya Lowlands*. Oxford: BAR Publishing.

Jobbová, Eva, Christophe Helmke, and Andrew Bevan. 2018. "Ritual Responses to Drought: An Examination of Ritual Expressions in Classic Maya Written Sources." *Human Ecology* 46 (5): 759–81.

Kennett, Douglas J., and David A. Hodell. 2017. "AD 750–1100 Climate Change and Critical Transitions in Classic Maya Sociopolitical Networks." In *Megadrought and Collapse: From Early Agriculture to Angkor*, edited by Harvey Weiss, 205–30. New York: Oxford University Press.

Lacadena García-Gallo, Alfonso, Dominique Michelet, and M. Charlotte Arnauld. 2019. "Uno en tres: El glifo-emblema de Río Bec." *Revista Española de Antropología Americana* 49: 97–119.

Lucero, Lisa J. 2006. *Water and Ritual: The Rise and Fall of Classic Maya*. Austin: University of Texas Press.

Michelet, Dominique. Forthcoming. "La difficile acceptation du rôle joué par des crises climatiques dans l'extinction du monde classique des Basses Terres mayas du Sud." In *Et pourtant elle tourne! Blocages épistémologiques en archéologie*, edited by Sophie A. de Beaune and Laure Fontana. Paris: CNRS Éditions.

Michelet, Dominique, Philippe Nondédéo, Julie Patrois, Céline Gillot, and Emyly González G. 2013. "The Structure 5N2 ('Group A'): A Río Bec Paradigmatic Palace?" *Ancient Mesoamerica* 24 (2): 415–31.

Michelet, Dominique, Philippe Nondédéo, Grégory Pereira, Julie Patrois, Alfonso Lacadena, and M. Charlotte Arnauld. 2010. "Rituales en una sociedad 'sin reyes': El caso de Río Bec y del Edificio A (5N2) en particular." In *El ritual en el mundo maya: De lo privado a lo público*, edited by Andrés Ciudad R., María Josefa Iglesias P. de L., and Miguel Ángel Sorroche C., 153–80. Madrid: Sociedad Española de Estudios Mayas.

Mock, Shirley B., ed. 1998. *The Sowing and the Dawning: Termination, Dedication, and Transformation in the Archaeological and Ethnographic Record of Mesoamerica*. Albuquerque: University of New Mexico Press.

Moyes, Holley, Jaime J. Awe, George A. Brook, and James W. Webster. 2009. "The Ancient Maya Drought Cult: Late Classic Cave Use in Belize." *Latin American Antiquity* 20 (1): 175–206.

Nondédéo, Philippe, M. Charlotte Arnauld, and Dominique Michelet. 2013. "Río Bec Settlement Patterns and Local Sociopolitical Organization." *Ancient Mesoamerica* 24 (2): 373–96.

Nondédéo, Philippe, Julie Patrois, Alfonso Lacadena, M. Charlotte Arnauld, Éric Taladoire, and Dominique Michelet. 2010. "De la autonomía política y cultural de la provincia de Río Bec." *Estudios de cultura maya* 36: 37–66.

Patrois, Julie, and Philippe Nondédéo. 2014. "Iconografía y secuencia estilística de las cresterías en la micro-región de Río Bec." In *Artistic Expressions in Maya Architecture: Analysis and Documentation Techniques*, edited by Cristina Vidal L. and Gaspar Munoz C., 125–52. Oxford: BAR Publishing.

Puleston, Dennis E. 1979. "An Epistemological Pathology and the Collapse; or, Why the Maya Kept the Short Count." In *Maya Archaeology and Ethnohistory*, edited by Norman Hammond and Gordon R. Willey, 63–74. Austin: University of Texas Press.

Rice, Prudence M. 1999. "Rethinking Classic Maya Pottery Censers." *Ancient Mesoamerica* 10 (1): 25–50.

Smith, Pierre. 1979. "Aspects de l'organisation des rites." In *La Fonction symbolique: Essais d'anthropologie réunis par Michel Izard et Pierre Smith*, 139–70. Paris: Gallimard, Bibliothèque des Sciences humaines. [1982. "Aspects of the Organization of Rites." In

Between Belief and Transgression: Structuralist Essays in Religion, History and Myth, edited by Michel Izard and Pierre Smith, 103–28. Chicago: University of Chicago Press.]

Stone, Andrea, and Marc Zender. 2011. *Reading Maya Art: A Hieroglyphic Guide to Ancient Maya Painting and Sculpture*. London: Thames and Hudson.

Taladoire, Éric, Sara Dzul, Philippe Nondédéo, and Mélanie Forné. 2013. "Chronology of the Río Bec Settlement and Architecture." *Ancient Mesoamerica* 24 (2): 253–372.

Titiev, Mischa. 1960. "A Fresh Approach to the Problem of Magic and Religion." *Southwestern Journal of Anthropology* 16 (3): 292–93.

Tobias, María Dolores. 2011. *Ritual Change at the End of the Maya Classic Period: A Study of Incense Burners from the Southern Lowlands*. Oxford: BAR Publishing.

Valencia Rivera, Rogelio. 2022. *K'awiil: El dios maya del rayo, la abundancia y los gobernantes*. Oxford: Archeopress Publishing.

4

Ritual Speech and the Transformation of Time

The Grammar and Voice of Temporalization in Yucatec Maya Rituals

VALENTINA VAPNARSKY

INTRODUCTION

RITUAL TEMPORALITY AND TEMPORALIZATION

Maya ritual speech, across languages and periods, has been the focus of numerous studies, particularly with regard to its rhetorical composition and poetic qualities. Linguistic anthropological studies have focused especially on the highly polyphonic nature of this speech, the transformations of spatial and interactional frames it activates, and the forms of agency and shared or unshared knowledges that it involves (Gossen 1974; Hanks 1996, 2006; Haviland 2000; Hull and Carrasco 2012; Monod Becquelin 2000; Monod Becquelin and Breton 2002, among others). Little has been said, however, of the temporal characteristics of this speech and the manner in which it contributes to the establishment of ritual temporalities. In ritual analysis more broadly too, the issue of temporality has often been approached all too schematically (see the introduction to this volume). This is despite the fact that the temporal composition of rituals is typically multiple and imbricated. By contrast, I will argue here that what some have even gone so far as to deem the "atemporality" of ritual corresponds, in fact, to the establishment of complex temporal configurations, separating the performance from the ordinary flow of time even while marking certain essential links with the latter.

In this chapter, I examine certain processes by which ritual speech contributes to setting up such complex temporal configurations. These processes are rooted in ways of speaking, and the transformations thereby engendered in the situation

https://doi.org/10.5876/9781646426829.c004

and in the experience of time. The processes hinge on specific discursive forms that are shaped by rhetorical figures, lexical choices, and grammatical markers, together with prosodic and vocal techniques. Focusing on some of these through a study of contemporary Maya ritual speech, I analyze the resulting *multitemporality* that is particular to ritual. The processes I discuss—deictic anchoring, aspectual marking, voice manipulation—are central to Maya ritual speech, and are arguably also typical of the discursive tools assumed to be at work in rituals more generally.

I approach the issue of temporality in ritual speech through what I term the *process of temporalization*, the phenomenon of handling and carving out time. In accordance with this approach, I view ritual time as a construct: it is emergent, processual, procedural, generative, and selective. Discursive forms play an essential role in the processes of constructing ritual temporalities. The process of temporalization is key to ritual actions and their effects.

In previous studies, I have analyzed Yucatec Maya rituals' constitutive modes of temporalization observed and recorded amongst the descendants of the Cruzo'ob Maya in the state of Quintana Roo in southeast Mexico, where I have conducted long-term fieldwork.[1] This chapter extends the corpus studied to a set of rituals performed throughout the Yucatan peninsula and recorded by other researchers over the past forty years (Arzápalo 1970; Gubler 2017; Hanks 1984). This allows us to compare the ritual speech of experts who live hundreds of kilometers apart, belong to distinct lines of transmission lineages, and have had no direct relations with each other. Note that the transmission and learning of these rituals is exclusively oral.

Anthropological comparison is particularly challenging in case of the Maya. This is on account of the highly developed art of variants and variation, which has led to the continual recomposing of genres over time, be it over the longue durée or over biographical and microhistorical time, from one community of practice to another, from one ritual speech expert to another, and for the latter, from one life stage, even one event, to another (Monod Becquelin, Breton, and Ruz 2010). This Maya art of variation derives not only from the need to adapt to the context but also from the need for inventiveness, essential if the words are to possess meaning, power, and life. To these necessities is wedded a poetic taste for the exploration of new forms and combinations. This poetics of the unstable originates with the creation of difference from sameness, with the introduction of microvariations into repetition, with the infinite rearrangement of units that seem fixed, until they themselves get swept up in the flow of this delicate entropy. The Catholic liturgy, with its abundance of prayers, saints, and ritual gestures, has been incorporated by the Maya for nearly five centuries as one more source of these rhetorical and aesthetic games that forge the pragmatics of their ritual.

It is against this background of a continual and constitutive variation of the genre that I seek to shed light on present-day Maya ritual speech's modes of composing temporalities. I will focus particularly on the relatively constant elements, which form the active principles of ritual's temporal composition, and from which variations unfold.

YUCATEC MAYA RITUALS: ACTORS AND SPATIOTEMPORAL CONFIGURATIONS

The rituals from which the speech analyzed is taken are of three related orders. The first are associated with the agricultural cycle, in particular: the *waajil kool*, the "bread [tortillas] of the cultivated field" rituals, celebrated annually to close the cycle of exchange with the guardian spirits who aid agricultural work; the *ch'acháak*, the "take-thunder" rituals, to attract rain; and the *jo'olbesaj nal*, to celebrate the first fruits of the corn harvest. Rituals of the second order include the *jeets'*, rituals of "appeasement." These are performed to protect particular spaces: a piece of land, an enclosure, or a well (*jeets' lu'um, jeets' kooral, jeets' ch'e'en*, "appeasement of the land, the enclosure, the well"). The rituals are performed prior to the occupation or use of these spaces, and, above all, when misfortunes reveal the discontent of the guardian spirits of those spaces. The third order includes therapeutic rituals of a type frequently performed, as when a person is "caught" by one or more of those noxious, agentive airs that abound amongst the Maya. Depending on the region and subtype, the rituals are named as follows: *púus* (literally "to dust" or "dusting"), *sáantigwar* (literally, "to sanctify"), or *pa'iik'* ("to shatter the winds"). From guardian spirits to noxious airs, all these rituals involve invisible entities with various powers and roles. These entities are generically named *iik'*, translated here as "air" or "wind," though the term also means "breath." Some *iik'* are more personified than others and are given specific collective names within the ritual context.

The agricultural rituals form part of the annual cycle of seasonal tasks. The main aim of these rituals is to offer thanks to the guardian spirits of the cultivated forest areas in their various roles, and to the saints and divinities, for help given to farmers. To this end, the ritual specialist (the *jmeen*, "the doer") must "bring down" (*éensik*, literally "cause to descend"), or "pile up" (*junts'ankúunsik*, "bring together and pile up"), the spirit entities summoned to where the altar is erected, and where the offerings are placed. He must hold them there so that they may consume the offerings, and then send them away by "raising" (*líisik*) them to the specific places to which they are attached. The protection rituals of the different spaces work in a similar way, because they must often remedy the shortcomings of the offerings and sacrifice made to the spirit inhabitants of the places concerned. It is also sometimes necessary to dispel certain ill winds from the place affected, an aspect that brings these rituals closer to the third type, the therapeutic order. This last includes formulas involving the actions of "sweeping" (*míistik*), "dusting" or "clearing" (*púustik*), and "breaking and shattering" (*pa'ik'tik*) the ill winds. Here, the interaction is clearly agonistic, even if the aid of souls, saints, and divinities is simultaneously sought. In all these cases, the rituals must displace the spirit entities, whose presence is a guarantee of appeasement, yet fraught with danger.

The specific conjuncture of the ritual and the entities invoked—or repelled, even combated—can yield a concentration of very different temporal frameworks during the performance (see also Hanks 1996, 2017). These include, nonexhaustively:

- the performance and its sequences;
- the events immediately leading to a ritual performance;
- the ritual cycles or series within which a given performance takes place;
- the temporality of the guardian spirits, which weaves links with the ancestors and previous humanities, that is, the Maya time of the longue durée;
- the time of saints and divinities attached to present humanity;
- and also, the time of the genealogies of deceased ritual specialists who may be summoned to intercede during the ceremonies.

The entanglement of events and presences belonging to these different frames, manifest in the same place, creates a multitemporality. This is a composite temporality, at once expanded and condensed, both temporally and spatially, that is specific to each ritual. Studies have generally focused on the ways in which rituals may activate mythic and historical frames, but other dynamics specific to accomplishing rituals must be added to this. I refer, in particular, to the essential dynamic that plays out at the most originary and intimate level, that of the creation of a ritual *hic et nunc*, its distinctive temporal flow fostering the presence and the relationship of key entities and actions. This level is, by definition, always at work in the rituals, even if little attention has hitherto been paid to it.

I discuss below how this essential ritual dynamic is created through the mobilization of three key dimensions of linguistic temporality, namely, indexical anchoring, aspectuality, and rhythmicity. I will analyze the specific elements of Yucatec Maya that serve to produce this transformation of time.

DISCURSIVE TEMPORALIZATION
INDEXICAL ANCHORING: REFERENTIAL MOORING, SINGULARIZING THE ACT, AND MAINTAINING THE RITUAL'S TEMPORAL FLOW

All ritual enunciations within Maya performances involve an explicit anchoring in an external temporal—typically calendrical—frame of reference. In the rituals studied here, the calendar is used minimally, with only the day of the week and, generally, the hour or time of day of the ritual's performance being mentioned. Sometimes, the ritual's insertion within a series of associated rituals is also referenced. These expressions are often accompanied by a temporal deictic for "today" (*béejla'*), as we see twice in excerpt (1), highlighted in lines 1 and 12.[2]

1. Excerpt from a *jeets' lu'um* ritual ("appeasement of the land"), Victor Hau, Teabo, circa 1990 (Gubler 2017, 12; transcriptions and translations revised here)

Le dia <u>béejlae'</u> *ti'al jump'éel* <u>myeerkoles</u>	On this day, today, for a <u>Wednesday</u>
te' santo meyaja'	of this holy work
yumen	lord
inka'a intsik óol le x-k'aanpool míiso'	I will express my respect to the k'ampool míis
tuláakal x-moson iik'	all the whirlwinds
meejil iiko'ob	the working winds
mejen iik'o'ob	the little winds
tulaaka le yiik'ale' x Yo' áaktuno'	all the winds of the caves
treese áaktuno'ob	the thirteen caves
treese múulo'ob xan	the thirteen mounds too
ti'al le santo priminsya	for these sacred first fruits
(. . .) *te' dia* <u>béejlae'</u>	(. . .) **of this day, today.**
Bey xan tuno'oj k'abil xan	Thus also to the right hand
ti' umeetal le santo primisya tumen le 'ermaano	that these sacred first fruits be celebrated by this brother
<u>ti las doose</u>	<u>at noon</u>

Apart from the existence of ceremonial days and hours that are more or less propitious, this calendrical mention effectuates two things. It is a mooring to the conjunctural reference frame that triggers the ritual (for example, the first fruits of the harvest, misfortunes on a piece of land, the "taking" of a child by an ill wind). It simultaneously singularizes the performance, making of it a unique event (performed on a specific day, at a given hour), even if it is related to other performances. Both mooring and singularization are conditions of efficacy. These two processes are, furthermore, expressed in other aspects of the ritual, for instance, in the mention of the name of the person for whom the ritual is performed (the cultivator, the patient, etc.) or the more complex mention of the forest or corporeal area concerned.

However, while such calendrical anchoring is one of numerous processes by which each performance is singularized, such anchoring seems equally necessary

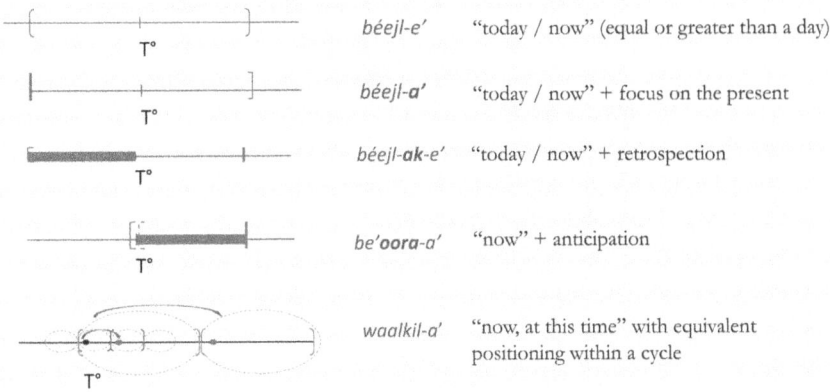

béejl-e'	"today / now" (equal or greater than a day)
béejl-a'	"today / now" + focus on the present
béejl-ak-e'	"today / now" + retrospection
be'oora-a'	"now" + anticipation
waalkil-a'	"now, at this time" with equivalent positioning within a cycle

Figure 4.1. Deictics for "today" and "now" in Yucatec Maya

in a somewhat opposed movement. This is a movement of detachment from the mundane world, through which emerges the ritual's own particular space-time, its imbricated temporalities and their flow unfolding according to specific modalities.

One of the key processes of this detachment is based on another Yucatec Maya temporal deictic for "now." This is no longer *béejla'* (the "now-today" of the preceding excerpt) but instead *be'oora* ("now"), which, among Maya temporal adverbs (see figure 4.1), is based on the notion of "moment." It is constructed from *oora* ("hour" in Spanish, "moment" in Maya). *Be'oora* refers to a moment of time, including the time of utterance, generally shorter than a day. It is also a projected moment, involving a prospective, rather than retrospective, horizon. In ordinary speech, *be'oora* is thus the deictic for "now," used in utterances that express the start of an action, even an anticipation of something imminent. Other forms of "now" in Maya, by contrast, are reserved to indicate the final moment or stage of a situation extending from the past (Vapnarsky 2017).

Records of ritual speech, despite being separated by decades and by hundreds of kilometers, and involving numerous variations, manifest similar sustained reiterations of the deictic *be'oora* ("now, in this moment") or of a verbal derivative of the root *oora* ("moment"), namely, *oorapajal* ("become the hour"). Although they are used in different linguistic constructions, these terms always serve, through their incessant repetition, to produce the same prospective tension of a moment-instant in the process of becoming, as is illustrated in the three excerpts below.

Excerpt 2 is from another *jeets' lu'um* (ritual of appeasement of the land), performed in 1994 by Adolfo Suarez Bautista at Mani (Gubler 2017). It manifests the repeated use of the deictic *be'oora* ("now") and its contrast with *béejla'* ("today"), the latter being used far more punctually, and only in case of calendrical anchoring. Excerpt 3 is from a ceremony performed to appease the resident spirits (Arzápalo 1970). It was performed over several days in 1959 in the Balankanche cave near Chichen Itza, before the place was explored by archaeologists. In the repertoire of prayers that make up this long ceremony, the temporal deictic *be'oora* is repeated very frequently. It is almost always introduced by the borrowed term *desde* ("from"), a preposition that accentuates the projective dynamic already contained in *be'oora*, to mean "from now on." Excerpt 4 is from a first-fruits ritual that I recorded in 1995 with Adriano Mex May at Kopchen in the eastern part of the Yucatan peninsula. In this case, *oora* is derived as a processual verb, meaning "to become the moment [or hour]," but also occurs repeatedly throughout the prayer.

2. Excerpt from a prayer of *jeets' lu'um* (appeasement of the land), Mani, 1994, 11 seconds of a prayer that lasts 7 minutes, 45 seconds (Gubler 2017, 19; transcriptions and translations revised here)

ka bin tinchi'it'antaj	and I invoked them
*tinsujuyt'antaj bakan xan **be'oora'***	I invoked them in purity truly also **now**
men uchik intsikbe'eno'obe'	because I have respected them
táan uchik insujuyt'antikech bakan xan	I invoke you in purity truly also
***be'oora'** amen*	**now** amen
ikil inpéeksajt'antik xan	while I invoke them by moving them also
kinsujuyt'antik anoj poder	I invoke in purity your great power
*anoj bendisyon bakan **be'oora'***	your great blessing truly **now**
men ti'al bakan	for truly
ink'áatik xan	that I also ask
insujuyt'antikech xan bakan	I invoke you in purity also truly
***be'oora'** amen*	**now** amen
(. . .)	*(. . .)*
kexi' bakan	let us hope truly
kinwéensajt'aan	I invoke by bringing [them] down
kinxansujuyt'aan	I invoke also in purity
ichil bakan xan	while truly also
*bey **béejla'** xan*	like **today** also

ti'al le sujuy **martes**	for this sacred Tuesday
ka' k'uchuk intsikbeno'ob	may my tokens of respect reach (you)
ka' beetak xan **be'oora'** *amen*	let it be done also **now** amen

3. Excerpt from the ritual of the Balankanche cave, 1959, from the Invocation of the Balam (jaguar guardians; Arzápalo 1970, 94; transcriptions and translations revised here)

desde be'oora, *inyum*	**from now on**, my lord
tech bakan	You truly
[k]ki'k'ubik xaan	we also give as offerings
desde be'oora	**from now on**
ti' saanto ah kanan saya'	to the sacred guardians of the sources
ti' treese santo báalam	to the thirteen sacred Balam (Jaguars)
kuki'kanantik xaan	who protect well also
treese yuntsilo' xaan	(to the) thirteen guardian spirits also
kuki'k'áat'otko'	they implore also
desde be'oora *bakan*	**from now on** truly
yan aki'k'áat'otik xan	you should implore also
desde be'oora *in yuum*	**from now on** my lord
tech bakan	you truly
anuk e t'aan bakan	respond to words truly
desde be'oora *bakan*	**from now on** truly

4. Excerpt from a *jo'olbesaj nal* (first-fruits ritual; Kopchen 1995)

way tuxuul meesa inyumeen	here at the tip of the altar my lord
way **tuyoorapaja** *tumen yet injajal ko'lel*	here **is the hour now becoming**, by my true lady
yeet junts'íit usujuy saanto jurameento	with a pure and sacred vow [materialized in the form of a candle]
usáasibal [let]	its clarity
uti'il inlíi'bansik injajal yuum	that I may raise my true lord
uti'il ulíi'bal ajajal ki'ichkemiléex	that your true beauty be raised
yóok'ol jump'el aki'ichkelem sujuy saanto meesa'éex	upon one of your beautiful and holy sacred altars

mukaj 'oorapaj men yet injajal ko'lel	**the hour will [now] become**, by [my lord] and my true lady
uti'il injunts'aankunsik biin	that I may reunite them, it is said,
u aj kanan-k'áak'bilóo' xaan	the guardians of fertile lands
(…)	(…)
beej San josé'	on the path of San José
way **kuyoorapaja** *tumen tinjajal ko'lel xane'*	here **the hour now becomes**, by my true lady also
way **kuyoorapaja** *te tunoj uk'a tinjajal ko'lel*	**here the hour now becomes**, there, to the right hand of my true lady

One of the most frequent leitmotifs, *(be')oora* thus veritably takes over this ritual speech. The rhythmic repetition of this "now" of the ritual instant, and of the projected moment, works to literally create the emergence of this time that is necessary for the actions and interactions undertaken within the ritual performance. The repetition also maintains this time in tension and in activity. It contributes, crucially, to create the temporal bubble, as it were, of the ritual performance. This dynamic of emergence and maintenance can be compared to the preparation of the *júuy k'óol*, the corn-based sauce prepared for the spirits that one must stir rapidly and continuously during its cooking, without which it does not set. Or, it may be compared to the continuous shaking of one's hand when one tries to keep a feather, trembling in the wind, suspended in the air, by stirring the air below the feather. The intimate time of the ritual would be similarly fragile and evanescent were it not carried by words, speech, and voice.

ASPECTUALITY: PROJECTIVE TENSION AND TEMPORAL FUSIONS

The temporal dynamic borne by *(be')oora* is of an originary and vital order. It is further shaped by other temporal markers that qualify the actions performed, whether by gesture or in speech, during the ceremony. Yucatec Maya, like other languages of the Maya family and the majority of Mesoamerican languages, is aspect-dominant. Notions of time are relative, especially, to the internal configuration of processes, and to their completive or incompletive nature, a large spectrum of transitions and perspectives being possible between and within these two, which are necessarily indicated in the verb. As table 4.1 illustrates, the Maya aspectual system, which combines with the modal and peripherally with tense, is very rich. How is this mobilized in ritual speech?

TABLE 4.1. (Tense-)Aspect-Mode markers in Yucatec Maya

(jo'o)**p'**-	inceptive
t(áan)-	progressive
k-	incompletive
ts'(o'ok)-	terminative
-**m**/ -**a'an**	perfect, resultant state
sáam	hodiernal retrospective
úuch	remote retrospective (> + days)
ken	topical prospective
mik(a'aj)	prospective + imminent
yan	deontic, projective
bíin	predictive-prophetic future

The Taut Line of the Incompletive

Quotidian speech, like narrative, is generally characterized by aspectual variability, with frequent shifts in perspective on the processes described or evoked. The ritual speech of the performances studied here, by contrast, for the most part manifests a very clear simplifying of the aspectual forms used. In fact, one form always appears as dominant, if not almost exclusive, namely, that of the generic incompletive, expressed by the prefix *k-*, bolded in the transcription of the Maya, and which I translate by the present.[3]

5. Excerpt from a ritual of *jeets' ch'e'en* (appeasement of the well), Felipe Manrique, 1997, (Gubler 2017, 8–9, transcriptions and translations revised here)

Síi ten a beendisyon Padre mío	Give me your blessing my father
le sáanto sakab	of the holy *sakab* drink
***ikil** int'anik San Dimas bakan*	as I invoke Saint Dimas truly
uti'al walkil bin un 'aanyoa' inyumen	for in a year, it is said, my father.
síi ten le bendisyion	Give me the blessing
ts'aa ten le feelisidad way	bring me happiness here
uti'al le ermaanoso'ob	for the brothers
***kuxíimbatiko'ob** ubo'oy le sáanto lu'um bakan*	who walk in the shade of the holy earth truly
*tu'ux **kuki'xíimbalo'ob** bakan*	there where they walk with fervor truly

*tu'ux **kuki'** meyajo'ob bakane' in yumen*	there where they work with fervor truly my lord
*le **kt'anik** uyiik'alo'ob bakan*	thus do we invoke their airs truly
*le **ktséentbesik** uyiik'alo'ob*	thus do we nourish their airs
*le **kpa'ik'tik***	thus do we break them
*le **kch'ooch'itik***	thus do we extract them
*le **kmíistik** bakane'*	thus do we sweep them truly
*le **kinxolampixtik** bakan tu chúumuk*	thus do I kneel truly at the center of
le sáanto lu'uma'	this holy earth here
tu kanti'its'i ka'an	to the four corners of the sky
tu kanyáalil muuyal	to the four layers of clouds
tu kan ti'its'i bakan uk'áaxil bakan	to the four corners truly of the forest truly
ulu'umil bakan	of the earth truly
ti' bakan san dimas bakane' in yumen	for truly Saint Dimas truly my father

This drawing of perspectives on events and actions in the ritual speech fulfills several functions. On the one hand, the mark of the generic incompletive (***k-***, with ***-ik*** for transitives) serves here as the canonical form for performative verbs such as those below, which are used in large numbers in invocations:

6. Examples of performative locutions in Yucatec Maya ritual speech

Kinsujuyt'antik	I call [or invoke] in purity
Kinki'ki't'anik	I call in sweet words
Kinwéensajt'antik	I call by bringing [them] down
Kinpéeksajt'antik	I call by making [them] move
Kinch'a'achi'tik	I chew [such names] (or, I call them one after the other continuously)

However, this usage does not suffice to explain the significance of this form of the incompletive in other types of verbs. In Excerpt 7, for example, a phase of finalization is expressed using a visualization that is incompletive, even though Maya possesses terminative aspectual marking. Thus, in the Balankanche prayer, the end of the ritual is marked by the use of *ts'o'ok*, which exists in the language as a terminative aspect marker but is here used in the first instance as a full verb, introduced by the incompletive marker *k-* (*kuki'ts'o'oko*, "it ends well"), and then within a noun phrase (*le ts'ok tsikbal*, "these words of completion"):

7. Excerpt from the ritual of the Balankanche cave, 1959 (Arzápalo 1970)

kuki'ts'o'oko to'on	this **ends** well for us
kuki'ts'o'ok xan	this **ends** well also
le ts'ok tsikbal	these words of completion

Beyond the performative condition, it seems that the repeated use of the generic incompletive serves to reinforce the dynamic of creation and maintenance of the ritual's temporal flow to which the leitmotif of *be'oora* ("now"), incessantly repeated, already contributed. What matters, then, is the continued incompletive character of the actions evoked, or rather generated, at the very moment of the performance. Finally—and this is far from incidental—this taut line of incompletives also permits the highlighting of certain moments or key actions, which are uttered with distinct tense-aspect marking.

Aspectual Contrasts, Actional Fusion and Fission

Within the ritual speech, the sudden appearance of the progressive *táan*—frequent in daily speech but generally avoided in this genre—underscores the relationship of causality between two types of actions by presenting them as concomitant: the moving actions of the spirits and the discursive actions of the ritual performer:[4]

8. Excerpt from a ritual of *jeets' lu'um* (appeasement of the land), Victor Hau, Teabo, circa 1990 (Gubler 2017, 14, transcriptions and translations revised here)

Waye' kikt'anik,	Here we call them
kikk'ubik tu no'oj k'abilo'ob xan	here we hand over to their right hands also
táan ubin uki'taal uxíimbalto'on,	they are keenly com**ing** to visit us
táan utal uki'pa'pa'laj	they are com**ing**, [and their hands] keenly clap-tap
táan inki'iki'ikt'aniko'ob	I am call**ing** them with my sweet words
te' kan tu'uk'o'	to the four corners (of the earth)

Ritual speech can also play with the juxtaposition of completive and incompletive forms toward setting in motion a causal dynamic. For example, this process plays a crucial role in the speech of curing rituals, where reference to the action of the body's being caught by illness-causing airs is juxtaposed with reference to their expulsion ("shattering the winds"), which is triggered by the performance. The whole is expressed through parallelism, which accentuates the matching of events that have clearly occurred at different moments.

9. Excerpt from a therapeutic ritual of *sáantigwaar* or *pa'iik'*, don Toribio Pat, San Andrés, Quintana Roo, 2006

wáa' ti' las syeete, ocho, nweebe, dyees, onsee' del diya;	if it is at the hours of seven, eight, nine, ten, eleven
ka' tuchukpacht e kweerpo [completive]	**that it caught up with the body**
to'one' ti'il jumpe' saanto' maarte xan ti las	we, on a holy Tuesday also, at
'oonse wáa las doose del diya; wáa ti la 'uuna del diya;	the hour of eleven or at noon, or even at one
táan kpa'iik'tik [progressive incompletive]	**we are shattering the winds**

The incompletive/completive juxtaposition can, conversely, concern the same actions. Such is the case in the next excerpt, from a ritual of appeasement of the land. In it, at a key moment, in which the ritual performer's voice displaces the spirits, the actions of invocation are each uttered twice, using the incompletive and the completive forms. The double aspectual visualization, discordant yet complementary, seems to intensify the agentive power of the speech, while contributing to the temporal texture's nonordinary character particular to ritual performance. Extending the theory of ritual condensation (Houseman and Severi 1998), one could say that it makes paradoxical temporal perspectives coalesce in the condensed, hence generative, chronotope of this sequence of the ritual (see also Lira 2017).

10. Excerpt from a ritual of *jeets' lu'um* (appeasement of the land), Adolfo Suárez Bautista, Maní, 1994 (Gubler 2017, 18, transcription and translation revised here)

...	...
Ikil inwéensajt'anik xan	**By invoking them and bringing them down** also
kinsujuyt'anik xan	**I invoke in purity** also [incompletive]
a noj poder	your great power
a noj bendisyon xan	your blessing also
bakan xan	truly also

beorae'	now
kinch'o'ocho'ojt xan	I chew their names also
kin *ti'il* **insujuyt'antik** *xan*	**I invoke them in purity** also
ti' k'aak'as iik'o'ob	for the ill winds
ti' sujuy iik'o'ob	for the pure winds
(…)	*(…)*
ka **tinpéeksajt'antaj** *xan*	and **I invoked them by making them move** [completive]
ka **tinsujuyt'antaj**	and **I invoked in purity** [completive]
ti'al inch'a'achi'itik xan	to chew their names also
bakan xan	truly also
men tuyik'al	because of their wind
ti tuláakal santos milagrosos	for all the miraculous saints
ti espirituales	for all the spirits
kink'áatiko'ob	I ask them
kinsujuyt'aantiko'ob *xan bakan*	**I invoke them in purity** [incompletive]
beora amen	now amen.

We find a similar process of double temporal visualization, effected through more lexical means, when the *jmeen*, in order to send the spirits away, must mention as simultaneous the ongoing action of making them depart ("to make them rise") and the already accomplished action by which he made them come ("to reunite them and make them pile themselves up").

11. Excerpt from the phase of sending back the spirits during a *jo'olbesaj-nal* (agricultural first-fruits ritual), Adriano Mex May, Kopchen, 1995

Bey tuyoorapaja men	As the hour is becoming now, by
yet in jajal ko'lel	[my lord] and my true lady
uti'il **injunts'ankúunsik**	**for me, to reunite and to make**
injajal yúum;	**[them] pile up**
	my true lord
uti'il **injunts'ankúunsik** *ajajal*	**for me, to reunite and to make**
ki'ichkemiléex	**[them] pile up**
	your true beauties
jats'aknak topoknaak	*jaats'aknak topoknaak*

uwach'a jump'el aki'ichkelem sujuy	one of your holy and pure altars
sàanto mèesa'éex	has come **undone**
jats'aknak topoknaak	*jaats'aknak topoknaak*
*uti'il **inlíi'bansk** ajajal*	**for me, to make [them] rise,** it is
ki'ichkemiléex;	said, their true beauties

Of interest in these cases is how ordinary causality is complexified, even disrupted, through a fusion of actions that are chronologically dissociated or, on the contrary, through the fission of a single action into multiple visualizations. The ritual performers produce this complexification by means of aspectual combinations that are minimal but highly calibrated. The framework of parallelism across lines and the taut line of incompletives brings these aspectual combinations into relief.

Projection and Purpose

Finally, there is another recurring form in ritual discourse that maintains the prospective temporal horizon characterizing this speech, all the while imbuing it with purpose. This is the conjunction *uti'al*, which may be translated as "for" or "in order that." Significantly, in ritual speech, this conjunction of purpose introduces not so much the medium- and long-term aims of the ritual as the actions that are supposed to occur during the performance. Most often, the matrix verb is a verb of invocation, and *uti'al* renders explicit the necessary precedence of any speech act over what is accomplished (see excerpts 11 and 12). Even in cases where the matrix verb of invocation is erased, the systematic presence of this conjunction of purpose makes the ritual enunciation emerge as the cause of the actions undertaken.

12. Excerpt from a ritual of *jeets' lu'um* (appeasement of the land), Adolfo Suárez Bautista, Maní, 1994 (Gubler 2017, 17, transcription and translation revised here)

kinsujuyt'antik xan	I invoke them in purity also
kinwéensajt'antik xan	I invoke them by bringing them
bakan xan	down also
be'oora xan	truly also
	now also
ti' tuláakal usujuy ik'ilo'ob	all the pure winds
tumen táanilo'ob yamarta'an bolon jmeen	because first nine *jmeen* (ritual specialists) were called
***uti'al** utsikbalo'ob tinwéetel xan*	**in order to** talk with me also

tu presensya paadre saanto xan	in the presence of the holy father
kamba	also
tu presensya leti' xan	in his presence also
kinsujuyt'antik	I invoke them
uti'al *inwéensajt'antik xan*	**in order to** bring them down also
ti tuláakal iik'o'ob	all the winds
tumen táanilo'ob xan	because they are in front also
bakan xan	truly also
be'oora. Amen.	now. Amen
uti'al *intsikbe'eno'obe'*	**in order to** offer them respect
kinjant'antik xan	I invoke them promptly also
uti'al *insujuyt'antik xan*	**in order to** invoke them in purity also
ti'al *ink'áatko'on upoder,*	**in order that** we may ask them for
unoj bendisyon	their power,
	their great blessing

The various types of repetitions mentioned above make the ritual speech seem somewhat monotonous even as they subtly shape its rhythm. However, this monotony dissipates rapidly with the constant variation and the rhythmic elaboration of the ritual speech.

RHYTHMICITY OF TEXT AND VOICE

The rhythmic variations and elaborations draw on several mechanisms and linguistic materialities: lexical and grammatical forms but also rhetorical structures, prosody, and vocal rhythms. Beyond their function of singularizing the performance, these contribute crucially to creating a "particular manner of flowing," to borrow Benveniste's expression (1971, 286), that is, particular to ritual.

Let us briefly explore how this rhythm is established. The main rhetorical structures undergirding Maya ritual speech registers are the well-known ones of parallelism, rhythmic series, and cyclicity, in their local forms. These do not function based on a metric but are, rather, based on the play of articulations between structures, units, and elements of repetition, so as to produce the irregularly regular rhythms so characteristic of Maya ritual speech genres (see Hull and Carrasco 2012; Monod Becquelin and Becquey 2008; Vapnarsky 2008; and the references therein). According to the types of ritual and the ritual performers, many variants on these combinations may be observed. I can only illustrate these here through a comparison of two textual rhythms transposed onto the page. Excerpt 13 illustrates the cyclic structure of an agricultural first-fruits prayer, each textual cycle corresponding to a group of spirits that the ritual performer seeks with his voice in a given place, mentioned at the end of the cycle. Excerpt 14 corresponds to therapeutic speech from the *sáantigwar* or *pa'iik'* ritual ("shatter the winds"), wherein long series of names of ill winds are recited in order to expel from the body those responsible for the illness. These rhetorical and rhythmic structures are associated with specific dispositions and actions: parallelism is the sine qua non of speech that strongly engages the ritual performer (see Gossen 1974; Monod Becquelin and Breton 2002; among others). Cyclicity is associated with the course of invocation and sacralization (Hanks 2017; Vapnarsky 2003). Series like the litany of ill winds (related to pains, poisonous animals, ancient spaces, etc.) function to comprehensively grasp various experiential and symbolic domains that are defined by specific features (Monod Becquelin and Breton 2002).

13. Excerpt of *jo'olbesaj-nal* (agricultural first-fruits prayer), Adriano Mex May, Kopchen, 1995 (the numbers within brackets correspond to the textual cycles)

[12] *jatsaknaaak; topoknaak*
     kubin int'aan
     my words go
         tu noj uk'a bin u'aj kanan-káakbilóo'
         to the right hand, it is said, of the guardians of fertile lands
             aj kanan-montaanya'ilóo'
             the guardians of the high forests
                 bej Sajkach'e'ene'
                 path to Sajkach'e'en

[13] *jatsaknak; topoknak*
     kubin int'aan
     my words go
         tunoj uk'a bino aj kanan-káakbilóo'
         to the right hand, it is said, of the guardians of fertile lands
             bej Yo'ts'ono'ote'
             path to Yotsono'ot

[14] *jatsaknaaak; topoknaak*
     kubin int'aan bin
     my words go

u noj uk'a bin u'aj kanan-káakbilóo'
to the right hand, it is said, of the guardians of fertile lands
 aj kanan-montaanya'ilóo'
 the guardians of the high forests
 ti bin u'aj balam-k'áaxilóo'
 of the, it is said, jaguars of the forests
 ti bin u'aj tepalilóo'
 of the, it is said, sovereigns
  le Ts'utsinbaake'
  of Tutsenbak

14.Excerpt from a therapeutic ritual of *sáantigwaar/pa'iik'*, don Toribio Pat, San Andrés, Quintana Roo, 2006

uyiik'al xan kruseero i kaayes	winds of the crossroads and the streets
uyiik'al kruseeroi beejo'	winds of the crossroads and the paths
uyiik'al la'la' soolare'	winds of the old patios
uyiik'al la'la' ch'e'en	winds of the old wells
uyiik'al la'lajkajtali	winds of the old villages
uyiik'al x kala'ap	winds of the ditches
uyiik'al xmulu'uch	winds of the mounds
uyiik'al muulu'	winds of the ruins
uyiik'al aj kanul	winds of the guardians
uyiik'al xan kulpach iik'	winds also of the backward airs
yiik'al xkuulpach taankaso'	winds of the backward *tankas*
uyiik'al xan k'asap iik'al	winds also of the *k'asap* wind
k'asap taankaso'	*tankas* of the *k'asap*
uyiik'al xan	the winds also
k'ak'al moson iik'o'	of the whirlwinds
k'ak'al moson taankaso'	of the *tankas* whirlwind

However, this textual organization cannot manifest itself without the voice that utters it. I have previously analyzed this in detail (see Vapnarsky 2022) and will synthesize certain key points here. The utterance of ritual speech involves voice manipulations that are essential to performativity. In case of the rituals I focus on here, these voice manipulations affect not so much the timbre or the pitch but rather the speech rhythm. These manipulations have various effects, one of them being to transform the sensorial experience of the passage of time. For does it not suffice to accelerate or slow down exaggeratedly one's speech to produce a different impression of the flow of time? Ritual utterances seem to exploit these phenomenological qualities of voice in order to, among other things, manipulate participants' subjective experience of time.

Maya ritual speech is generally very rapid—as often ritual tempos are, cross-culturally—with significant accelerations and decelerations. Utterances are organized in breath groups, which may be lengthened to the point of breathlessness, attaining lengths unused in nonritual contexts. The lengths of breath groups and pauses may vary within a performance, depending on the phase. To this, intonation curves and marked vocalic lengthening at the end of certain breath groups add an additional cadence.

Furthermore, the opening and closing formulas have a rhythm that is clearly slower and unmeasured. They seem to operate as rhythmic boundaries of transition between ritual time and ordinary time. Other utterances involving a clear slowing down may punctuate the sections. These correspond often, though not always, to canonical formulas of the Catholic liturgy (*dyoos yuumbil, dyoos mejenbil, dyoos espiiriu saanto*, "God the Father, God the Son, God the Holy Ghost"). In the first-fruits prayer performed by Don Yano (cf. excerpt 13), what is marked by a slowing-down is the formula *jats'anaak topoknaak* that introduces each textual cycle. In the *jeets' lu'um*, the ritual of appeasement of the land, the ritual performer contrasts an extreme lengthening of the second syllable—*wayeeeeeee* or "here" (the opening words of the textual cycles, which may be extended to 4.5 seconds)—with the accelerated rhythms of the words that follow, where he may utter twenty-five to thirty syllables in the same time span, as is visible in the sonogram in figure 4.2.

These voice rhythms then articulate in significant ways with the textual rhythmicities evoked earlier. While the limits of breath groups may coincide with those of textual groups, there are time lags between textual and vocal units. For example, when, instead of pausing at the end of a cycle, the ritual performer stops in the middle, time and text are suspended . . . before restarting, though he recommences with the end of the cycle instead of the beginning of the next one. In other instances, several cycles or verses are uttered one after the other without interruption. I have shown that such temporal "disalignments," to coin a term, are far from arbitrary and that they occur at specific phases of the ritual, appearing as the veritable motor of certain actions and transformations (Vapnarsky 2022). In particular, these temporal disalignments are linked to a fundamental action of the rituals analyzed here, namely, the action of moving spiritual entities, whether to summon them to the altar and then send them back to their place of origin or to expel them from an ailing body. In each of these cases, the temporal disalignment seems to mark a spatial displacement. Moreover, in a therapeutic curing ritual, the stated aim of which is

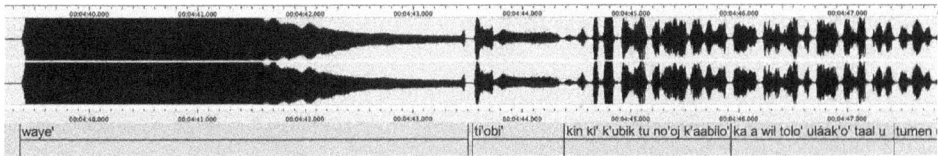

Figure 4.2. Sonogram of an excerpt of the prayer of *jeets' lu'um* (appeasement of the land), Victor Hau, Teabo, circa 1990 (in Gubler 2017). The first wave corresponds to the utterance of *wayeeeeeee'* ("here" [with the final *e'* lengthened]), between code times 04:39.5 and 04:43.5. After that, there is a faster line (starting at 04:44.7), where the short waves show that the utterance rhythm clearly accelerates.

to extract ill winds from the patient's body, the rhythmicity with very rapid speech rate, long breath groups, and short, regular pauses, combined with minimal temporal differences of alignment, creates the effect of a rapid and uninterrupted flow with a centripetal dynamic (similar to the blowing of alcohol that also accompanies this ritual). This flow certainly contributes to the desired effect—the expulsion of winds—through the play on sonic iconicity, although it does so more physically than metaphorically.

I propose that, additionally to the effects of spatiotemporal displacement and the transformation of the ritual situation evoked above, the combinations of rhythms also create a specific temporal flow that constitutes a palpable sensorial experience of temporal alterity for different ritual participants. This is particularly the case for the nonspecialists. For, although ritual speech is semiopaque, the sonic vibrations of voice may be perceived by anyone. The particular rhythm also acts on people, because it indexes the interactions in progress between the ritual specialist and the spiritual entities involved. So, vocal rhythmic patterns in Maya rituals function as indexes of the presence and movements of these entities during certain phases of the performance. In the ritual framework, the same rhythmic elaborations will thus have different effects on different types of participants. To return to our example of the curing ritual, the specific rhythmicity of the words contributes to moving and expelling invisible entities while helping to heal the patient, by virtue of his or her sonic perception of the ongoing interaction. This rhythmicity also helps in light of its other qualities such as the soothing properties of the regular and rapid rhythm also found in other Maya practices like childcare.

CONCLUSION

The analysis of ritual has been at the heart of anthropology since its beginnings, and attention has long been paid to ritual's relation to time external to it (see the introduction to this volume). Temporality, however, as it is constructed and unfolds within ritual, has been neglected. The research discussed here, and more broadly in this volume, reveals the importance and complexity of the processes at stake. The discursive processes that I have discussed are established in ritual speech to instantiate relations between distinct temporal frameworks and to create a hic et nunc specific to the ritual performance, wherein time unfolds and is composed in specific ways. This composite and altered temporal flow is generated by a set of manipulations—of word use, syntactic constructs, and voice, in particular. I have tried to elucidate some of these in the cases of several Yucatec Maya rituals. Much remains to be done, nevertheless, from a comparative perspective and with regard to the articulation of discursive and vocal techniques and other domains of ritual expression and action.

This analysis of the mechanics of ritual temporalization has taken into account various levels: those of grammar, utterance, and gesture and, more broadly, those of "co-expressivity" (Haviland forthcoming)[5] and praxis. The analysis contributes to our understanding of the so-called efficacy of ritual speech. This efficacy is certainly, in part, symbolic (Lévi-Strauss 1949), but it is mostly pragmatic, founded as it is in all dimensions of the utterance and of its contextual projections. Advances over recent decades in discourse analysis, pragmatics, and the study of multimodality allow us to understand these dimensions both more subtly and holistically (see the introduction to this volume).

A comparative exercise focused on a circumscribed cultural area, that of a part of the Maya world, enables us to discern a matrix of fairly stable ritual procedures and techniques transmitted over generations without formal training. Confirming the great stylistic freedom cultivated by these ritual performers, this study also reveals the creativity of the art of ritual speech. This involves a poetics of time that plays with grammar and breath to inscribe words and acts, humans and spirits in the longue durée, simultaneously engendering an altered temporality immediate to the ritual, one that is constantly renewed.

NOTES

I dedicate this chapter to Adriano May Mex, who introduced me to Maya ritual oratory and its infinite subtleties. This chapter is a revised version of "La composition des temporalités au sein des discours rituels: Voix mayas de la transformation du temps," published in Comptes rendus des séances de l'Académie des Inscriptions et des Belles Lettres, Année 2018, 1517–1543 (Paris: Éditions de l'Académie). Translation from French by Urmila Nair.

1. There are over 800,000 speakers of Yucatec Maya, living chiefly in their region of origin, which covers the entire Yucatan peninsula in Mexico and northern Belize, and also, following migration in recent times, the United States. The Maya known as the Cruzo 'ob refer to themselves as the Máasewal (Macehual). They are the descendants of mid-nineteenth-century Yucatec Maya rebels who founded a new Maya society on territory to the east of the Yucatan peninsula, retaining their autonomy until the start of the twentieth century.

2. *Béejla'* appears here followed by the topic marker *-e'*.

3. Other forms present in the text are equivalent as far as we are concerned, such as the conjunction *ikil* and the use of action nouns without aspectual marking (see Vapnarsky 2018, footnotes 12 and 13).

4. This specific aspectual function apart, the virtual absence of the progressive *táan*, an aspect commonly used in ordinary language, may additionally result from the need for a demarcation between the ritual flow and the temporal flow of daily life.

5. As Haviland conceptualizes it, co-expressivity is how multiple simultaneous modalities of expression and levels of interactional structure conspire to produce utterances and actions that may lean upon but ultimately transcend words. Co-expressivity concerns "not only multimodal aspects of utterance . . . but also monomodal elements, sometimes something as small as a single spoken form, but also something as large as constructions that produce multiple expressive effects at once, simultaneously, or sometimes spread across a range of other conjoint actions (even with different actors)" (Haviland forthcoming).

REFERENCES

Arzápalo Ramón I. 1970. "The Ceremony of Tsikul T'an Ti' Yuntsiloob at Balankanche: Transcription and Translation of the Maya Text." In *Balankanche: Throne of the Tiger Priest*, edited by Wyllys Andrews IV, 79–164. New Orleans: Middle American Research Institute, Tulane University.

Benveniste, Emile. 1971. "The Notion of 'Rhythm' in Its Linguistic Expression." *Problems in General Linguistics*, translated by M. E. Meek, 281–88. Coral Gables, FL: University of Miami Press.

Gossen, Gary H. 1974. "To Speak with a Heated Heart: Chamula Canons of Style and Good Performance." *Explorations in the Ethnography of Speaking*, edited by R. Bauman and J. Sherzer, 389–413. Cambridge: Cambridge University Press.

Gubler, Ruth. 2017. *Ritos y ceremonias curativas en Yucatán*. Izamal, Yucatan: UNAM / Gobierno del Estado de Yucatán.

Hanks, William F. 1984. "Sanctification, Structure and Experience in a Yucatec Maya Ritual Event." *Journal of American Folklore* 97 (384): 131–66.

Hanks, William F. 1996. "Exorcism and the Description of Participant Roles." In *Natural Histories of Discourse*, edited by Michael Silverstein and Greg Urban, 160–200. Chicago: University of Chicago Press.

Hanks, William F. 2006. "Joint Commitment and Common Ground in a Ritual Event." In *Roots of Human Sociality*, edited by Nick J. Enfield and Stephen C. Levinson, 299–328. New York: Berg.

Hanks, William F. 2017. "The Plurality of Temporal Reckoning among the Maya." *Journal de la Société des Américanistes* 103: 497–520. https://www.jstor.org/stable/26606807.

Haviland, John B. 2000. "Warding Off Witches: Voicing and Dialogue in Zinacantec Prayer." In *Les rituels du dialogue*, edited by Aurore Monod Becquelin and Philippe Erikson, 367–400. Nanterre: Société d'Ethnologie.

Haviland, John B. Forthcoming. "Mastery, Modality, and Co-Expressivity." *Languages*, special issue, *Coexpressivity, Gesture, and Language Emergence: Modality, Composition and Creation*.

Houseman, Michael, and Carlo Severi. 1998. *Naven; or, The Other Self: A Relational Approach to Ritual Action*. Leiden: J. Brill.

Hull, Kerry, and M. D. Carrasco. 2012. *Parallel Worlds: Genre, Discourse, and Poetics in Contemporary, Colonial, and Classic Maya Literature*. Boulder: University Press of Colorado.

Lévi-Strauss, Claude. 1949. "L'Efficacité Symbolique." *Revue de l'histoire des religions* 135 (1): 5–27.

Lira, Regina. 2017. "Caminando en el lugar del día (tukari), caminando en el lugar de la noche (tikari): Primer acercamiento al cronotopo en el canto ritual wixárika (huichol)." In *Mostrar y ocultar en el arte y los rituales: Perspectivas comparativas*, edited by Guilhem Olivier and Johannes Neurath, 537–62. Mexico City: UNAM.

Monod Becquelin, Aurore. 2000. "Polyphonie thérapeutique: Une confrontation pour la guérison en Tzeltal." In *Les rituels du dialogue*, edited by Aurore Monod Becquelin and Philippe Erikson, 511–54. Nanterre: Société d'Ethnologie.

Monod Becquelin, Aurore, and Cédric Becquey. 2008. "De las unidades paralelísticas en las tradiciones orales mayas." *Estudios de Cultura Maya* 32: 111–53.

Monod Becquelin, Aurore, and Alain Breton. 2002. *La "guerre rouge" ou, Une politique maya du sacré: Un carnaval tzeltal au Chiapas, Mexique*. Paris: CNRS Éditions.

Monod Becquelin, Aurore, Alain Breton, and Mario H. Ruz, eds. 2010. *Figuras mayas de la diversidad*. Mérida: Mexique Centro Peninsular en Humanidades y Ciencias Sociales, UNAM.

Vapnarsky, Valentina. 2003. "Recorridos instauradores: Configuración y apropiación del espacio y del tiempo entre los mayas yucatecos." In *Espacios mayas: Usos, representaciones, creencias*, edited by Alain Breton, Aurore Monod Becquelin, and Mario H. Ruz, 363–81. Mexico, UNAM.

Vapnarsky, Valentina. 2008. "Paralelismo, ciclicidad y creatividad en el arte verbal maya yucateco." *Estudios de Cultura Maya* 32: 155–99.

Vapnarsky, Valentina. 2017. "Senses of Time: Exploring Temporality in Mayan Discourses, Experiences and Remembrances." Habilitation à Diriger des Recherches, École des Hautes Études en Sciences Sociales, Paris.

Vapnarsky, Valentina. 2018. "La composition des temporalités au sein des discours rituels: Voix mayas de la transformation du temps." *Comptes rendus des séances de l'Académie des Inscriptions et des Belles Lettres*, 1517–43. Paris: Éditions de l'Académie.

Vapnarsky, Valentina. 2022. "Voice Matters: The Vocal Creation and Manipulation of Ritual Temporalities." In *Materializing Ritual Practices*, edited by Lisa Johnson and Rosemary Joyce, 70–94. Boulder: University Press of Colorado.

PART II

Ritual Multitemporalities

5

Time Compression in Aztec Ritual Artifacts and Gods

DANIÈLE DEHOUVE

Any time-dependent principle defines by itself an order, since one instant always precedes the other (Crump 1995, 23). In accordance with this remark, rituals have long been studied as a succession of moments, for example the stages structuring the sacrificial act according to Hubert and Mauss ([1899] 1968) and the phases organizing the rites of passage or transition according to Van Gennep ([1909] 2011) and Turner (1969). The Aztec rituals themselves subdivided time into small modules and combined them in a complex way (Dehouve 2014, 277–312). In this type of analysis, the articulation of temporalities usually respects the order based on the flow of time.

However the latest series of works have shown that in the same ceremonies, several temporal layers coexist. For Mesoamerica, Hanks (2000, 223–24) was probably one of the first to consider the manipulation of time in Yucatan rituals. More recently López Austin (2015, 2018) proposed the paradigm "Ecumene Time and Anecumene Time." In the present collective publication devoted to ritual time, other approaches converge to highlight different ways of combining distinct temporal dimensions.

This work focuses specifically on the processes that create time compression, or *collapsus temporis*, in Aztec ceremonies, by which I mean the compression of two distant moments in the temporal order, such as the ritual act and the phenomenon it is supposed to activate, or the capture-to-sacrifice and rain-to-vegetation growth sequences. It presents different theories and methods of analysis that can be used

https://doi.org/10.5876/9781646426829.c005

to highlight time compression, and I will show that ritual artifacts constituted a privileged medium for it. And since, in central Mexico, analyses show that the deities were literally made up of ornaments and objects (see Bassett 2015; Boone 1989, 2007; Dehouve 2016a; Vauzelle 2018), the gods themselves can be seen as beings compressing different temporal dimensions.

THEORETICAL APPROACHES

The following lines present theories from semiotic and cognitive research that have reached the same result—the highlighting of time compression—while offering various methods of analysis from which researchers can choose according to their predilections or the type of their materials.

THE METALEPSIS

The branch of research concerned with the constitution of meaning appears to be highly useful in deciphering ritual, plastic, and linguistic acts. In this context, a whole field of studies derives from Lakoff and Johnson's book (Lakoff and Johnson 1980). Its basic premise is that metaphor is not simply a stylistic feature of language but that thought itself is fundamentally metaphorical in nature. This means that one conceptual domain is systematically structured in terms of another, what has been called the conceptual metaphor (Kövecses 2010).

Some researchers have extended the notion of conceptual metaphor to that of conceptual trope. For example, an Egyptologist has developed a visual semiotic theory of tropes (Angenot 2005) that she recently presented as follows:

> This theory distinguishes itself from rhetorical semiotics in that it does not consider the tropes as ornamental or argumentative devices resorting to language, as has been the case since the ancient rhetoric of the Greeks up to now, but rather as cognitive mechanisms at the core of human meaning production. My definition of each trope remains nonetheless close to the way they have been defined by rhetoric. (Angenot 2020–2021, 17)

Among the conceptual tropes considered is metalepsis, a figure of speech that consists of taking the before for the after, and vice versa. Defined as a figure of style (in a perspective that has been described as microstructural), the word is used as a trope "which makes one pass gradually from one meaning to another, taking the antecedent for the consequent or vice-versa" (Dumarsais [1730] 1988, 104–12; my translation). For example, to mean "he died," we can say "he lived" (the antecedent for the consequent) or "we mourn him" (the consequent for the antecedent)

(*Dictionary Littré*,[1] quoted by Salvan 2007). Considered within the framework of the analysis of the story (in a perspective qualified as macrostructural), metalepsis is a figure of thought consisting not of an isolated word but of a proposition or phrase: "metalepsis designates a transgression in following a homogeneous level of narration" (Mazaleyrat and Molinié 1989, 213; my translation). For example, in Racine's *Berenice*, Titus proclaims: "I wanted to comfort the sad Berenice." "However," as Angenot describes, "Berenice is not yet sad as he speaks, because she does not yet know that she will be abandoned. Two temporal orders are thus overlapped in this sentence, one past, the other future" (Angenot 2005, 6; my translation). Considering metalepsis not as a stylistic figure existing in the language but as a cognitive process makes it possible to search for it in pictorial and material representations.

Analysis in terms of conceptual metalepsis can not only be applied to Mesoamerican material but also contribute powerfully to illuminating it. Take the example of the Cacaxtla Murals, made between AD 650 and 950 and analyzed by Brittenham (2011). They stage a battle between bird- and jaguar-warriors. The author highlights a transgression in the homogeneous narrative that concerns the fact that the bird warriors are already dressed as sacrificed, whereas the mural is supposed to represent war:

> This depiction of victory in the Battle Mural is so forceful, the combat so unequal that many authors have questioned whether the painting represents a battle at all, preferring to read it as a sacrifice, perhaps of war captives. Rather than presuming that the mural accurately records a single moment in combat, it may be more fruitful to consider it as an exercise in rhetoric. The Battle Mural may refer both to the battle and to the sacrifices that inevitably follow it, all in an image designated to aggrandize the victors. The painting compress time, anticipating the display and sacrifice of captives after the battle. (Brittenham 2011, 79)

Brittenham convincingly shows that the painting should not be conceived as a realistic representation of a battle. In my opinion it is a good example of conceptual metalepsis, conflating the before for the after, and the antecedent for the consequent, in a single moment. This is due to the technical constraints of the representation but also to a cultural representation deeply rooted in central Mexico. Indeed, the metalepsis war-sacrifice was extremely common in the Aztec world. A pictorial and material example of it is the shield decorated with down feathers.

In the pictorial manuscripts of central Mexico war was depicted in several ways: as a double stream of water and fire, a burnt field, or a combination of shield and weapons (Mikulska 2015, 375–87). This last representation will be examined here (figure 5.1a). At the same time, the most common representation of the sacrifice

Figure 5.1. (a) Representation of war as darts and shield—shield, arrows, net, lance thrower, and thorny stem (Codex Borgia 13) (drawing by D. Dehouve). (b) Representation of sacrifice as white down, feathers, and banners (Codex Borbonicus 17) (drawing by N. Latsanopoulos). (c) Representation of war-sacrifice as darts and shield with down balls and a banner (Codex Borgia 63) (drawing by D. Dehouve)

consisted of balls of white down, possibly associated with a twofold ornament of white feathers and a white banner, which either adorned the sacrificed or appeared as an isolated sign (figure 5.1b). When the set of darts and shield was adorned with white down, the war-sacrifice pair was achieved (figure 5.1c). In fact, in the pictographic manuscripts of central Mexico, particularly the Codex Borgia, it is rare that the darts and shield are not accompanied by down or a white banner (see Mikulska 2015, 381–86). This shows that the association of the weapons and down signs offered a privileged means of jointly representing the two successive moments of the capture of the warrior and his ritual killing.

To analyze the feathered shield using a trope-based method, one must first highlight the nature of the link between the sign and its object. How does the mental representation of weapons come to refer to war? It is a metonymy that is "a trope in which an object is referred to through [the depiction of] something which is closely related to it, in a relation of contiguity or causality" (Angenot 2020–2021, 10). Weapons are used in war, they are therefore an extension of it, a trope by contiguity, that is, a metonymy. In the same way, down balls, feathers, and white banners are the attire of the sacrificed and represent a metonymy of the victim and sacrifice.

When weapons and white feathers are joined together, they constitute a material metalepsis, which condenses the time of capture and the time of ritual death. In the case of the Mural of Cacaxtla, the metalepsis can be seen directly in the representation of the warriors. In contrast, when embodied in an artifact, metalepsis is a secondary trope, which applies to other tropes, in this case, metonymies. But the connection between these two cases suggests that the compression of wartime and sacrifice was common in central Mexico.

Analysis based on conceptual tropes thus offers a simple way to highlight time compression in the artifacts and their figuration. The identification of this process allows further studies to reveal other cases of ritual metalepsis.

THE BLENDING THEORY

Another school stemming from cognitive linguistics highlights time compression: the cognitive theory of conceptual blending, developed by Fauconnier and Turner (2002). For them, imagination, through a process of multiple and constant "blendings" of mental spaces, is the principal basis of the functioning of the human mind.

This idea took shape in Fauconnier's work (Fauconnier 1994, 1997), and for him, the construction of meaning involves two processes: the building of mental spaces and the establishment of mappings between them. Fauconnier and Turner (2002, 40) define mental spaces as "small conceptual packets constructed as we think and talk, for purposes of local understanding and action." The essence of the "blending" is to construct a partial match between two input mental spaces and to project selectively from those inputs into a novel "blended" mental space (also called "the blend") which then dynamically develops an emergent structure (Fauconnier and Turner 2003, 58–59).

As I have shown (Dehouve 2019) in commenting on Sweetser's (Sweetser 2000), Fauconnier and Turner's (Fauconnier and Turner 2000, 295–96), and Sørensen's work (Sørensen 2007), a ritual can be approached as the blending of three mental spaces or inputs: input 1 corresponds to the ritual act (a mental space that is a representing space), input 2 corresponds to future life (it is the mental space that is the space represented), and input 3 corresponds to mythical space (the other represented space). In the blend, the ritual representation and the represented spaces are merged, resulting in a modification of reality for the ceremonial actors.

For the blend to be created, it is necessary to compress various kinds of "vital relations." The most important for us is the compression of time and cause/effect. In the ritual blend, as we are in a performative context, "now" (the ritual) is compressed into "tomorrow" (the future life) and the cause into its effect. It consequently achieves in the blend the compression into uniqueness of the structure of the two events (ritual and its corresponding event in the future life) and their simultaneity. If myth is introduced as an input in the shaping of blended space, this means that alongside ritual time and the immediate future, a third timeframe is introduced, that of original times. Compression of time thus takes on an exceptional density.

Blends may be conceptual, linguistic, and material. I have taken (Dehouve 2019) the example of a material blend expressed in an artifact associated with the rain god, for which we have information from archaeological and written sources: the rattle stick or rattle boards (figure 5.2).

Figure 5.2. The rattle stick of Atlacoaya, a fertility goddess (Codex Magliabechiano 75r) (drawing by N. Latsanopoulos)

Tlaloc was the Aztec rain god of fertility, mountains, thunder, the rainy season, and new vegetation. His ornaments constituted his identity. Consequently, it was possible for the god to be incarnated in a statue or in a human impersonator who took on his personality by adorning himself in his array (for the notion of *ixiptla* [impersonator], see Bassett 2015; Dehouve 2016a, 2016b; Hvidtfeldt 1958). His music instrument was the "mist rattle boards," *ayauhchicahuaztli*. Generally the rattle boards in the form of a hollow stick named *chicahuaztli* were held by several classes of deities, but when the word was prefixed by *ayahu[uh]*, "mist" or "cloud," it designated an instrument proper to the rain deities. In this case, the instrument was painted blue (figure 5.2).

The instrument was shaken by the priests and impersonators of Tlaloc during the ceremonies. In fact, it is an object which, through auditory sensorial mapping, represents one of the typical sounds of the rainy season—the sound of rain striking the ground—because it is made of a hollow gourd filled with seeds that produces a repetitive rustling sound when shaken. The ritual shaking thus activates two mental spaces, that of the shaken rattle boards and that of falling rain. It furthermore reaffirms a third mental space, that of myth, because among the Aztecs, the kingdom of the god Tlaloc, named Tlalocan, represented the archetypical domain of fertility.[2]

The Rattle Stick Ritual can be formally analyzed, following the blending theory method:

Input 1: the rattle stick is shaken (the representing space)

Input 2: rain falls (the represented space)

Input 3: rain falls in Tlalocan (the mythic space)

This model is based on the compression of time. Let us first consider the compression produced between input 1 and input 2. The lapse of time separating the rituals from the rainy season is compressed into simultaneity. According to the manuscripts, the Aztec twenty-day months during which the rituals to Tlaloc using this percussion instrument were performed were Atemoztli (December 9–28) and Etzalcualiztli (May 3–June 11) (following a correlation established by Broda [2000], based on texts from Sahagún). But in Mexico the rainy season begins in May and ends in November. The first ritual was thus five months before the first showers, while the second one was carried out almost at the same time as the first rains. The compression of time was accompanied by the compression of cause/effect into uniqueness, since the ritual as a cause and rain as an effect were condensed in the blend.

This compression of time and cause/effect appears clearly in the invocation of Tlaloc's priest referring to the sound of the rain falling in the future: "May mist rattle boards billow, may cloud rattle boards shake" (FC VI, 39). So the priest asking for the rains to come does not request us to listen to the noise of the falling rain but that we "listen to the noise of the rattle stick," which he shook prior to asking for rain. The phrase pronounced by Tlaloc's priest takes the ritual for the natural phenomenon, the cause for the consequence, and the before for the after.

It should be noted that it was not uncommon for the same verbs to refer both to ritual action and the natural phenomenon. So *moloni* had several meanings besides "to shake the rattle boards"—"to flow from the source" (Molina 1966, 398); "to boil, bubble, foam" (Wimmer 2004)—and could describe the movement of the clouds and churning of running water. It thus includes two categories of meanings: those referring to a natural phenomenon (to flow from the source, boil, bubble, foam) and those designating a human action (to shake, spread out). The verb *huihuixahui*, which stems from *huihuixoa* ("to shake"), was used also to describe a heavy rain.[3]

The ritual time (in input 1) and the time of the future phenomenon (in input 2) are thus compressed in the blend. But this is not the complete picture, since another type of time, the timelessness of the myth (input 3), is also a component in this blending. A precise time is not assigned to Tlalocan: it has existed, it exists, and it will exist, since it refers to the archetypical image of the rainy season and fertility. It draws together in its nature the model of all the rainy seasons, both those past and those to come in the future. The Rattle Stick Ritual thus consisted in the blending of three mental spaces representing three distinct and compressed temporalities.

AN AQUATIC GODDESS AND HER RITUAL ARTIFACTS

So there are two ways to highlight time compression in the ritual artifacts: conceptual metalepsis and blending theory. These theories, derived from semiotics and cognitive linguistics, can be applied to any human society, since they concern the operating mechanisms of the human mind, characterized by its ability to establish connections between concepts and mental spaces. But this does not mean that all cultures use metalepsis or make blends for the same purpose. In Aztec rituals, there is no "fiction" as in Western societies but a performative act that automatically creates time compression. The ritual artifacts are the operators of it. We will demonstrate this by analyzing the case of an aquatic goddess.

As has been said, a god was built by his ornaments, whether he was represented in two dimensions in the manuscripts, or in three dimensions in the statues and in the impersonators (priests, participants, or sacrificed). Huixtocihuatl, goddess of the salt manufacturers, was a goddess of water and fertility, because salt is extracted from the lagoons and lake areas, that is, from the great extensions of water. She was said to be the sister or wife of the rain gods Tlaloqueh (FC II, 91). During the feast of Tecuilhuitontli,[4] the group of salt makers would gather around a woman dressed like her and destined for sacrifice. The description of this feast is exceptional, because it shows how the ornaments and ritual objects of the impersonators of the deities were used in real-life situations.

It will be shown that the ornaments that covered the body of Huixtocihuatl represented the natural phenomena hoped for, so that the deity was literally made of the ritual objects that foreshadowed the arrival of rain and the growth of new vegetation. Her ornamentation was itself a *collapsus temporis*, as the description of the ceremony by Friar Sahagún's informants allows us to understand. For the purposes of the demonstration, our analysis will focus on the array of the goddess and will not study the objects she holds in her hand (figures 5.3a and figure 5.3b).

Introduced by the sentence "And the array of [the likeness of] Uixtocihuatl was [thus],"[5] a description in Nahuatl accompanies the two illustrations showing the arrival of the impersonator of the goddess and her sacrifice (figures 5.3a and 5.3b). It is interesting that this description makes explicit the meaning of the ornaments, either directly ("her skirt is painted with the patterns of water") or by means of

Figure 5.3. The goddess of saltwater areas (Sahagún 1979, vol. 1, book II, chap. 26, figures 24–25), Alessandra Pecci, public domain, via Wikimedia Commons (https://commons.wikimedia.org /wiki/File:Florentine_Codex _Chapter_26_Huixtocihuatl%27s _Sacrifice.png)

iuhqui, "as if"; when the commentary states "it was as if," it gives the meaning of the object for the ritual actors. This allows us to understand that the goddess was made up of two large sets: water and vegetation.

WATER AND CLOUDS

And her shift was designed like water; it was designed as if with water. And the border of her shift had a design of green stones; it was designed as if of green stones; the border was of billowing clouds; it had a cloud design. And her skirt was designed in the same fashion.[6]

The shirt and skirt therefore bear the design (from the term *ihcuilolli*, which refers to the writing as well as the image) of the water. The illustrations (figures 5.3a and 5.3b) show that this design is composed of wavy lines, so that Sahagún's interpreter translated the expression by the following words: "They had the shirt adorned with waves of water."[7] As for the clouds, they are represented by a border of oval-shaped stones, green like jade (*chalchihuitl* in Nahuatl). Shirts and skirts are therefore covered with signs that conventionally designate water and clouds.

> And her sandals, her foam sandals [had] side pieces. The side pieces were of loose cotton yarn with flecks of raw cotton woven in, put in by hand. And the tassels of her sandals were similarly of loose [cotton]. And her sandal thongs were of the same loose [cotton].[8]

Here, two words make explicit the meaning of sandals. The one that describes the material of which the object is made (i.e., the signifier) is *poton*. Coming from the verb *potonia*, "to feather," it refers to the white feathers with which the persons to be sacrificed were adorned (as in figure 5.1b). In a sacrificial context, *potonqui*, "he who feathers" certainly refers to this sacrificial array. But the same term, *poton*, was also used in fertility rituals. Thus, in the Nahuatl-speaking region of today's state of Guerrero, in the early seventeenth century, a priest observed the use of "cotton threads": "With this [the penitent] went on his journey, taking for his first offering copal, which is incense from the earth, and some skeins of thick, poorly spun cotton thread, in the manner of a wick, or some handkerchief woven of that kind of thread that they call *poton*: it means that the cotton is not very well twisted, as I found it in the offerings of the stone piles."[9] These bloated white cotton threads evoked images of clouds and water.

Actually, the word that reveals the meaning (i.e., the signified) of *poton* is "foam" (*pozolli*); the term describes the dish made of boiled corn (maize) after being whitened in a mixture of lime, nowadays called *pozole*, from the verb *pozoni*, "to boil the pot or the sea" (Molina 1966, 453) and "to boil, bubble, shake, speaking of a liquid" (Siméon 1977, 390). These words highlight the comparison made by the speakers between the boiling water in the pot and the sea foam. This meaning enhances the images of water and clouds contained in the shirt and skirt.

RAIN

> And on her ankles she had placed bells, golden bells, or rattles. On the calf of her legs she had bound ocelot skins on which were the bells. And when she walked, much did she rustle, clatter, tinkle, continuously tinkle.[10]

The jingles could be used in a war context (then their sound was assimilated to the shouts of the fighters on the battlefields; Vauzelle 2018, 469–70) or in fertility cults, which is the case here. In the latter, "the bells attached to the ankles of the Tlaloquê impersonators were often used in conjunction with rattle sticks—instruments that were shaken by the priests—as well as censers that were used to produce smoke in order to call the Tlaloquê, to ask for rain" (Vauzelle 2018, 468, my translation). The terms that describe the sound emitted by the jingles are significant. *Tzitzilica* and *ixahuaca* apply only to bells and rattle boards. The Karttunen dictionary (Karttunen 1983, 122) transcribes *ixxahuaca* and translates it by "to make a noise as of rushing, spouting water."[11] As for the din of rain showers, it was referred to in Nahuatl poetry by the term *ixamaca* or *xaxamaca* used here to describe the sound of the bells (e.g., *Cantares Mexicanos*, Bierhorst 1985, 154–155, quoted by Vauzelle 2018, 469). In other words, these verbs behave like *moloni* and *huihuixahui* mentioned above, which refer to both the sound of the rattle boards and of the rain.

> And [the women] went singing; they cried out loudly; they sang in a very high treble. As the mockingbird takes it, [so] was their song. Like bells were their voices.[12]

The women's song, made to imitate the jingles, as *iuhquin* ("it is as if") points it out, produces a sound comparable to the one we have just analyzed and which imitates the rain.

SPOUTING OF A STREAM

Finally, at the moment of sacrificing the woman who represented the goddess, the priest took care to make her blood spring forth, as if it were a powerful flow of water:

> they laid [the impersonator of Huixtocihuatl] down on the offering stone [...] And the slayer stood ready; he arose upright for it. Thereupon he cut open her breast. And when he had opened her breast, the blood gushed high; it gushed fat. It was as if it rose; it was as if it showered; it was as if it boiled up.[13]

The word *iuhquin* ("it is as if"), which is used again, explains here the meaning of the blood spurt. The chosen verbs describe the form of the gushing stream: *mopipiyaquetza* and *mopiyazoa* are formed from *piyaztli*, which refers to a tube to suck up the liquid, or an oblong squash. The comparison ("it's as if") is made with three verbs dedicated to the flow of water: *momoloca* ("to bubble the water"; Molina 1966, 399), from *moloni* ("to flow speaking of a fountain"; Molina 1966, 398), *pipica* ("to drip"; Molina 1966, 450), *popozoca* (from *pozoni*, "to boil up, to bubble"; Molina 1966, 453; Siméon 1977, 390). Here the body is used to create the thing that looks like the required running water, that is, the gushing of blood.

VEGETATION

And her paper cap had quetzal feathers in the form of corn stamens; it had many quetzal feathers; it was full of quetzal feathers. It was as if they turned it green; it was all turned green; they were outspread; they spread out; it was as if it were vivid green; it became green.[14]

Quetzal feathers carried many potential meanings, but in an agricultural context they evoked vegetation, especially corn (Aguilera 2001; Vauzelle 2018, 527, 522). Here they form part of the goddess's headdress in the form of corn stamens. This precision, together with the abundance of verbs that evoke a stream of greenery, is reminiscent of a cornfield.

SQUASH FLOWER

And there were her golden ear plugs. She had golden ear plugs. And the golden ear plugs glittered, flashed. They were very yellow; they were like squash blossoms.[15]

The golden ear plugs were "as if" (*iuhquin*) they were squash blossoms. The presence of squash thus completes the green corn represented by the quetzal feathers, since corn and squash were grown in the same fields.

METALEPSIS

As has been said, in ritual artifacts metalepsis is a secondary trope that is superimposed on synecdoche, metonymy, and metaphor. On Huixtocihuatl's skirt and shirt, the wavy lines represent water by synecdoche (the part—the waves—for the whole, the body of water).[16] The jade beads designate the clouds by a double metaphor:[17] both have an oval shape, and the green color evokes the realm of vegetation and fertility.

It is also by metaphor that the sandals of loose cotton threads designate the clouds, the sound of the bells the sound of rain, the gushing of blood that of a stream, the feathers of quetzal the leaves of corn, the gold earrings the flowers of squash. It is necessary to have deciphered these first-level tropes to arrive at the level that interests us here: the compression of time.

Two kinds of metalepsis can be identified. The first conflates the time of the ritual and the time of the natural phenomenon represented. As we said about Tlaloc's rattle boards, a ritual is performative, because a representation in the ritual merges with the natural phenomenon it evokes. There is always a certain amount of time between the ritual dedicated to the rain deities and the arrival of the rains. The existence of verbs that designate both the sound that imitates rain by means of bells and the sound of falling rain (*ixamaca, xaxamaca, huihuixahui*), those that designate both the gushing of the blood of the sacrifice and the spouting of water (*moloni*), and those that describe the swelling of the white cotton thread and the piling up of clouds (*pozoni*) offer concrete evidence of this compression of time. These are metaleptic verbs.

The second type of metalepsis is obtained by the joint representation of material tropes for rain and material tropes for vegetation. Clouds, rain, and running water are present in the wavy lines, jade balls, sandals of white cotton thread, the sound of bells, and the gushing of blood. Vegetation—corn and squash—is represented by quetzal feathers and gold earrings. However, the arrival of the rains precedes the growth of the vegetation by several months and is also its cause. It is the body of the goddess Huixtocihuatl that brings together the objects that make up this metalepsis. The "rain-vegetation" couple is of the same type as "war-sacrifice" examined above and just as conventional in the Aztec world.

BLENDS

Analyzed through blending theory, each of the objects covering the deity's body represents a blend between three mental spaces corresponding to three different types of time, taking sandals made of white cotton threads as an example:

Input 1: the sandals of loose cotton threads (the representing space: the ritual time)

Input 2: piling up of clouds (the represented space: the future lifetime)

Input 3: falling of rain in Tlalocan (the mythic time)

The sandals that represent the clouds are placed at the feet of the goddess; as the goddess moves, she sets the sandals-clouds in motion and embodies the arrival of the clouds (see Vauzelle 2014, for the meaning of the objects worn on the feet). The represented space-time (in ritual) merges with the represented space-time (the arrival of the rains). Finally the Tlalocan as a mythic space is also really present. The text that we have analyzed indeed specifies this: "This Huixtocihuatl, so it was said, was thought to be the elder sister of the rain gods. And it was thought that the rain gods were her brothers. In one thing she angered them, she offended them: that she mocked at her brothers. And then they banished their elder sister to the salt beds" (FC II, 91). The place where Huixtocihuatl reigns is therefore an ersatz of the Tlalocan, the mythical space of fertility. In the terms of Fauconnier and Turner, the basic mental spaces or inputs are blended by means of compression of time accompanied by the compression of cause/effect into uniqueness.

The same pattern can be applied to each of the artifacts that cover the body of the goddess, which thus constitute newly emerging mental spaces. These have a predisposition to combine with other emerging mental spaces: "In general, as we move from blend to megablend and from earlier megablends to later ones, the frames become more complex and perform greater compressions" (Fauconnier and Turner 2002, 153). A first megablend is formed by bringing together all the artifacts that designate clouds, rain, and water, thus compressing the time of the ritual and the time of the atmospheric phenomenon. A second megablend consists of artifacts that designate vegetation, using the same type of time compression. And finally, a more complex megablend compresses the two previous megablends, that is, rain and vegetation. It does this by conflating the time of arrival of the rains and the time of vegetation growth, as well as the cause/consequence. The Tlalocan, the mythical place of Tlaloc, is made up of this "super megablend." The application of the blending theory thus makes it possible to highlight the same two types of time compression as metalepsis, by other means.

CONCLUSION

Metalepsis and blending theory have shown that the ritual artifacts that cover the bodies of the deities' impersonators during the Aztec ceremonies contemplated—Tlaloc and Huixtocihuatl—constitute time compression and cause/consequence compression. These are of two kinds: the compression of the time of the ritual and of the natural phenomenon; and the compression of two successive natural phenomena—rain and the growth of vegetation. Surely other types of analysis (e.g., Alejos García 2017, 2018; López Austin 2018) could be used to bring out the same observation. The important thing is to recognize that the compression of time is organic, because it determines the effectiveness of the ritual. We tend to neglect this dimension when the phenomenon is undoubtedly so constant that it is legitimate to consider it as an integral part of the definition of the ritual act.

As the attributes represented on the bodies of the impersonators in the course of the rituals constituted the essence of the deity, Tlaloc was literally made of material tropes, as stated in the comment of the author of the Codex Ixtlilxochitl (*Codex Ixtlilxochitl* 1976, 110r) concerning the image of the god (110v): "every part of his array signified rain and abundance of crops." The same was true of Huixtocihuatl. Since these ritual artifacts were also instances of metalepsis (or blended spaces based on the compression of time), it can be concluded that these gods, in their representation, their ornaments, and their actions, constituted the essence of the propitiatory ceremony of the natural phenomenon they embodied, so that they were in themselves metaleptic beings, in which the ritual cause and its meteorological consequence were merged.

NOTES

ABBREVIATIONS

FC: Florentine Codex, see Sahagún 1950–1982
HG: Historia General, see Sahagún 1956

1. *Dictionnaire Littré*, "métalepse," http://littre.reverso.net/dictionnaire-francais/defini
tion/métalepse.

2. Among the Aztecs, the kingdom of the god Tlaloc, the Tlalocan, was conceived of as
a chest holding all seeds and plants (López Austin and López Luján 2009, 323). Described
by scholars as the underground paradise of perennial vegetation (López Luján 2014, 39),
Tlalocan represented the archetype of all places and times where fertility reigned.

3. *A ca oipan ompixauh, ca oipan huihuixauh*: "it drizzled on it, it rained on it" (FC VI, 4).

4. Annual festival of Huixtocihuatl, goddess of the salt makers, which was held at the
time of the spring solstice.

5. *Auh in Huixtocihuatl, in inechichihual catca* (FC II, 91). Translation by Dibble and
Anderson (Sahagún 1950–1982).

6. *Ihuan ihuipil tlaaihcuilolli, aihcuiliuhqui: auh in iten in ihuipil, tlachalchihuihcuilolli,
chalchihuihcuiliuhqui, temmixmolonqui, tlatemmixihcuilolli: auh in icue zan ye no iuhqui
inic tlahcuilolli* (FC II, 91). The spelling of quotations in Nahuatl has been standardized
according to Wimmer (2004). In particular, it should be noted that the phoneme named
saltillo is expressed with an "h." The English translation adopted here comes from Dibble
and Anderson (Sahagún 1950–1982, II: 91–94), unless otherwise stated.

7. *Tenían el huipil labrado con olas de agua*, HG (Sahagún 1956, vol. II, chap. 26, 119).

8. *Ihuan icahcac ipozolcac, in icacnacaz, in cacnacaztli, icpatl potonqui inic tlahquittli,
inic tlamaihquittli: auh in icacxochiyo, zan no ye in potonqui: auh in icacmecayo, zan ie no ic
in potonqui* (FC II, 92).

9. *Con esto salía [el penitente] a su viaje, llevando para su primera ofrenda copal que es
incienso desta tierra, y unas madejas de hilo grueso de algodón mal hilado, al modo del que se
hace el pabillo, o algún pañuelo tejido de aquel género de hilo, que por esto llaman poton: quiere
decir poco torcido que a trechos descubre el algodón, así lo he hallado yo en las ofrendas de los
montones de piedra* (Ruiz de Alarcón 1892, 140; my translation; see also 134).

10. *Ihuan icxic contlalia coyolli, teocuitlacoyolli, ahnozo tzitzilli: itlanitzco in quilpiaya,
oceloehuatl in ipan onoc coyolli: in ihcuac nehnemi cencah ixahuaca, ixamaca, xaxamaca,
tzitzilica, tzitzitzilic* (FC II, 92).

11. *Ruido del chorro de agua*, according to Brewer and Brewer 1971.

12. *Ihuan cuicatihuih, cencah tzahtzih, cencah tlapitzahuah: iuhquin tzontli canah incuic:
iuhqui in coyolli intozqui* (FC II, 93). The bird *Mimus polyglottus*, called *centzontlahtoleh* (the
one with four hundred voices or words), is conceived as an imitator (*ehecalhuia*; he imitates).

13. *Ye ic contecah in techcac [. . .] Auh in tlamictih, za ye ihcac, omach ic moquetz, niman ye ic queltehtequi: auh in ompet iielchiquiuh, in eztli hualmopipiyazquetza, huehca in onmopiya-zoa, iuhquin momoloca, iuhquin pipica, yuhqujn popozoca* (FC II, 94).

14. *Ihuan iamacal, quetzalmiyahuayoh, quehquetzalloh, moca quetzalli, iuhquin, xoxo-quihui, xoxoquiuhtimani, momoyahua, xexelihui, iuhquin xoxopalehua, xohxoxohuiya* (FC II, 91). I translate "corn stamens" instead of "a tassel of maize corn" as do Dibble and Anderson, and "they spread out" instead of "they were divided."

15. *Ihuan iteocuitlanacoch teocuitlanacocheh: auh in teocuitlanacochtli pepetlaca, pehpepet-laca, cencah coztic, iuhquin ayohxochquilitl* (FC II, 91).

16. "Synecdoche is a trope in which an object is referred to through [the depiction of] one of its part standing for the whole (or vice versa)" (Angenot 2020–2021, 9–10).

17. "Metaphor is a trope in which a thing is referred to through [the depiction of] another one with which it shares common sensitive or conceptual qualities" (Angenot 2020–2021, 11).

REFERENCES

Aguilera, Carmen. 2001. "El simbolismo del quetzal en Mesoamérica." In *Animales y plan-tas en la cosmovisión mesoamericana*, edited by Yólotl González Torres, 221–40. Mexico City: Plaza y Valdes.

Alejos García, José. 2017. "Ïikin y kéex: Cronotopos del ritual terapéutico maya." *Estudios de Cultura Maya* 44: 247–71.

Alejos García, José. 2018. "El principio fundacional en la mitología y el ritual entre los tzotziles de San Andrés Larráinzar." *Estudios de Cultura Maya* 52: 139–60.

Angenot, Valérie. 2005. "Pour une herméneutique de l'image égyptienne." *Chronique d'Égypte* 80: 11–35.

Angenot, Valérie. 2020–2021. "Eating in Ancient Egypt: Semiotics of an Iconographic Absence." *Journal of the Society for the Study of Egyptian Antiquities* 4: 3–38.

Bassett, Molly H. 2015. *The Fate of Earthly Thing: Aztec Gods and God-bodies*. Austin: University of Texas Press.

Bierhorst, John. 1985. *Cantares mexicanos: Songs of the Aztecs*. Stanford: Stanford University Press.

Boone, Elizabeth H. 1989. *Incarnations of the Aztec Supernatural: The Image of Huitzilopochtli in Mexico and Europe*. Philadelphia: American Philosophical Society.

Boone, Elizabeth H. 2007. *Cycles of Time and Meaning in the Mexican Books of Fate*. Austin: University of Texas Press.

Brewer, Forrest, and Jean G. Brewer. 1971. *Vocabulario de Tetelcingo, Morelos*. Mexico City: Summer Institute of Linguistics.

Brittenham, Claudia. 2011. "About Time: Problems of Narrative in the Battle Mural at Cacaxtla." *RES*, nos. 59/60, 75–92.

Broda, Johanna. 2000. "Ciclo de fiestas y calendario solar mexica." *Arqueología Mexicana* 7 (41): 48–55.

Codex Borbonicus: Manuscrit mexicain de la Bibliothèque du Palais Bourbon (Livre divinatoire et rituel figuré). 1899. Facsimile. Edited by Ernest Théodore Hamy and Ernest Ledoux. Paris: E. Leroux.

Codex Ixtlilxochitl: Bibliothèque nationale de Paris (Ms. Mex. 65–71). 1976. Edited by Jacqueline de Durand-Forest. Graz: Akademische Druck- und Verlagsanstalt.

Crump, Thomas. 1995. *Anthropologie des nombres: Savoir-compter, cultures et sociétés*. Paris: Seuil.

Dehouve, Danièle. 2014. *El imaginario de los números entre los antiguos mexicanos*. Mexico City: Centro de Investigaciones y Estudios Superiores en Antropología Social / Centro de Estudios Mexicanos y Centro-Americanos.

Dehouve, Danièle. 2016a. "El papel de la vestimenta en los rituales mexicas de personificación." *Nuevo Mundo Mundos Nuevos*. Accessed February 2023. http://nuevomundo .revues.org/69305.

Dehouve, Danièle. 2016b. *La realeza sagrada en México (siglos XVI–XXI)*. Mexico City: Secretaría de Cultura / Instituto Nacional de Antropología e Historia / El Colegio de Michoacán / Centro de Estudios Mexicanos y CentroAmericanos.

Dehouve, Danièle. 2019. "The Aztec Gods in Blended-Space: A Cognitive Approach to Ritual Time." *Journal of Cognition and Culture* 19: 385–410.

Dumarsais, César Chesneau. (1730) 1988. *Des Tropes*. Paris: Flammarion.

Fauconnier, Gilles. 1994. *Mental Spaces: Aspects of Meaning Construction in Natural Language*. Cambridge: Cambridge University Press.

Fauconnier, Gilles. 1997. *Mappings in Thought and Language*. Cambridge: Cambridge University Press.

Fauconnier, Gilles, and Mark Turner. 2000. "Compression and Global Insight." *Cognitive Linguistics* 11 (3/4): 283–304.

Fauconnier, Gilles, and Mark Turner. 2002. *The Way We Think: Conceptual Blending and the Mind's Hidden Complexities*. New York: Basic Books.

Fauconnier, Gilles, and Mark Turner. 2003. "Conceptual Blending, Form and Meaning." *Recherches en communication* 19: 57–86.

Hanks, William F. 2000. *Intertexts: Writings on Language, Utterance, and Context*. New York: Rowman and Littlefield Publishers.

Hubert, Henri, and Marcel Mauss. (1899) 1968. "Essai sur la nature et la fonction du sacrifice." In *Œuvres. 1, Les fonctions sociales du sacré*, 193–307. Paris: Minuit.

Hvidtfeldt, Arild. 1958. *Teotl and Ixiptlatli: Some Central Conceptions in Ancient Mexican Religion*. Copenhagen: Munksgaard.

Karttunen, Frances. 1983. *An Analytical Dictionary of Nahuatl*. Austin: University of Texas Press.

Kövecses, Zoltán. 2010. *Metaphor: A Practical Introduction*. Oxford: Oxford University Press.

Lakoff, George, and Mark Johnson. 1980. *Metaphors We Live By*. Chicago: University of Chicago.

López Austin, Alfredo. 2015. "Ecumene Time, Anecumene Time: Proposal of a Paradigm." In *The Measure and Meaning of Time in Mesoamerica and the Andes*, edited by Anthony F. Aveni, 29–52. Washington, DC: Dumbarton Oaks.

López Austin, Alfredo. 2018. *Juego de tiempos*. Mexico City: Academia Mexicana de la Lengua.

López Austin, Alfredo, and Leonardo López Luján. 2009. *Monte Sagrado-Templo Mayor*. Mexico City: Instituto Nacional de Antropología e Historia / Universidad Nacional Autónoma de México / Instituto de investigaciones antropológicas.

López Luján, Leonardo. 2014. "Tierra, agua y fuego al pie del Templo Mayor de Tenochtitlan: Un conjunto de bajorrelieves de la época de Motecuhzoma Ilhuicamina." *Estudios de Cultura Náhuatl* 47 (1): 7–51.

Mazaleyrat, Jean, and Georges Molinié. 1989. *Vocabulaire de la stylistique*. Paris: Presses Universitaires de France.

Mikulska, Katarzyna. 2015. *Tejiendo destinos: Un acercamiento al sistema de comunicación gráfica en los códices adivinatorios*. Warsaw: University of Varsovia / El Colegio Mexiquense.

Molina, Alonso de. 1966. *Vocabulario Nahuatl-Castellano, Castellano-Nahuatl*. Mexico City: Ediciones Colofón.

Ruiz de Alarcón, Hernando. 1892. *Tratado de las supersticiones y costumbres gentílicas que oy viven entre los indios naturales desta Nueva España, Año 1627*. Mexico City: Imprenta del Museo Nacional.

Sahagún, Bernardino de. 1950–1982. 12 vols. *Florentine Codex: General History of the Things of the New Spain, A.J.D.*, edited and translated by Anderson and C. E. Dibble. Santa Fe, NM: School of American Research, University of Utah.

Sahagún, Bernardino de. 1956. *Historia general de las cosas de Nueva España*. Mexico City: Editorial Porrúa.

Sahagún, Bernardino de. 1979. *Códice Florentino*. Facsimile. 3 vols. Mexico City: Secretaría de Gobernación.

Salvan, Geneviève. 2007. "Pragmatique de la métalepse." *Fabula: La recherche en littérature*. http://www.fabula.org/atelier.php?Pragmatique_de_La_M%26eacute%3Btalepse.

Siméon, Rémi. 1977. *Diccionario de la lengua náhuatl o Mexicana*. Mexico City: Siglo XXI.

Sørensen, Jesper. 2007. *A Cognitive Theory of Magic*. Lanham: AltaMira.

Sweetser, Eve. 2000. "Blended Space and Performativity." *Cognitive Linguistics* 11 (3/4): 305–33.

Turner, Victor. 1969. "Liminality and Communitas." In *The Ritual Process: Structure and Anti-Structure*, edited by Victor Turner, 94–113, 125–30. Chicago: Aldine Publishing.

Van Gennep, Arnold. (1909) 2011. *Les rites de passage*. Paris: Picard.

Vauzelle, Loïc. 2014. "Partition du corps et ornements des dieux aztèques." *Ateliers d'anthropologie* 40. https://doi.org/10.4000/ateliers.9612.

Vauzelle, Loïc. 2018. "Tlaloc et Huitzilopochtli: Eléments naturels et attributs dans les parures de deux divinités aztèques aux XVe et XVIe siècles." PhD diss., Université de recherche Paris Sciences et Lettres PSL Research University/ Ecole Pratique des Hautes Etudes, Paris.

Wimmer, Alexis. 2004. *Dictionnaire de la langue nahuatl classique*. http://sites.estvideo.net/malinal.

6

Witz and *Tz'uultaq'a*

Ritual Temporality in Caves at Raxruha, Alta Verapaz, Guatemala

CHLOÉ ANDRIEU, CARLOS EFRAÍN TOX, DIVINA PERLA-BARRERA,
JULIEN SION, AND FIDEL TUYUC NIJ

INTRODUCTION

Mountains and caves have sometimes been described as "boundary line-settings" between the underworld and this one (Bassie-Sweet 1996; Cook 2000, 164; Christenson 2008, 108; Moyes and Brady 2012; Vogt and Stuart 2005, 155). Numerous Mesoamerican myths also describe them as the places of origin for numerous things such as corn, rain (Adams and Brady 2005, 305), the planets (Brady and Garza 2009; Garza 2009), new inventions, ancestors' houses (Bergeret 2012), and the houses of the dead (Cook 2000, 164). Time and space seem to blur in caves, for many narratives relate the compression of time for people who get lost in underground spaces (Bergeret 2012, 637–38; Cruz Torres 1978, 117–26, 319–26).

The importance of caves is very well known both for the Classic period (Brady and Prufer 2005; Domenici 2012; Stuart 1997), and for contemporary Maya rituals (Garza, Brady, and Merino 2007; Vogt 1976, 16–17). Many works use analogies with pre-Columbian rites in order to understand continuity or change in contemporary ones (Garza, Brady, and Merino 2007; Permanto 2015) or, conversely, suggest studying contemporary practices in order to understand the pre-Columbian ones (Adams and Brady 2005; Moyes and Brady 2012; Woodfill and Henderson 2016). However, few studies have raised the subject of the co-presence of the material remains of all of these ritual activities accumulated through time in the same places, and the impact these have had on the perception of such places, in which

https://doi.org/10.5876/9781646426829.c006

the remains of different temporal orders interrelate between themselves and contemporary ritual activities.

In northern Alta Verapaz, albeit with interruptions, displacements, abandonment, and reoccupations, certain caves have been places of ritual activity from the Early Classic, or even sometimes from the Preclassic, until today. Given that there was no continuity of occupation in the period from the Classic up to now, we cannot assert any direct permanence of ritual practices through time. In fact, the Late Classic sites around the actual city of Raxruha seem to have been abandoned at the end of the eighth century, together with the neighboring lowland region (Andrieu et al. 2023; Demarest et al. 2020). The area appears to have been little occupied after the end of the Classic, though colonial data indicates the presence of both Q'eqchi' and Chol villages along the transversal strip (Caso Barrera and Aliphat 2007; Feldman 2000). Another wave of settlement began around the 1960s with the discovery of petroleum and the founding of the modern city of Raxruha. During the war, the region was highly strategic for the control of the country and suffered many forced population displacements by the military. In particular, the army prohibited anyone from living close to a certain perimeter of any cave, for fear they might be hiding guerilla fighters (Wilson 1995). Throughout their history, the caves have been a reason for movements of populations, pilgrimages, occupations, and displacements in this part of Alta Verapaz. Over time, caves accumulated the functions of landscape anchors, boundary settlers, and pilgrimage centers, and, today, in many cases, they are home to Tz'uultaq'a, the vivid entities of a living landscape.

Because of this history, remains of rituals of different temporalities are, in some cases, still visible. Thanks to the methods and objectives of archaeology, these dramatic interactions between time and space can be revealed by studying these vestiges over the long term (Ingold 1990). Each of these material remains corresponds to a singular frame of time and space that has accumulated in caves for more than a thousand years. By disentangling them, we will try to comprehend how these different layers of time interacted with the rituals of each period.

THE ALTA VERAPAZ CLASSIC LANDSCAPE: CAVES AND HILLS

Alta Verapaz, Guatemala, is a karstic region with numerous caves. The northern part is also a frontier zone between the distinct geographic and cultural areas of the Maya in the highlands and lowlands. Although highly strategic for exchanges of their respective resources, until now, very few hints of occupation have been found in the Alta Verapaz region before the Late Classic (Andrieu et al. 2023; Woodfill 2019). However, we know that this zone was very often transited, at least from the

Early Classic (AD 250–600), thanks to the presence of important quantities of offerings in the numerous surrounding caves (Woodfill 2011, 2019; Woodfill and Andrieu 2012), many showing stylistic similarities with the central Petén ceramics. This data has long been interpreted as proof that these caves were probably pilgrimage places for people coming from, or, at the least, closely related to, the lowlands, at that time (Andrieu et al. 2020; Carot 1989; Woodfill 2011, 2019).

The founding of the town of Raxruha Viejo dates from the Late Classic (AD 600–800) (Andrieu et al. 2018, 2019, 2023) and seems to have been concurrent with an important population movement, since it was both monumental and apparently rapid (Andrieu et al. 2018, 2023). Its establishment appears to be contemporary with that of Cancuen, a lowland site that was closely involved in highland-lowland trade and was located only 17 km from Raxruha Viejo (Demarest 2013; Demarest et al. 2014a, 2014b, 2016, 2020). Despite its geographic proximity to the lowlands and to Cancuen (figure 6.1), and despite the fact that the two cities were contemporaneous, the architecture and ceramic style of Raxruha and its surrounding region was distinct from that of Cancuen (Andrieu et al. 2020, 2023). In fact, preliminary results show that the Raxruha local ceramics share no common features with the lowland ceramic sphere (Saravia 2018, 2019) and, conversely, that it has considerable modal and typological similarities with other sites from the transversal region and from the northern highlands (Andrieu et al. 2023).

Mountains and caves have structured urbanism in that region. Raxruha, like many other highland sites, is organized around two mountains that have been "pyramidized" by means of platforms (figure 6.2). On the other side of the main plaza, in front of the palace, the western karst mound was converted into a pyramid by the construction of a huge platform bearing five stelae (Andrieu et al. 2018, 2023). That same mound-pyramid contains two caves that were part of the town urbanism (Tox 2017). Given that the word sometimes used for designating temples in Maya Lowland inscriptions is *ch'een*, meaning "cave," whereas the pyramids are often referred to as *witz*, meaning "mountain" in Cholean languages (Stuart 1997; Vogt and Stuart 2005), we may consider that there was a direct analogy between the mountain-pyramids and the cave-shrines.

The organization of the regional architectural groups was closely related to the presence of caves, many sites being oriented toward the hills and facing a cave (Sion, Perla-Barrera, and Quiñónez 2019). But it also appears that the Raxruha polity directly controlled the Candelaria cave system. In fact, our prospections showed that the Raxruha Viejo site extended 4 km westward (Cambranes 2019), to where a Late Classic group is located, called La Lima, and which topographically controls certain entrances to the Candelaria Caves. This is an important conclusion, since the Candelaria cave system represents more than 30 km of caves (Bassie-Sweet 1996;

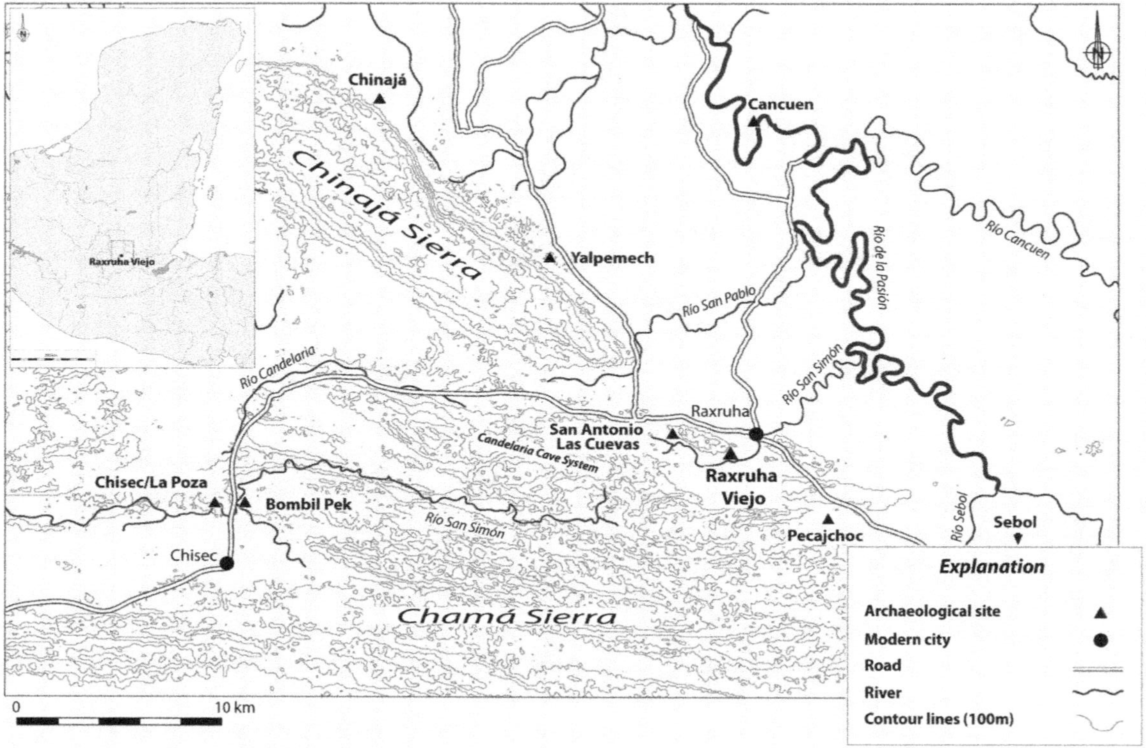

Figure 6.1. Location of Raxruha Viejo (modified by Julien Sion)

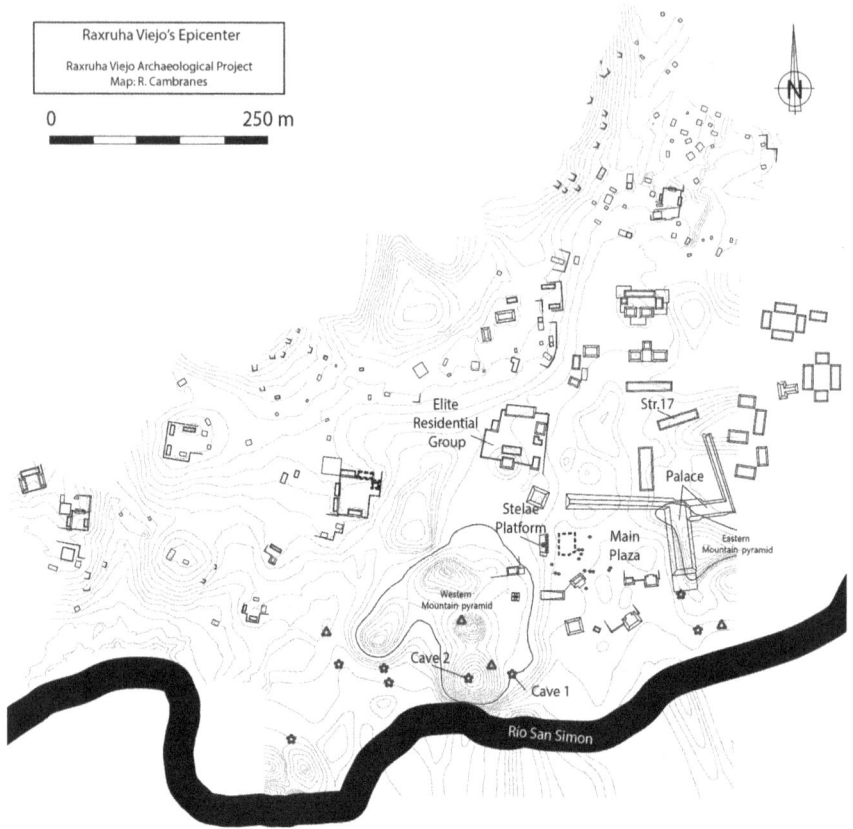

Figure 6.2. Map of the epicenter of Raxruha Viejo (modified from Cambranes 2019 by Julien Sion)

Van Akkeren 2012; Woodfill 2019) and is often considered to be one of the largest such systems in Latin America.

All these elements show that caves were major structuring elements in the ritual, political, and economic landscape of the entire Classic period, until the abandonment of the Late Classic centers in the region at the end of the eighth century.

THE *TZ'UULTAQ'A* CULT IN CAVES

Many of these hills and caves are considered today as living beings by the Maya Q'eqchi'. These entities called *tz'uultaq'a* (spirits of the mountains and valleys) (Adams and Brady 2005; Bergeret 2012; Brady and Prufer 2005; Permanto 2015; Wilson 1995) are the depository of life and ensure fertility to those living on their territory (Weeks 1997, 88; Wilson 1999, 54). Consequently, the need to maintain a relationship with the *tz'uultaq'a* by means of offerings and prayers is crucial (Wilson 1991), and implies a profound knowledge of the name, history and personality of each *tz'uultaq'a* (Wilson 1991, 44). *Tz'uultaq'a* are geographic anchors in the Q'eqchi' landscape, but they can be displaced, leave, and return (Bergeret 2012). New *tz'uultaq'a* may also appear, since, recently, certain archaeological sites have become *tz'uultaq'a* (Garcia 2007). Some narratives mention the existence of only thirteen *tz'uultaq'a*, whereas others consider that they are far more numerous, but only thirteen are the most powerful (Bergeret 2012, 219; Permanto 2015, 67), while people believe that smaller hills are integrated to other *tz'uultaq'a* in order to obtain the number thirteen (Estrada Ochoa 2006, 154–55). In fact, not all the *tz'uultaq'a* seem to have the same importance, and only certain caves seem to be associated with them. All these mountain valleys compose a living territory, since each *tz'uultaq'a* has its own culture, history, characteristics, hierarchy, and jurisdiction (Permanto 2015, 66). Consequently, they do not belong to the same community (Brady and Garza 2009; Garza 2005); each appears to have what some call their own "area of protection."

Caves are often considered to be the dwellings of the *tz'uultaq'a* (Brady and Prufer 2005, 367). In reference to the human body, they are also sometimes called the uterus or the mouth of the hill (Bergeret 2012, 222). The *tz'uultaq'a* have been the subject of various studies (Bergeret 2012; Permanto 2015; Schackt 1984; Wilson 1995), but while these all stress the importance of caves in the interactions with the *tz'uultaq'a*, they contain very few ethnographic descriptions of the actual stages of the rituals held in these caves. We know that these rituals often begin with an offering at the entrance of the cave and that incense is burned before entering them (Adams and Brady 2005). The rituals inside are mostly secret; many accounts highlight the fact that they require strict sexual prohibition (Kieffer, Garza, and Brady 2009; Permanto 2015, 167) and are, in most cases, forbidden to women (Brady and Adams 2005, 315; Bergeret 2012, 277; Carot 1989, 26).

The major cave ritual is the *mayejak*, a word meaning "to offer" or "to give and to receive." It is a collective ritual held prior to the planting of milpa (Permanto 2015, 164) or to avoid environmental theft, droughts, or floods (Permanto 2015, 171). But it can also be performed on an individual basis to prevent illnesses or accidents. The ritual usually begins in a church and is followed by a nocturnal ceremony in one or several caves (Permanto 2015, 167). The people who enter must be purified beforehand. Many accounts insist on the fact that the actors in this rite must remove all foreign objects before entering the cave (Adams and Brady 2005, 310; Bergeret 2012, 478; Permanto 2015, 168; Siebers 1999, 67) and that the offerings made to the *tz'uultaq'a* have to be native (Bergeret 2012, 479). A central part of the *mayejak*, whether it is being done collectively or individually, is the feeding, or *wa'tesink*, "to give or to eat," of the *tz'uultaq'a*. Most descriptions mention the offering of candles, *pom* (incense), and *b'oj* (moonshine) (Permanto 2015, 168), and sometimes a hen or a turkey as well as tortillas, tamales, and cacao (Bergeret 2012, 474). Certain priests have tried to integrate the *tz'uultaq'a* to the Catholic mass. Consequently, certain caves also contain crucifixes, and masses have even been held inside them (Bergeret 2012, 251; Wilson 1995, 60). Another important cave-related ritual concerns water, which is recovered from the stalactites and used, in particular, for cures (Tox 2017, 178).

A *tz'uultaq'a* is much more than a cave; it is a living being, a territory that is both moving and alive and with which relationships and negotiations include feeding, which mostly takes place inside the caves. Many of the major sites in Q'eqchi' sacred geography were also in ritual use during the Classic period and still show the visible remains of such practices.

MATERIALITY OF TIME IN CAVE RITUALS IN THE *TEMPS LONG*

What are the material remains of this long-term ritual activity, and how do they appear through time in the caves? The ethnographic information shows that contemporary rituals leave very few traces, even the more important *wa'tesink* only leaves traces of hearths and combustion, charcoal, candles, plastic bottles, chicken bones, and plastic bags on the stalactites for catching the water from them.

Nor do Catholic masses leave many traces, unless a crucifix or an altar had been placed inside the cave. In fact, some of the pre-Columbian rituals are more visible in the material culture, since a portion of them included offerings of nonperishable materials, such as ceramic or lithic items, as well as charcoal and bones.

With these elements in mind, we proceeded to a superficial identification of ten of the caves surrounding Raxruha (Tox 2017, 2018; Tox, Perla-Barrera, and Quiñónez 2019), which we crossed with bibliographical data on twelve others' cavities in the same area (Ohnstadt 2006) (figure 6.3) in order to determine their use and occupation. All, with no exception, presented pre-Columbian sherds visible on the surface. These were not buried but scattered on the ground. Although no systematic quantitative analysis has been carried out, the most commonly found sherds appear to be Early Classic Lowland ceramics (Tzakol sphere) (Carot 1989; Tox 2017, 2018; Tox et al. 2019; Woodfill 2011), confirming the frequency of the Early Classic pilgrimages in this region. The pre-Columbian deposits follow different patterns, each cave showing particular accumulations depending on its spatial configuration and its use over time, sometimes present in remote and difficult-to-access areas (Tox, Perla-Barrera, and Quiñónez 2019).

Figure 6.3. Regional map of the San Simon Valley indicating the sites and studied caves (map by Jean François Cuenot, from data by Cambranes 2019 and Ohnstad 2006)

Five of these caves were clean of any modern waste but showed the remains of possible contemporary ritual practices (candles and hearths), which tended to be at the entrance and in the deepest part of the cave. Conversely, the caves that were easier to access seemed to be used for trash deposits, as shown by the presence on the floor of soda cans, condoms, excrement, and a variety of other such waste (figure 6.4). We do not know if any direct causal relationship can be established between these factors (trash, difficulty of access, presence of contemporary ritual), or which factor might be the cause of the other, but this aspect would be interesting to verify in the future. In addition, none of the caves we visited contained Christian crucifixes, though it is a pattern often described in the region.

Out of all the caves, we decided to excavate the two that lay within Raxruha Viejo, and such investigations were carried out by Carlos Efraín Tox (2017). Since they were part of one of the mountain-pyramids of the site, we thought they could have been shrines in the ancient epicenter (figure 6.2). Also, both caves are small and their entrances on the southern side of the mountain facing the San Simón River have a relatively easy access.

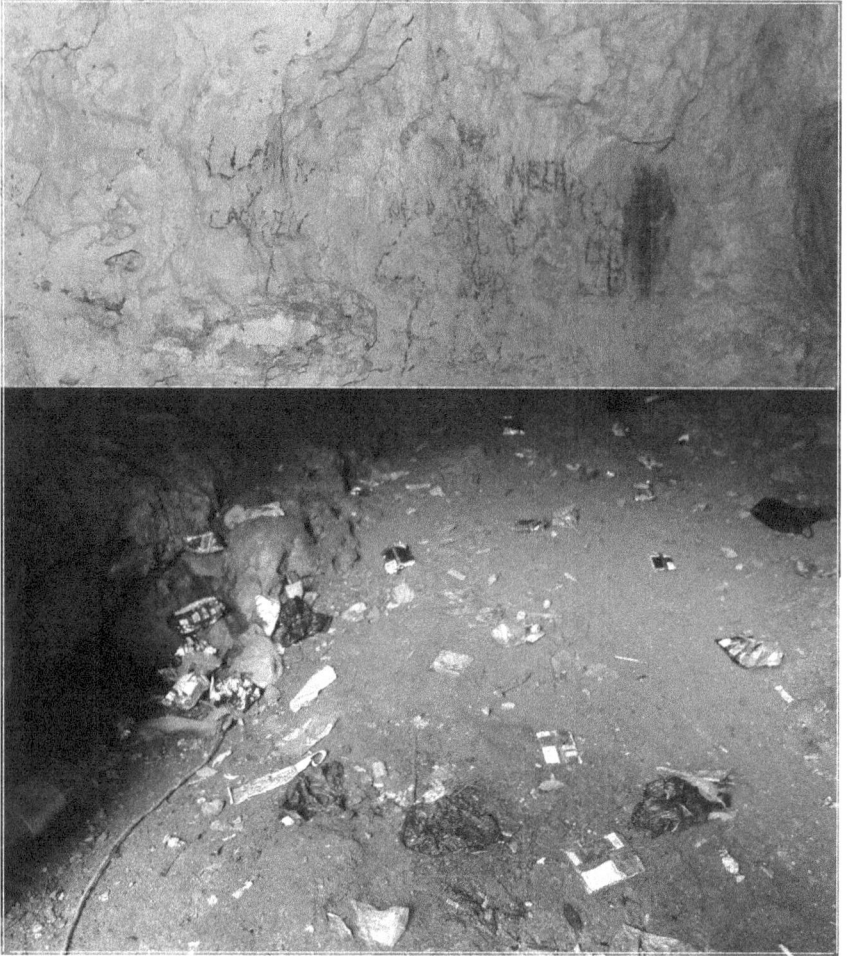

Figure 6.4. Graffiti and trash in caves of the San Simon Valley (photo by Carlos Efraín Tox)

CAVE 1

The cave with the easiest access was littered with various kinds of waste on the ground and graffiti on the walls, which shows a contemporary use. In order to map and to excavate three test pits, we had to clear the area and the surface, on which was present important quantities of ceramic material mixed with contemporary trash debris. Despite the intensive looting in the area, we found a possible pre-Hispanic hearth in one of the test pits, associated with an important concentration of charcoal (Tox 2017).

Figure 6.5. Ritual hearth from Cave 2, Raxruha (photo by Carlos Efraín Tox)

CAVE 2

The second cave, with an access slightly harder, is situated 10 meters away from Cave 1. Strangely, this cave was perfectly clean, unlike the first one, and without any modern graffiti. A ritual altar was found at the entrance, identified as such by Carlos Efraín Tox and the Q'eqchi' excavators (figure 6.5). Because of this find, we were told that no archaeological work could be carried out here unless we found the person in charge of the cave, so that we might ask for permission to work in it and possibly hold a ceremony.

The search for the ritual specialist in charge proved to be difficult, since nobody knew or could tell us who to ask for. After various denials, we were finally told that an elderly woman, a ritual specialist and owner of a funeral home who lived near the mountain, would have the information we were looking for, and, when found, she agreed to talk with us. The conversation was entirely in Q'eqchi', handled by Carlos Efraín Tox, who translated. After a very long discussion to situate Carlos Efraín Tox's family in Alta Verapaz, and then about the cave in question within the landscape, the informant refused to hold such a ritual since she was not the person in charge for that specific *tz'uultaq'a*, which was outside her protection area, and stated that she did not know who was in charge of it. This not only inferred that each *tz'uultaq'a* has a personality, a name, a gender, an age, and kin relationship with others (Brady and Prufer 2005, 367; Wilson 1995), but also that certain ritual specialists are assigned to certain *tz'uultaq'a* and not to others. This confirms Garza's observation about the strong territoriality in the use of certain caves and the restriction of access from one community to another with regard to performing rituals in each other's caves (Brady and Garza 2009; Garza 2005). The informant also said that since this *tz'uultaq'a* was probably no longer known, no one could tell whether it was a dangerous *tz'uultaq'a* or not, and that therefore no one would accept to perform any ritual inside it.

Once it was clear that nobody knew the person empowered to hold the ritual in that cave, the Q'eqchi' workers told us that we could work in that place, "since nobody was taking care of it any longer." However, they specifically asked to work not inside the cave but in the other excavations that were held in the rest of the epicenter.

We decided not to excavate the ritual hearth, but we carefully removed the plastic receptacles found inside the cave, as well as the candles and some ashes, which we placed inside a bag in order to replace them after the excavation. With the help of other Ladino workers who accepted to work there, we dug six test pits in this cavity that enabled us to find important ceramic concentrations in the deepest parts of the cavity, as well as large quantities of obsidian and shells and some figurine fragments. In the deepest part of the cave we found a deposit that was oriented north-south/east-west, which had been looted but contained buried remains of charcoal, ceramics, and offerings (Tox 2017). Once we refilled the excavation, we replaced the plastic bottles and the ashes, without any special ceremony.

The excavations in front of the caves enabled us to find a platform as well as possible stairs leading from the San Simón River to these spaces, indicating that they could have been a stage point for those coming from the river before entering to the Late Classic epicenter (Tox 2017, 176–77).

USE AND REUSE OF TIME AND POTS

However, the most interesting and surprising aspect of our work in the epicenter caves did not lie in the excavations themselves but came from the analysis of the material. Indeed, the ceramic collection of Raxruha's microregion can be divided into two preliminary groups. The first one, namely Northern Highland style, includes ceramics of the Classic period that can be found both in the transversal region and in the northern highlands of Guatemala, and encompasses particularly the Chichicaste, Cebada, Raxruha, and Nopal groups, as well as the Engobe Naranja Local and the Engobe Rojo Local groups, which have yet to be better defined (Andrieu et al. 2020, 2023). Conversely, a second set, for which the preliminary name is Southern-Central Lowland style, is conformed by ceramics of

TABLE 6.1. Distribution of the diagnostic ceramics of the Late Classic period in Raxruha Viejo epicenter

Late Classic ceramic style	Epicenter architectural groups (n=3,249)	Epicenter Caves (n=243)
Northern Highland style	83.3% (n=2,708)	16.9% (n=41)
Southern-Central Lowland style	16.7% (n=541)	83.1% (n=202)

the Tzakol and Tepeu spheres. On one hand, the Early Classic pottery (Tzakol) includes the Águila, Dos Arroyos, Balanza and Quintal groups. On the other hand, the Late Classic ceramics (Tepeu) are represented by the Cambio, Saxché-Palmar, Tinaja and Remate groups, as well as specific ceramic groups of Cancuen, namely, the La Isla and Sendero.

The vast majority of the material found in the Raxruha Viejo epicenter corresponds to diagnostic sherds of the Late Classic Northern Highland style (table 6.1). Despite the proximity with the lowlands, only a very small quantity of material of this period related to this area was found in the excavations. Interestingly, the only exception was the material found in Caves 1 and 2. In fact these two contexts showed a very high concentration of ceramics—83 percent of the Late Classic diagnostic sherds—that have not local but Southern-Central Lowland characteristics (table 6.1).

Thus, this clear-cut difference in the distribution of the ceramics between the architectural groups and the caves of the Raxruha Viejo epicenter could indicate that these caverns were places of religious cults and pilgrimages for the Lowland people, probably from Cancuen, during the Late Classic period (Andrieu et al. 2019, 2020).

Additionally, if we consider the distribution of the ceramics from one cave to another, another very striking difference appears. In Cave 2, the pots deposited correspond almost exclusively to the Lowland style, whereas in Cave 1, although the majority of the pottery is still related to that style, it seems to have been used more by local inhabitants during the Late Classic (table 6.2).

This clear-cut difference in the ceramic distribution patterns from one cave to the other cannot be explained by a lack of knowledge of the existence of Cave 2 by the inhabitants of the site, since both caverns formed part of the urbanism of the Late Classic epicenter, and one entrance was only 10 meters distant from the other. This implies that it was the result of a community decision for exclusively attributing the use of one cave to deposit Lowland-style vessels. Therefore, it seems to reflect a sociopolitical control over the practices carried out in the different caves during the Late Classic.

TABLE 6.2. Distribution of the diagnostic ceramics of the Early and Late Classic periods in the caves of the Raxruha Viejo epicenter and of Jul Ix

Period	Ceramic Style	Raxruha: Cave 1 (n=106)	Raxruha: Cave 2 (n=231)	Candelaria: Jul Ix Cave (n=507)
Late Classic	Northern Highland style	34.7% (n=35)	4.2% (n=6)	37.6% (n=47)
	Southern-Central Lowland style	65.3% (n=66)	95.8% (n=136)	62.4% (n=78)
	Total	100% (n=101)	100% (n=142)	100% (n=125)
Early Classic	Northern Highland style	0% (n=0)	91.0% (n=81)	0.3% (n=1)
	Southern-Central Lowland style	100% (n=5)	9.0% (n=8)	99.7% (n=381)
	Total	100% (n=5)	100% (n=89)	100% (n=382)

Interestingly, this differential distribution also applies to the ceramics from the older periods that had been deposited over the entire region before the founding of Raxruha Viejo. Material from the Early Classic period is usually found in large quantities in a lot of caves of the region (Carot 1989; Woodfill 2011); indeed, the pottery distribution from this period in the epicenters of the caves is also surprising. Cave 2 is the only one to contain Early Classic material, which is almost absent in Cave 1 (table 6.2). The lack of such material in Cave 1 is probably significant, since such contrast seems to indicate that not only were certain spaces assigned to specific functions or people but also to a certain temporality.

THE CANDELARIA CAVE SYSTEM

However, despite their central location in the town of Raxruha Viejo, these caves of the epicenter probably show a lower use over time than the Candelaria cave system, with regard to the quantity of remains. In fact, these 30 km of caves are thought to have been a major ritual site in the Maya world because of their size and location (Woodfill 2019, 117). Some authors have even suggested that the Candelaria system could have been the Xibalba of the Popol Vuh (Bassie-Sweet 1996; Van Akkeren 2012). Despite its importance, this cave system is both well known and little studied, since it lies at the center of many contemporary unresolved territorial conflicts between Q'eqchi' communities and a French landowner (Woodfill 2019, 127–33; Ybarra 2018). Previous works by Patricia Carot (Carot 1989) and Brent Woodfill (Woodfill 2010, 2011) show the importance of the use of this cave system over time, with hints of visits from the Preclassic to the Postclassic periods.

Certain parts of the Candelaria caves are still sacred places for the Q'eqchi' communities located nearby (Woodfill 2019, 128; Ybarra 2018). This explains why we did not obtain permission to excavate the central part of the caves, given that they are places where major contemporary ceremonies are held. However, the eastern part of this system (Los Nacimientos section) is not used for rituals by the local communities but for touristic purposes by a Ladino owner. As a result, we were able to map and test-pit three caves of this section, namely: Jul Ix, Los Metates, and El Gorrión (figure 6.3) (Saravia and Tox 2018; Tox 2018; Tox, Perla-Barrera, and Quiñónez 2019).

In Jul Ix and Los Metates, our mapping work enabled us to discover the presence of huge built platforms that led from the entrance of the caves to the Candelaria River in both caverns (Tox 2018; Tox, Perla-Barrera, and Quiñónez 2019). In the El Gorrión cave, a "balcony" near the final window had been built and appears to be one of the major places for religious ceremonies, given the concentration of materials and constructions (Tox, Perla-Barrera, and Quiñónez 2019). This is a first strong indicator that these caves were used often enough to be built up. Overall, the three caves we studied show similar features: they had all been shaped and built by means of platforms and walls that appear to date to the Late Classic. In all cases, such construction fills contained sherds similar to those found in the Raxruha Viejo epicenter (Andrieu et al. 2020; Andrieu et al. 2023). Therefore, all these data—the arrangements in the caves, the establishment of architectural groups nearby their entrances, and the foundation of Raxruha Viejo—confirm that during the Late Classic, this section of the Candelaria system, at least, formed part of the Raxruha polity, which probably controlled its usage.

Preliminary results of the Jul Ix ceramic analysis show that we have the same distribution pattern as in the caves from the epicenter, which means that the Southern-Central Lowland style for the Late Classic is more frequently represented than the Northern Highland diagnostic sherds, unlike our observations at Raxruha Viejo (tables 6.1, 6.2, and 6.3). These analyses also indicate that in this cave there are a lot of Early Classic remains and almost all the diagnostic sherds of this period are related to the Southern-Central Lowland style, in contrast to what has been observed in the epicenter caves (tables 6.2 and 6.3). Additionally, we were able to identify that particular parts of this cavern have had a differential use over time, as is the case in the painting chamber, which only presents Lowland-style material from the Early Classic period, while others, as the deepest chamber, concentrated the greatest variety of artifacts (Tox 2018; Tox, Perla-Barrera, and Quiñónez 2019).

TABLE 6.3. Distribution of the diagnostic ceramics of the Early and Late Classic periods in different branches of the Jul Ix Cave

Period	Ceramic Style	Entrance— Surface (n=95)	Entrance— Test Pits (n=281)	Deepest Chamber— Surface (n=12)	Western Branch— Surface (n=13)	Painting Chamber— Surface (n=106)
Late Classic	Northern Highland style	12.0% (n=3)	43.0% (n=40)	66.7% (n=4)	0% (n=0)	– (n=0)
	Southern-Central Lowland style	88.0% (n=22)	57.0% (n=53)	33.3% (n=2)	100% (n=1)	– (n=0)
	Total	100% (n=25)	100% (n=93)	100% (n=6)	100% (n=1)	– (n=0)
Early Classic	Northern Highland style	1.4% (n=1)	0% (n=0)	0% (n=0)	0% (n=0)	0% (n=0)
	Southern-Central Lowland style	98.6% (n=69)	100% (n=188)	100% (n=6)	100% (n=12)	100% (n=106)
	Total	100% (n=70)	100% (n=188)	100% (n=6)	100% (n=12)	100% (n=106)

The platforms had been built in the Late Classic; however, in many cases, the Early Classic material was collected above them (Andrieu et al. 2020). Such a pattern could be explained by the fact that these pots and sherds had been replaced by the Maya themselves after they constructed the platforms (Andrieu et al. 2019, 2023), indicating that the ceramics deposited before the rise of the Raxruha polity always received special treatment and were redeposited hundreds of years after.

This shows that these caves were pilgrim centers, and probably ones that represented temporal and spatial markers shared by different groups, sometimes as distant as central Peten, during the entire Classic period. It also shows that the material remains from those ancient pilgrimages were probably recognized as such by the Late Classic users of these caves and consequently received particular attention and were maybe involved in later rituals.

FINAL REMARKS: FILLING OF TIME AND RITUAL DENSITY

Despite their prevalence in social and religious space, not all caves seem to have had the same function and use over time. That is also the case today, as can be demonstrated by the fact that rituals are still performed in certain caves, whereas others are filled with trash or are no longer "cared" for, while still others are strictly prohibited. In a different way, this was also the case during the Classic period, since not all the caves, or the rooms within a cave, had the same material or the same temporalities, some only containing Early Classic material, and others more pottery with Highland stylistic features.

In all cases, however, the repetition of these deposits through time is visible in the accumulation of material over the centuries, and this accumulation may have contributed to the ritual load of these places. In fact, one of the specificities of the caves is the lack of normal natural filling phenomena that can be observed on the outside (except nearby the entrances or in the river overflow areas). The filling is much slower on the caves' surfaces, and a deposited object remains visible on the surface centuries later. There are very few perturbation elements—except where people have moved things.

Deposits from the pre-Hispanic period are still visible to the human eye on the same level as the contemporary ones; they accumulate with one another, conferring a strong "ritual density" on these places (Bell 1997, 173). A lot of objects are disposed on the ground, in anfractuosity, all time periods mixed together, giving a notion of crowding in the surfaces (Andrieu et al. 2018), contrary to what happens on Classic Maya sites, where the majority of the deposits are buried ones (e.g., Schwake and Iannone 2010), except for the abandonment deposits that are also found on the surface (e.g., Dussol, Sion, and Nondédéo 2019). Such difference implies that everyone entering the caves, both archaeologists and the pre-Hispanic Maya people, could perceive in a single glance that there were vessels from different time periods. This suggests that caves are places in which temporality takes on a very palpable form, where the co-presence of artifacts from various epochs in the same place probably contributed to create another perception of time. Indeed, the impression of accumulation and return over time are also observed in some way in the buried deposits, in which there was a memory of the place where the offerings were made. However, the fundamental difference is the visibility of these actions that show the ritual regularity in the caves, where nothing disappears, or very little does, and everything accumulates and remains visible.

This visibility of return is probably also important today, since recent descriptions of contemporary rituals in Candelaria mention the use of the ancient ceramics.

> People [. . .] came from as far as Peten and both the highlands and lowlands of Alta
> Verapaz. They gathered flowers and avidly discussed the best arrangements to mark
> the four cardinal points, trimmed the ecotourism center's lawn, and prepared massive quantities of food. [. . .] The elaborate ceremony lasted until dawn, and a priest

employed ancient Mayan ceramics from the caves (including the tall pot center-right at the edge of the offering in Figure 7) and offerings including moonshine (*b'oj*), incense, and candles. The *mayejak* itself consisted of long prayers, ritual dancing, and the healing of sick people. (Ybarra 2018, 126)

In that sense, we could say there is a cumulative aspect of time in caves that could contribute to the efficiency of the rituals over time. For instance, the contemporary ritual remains in the Raxruha epicenter's cave were so old that nobody remembered who was in charge of it. Nevertheless, they were still visible and complete. The visibility of the ritual remains have somehow conferred protection on the place, for we were not allowed to excavate it until it had been verified that nobody was taking care of it. Such visibility may also be played with, integrated in rituals in a palimpsest of times, with Early Classic potteries being moved and replaced on Late Classic platforms and, today, pre-Hispanic ceramic being used in contemporary Q'eqchi' ceremonies.

Acknowledgments. We would like to thank the Instituto de Antropologia e Historia de Guatemala (IDAEH), the Centre National de la Recherche Scientifique (CNRS, UMR 8096, Archéologie des Amériques), the Cancuen Project, in particular Arthur Demarest and Paola Torres, the French Ministry of Foreign Affairs (MEAE), the GDRI RITMO, the Centre d'Etudes Mésoaméricaines et Centre Américaines (CEMCA), as well as Brent Woodfill and the Salinas de Nueve Cerros Project for their help and collaboration. We would also like to thank Airaiel Álvarez, Celso Cucul, Miguel Cucul, Carlos Choc, Antonio Lobos, Edgar Cucul, Reginaldo Yaxcal, Pedro Chun, Juan Manuel Perla, Victor Santiago Mejía, Julio Tox, Marco Tulio Caal, Eduardo Morales, Leonardo Caal, Esteban Toj, Belsasar Morales, Francisco Morales, Cornelio Morales, Marilin Perla, Alejandra Diaz, Juan Francisco Saravia, Rafael Cambranes, Ricardo Rodas, Paulo Estrada, Fidel Suyuc, and Cesar Borjoquez, who all contributed to gathering the information we have used in this work; and to Krystyna Horko for correcting the English in this article.

REFERENCES

Adams, Abigail E., and James E. Brady. 2005. "Ethnographic Notes on Maya Q'eqchi' Cave Rituals: Implications for Archaeological Interpretation." In *In the Maw of the Earth Monster: Mesoamerican Ritual Cave Use*, edited by James Brady and Keith Prufer, 301–27. Austin: University of Texas Press.

Andrieu, Chloé, Julien Sion, Arthur Demarest, Divina Perla-Barrera, Jackeline Quiñónez, Juan Francisco Saravia, and Carlos Efraín Tox. 2019. "Entre cuevas, montañas y ríos: El territorio político-religioso de Raxruha Viejo en el Clásico Tardío." In *XXXII Simposio de Investigaciones Arqueologicas de Guatemala, 2018*, edited by Barbara Arroyo, Luis Méndez Salinas, and Gloria Ajú Álvarez, 627–42. Guatemala: Ministerio de Cultura y Deportes / IDAEH / Asociación Tikal.

Andrieu, Chloé, Julien Sion, Divina Perla-Barrera, Jackeline Quiñónez, Rafael Cambranes, Carlos Efraín Tox, and Felipe Trabanino. 2020. "Raxruha Viejo: La historia de una frontera cambiante entre Tierras Altas y Bajas mayas." In *XXXIII Simposio de Investigaciones Arqueológicas de Guatemala, 2019*, edited by Barbara Arroyo, Luis Méndez Salinas, and Gloria Ajú Álvarez, 627–42. Guatemala: Ministerio de Cultura y Deportes / IDAEH / Asociación Tikal.

Andrieu, Chloé, Julien Sion, Divina Perla-Barrera, Carlos Efraín Tox, and Jackelin Quinonez. 2023. "On The Frontier: Raxruha Viejo, a Late Classic Highland Exchange Center." In *Highland Archaeology: New Debate and Data*, edited by G. Davis and E. Robinson, 259–280. London: Routledge.

Andrieu, Chloé, Julien Sion, Paula Torres, Arthur Demarest, Moises Aldana, Rafael Cambranes, Alejandra Diaz, Paulo Estrada, Jaquelin Quiñonez, Juan Francisco Saravia, and Carlos Efraín Tox. 2018. "Raxruha Viejo, una ciudad frontera entre Tierras Altas y Bajas." In *XXXI Simposio de Investigaciones Arqueológicas en Guatemala, 2017*, edited by Barbara Arroyo, Luis Méndez Salinas, and Gloria Ajú Álvarez, 327–48. Guatemala: Ministerio de Cultura y Deportes / IDAEH / Asociación Tikal.

Bassie-Sweet, Karen. 1996. *At the Edge of the World*. Norman: University of Oklahoma Press.

Bell, Catherine. 1997. *Ritual Practice, Ritual Theory*. New York: Oxford University Press.

Bergeret, Agnès. 2012. "La quête d'autonomie des paysans Mayas Q'eqchi' de Cahabon, Guatemala, 1944–2011." PhD diss., Université Sorbonne Nouvelle–Paris 3, Paris.

Brady, James E., and Sergio Garza. 2009. "A Reassessment of Ethnographic Data on Cave Utilization in Santa Eulalia." In *Archaeology and Ethnography in Huehuetenango, Guatemala*, edited by James Brady, 73–80. Austin: Association for Mexican Cave Studies.

Brady, James E., and Keith M. Prufer. 2005. "Introduction: A History of Mesoamerican Cave Interpretations." In *In the Maw of the Earth Monster: Mesoamerican Ritual Cave Use*, edited by James Brady and Keith Prufer, 1–17. Austin: University of Texas Press.

Cambranes, Rafael. 2019. "Operación RAX 14: Reconocimiento y mapeo en los sitios arqueológicos Raxruha Viejo y La Lima." In *Proyecto Arqueológico Regional Cancuén, Informe Final n°18, Temporada de Campo 2018, Tomo II*, edited by Julien Sion, Chloé Andrieu, Paola Torres, and Arthur Demarest, 329–40. Guatemala: Instituto de Antropología e Historia.

Carot, Patricia. 1989. *Arqueología de las Cuevas del Norte de Alta Verapaz*. Mexico City: Cuaderno de Estudios Guatemaltecos I. / CEMCA.

Caso Barrera, Laura, and Mario Aliphat. 2007. "Relaciones de Verapaz y las Tierras Bajas Mayas Centrales en el siglo XVII." In *XX Simposio de Investigaciones Arqueológicas en Guatemala, 2006*, edited by Juan Pablo Laporte, Barbara Arroyo, and Hextor Mejía, 48–58. Guatemala: Museo Nacional de Arqueología y Etnología.

Christenson, Allen J. 2008. "Places of Emergence: Sacred Mountains and Cofradía Ceremonies." In *Pre-Columbian Landscapes of Creation and Origin*, edited by John E. Staller, 95–121. New York: Springer.

Cook, Garret W. 2000. *Renewing the Maya World: Expressive Culture in a Highland Town*. Austin: University of Texas Press.

Cruz Torres, M. E. 1978. *Rubelpec, cuentos y leyendas*. Guatemala: Editorial del Ejército.

Demarest, Arthur. 2013. "Ideological Pathway to Economic Exchange: Religion, Economy and Legitimation at the Classic Maya Royal Capital of Cancuen." *Latin American Antiquity* 20 (4): 371–402.

Demarest, Arthur, Chloé Andrieu, Paola Torres, Mélanie Forné, Tomas Barrientos, and Marc Wolf. 2014a. "Economy, Exchange, and Power: New Evidence from the Late Classic Maya Port City of Cancuen." *Ancient Mesoamerica* 25 (1): 187–219.

Demarest, Arthur, H. Martinez, Paula Torres, Monica Urquizu, Mathew O'Mansky, Marc Wolf, Miriam Saravia, Y. Cifuentes, Iyachel Cotji, Chloé Andrieu, Juan Francisco Saravia, Luis Luin, Fidel Tuyuc, and J. Braken. 2014b. "Las dinámicas de interacción de Tierras Bajas con el Altiplano: Descubrimientos en Cancuen y la Alta Verapaz." In *XXVII Simposio de Investigaciones Arqueológicas en Guatemala 2013*, edited by Bárbara Arroyo, Luis Méndez Salinas, and Andrea Rojas, 655–70. Guatemala: Museo Nacional de Arqueología y Etnología.

Demarest, Arthur, Paola Torres, Horacio Martinez, Miriam Saravia, Juan Francisco Saravia, Fidel Tuyuc, S. Sanchez, Chloé Andrieu, Marc Wolf, and Luis Luin. 2016. "Los Reyes de los Ríos y Valles: Cancuen, Raxruha Viejo, Sebol, Sesakkar y el control de las fronteras y de las rutas mayas." In *XXIX Simposio de Investigaciones Arqueológicas en Guatemala, 2015*, edited by Bárbara Arroyo, Luis Méndez Salinas, and Gloria Ajú Álvarez, 49–62. Guatemala: Ministerio de Cultura y Deportes / IDAEH / Asociación Tikal.

Demarest Arthur, Bart Victor, Chloé Andrieu, and Paola Torres. 2020. "Monumental Landscapes as Instruments of Radical Economic Change: Innovation, Apogee, and the 'Monumental' Collapse of the Southwestern Innovation Networks." In *Monumental Landscapes: How the Maya Shaped Their World*, edited by Brett Houk, Bárbara Arroyo, and Terry Powis, 242–67. Miami: University Press of Florida.

Domenici, Davide. 2012. "Un posible caso de sacrificio de niños del Clásico Tardío en el área Zoque: La cueva del Lazo (Chiapas)." *Estudios de Cultura Maya* 41: 63–91.

Dussol, Lydie, Julien Sion, and Philippe Nondédéo. 2019. "Late Fire Ceremonies and Abandonment Behaviors at the Classic Maya City of Naachtun, Guatemala." *Journal of Anthropological Archaeology* 56: article 101099.

Estrada Ochoa, Adriana C. 2006. "Li tzuultaq'a ut li ch'och: Una visión de la tierra, e mundo y la identidad a través de la tradición oral q'eqchi' de Guatemala." *Estudios de Cultura Maya* 27: 149–63.

Feldman, Lawrence. 2000. *Lost Shores, Forgotten Peoples: Spanish Explorations of the South East Mayan Lowlands*. Durham, NC: Duke University Press.

Garcia, David. 2007. "Territorio y espiritualidad: Lugares sagrados q'eqchi'es en Chisec." In *Mayanización y Vida Cotidiana: La ideología multicultural en la sociedad guatemalteca*, vol. 2, *Estudios de casos*, edited by Santiago Bastos and Aura Cumes, 273–306. Guatemala: FLACSO / CIRMA / Cholsamaj.

Garza, Sergio. 2005. "Ethnographic Models of Cave-Community Relations." Paper presented at the symposium Caves and Settlement: The Socio-Religious Context of Mesoamerican Cave Use (Keith Prufer and James Brady, organizers), 70th Annual Meeting of the Society for American Archaeology, Salt Lake City, UT.

Garza, Sergio. 2009. "The Social and Cosmological Significance of Quen Santo in Contemporary Maya Society." In *Archaeology and Ethnography in Huehuetenango, Guatemala*, edited by James Brady, 49–54. Austin: Association for Mexican Cave Studies.

Garza, Sergio, James E. Brady, and Emilio Merino. 2007. "Una perspectiva etnoarqueológica sobre la utilización del espacio en cuevas en Santa Eulalia, Huehuetenango." In *XX Simposio de Investigaciones Arqueológicas en Guatemala, 2006*, edited by Juan Pablo Laporte, Bárbara Arroyo, and Hector Mejía, 1213–18. Guatemala: Museo Nacional de Arqueología y Etnología.

Ingold, Tim. 1990. "The Temporality of the Landscape." *World Archaeology* 25 (2): 152–74.

Kieffer, C. L., Sergio Garza, and James E. Brady. 2009. "The Gendered Use of Caves in the Jakaltec and Chuj Areas." In *Exploring Highland Maya Ritual Cave Use: Archaeology and Ethnography in Huehuetenango, Guatemala*, edited by James Brady, 61–65. Austin: Association for Mexican Cave Studies.

Moyes, Holley, and James E. Brady. 2012. "Caves as Sacred Space in Mesoamerica." In *Sacred Darkness: A Global Perspective on the Ritual Use of Caves*, edited by Holley Moyes, 151–70. Boulder: University Press of Colorado.

Ohnstadt, Arik. 2006. "Investigaciones en el Valle del Río San Simon." In *Proyecto Arqueológico Cancuén, Temporadas 2004–2005*, edited by Tomás Barrientos, Arthur Demarest, Luis Luin, and Brent Woodfill, 549–611. Guatemala: Instituto de Antropología e Historia.

Permanto, Stefan. 2015. *The Elders and the Hills, Animism and Cosmological Re-Creation among the Q'eqchi' Maya in Chisec, Alta Verapaz*. Gothenburg: School of Global Studies / University of Gothenburg.

Saravia, Juan Francisco. 2018. "Resultados del análisis cerámico del sitio Raxruha Viejo, Temporada 2016." In *Proyecto Arqueológico Regional Cancuén, Informe Final no. 17, Temporada de Campo 2017, Tomo I*, edited by Arthur Demarest, Paola Torres, Julien Sion, and Chloé Andrieu, 214–67. Guatemala: Instituto de Antropología e Historia.

Saravia, Juan Francisco. 2019. "Resultados del análisis cerámico del sitio Raxruha Viejo, Temporada 2016 (Operación 10C)." In *Proyecto Arqueológico Regional Cancuén, Informe Final no. 18, Temporada de Campo 2018, Tomo II*, edited by Arthur Demarest, Paola Torres, Julien Sion, and Chloé Andrieu, 341–51. Guatemala: Instituto de Antropología e Historia.

Saravia, Juan Francisco, and Carlos Efraín Tox. 2018. "Operación RAX 12: Documentacion preliminar de las pictografias rupestres de la cueva de Jul Ix." In *Proyecto Arqueológico Regional Cancuén, Informe Final no. 17, Temporada de Campo 2017, Tomo II*, edited by Julien Sion, Chloé Andrieu, Paola Torres, and Arthur Demarest, 612–91. Guatemala: Instituto de Antropología e Historia.

Schackt, Jon. 1984. "The Tzuultak'a: Religious Lore and Cultural Processes among the Kekchi." *Belizean Studies* 12 (5): 16–29.

Schwake, Sonja, and Gyles Iannone. 2010. "Ritual Remains and Collective Memory: Maya Examples from West Central Belize." *Ancient Mesoamerica* 21 (2): 331–39.

Siebers, Hans. 1999. *"We Are Children of the Mountain": Creolization and Modernization among the Q'eqchi'es*. Amsterdam: CEDLA.

Sion, Julien, Divina Perla-Barrera, and Jackeline Quiñónez. 2019. "Operación RAX 14: Excavaciones en el Grupo A de La Lima—La Plaza y las Estructuras 3 y 4." In *Proyecto Arqueológico Regional Cancuén, Informe Final no. 18, Temporada de Campo 2018, Tomo II*, edited by Julien Sion, Chloé Andrieu, Paola Torres, and Arthur Demarest, 300–328. Guatemala: Instituto de Antropología e Historia.

Stuart, David. 1997. "The Hills Are Alive: Sacred Mountains in the Maya Cosmos." *Symbols* (Spring): 13–17.

Tox, Carlos Efraín. 2017. "Operación RAX 12: Investigaciones espeleológicas en Raxruha Viejo." In *Proyecto Arqueológico Regional Cancuén, Informe Final no. 16, Temporada de Campo 2016, Tomo II*, edited by Julien Sion, Chloé Andrieu, Paola Torres, and Arthur Demarest, 549–611. Guatemala: Instituto de Antropología e Historia.

Tox, Carlos Efraín. 2018. "Operación RAX 12: Investigaciones arqueo-espeleológicas en la Cueva de Lodo y la Cueva de Jul Ix." In *Proyecto Arqueológico Regional Cancuén, Informe Final no. 17, Temporada de Campo 2017, Tomo II*, edited by Julien Sion, Chloé Andrieu,

Paola Torres, and Arthur Demarest, 431–54. Guatemala: Instituto de Antropología e Historia.

Tox, Carlos Efraín, Divina Perla-Barrera, and Jackeline Quiñónez. 2019. "Operación RAX 12: Investigaciones arqueo-espeleológicas en las Cuevas del Gorrión, de Lodo (Los Metates) y de Jul Ix." In *Proyecto Arqueológico Regional Cancuén, Informe Final no. 18, Temporada de Campo 2018, Tomo II*, edited by Julien Sion, Chloé Andrieu, Paola Torres, and Arthur Demarest, 260–99. Guatemala: Instituto de Antropología e Historia.

Van Akkeren, Ruud. 2012. *Xib'alb'a y el nacimiento del Nuevo Sol: Una visión posclásica del colapso maya*. Guatemala: Piedra Santa Editorial.

Vogt, Evon Z. 1976. *Tortillas for the Gods: A Symbolic Analysis of Zinacanteco Rituals*. Norman: University of Oklahoma Press.

Vogt, Evon Z., and David Stuart. 2005. "Some Notes on Ritual Caves among the Ancient and Modern Maya." In *In the Maw of the Earth Monster: Mesoamerican Ritual Cave Use*, edited by James Brady and Keith Prufer, 155–85. Austin: University of Texas Press.

Weeks, John M. 1997. "Subregional Organization of the Sixteenth-Century Q'eqchi' Maya, Alta Verapaz, Guatemala." *Revista Española de Antropología Americana* 27: 59–93.

Wilson, Richard. 1991. "Machine Guns and Mountain Spirits: The Cultural Effects of State Repression among the Q'eqchi' of Guatemala." *Critique of Anthropology* 11 (1): 33–61.

Wilson, Richard. 1995. *Maya Resurgence in Guatemala: Q'eqchi' Experiences*. Norman: University of Oklahoma Press.

Wilson, Richard. 1999. *Resurgimiento maya en Guatemala (Experiencias Q'eqchi'es)*. Antigua, Guatemala: CIRMA / PMS.

Woodfill, Brent. 2010. *Ritual and Trade in the Pasión-Verapaz Region, Guatemala*. Nashville, TN: Vanderbilt University Press.

Woodfill, Brent. 2011. "The Central Role of Cave Archaeology in the Reconstruction of Classic Maya Culture History and Highland-Lowland Interaction." *Ancient Mesoamerica* 22 (2): 213–27.

Woodfill, Brent. 2019. *War in the Land of True Peace: The Fight for Maya Sacred Places*. Norman: University of Oklahoma Press.

Woodfill, Brent, and Chloé Andrieu. 2012. "Tikal's Early Classic Domination of the Great Western Trade Route: Ceramic, Lithic, and Iconographic Evidence." *Ancient Mesoamerica* 23 (2): 189–209.

Woodfill, Brent, and Lucia Henderson. 2016. "The Classic-Period Pictographs at Juliq' Cave, Alta Verapaz, Guatemala: An Interdisciplinary Approach to Cave Art as Organizing Principle." *Journal of Field Archaeology* 41 (2): 177–92.

Ybarra, Megan. 2018. *Green Wars: Conservation and Decolonization in the Maya Forest*. Berkeley: University of California Press.

7

Myth and Ritual

Temporality through the Lens of Analogy

PERIG PITROU

The relationship between myth and rite is often approached from the perspective of temporality. In response to Victor Turner's analysis of the "ritual process" (Turner 1969) as a lived experience, the final chapter of *The Naked Man* distinguishes between the continuity of time experienced during a rite and the discontinuity produced by the myth, described as an intellectual operation of classification of the perceived world (Lévi-Strauss 1971). Despite this contrast, it is also possible to highlight similarities between past actions described in the myths and their reenactment in the present of the rite. From this point of view, ritual actions can be described as a repetition of mythical actions, a kind of continuity apprehended, for example, with the idea of "archetypal action" (Humphrey and Laidlaw 1994). In these contexts, the marks of "deference" (Bloch 2020) participate in the establishment of the authority of these ritual practices and their effectiveness: indeed, in Bloch's conceptualization, the "deference" is a claim for obedience to a tradition, that is to say, the will to repeat a past or mythical action—as is the case when ritual discourses contain sentences such as "we act as our ancestors did." In Mesoamerica it is frequent to interpret rites, especially ceremonial deposits accompanied by sacrifices, as the reiteration of past actions performed in mythical times. In *La leyenda de Los Soles* (*Códice Chimalpopoca* 2019), the description of the first sacrifice of the gods to set the cosmos in motion epitomizes this temporal order of succession where humans are cyclically obliged to reproduce actions performed in the past. The Carnival ceremonies described by Aurore Monod Becquelin and Alain Breton in *La "guerre*

https://doi.org/10.5876/9781646426829.c007

rouge" (2002) attest to the primordial character, for today's Amerindian populations, of collective engagement in this kind of regenerative enterprise.

As a complement to such retrospective interpretations that scrutinize the traces left by myths in rituals, I wish to show how conceptions of mythic actions also depend on a way of imagining the past from the present—which amounts to a different retrospective perspective. Conceptions about the past can indeed also be interpreted as constructions of a past period based on everyday experience and involving, in particular, human interactions with living beings and artifacts. To defend this idea, I will draw on the concept of "co-activity" I have presented in different texts (Pitrou 2016a, 2016b) to interpret ritual gestures and the manipulation of ritual artifacts as an attempt to cooodinate human and nonhuman activity. For instance, I have established how the ceremonial deposits of Amerindian groups of Mesoamerica and the Andes aim to establish a synchronization of sequences of ritual actions (e.g., the distribution of elements) with sequences of actions carried out at two scales: the human scale during sowing; the macrocosmic scale where entities of nature are called upon to distribute rain. The construction of the ritual space in gestures and words is made possible by the application of an analogical scheme putting in a relation of equivalence agencies of very distinct space-times. For instance, from the point of view of the act of distribution, the action of sowing and that of distributing rain can be considered as similar. The standard explanation of practices long described as "offerings" is summarized by the formula *do ut des*, which asserts the idea of a succession of sequences of actions performed by humans and nonhumans. According to the dynamics of gift or exchange, a two-step sequence takes place: humans give something and nonhumans render a service. However, while not being incorrect, such a division remains incomplete as long as it does not leave room for the description of situations of "co-activity" (Pitrou 2016b) and of "co-presence" (Hanks 2013) that ritual actions aim to establish. Ritual temporality benefits from being seen as a moment of "condensation" (Houseman and Severi 1998) where two temporalities are combined in both successive and simultaneous actions.

In this chapter, I want to explore how myths, in addition to being the foundations of repeated actions in rituals, can also be interpreted as a projection into the past of contemporary interactions between human and nonhuman agents. More precisely, I focus specifically on the "agency"—that is to say, the many ways of being active (see Monod Becquelin and Vapnarsky 2010)—of nonhuman entities when they are asked to make the maize grow or to protect the health of a person and more broadly to exert actions that produce vital processes such as growth, regeneration, reproduction, and so forth. Drawing on my fieldwork among the Mixe of Oaxaca, I have discovered that these nonhuman actions are often described as technical activities. For instance, an entity called "He Who Makes Being Alive" (*yikjujykyäjtpi*) will "distribute" the water to make the corn grow, and he will strengthen the body shell of a newborn baby in a process comparable to an activity of pottery. These observations are congruent with the work of Georges Canguilhem (1992) or Evelyn Fox Keller (1995), who aptly show that the understanding of organic processes is often based on an analogy made between life and technique; for instance, the heart is compared to a pump, or the inscription of the DNA in our cells to a text. The historicity of the knowledge of life is not only about the evolution of the understanding of the phenomenon over time. It manifests itself in the correlation between the mechanist analogies mobilized in theories of life and the elements of the material culture of a human group. Like the invention of automata at a time when organisms were beginning to be conceived as machines, only the development of contemporary technologies makes possible the comparison made by synthetic biology between biological processes and electrical circuits (Endy 2005; see also the metaphor of "molecular machines" [Loeve 2020]). These analogies are not intellectual abstractions: they guide practices. Conceiving life as a technical process opens up the possibility of treating living beings as artifacts (Pitrou 2017a). Analogical schemas are always approximations for the comprehension of something unknown from the observation of phenomena better understood: they depend on historical contexts and on the technical capacities human societies develop.

I wish to show that these analogical schemas that capture the power of entities capable of bringing life as technical actions are also at work in the way the actions narrated in mythic times are conceived. Myths can be described both as narratives of past actions that institute present actions, and as projections through which present-day populations represent a past they have not experienced. From this point of view, we can therefore consider that a mythical narrative establishes a situation of contemporaneity with the past. While the past continues to set the framework for action, it is also a projected form of praxis in which humans are engaged. If humans imitate what mythical figures once did, it is also because, in a certain sense, the intervention of the latter can be deciphered from the observation of present practices carried out by humans.

For this demonstration, I draw on my research in the field of the "anthropology of life," a comparative approach to the conceptions of life developed by human groups according to sociotechnical contexts (Pitrou 2022). All over the world, humans cannot fail to observe processes such as birth, growth, reproduction, disease, aging, and death, which manifest themselves in their bodies or in living nonhumans. In order to try to identify the causes producing these usually very obvious processes, all societies develop explanatory systems, which I call after Maurice Bloch "theories of life" (Bloch 2018). From this perspective, the description of technical actions in myths, actualized in rituals, provides useful information for identifying the theories of life prevailing in a human group. These hypotheses have already shed light on the various levels of interweaving of vital processes and technical processes in the Andes (Angé and Pitrou 2016), in the South American lowlands (Pitrou 2016b), and in Oceania (Coupaye and Pitrou 2018), with particular attention to figurative practices (Mauzé and Pitrou 2021). Following this thread, I wish to show how Mesoamerican myths and rituals relating to life, envisaged as a power that humans seek to control through ritual techniques, are based on an organization that seeks to articulate the temporality of vital and technical processes. The aim of my demonstration is therefore to show how technical actions performed by humans serve to represent and materialize the agency of entities who are able to exert the power of life. This can be seen in the temporal configurations that link ritual and myth.

Specifically, I aim to demonstrate how rites—of birth and agriculture—are based on a dual temporal operation that seeks to establish *synchronicity* between the activities of humans and nonhuman entities, and *contemporaneity* between past and present activities. Two examples are studied. First, a birth rite among the Mixe illustrates how humans attempt to synchronize their intervention on a child's body with the actions of nonhumans that "make it live." Simultaneously, the rite creates a dual connection between past and present. On one hand, ritual actions on the child reenact the world's creation and the birth of living beings by a demiurge. On the other, this creative activity, conceived analogously to human techniques, is linked to current human experience. While not denying the mythical past, the analogy establishes a form of contemporaneity with current human practices. In the second example, a myth collected by Monaghan among the Mixtecs suggests a similar hypothesis regarding agricultural rites. The myth describes the necessity of, through rites, synchronizing human labor in fields with nature's work, to grow corn. All subsequent rites are a reiteration of this initial episode, establishing analogies between social interactions and interactions with the Earth, an entity that grows corn and is treated as a collaborator for whom a meal is prepared and served. Again, the anteriority of a mythical episode does not prevent the past from being conceived from the present of social interactions.

For the anthropology of life, creation myths represent a wealth of information. First of all, they shed light on the fundamental conceptions of a human group when it comes to the question of why living beings appear in such different forms and how they maintain themselves in existence. Myths are never about life as such but about more specific problems concerning particular processes: why do humans, instead of being immortal, have a short life? Why are there different species? How can we explain the characteristic features (physiology, behavior) of this or that species? Moreover, as Lévi-Strauss demonstrates, myths often illustrate the transition from nature to culture, the tangible evidence of which is embodied in the invention of techniques with which humans transform the elements of the world—culinary activity being a paradigm.

A double historicity is then to be deciphered. Mythical events are treated as antecedent causes whose effects on the world of the living continue to be felt. But insofar as certain myths give an account of the state and use of the world in the present time, we can scrutinize the influence of a human sociotechnical context on the account of origins. For example, among the Mixe, birth rituals involving daily sessions of ritual bathing (*temazcal*)—for twenty or forty days—materialize the aim to warm the body of the newborn as a piece of pottery would be (Pitrou 2017b). The equivalence established between a technical process of shaping an artifact and reinforcing the child's body envelope—in particular the fontanel—implies a specific temporality, which in both cases combines the continuous effect of the heat with the succession of intermittent sequences. At another level, this practice can itself be analyzed as a way of coordinating the agency of humans with that of nonhuman agents who are called upon to prolong the action exerted by the parents on the body over a longer period. During a ceremonial deposit, for example, one hears the parents say:

ïjyxyäm npïktäknï	now we deposit it
ëëts ja tsejxk	the temazcal (= we make a deposit in the form of the structure where the ritual baths are given)
nyïkkukëxï nyik'apääti	we make it end, we make it touch its end (= we come to the end of the twenty days during which temazcal must be performed)
tsëënïtïp	let her sit (= let her live)
ëëts ja n'uu'nk ja unääjk	our daughter, our granddaughter
yäät mëjk ja xyëëw'unk	may it be strong the energy (or name) of our daughter
tpattëkïtït	when she starts to enter
tpatwääkïtït	when she begins to walk (= when she begins her existence)
yäät ïjyxyäm ëëts	now, we
npïktääky n'ejxtääky	we deposit it, we deposit it in front of your gaze
ïjyxyäm ja tsyejxk'u'nk	now, his dear temazcal

ïjyxyäm	now
ja xyëmatsyoo'ïn tsyoo'ntäknï	the counting of her days begins (= after the counting of the days of temazcal begins the counting of the days of the girl's existence)
ïjyxyäm ja yjumëjt	now, her year
tpattëjkïnyï	she begins to enter it
tpatwä'äkïnyï	she begins to walk there (= the girl begins her existence)
mëjk majääw	[may she be] strong, resistant

We thus observe a ritual scheme that interweaves two temporalities, the succession of a human action that ends while the intervention of a nonhuman agent begins. But, for this order of succession to be possible, there must also be a moment of junction between two levels of agency. This is precisely the function of the ceremonial deposit. In this case, the candle, wooden twigs, and foliage placed on the sacrificial stone around an anthropomorphic corn dough figure, representing the child, constitutes a ritual miniaturization of a ritual bath. The staging of a technical device illustrates both the action of parents on the organism and the action of life, conceived by analogy with the process of cooking.

This practice is itself articulated in a cosmological framework transmitted in a myth told to me in 2007 by Adrián Martinez González, a bilingual teacher from Santa María Tlahuitoltepec. Indeed, the activity of shaping the baby's body is attributed to the intervention of a nonhuman agent, the *täätyunpï* (*tääy* "idea," *tun* "to work, to be active," *-pï*, personificator), "He, Whose Activity Is to Have Ideas." With every newborn, *täätyunpï* repeats the same action, performed at the beginning of the creation of the world. The mythical description of this endeavor is described as a set of technical processes, which illustrates, again, how life is conceived as a technical process. And, in the same manner that technical analogy has a performative effect in establishing a form of synchronization between two levels of agency, we can suggest that it creates a sort of contemporaneity between mythical activity in the past and human activity in the present.

Like the passages in the Popol Vuh, the account of the activity of the *täätyunpï* is made to describe the creation (and destruction) of the world. While recounting events in the distant past, the agency of this entity is identified through present-day technical activities and material elements.

täätyunpï jatë'n	"He, Whose Activity Is to Have Ideas" (= the Creator) as well
yï majää'tyëjk	they [the] elders
yï tkäjpxti tmatyää'äkti	they talk about it, they discuss it (= they tell);
jaayip yi	at the beginning
tsyoo'ntää'äky tsoo'ntää'äkyïp	it starts, it starts
näxwii'nyït mëët	with the Earth
et näxwii'nyït mëët	with the extent, the surface of the land
	(= he starts by inventing [or creating] the land)
tsyoo'ntää'äkyi	he starts it;
yï täätyunpï	The Creator
mäji na'api mäji kojpï	like the potter, like the basket maker
na'api ëë'pyi	makes pottery, bends [the fibers in basketry] (= he creates the world like these craftsmen);
yë' yï näxwii'nyït	the Earth
nayitë'n	in the same way
tyanïpiktääjkip	he puts it down (= shapes it, builds it);
uk yë'ts	and this one
ja tsïnää'yïn tanää'yïn	sitting, standing (= our life, our way of living)
nayitë'n xmëë'yïmp	and so he gives it to us
täätyunpï ntejïnt	It is said that "He, Whose Activity Is to Have Ideas."
tyanïwejtsïp	he orders
sutsooj ja tyik̈'ëyït	how it will be built
ja tsïnaapyïti ja jää'tyi	the people
pën jatë'n tsïnaatyïp	who thus sit (= who live, exist)
ja jïyujktï ja ujtstï	animals, plants;
tuki'yï tum yë' ntejïnt	all this really, it is said,
yïktamïjää'wïp	it is believed
tnikëjxp'aty	is upon him (= the creator carries, maintains in existence these beings);
yë'ts tyikë'yïp	those he builds
ja ujts ja kipy ja tsääj	plants, trees, stones;
ku atëm nnii'myïntï	when we say:

ja nëëj ja tuuj	"water, rain"
ku atëm nnii'myïntï	when we say:
tuupï	"He who rains"
kïtäkpï	"He who brings down (who distributes)
ja nëëj ja tuuj	water, rain."
yë'ts jatë'n yïkʼëëʼyïp	that one so it builds them
	(= he creates the rain);
paty yïktiijy täätyunpï	for this he calls himself "Creator."
ku jatë'n	when
kutääyjanyaxy xïtë'n yë'	he gets his ideas across
	(= he makes what he invents exist)
wenkjaty ja' tyïkpitsimy	and he makes a lot of things up (= he often decides)
pïnï miti'pi yï tyanïwejtsïp	in accordance with its invention;
ejxïm ja ntejïnt	for example, we say
ja tsïnääʼyïn	the "sitting" (= existence, life)
miti ntajujykyʼäjtyïmp	the things "we live with."
ejxïm jï moojkïn	for instance maize
ejxïm jï xëjkïn	for instance the bean
jïts ja pään ja tuʼujts	and the millstone, the pot
yëʼ jatë'n	this one as well
atëm	we
ntajujykyʼäjytyïntïp	"what we are alive with."
	(= maize, the means of our livelihood)
yë'ts jïtë'n yïkʼëëʼyïp	so he builds it
yëʼ jïtë'n	this one
yïktamajääʼwïp	this is what we believe
pyïktäkkëjxtaapy	he puts everything on it
	(= he organizes the order of the world)
pïnï tiij jätë'n tsëjkyïmp	what we need
ejxïmi jëënïn	for example, the fire
ejxïmi tëjkïn	for example, the house
nay yëʼyï	himself

nyïjkëjxp'ajytypy	he wears it
nay yë'yï	himself
yiktanïpëjkp	he has them in his power
nay yë'yï	himself

This myth describes the beings that the Demiurge brings into existence: the Earth, the animals, the plants—in particular, corn ("what we live with")—the rain, the kitchen utensils. These elements are distributed over the surface of the world and assembled according to an organizing activity conceived as a "deposition." It is also a conventional system, a "way of sitting," that is, a "way of living" that is established through it and reproduced through tradition. Two cycles are implicitly mentioned: on the one hand, the one that makes the growth of maize dependent on rain; on the other hand, insofar as maize is, par excellence, a being "with which one lives" (*tajujyky'ajtpï*), that of culinary transformation carried out with kitchen utensils. More broadly, it is a question of a global cycle of creation and destruction, which delimits the beginning and end of the world and establishes a hierarchy—defining who eats whom, structuring the relationships between living beings. Life thus appears as an evolutionary ecosystemic phenomenon. Like the Popol Vuh (Tedlock 1996), which describes how the species punished by the Creators are condemned to live in the woods and be preyed upon by humans, the Mixe myth explains that at some point in the history of the world, humans are themselves at risk of being eaten by their pets—or even by the objects they use on a daily basis.

The agency associated with this dual activity of creating forms and organizing is based on an ability to form mental representations. Literally, the *täätyunpï* is "He whose activity (*tunk*) is to have ideas (*tääy*)." The creation of living beings, life cycles, technical processes, and a hierarchical order is attributed to this intentionality, described as a category of action of human technique. It is as if human agency serves as an analogy for representing actions carried out by a demiurgic entity that works before humans exist. "He Whose Activity Is to Have Ideas" is supposed to have made living beings like "a potter, like a basket maker, who shapes, who bends [textile fibers, as in basketry]." In just a few lines, we find condensed the constitutive elements of a theory of life thought by analogy with technical activity, in order to make the formation of organisms (analogy with pottery) and their structuring (analogy with basketry) intelligible. The insertion of living beings into cycles and systems of relationships is understood through the idea of a "deposition," a "distribution" which refers to a human activity of organization. The very fact of describing the act of creation by analogy with a human mental experience, which correlates the action with a mental representation, attests to the anthropomorphic character of the account of cosmogenesis.

The reference to technical actions thus provides a link between the present and the past, between humans and nonhuman entities. Very often, the description of a technique in a myth depicts an inaugural act, an invention, or even a "mythical operational sequence [*mythique chaîne opératoire*]" (Lemonnier 2004) that is subsequently imitated by humans.[1] These mythical episodes affirm more than chronological precedence: they delimit a legitimate framework within which each generation must inscribe its action. In Mesoamerica, stories of the invention of techniques–for example, agriculture, sacrifice, fermentation, and so forth—can always be interpreted as a way of identifying the new generation. But symmetrically, the actual techniques of a human group compose a repertoire of forms, materials, and processes from which the creation of living beings by demiurges is conceived. Despite the temporal hiatus with the time of origins, mythical thought establishes bridges between universes where transformations are observed, caused by human and nonhuman agents. With technology, a continuity and circularity between regimes of action is affirmed: if humans repeat the actions performed by the demiurges and the ancestors, the latter intervene in the world not in a miraculous way but with techniques similar to those of humans. In his commentary on the Popol Vuh, Dennis Tedlock explains: "the gods are preoccupied with the difficult task of making humans, and [. . .] humans are preoccupied with the equally difficult task of finding the traces of divine movements in their own deeds" (Tedlock 1996, 59). How better to express the idea of a continual resumption by humans of demiurgic actions?

Around the issue of life, the interpretation of creation myths often reveals a form of chiasmus where the order of the world depends on a past intervention—potentially repeatable in the future—an intervention whose modalities are themselves thought according to a praxis experienced in the present time. In some cases, the synchronization of temporalities is even at the heart of the myth, when collaboration between humans and nonhuman entities is presented as the very condition for the establishment of a sociotechnical order.

Mesoamerican myths sometimes feature situations of collaboration between humans and entities of nature. The issue is to relate the way in which humans coordinate their life techniques with the agency of beings endowed with the power of life. This means that the analogy between human and nonhuman actions does not rely exclusively on technical activities. It also involves social relations and values, which imply a temporal coordination between human and nonhuman agencies. This is well illustrated in *The Covenants with Earth and Rain: Exchange, Sacrifice, and Revelation in Mixtec Sociality*, a monograph in which John Monaghan (1995) examines the material and contractual relationships of the Mixtec with their natural environment. He reveals the homologies between social institutions that organize collective work, and the exchange of services and ritual practices involving the participation of nonhuman agents in a collective effort. The production of vital processes is less a biological issue than a technical and social problem of coordinating activity. This is the lesson that can be drawn from a Mixtec myth translated by Monaghan (1995, 204–207):

> The story says that there were two men who worked . . . who knows where?
> They went and cleared the forest and brush, they cut it down,
> And well, if it wasn't the next day they went again to where their piece of work was,
> And it was only forest, that regrew.
> The work they did was not there, because the forest regrew,
> And they thought that they would make a plea to the Earth, they spoke to the Earth.
> They said, they pleaded "Give us to eat, give us to drink, clothe us, because from the
>   Earth comes all we need, and thus is our lot"
> And so they asked, they made a covenant [nchisoyu'u ra],
> They asked that "that which gives us life come over the Earth."
> They asked that it gives them to drink, it gives them to eat, and that [the Earth] should
>   then take them in again, because there is no other place they will go [when they die].
> As the Earth gives them to drink, as the Earth gives them to eat, it will gather them in
>   again, we say and we realize this is true.
> "And now it will produce, and we will obtain what it is we need to eat, and thus we live,
>   we live from it," they said.
> "And as we live, sickness will arrive, which will enter into us, and where will we go? To
>   what side will we leave?"
> "We will go because in the Earth we will lie down again,"
> "There it will take us in," they said.
> The Earth acquiesced.
> They were able to do their work,
> Because they were not able to enjoy the work they did before.
> They went to look for . . . they pleaded with [the Earth] that there would be there . . .
>   that there would begin to exist, the work they did.
> What corn seed! What bean seed! What squash seed they sowed!
> "Yaah! It is going to bear fruit!" they said. But they asked a favor of it,
> And thus they were able to work, so the story says.

This story explains how a new institution, sacrifice, ensures coordination between technical and life processes. At the beginning, the peasants may work and cut wood—to grow maize, which is slash-and-burned—but their efforts are in vain because they are not in tune with the activity of the Earth, which keeps the plants growing back. The challenge is to establish an agreement with this entity that "gives life" through the food it produces. The elements of the Mixtecs' theory of life are then revealed, less concerned with the explanation of isolated vital processes (growth, reproduction, etc.) than with the respect of a contractual framework of fruitful collaboration with the Earth, which implies also a good synchronization. Before the covenant, the work done by humans disappeared "because the forest regrew"; after the covenant, an accurate coordination is possible. Instead of the omnipotence of "supernatural" deities acting in a transcendent way, the narrative recalls a particular form of *interdependence* that is woven through these joint actions. Although the participation of the Earth, and of the Rain, is indispensable for the provision of sustenance, the sacrificial institution places these partners in a less asymmetrical position than it seems. These entities must comply with an order that is imposed on them as much as on humans. Once the contract is established through sacrifice, they find themselves enrolled in a framework of action from which it is difficult to escape. Moreover, they are not only bound by obligations: they are subject to physiological constraints, and the efforts they make must be compensated. Humans need the entities of nature to obtain the fruits of their sustenance, but they depend on those who feed them in exchange for their participation.

The recognition of these situations of interdependence and synchronization of activity helps us to better understand the ritual temporality at work during ceremonial deposits. All archaeological, historical, and anthropological research agrees that these practices were oblations made in compensation for services rendered by nonhuman entities from whom Amerindian peoples solicited services. The use of food elements, fermented beverages, blood, and the bodies of sacrificial victims leaves little doubt as to the dietary nature of the transfer made. This is confirmed by Indigenous exegesis and prayers; in Mixe, for example, phrases such as "This is your broth, this is your drink" are heard during sacrificial deposits. Ritual temporality is thus based on the succession of complementary sequences: before (or after) the effort, food is transmitted as compensation for the effort.

The obvious nature of this dynamic should not, however, obscure another temporal regime aimed at establishing moments of synchronization. This applies of course to coordination between humans. In a plurimodal manner, gesture and speech ensure the joint execution of actions by the participants; whether these actions are complementary, as in the transmission of command sticks, or synchronized, as in the sowing of seeds or the pouring of alcohol. The work of William Hanks (1990) and Valentina Vapnarsky (2022), among the Yucatecan Maya, on the construction of a space where ritual specialists interact with the spirits, attests to the extension of this synchronization to relations with the spirits, which must be "co-present" (Hanks 1990), in a spatial as well as a temporal sense.

In detail, temporal markers indicate a hiatus between these spheres of activity, some concerning the action in progress ("we are distributing the elements on the ceremonial deposit"), others the activities to be carried out to promote growth ("we are going to distribute the grains in the field"; "you are going to distribute the rain"). In other words, the form of synchronization of the levels of action sought during the rite does not prevent this sequence from being inscribed in an order of succession. But the organizing power of rites makes it possible to condense these temporal logics.

The power of life inscribes the world in a general becoming where all living beings are traversed by a multiplicity of vital processes. Procreation, birth, growth, regeneration, metabolization, aging: these are all processes whose specific temporalities impose a set of constraints on the organisms of humans, animals, and plants and even, in certain cases, on the organisms of entities in nature that possess the power of life. Death itself, as a moment that closes or punctuates individual existences, appears as a mark of the irremediable with which all societies must deal. According to distinct conceptual modalities, the notions of "process" and "life cycle" insist on the idea of a succession of sequences or stages inherent to vital phenomena. With life, a temporal order based on a logic of succession is thus established: being born before dying, feeding before growing, and so forth.

Modeled and articulated to this temporal order, the techniques of the living put in place by humans take the form of processes in which actions are linked together with a view to an end: sowing in order to grow, procreating in order to reproduce, cooking in order to feed oneself and the others, and so forth. While it is difficult to think of technical activity without a sequencing of actions, the chains of operation do not only trace sequences: the coordination and synchronization of actions—similar or complementary—is equally important. Insofar as any action on the living is always an interaction *with* the living, investigations benefit from reconstructing "agentive configurations" (Pitrou 2017b), in order to describe, *at the same time*, what humans do to the living and what the vital processes running through these beings make humans do. The examples presented in this chapter demonstrate that, like the techniques coordinating human action, ritual techniques for enlisting nonhuman agents also combine a dual temporal logic of succession and synchronization. For the Mixe, this explains why the intervention of "He Who Makes Being Alive" on the corn or the body of a child is understood by analogy with the actions that humans themselves carry out on these organisms. This analogical logic is also found at the heart of mythical accounts of origins, where the creation of the world and living beings is conceived as a set of sociotechnical actions performed by metapersonal beings. In this case, a form of contemporaneity of agency regimes is asserted. Instead of thinking of humans as the image and likeness of God, the peoples of Mesoamerica draw the contours of the agency of the demiurges from the observation of human activities.

NOTE

1. All translations are mine unless stated otherwise.

REFERENCES

Angé, Olivia, and Perig Pitrou. 2016. "Miniatures in Mesoamerica and the Andes: Theories of Life, Values, and Relatedness." *Journal of Anthropological Research* 72 (4): 408–15.

Bloch, Maurice. 2018. *How We Think They Think: Anthropological Approaches to Cognition, Memory, and Literacy*. London: Routledge.

Bloch, Maurice. 2020. *Essays on Cultural Transmission*. Abington: Routledge.

Canguilhem, Georges. 1992. *La connaissance de la vie*. Paris: Vrin.

Códice Chimalpopoca: Anales de Cuauhtitlan y Leyenda de los soles. 2019. Translated by Primo Feliciano Velázquez. Foreword by Miguel León Portilla. Mexico: Universidad Nacional Autónoma de México / Instituto de Investigaciones Históricas.

Coupaye, Ludovic, and Perig Pitrou. 2018. "Introduction. The Interweaving of Vital and Technical Processes in Oceania." *Oceania* 88 (1): 2–12.

Endy, Drew. 2005. "Foundations for Engineering Biology." *Nature* 438: 449–453.

Hanks, William F. 1990. *Referential Practice: Language and Lived Space among the Maya*. Chicago: University of Chicago Press.

Hanks, William F. 2013. "Counterparts: Co-presence and Ritual Intersubjectivity." *Language and Communication* 33 (3): 263–77.

Houseman, Michael, and Carlo Severi. 1998. *Naven, or, the Other Self: A Relational Approach to Ritual Action*. Leiden: Brill.

Humphrey, Caroline, and James Laidlaw. 1994. *Archetypal Actions of Ritual: A Theory of Ritual Ilustrated by the Jain Rite of Worship*. Oxford: Clarendon Press.

Keller, Evelyn Fox. 1995. *Refiguring Life: Metaphors of Twentieth-Century Biology*. New York: Columbia University Press.

Lemonnier, Pierre. 2004. "Mythiques chaînes opératoires." *Techniques and Culture: Revue semestrielle d'anthropologie des techniques*, nos. 43/44. https://doi.org/10.4000/tc.1054.

Lévi-Strauss, Claude. 1971. *L'homme nu*. Paris: Plon.

Loeve, Sacha. 2020. "Comme si la nature imitait l'art: Les machines moléculaires artificielles et leurs analogues naturels." *Techniques and Culture* 73. https://doi.org/10.4000/tc.13953.

Mauzé, Marie, and Perig Pitrou, eds. *Reconfigurer le vivant*. Paris: L'Herne.

Monaghan, John. 1995. *The Covenants with Earth and Rain: Exchange, Sacrifice, and Revelation in Mixtec Society*. Norman: University of Oklahoma Press.

Monod Becquelin, Aurore, and Alain Breton. 2002. *La "guerre rouge" ou, Une politique maya du sacré: Un carnaval tzeltal au Chiapas, Mexique*. Paris: CNRS.

Monod Becquelin, Aurore, and Valentina Vapnarsky, eds. 2010. "L'agentivité vol. I: Ethnologie et linguistique à la poursuite du sens." *Ateliers d'anthropologie* 34. https://doi .org/10.4000/ateliers.8515.

Pitrou, Perig. 2016a. *Le chemin et le champ: Parcours rituel et sacrifice chez les Mixe de Oaxaca (Mexique)*. Nanterre: Société d'ethnologie.

Pitrou, Perig. 2016b. "Co-activity in Mesoamerica and in the Andes." *Journal of Anthropological Research* 72 (4): 465–82.

Pitrou, Perig. 2017a. "Life as a Making." *Natureculture* 4: 1–37.

Pitrou, Perig. 2017b. "Life Form and Form of Life within an Agentive Configuration: A Birth Ritual among the Mixe of Oaxaca, Mexico." *Current Anthropology* 58 (3): 360–80.

Pitrou, Perig. 2022. *Les anthropologues et la vie*. Sesto San Giovanni (Italy): Mimésis.

Tedlock, Dennis, trans. 1996. *Popol Vuh: The Definitive Edition of The Mayan Book of The Dawn of Life and The Glories of Gods and Kings*. New York: Simon and Schuster.

Turner, Victor. 1969. *The Ritual Process: Structure and Anti-structure*. London: Routledge.

Vapnarsky, Valentina. 2022. "Voice Matters: The Vocal Creation and Manipulation of Ritual Temporalities." In *Materializing Ritual Practices*, edited by Lisa Johnson and Rosemary Joyce, 70–94. Boulder: University Press of Colorado.

8

Male Pregnancy and the Rebirth of the Year

Actors and Temporalities in a Tseltal Instauration Ritual (Bachajon, Chiapas)

ALAIN BRETON, MARIE CHOSSON, AND AURORE MONOD BECQUELIN

This chapter examines a ritual constituting the first stage of what we term an "instauration ceremony" in Bachajon, a Tseltal Maya village in Chiapas, Mexico. The chronological succession of two events—the feast of Saint Sebastian and Carnival—and the strong symbolic link expressed by Tseltal glosses in regard to the former have led us to revisit what we previously considered a mere introductory sequence in an earlier work on the Bachajon Carnival (Monod Becquelin and Breton 2002). A closer analysis of the Saint Sebastian ritual has produced two hypotheses we tested. First: this festival, which the Tseltal describe as a prelude to Carnival, is an inherent and indissociable part of the whole; second: the performances seen and heard at Saint Sebastian and Carnival do indeed constitute a time instauration ritual, fundamentally distinct from other types of ritual, such as laying the foundations of a house, the propitiation of a new field, or a curative treatment.

Our description of the first act—the San Sebastian festival—in this ritual ensemble will be supported by an analysis of the various discourses and actions involved and the multiple modes whereby mythical characters are evoked alongside animals long gone from the region; conflicts, real or legendary, conflated with one another; and underground worlds, all associated with differing temporalities and discursive modes. We will demonstrate the specificity of these instauration discourses that make up a subgenre of what is commonly called *pat'o'tan* (ritual dialogue); then, we will show the ways in which the junction between differing referential worlds works, "inaugurating" a temporal axis on which the past and the

https://doi.org/10.5876/9781646426829.c008

future are expressed, thus aligning ourselves with other analyses of Mayan time as ancestral and cyclical.[1]

The Saint Sebastian ritual is performed in Bachajon, a village in northern Chiapas, located between Ocosingo and Palenque at an altitude of 900 meters, a temperate submontane zone between the highlands and lowlands. Its territory extends down to the warm valley of the T'ulilha' river (figure 8.1).

For forty years, the community, formerly made up of two districts or barrios of Bachajon (San Jerónimo and San Sebastián) has been split into two distinct administrative units—essentially two different communities—due to exacerbated tensions left over from the colonial era, and bloody conflicts born out of the consequences of the 1994 Zapatista uprising. Our focus will be entirely on San Sebastián and the very particular festival that it hosts.

The feast of Saint Sebastian (January 20) comes before Carnival, a movable date between February and March in the Christian calendar. In Bachajon, Saint Sebastian is the setting for a surprising ritual, probably unique in Mesoamerica, during which "wild men" (*kabinal*) appear, personifying beings of an earlier creation, worldly spirit-masters, and ancestors come from distant lowlands. The kabinal simulate an animal copulation with individuals called *kapitanes*, "captains," actors whose (politico-religious) authority and the renewal thereof constitute the central themes of the Carnival celebrations to follow. The insemination of these captains and the announcement of an already advanced pregnancy mark the start of a period of uncertainty and danger that will culminate in Carnival. For the Tseltal, both events are consubstantially linked. The encounter between these two groups introduces mythohistorical temporalities—the perilous return of ancient history, the brutal intrusion of the ancestors, the resurgence of chthonic beings from the darkness of the pre-Christian world—harking back to the community's two different origins five centuries earlier. Through the different sequences and discursive strategies used in the dialogues, this transition ritual expresses multiple temporalities by mingling them, while calling to mind historical spaces and periods (lowlands vs. highlands; pre-Hispanic vs. colonial era) that work toward the affirmation of continuity. As an allegory for the annual renewal and changes of the captains' offices, this ritual is an essential part of a complex whole unfolding amid the darkness of the "lost days" (*wayeb*) in ancient Maya calendars (*ch'ay.k'in* in Tseltal), when the forces of chaos and night reign, before the anticipated rebirth of the solar cycle, the warming of the cosmos, and the restoration of social order in the human world.

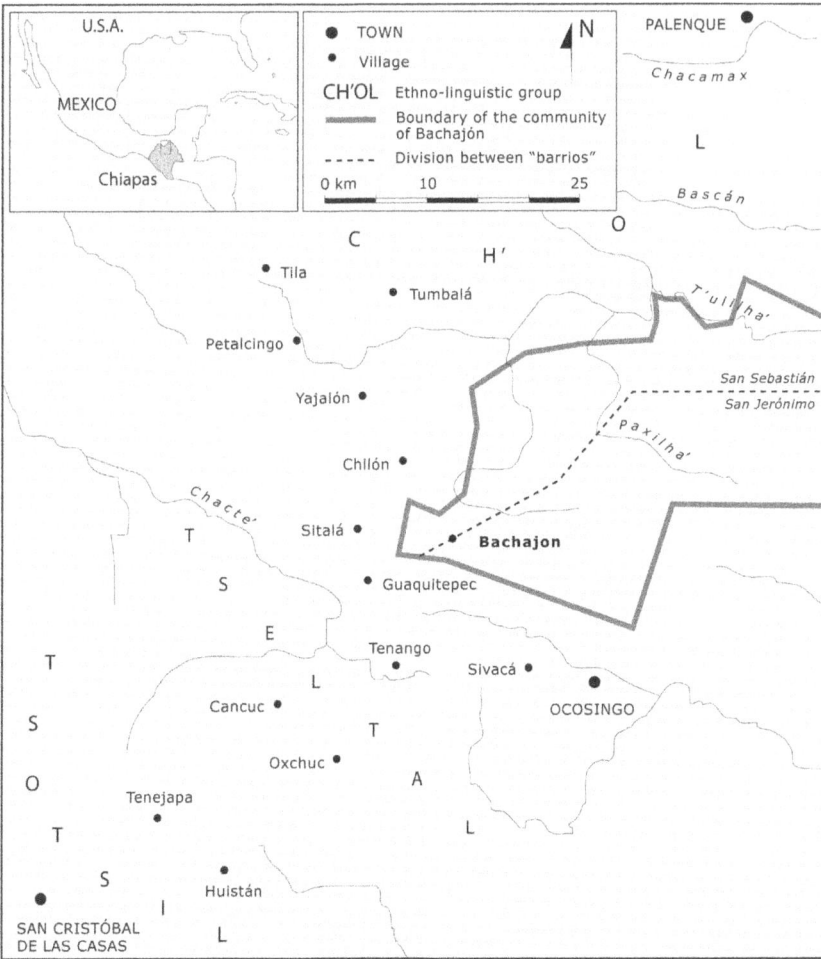

Figure 8.1. Bachajon and surrounding region (from Monod Becquelin and Breton 2002)

SOCIAL ORGANIZATION

The community of San Sebastián Bachajon is divided into four *kalpul*,[2] patrilineal groupings in which all members, men and women, are related (figure 8.2). Although the kalpul represent a geographically tangible space within the village area, this becomes irregular and discontinuous further out across the territory, the result of how the land has been distributed among the lineages that occupy it. By the Tseltal's own explanation, a kalpul constitutes a "group" (*k'atinajibal*) "warmed" under the eyes of the ancestors and through ritual alliance that ensures the protection of individuals and the wider community. Each of the four kalpul is headed by

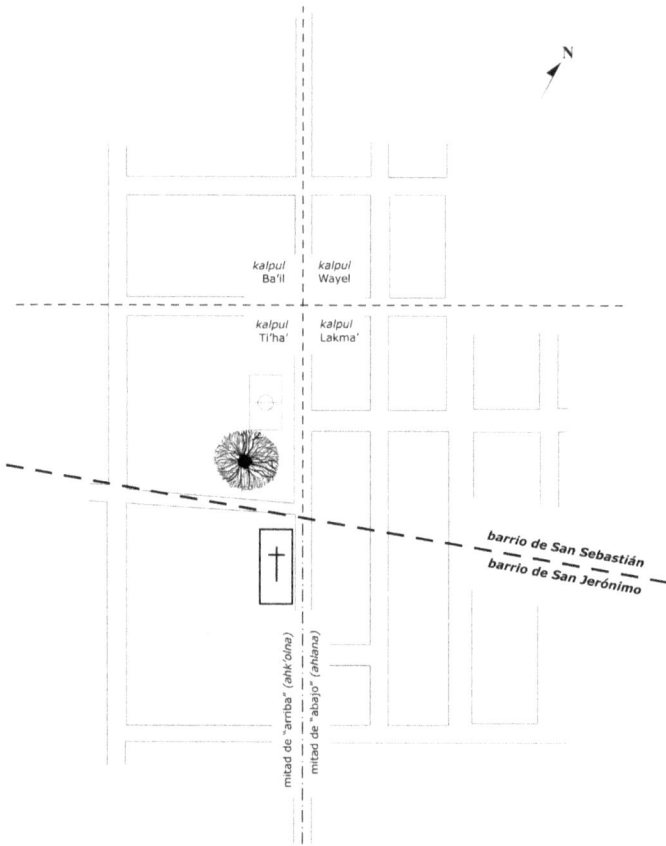

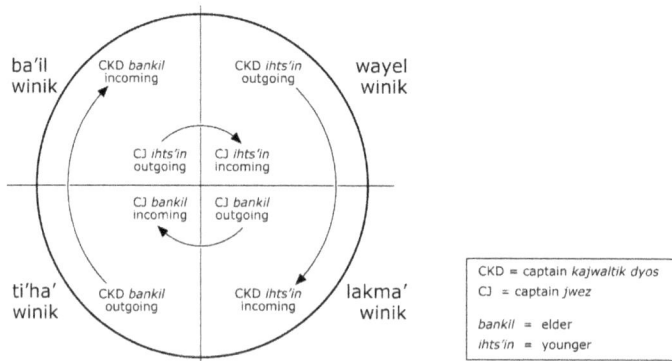

Figure 8.2. (a) Territorial divisions of Bachajon into moieties, San Jerónimo and *kalpul*, and San Sebastián (today these barrios have become two distinct communities); and (b) the principle of the rotating cargo system between the four *kalpul* (San Sebastián) (from Breton 1979)

a great *principal*, known as *k'atinab*, "he who warms": this is usually an older, experienced man chosen by his peers on the basis of an exemplary career (as demonstrated by his titles in the cargo system) and his qualities as a healer. He is endowed with considerable powers but also heavy responsibilities. His primary role is to protect, to "heal" people, and watch over them. Another term given for this high authority is *ts'umbajon* (the sewer), since, year after year, the heavy task falls to him to find, convince, and recruit the captains on whom the entire material organization of the Carnival depends. The public offices of the Carnival captains are organized into *kajwaltik dyos* (our lord god), and *jwes* (judge), then subdivided into "elders" (*bankilal*) and "youngers" (*ihts'inal*), who move clockwise from one kalpul to the next; a rotational logic which ensures that an outgoing captain will always be succeeded by an incoming captain from the next kalpul.

This model is weakened by modernity and the exorbitant costs today of bearing this authority; yet this four-way structure does remain, alongside a dynamic of alliances between the kalpul, presided over by the gerontocracy of the *principales*, who guarantee the restoration of social and cosmological order, reminiscent of an older structure and dynamic (Breton 1979).

A SHORT HISTORY

What little information we have regarding the establishment of Bachajon dates back to the first decades after the Spanish conquest of Mexico (1521) and Chiapas (1524). The policies of pacification, evangelization, and resettlement (*reducciones*) pursued by the mendicant orders of the time led to the formation of this community, according to chroniclers from three groups or *parcialidades* between 1550 and 1580, later reduced to two following the 1712 Tseltal rebellion (Ximénez 1930–31, 2:250). This configuration lasted from the colonial era in the form of barrios (San Jerónimo and San Sebastián) until the recent establishment of distinct autonomous communities today. The *parcialidad* of Tuni (whose geographical and ethnic origins remain unknown) disappeared during the eighteenth century following the repression, unrest, and epidemics that blighted the region. The Xuxuycapa were a local group from Joybe', not far from the village's present-day location, and probably the primitive settlement, of the future barrio of San Jerónimo. They were converted in situ (church ruins have been found here) before being resettled a few kilometers away with the Lakma' group, each group forming one barrio of a new community: Bachajon. According to contemporary chronicles, the Dominican missionary Friar Pedro Lorenzo de la Nada, played a crucial role in the establishment of new colonial villages and the conversion of Indians in the region between his arrival in Chiapas in 1560 and his death in Palenque in 1580. He was likely responsible for founding

Bachajon, where a group from these lowland regions was settled around 1564 as well (de Vos 1980). We have three clues to infer the distant origins of the people from the Bachajon barrio of San Sebastián: (1) the name (whether toponym or ethnonym is uncertain) Lakma[3] given to one of the four kalpul, still considered the "eldest" of the kalpul; (2) the four-way structure, itself typical of how these lowland societies were arranged (Hellmuth 1972; Thompson 1976), which at the time included Tseltal, Ch'ol, and Lacandon Ch'olti groups; (3) the use of the name or title "Kabnal," associated with chiefdom among these groups (Bricker 1973; Hellmuth 1972).

Kabnal, kabinal—together with "Lacandons," "red Caribs," "cannibals," and "enemies"—are words synonymous with "unsubdued" and "savage" that resonated with the Spanish and pacified Indians across the centuries. And accounts of Lacandon attacks between 1530 and 1586 on Christianized villages bound to the Crown are indeed found in chronicles: houses razed to the ground, pillaging, metal objects looted, women kidnapped. . . . The population of San Sebastián Bachajon found itself at the crossroads of this displacement and violence, assuming the dual heritage of the lowland "ancestors" and "enemies" that marked the history of the region during the sixteenth century and beyond (see Breton 1988). Several factors are worth keeping in mind regarding Bachajon's particular identity: its origins (from lowland resettled groups), the preservation of the four-way kalpul model, and the unconsciously transposed survival of the community's connection to this antagonistic, even warlike alterity. This singular identity is showcased each year at Carnival, for which the feast of Saint Sebastian sets the stage and assembles the actors involved.

A BRIEF DESCRIPTION OF THE FEAST OF SAINT SEBASTIAN

On January 20, 1992, *sbah k'in* (the prime day), the outgoing and incoming captains are confirmed, and the dates of the festivities are announced publicly. Also announced on this day are the leaving and return dates of the kabinal expedition into the forest. The kabinal are a group of Bachajon people who play the ambivalent role of the enemy and the ancestors. The main actors involved in the feast of Saint Sebastian are the same who will later take part in Carnival: the captains' group (including captains, musicians, and authorities) and the kabinal group. Both celebrations demand considerable work of the captains' kin and extended family: months, often years spent in preparation, responsible as they are for supplying the necessary resources, ingredients, and objects for humans and nonhuman actors.

The *auto* (proclamation), in which the number of days left before Carnival is declared, falls to the *piskal*. His role is to stand before the kabinal to announce the date they must "go out" of the village (*lok'el*), or "leave" (*bahel*) for the lowlands; the date the principales will collect them, at dusk, from a clearing on the edge of the village; and the date the captains will seclude themselves (*ochan ta ora*, literally, "enter a period of time-space").

> Listen, my respected elders,
>> to the dates and days I give you.
>> In twenty-nine days will come the small matins (*maitines*).
>> The *kabinal-karibyos* will arrive on the sixteenth (of February), Friday.
>> Saturday the seventeenth is the first matins, as they say [...]
>> Then only thirteen days remain before the end of February,
>> And the feast begins.
>
> (San Sebastián 1996)

Or, according to one comment overheard:

> It will soon be time to proclaim the new year; with offerings to Saint Sebastian.

And so the calendar is set.

The expedition sets off the next day, jealously guarded and unwitnessed. Between ten and fifteen men from the village—the kabinal—leave in order to return later bearing the "world"-spirits.

Yax bohon ta montaña,	*yax k'ohon,*	*yax k'op-k'ohon te bahlumilal,*
I go into the forest,	I arrive there,	and **I address-arriving** the world
Ya kalbey te bahlumilal	*yu'un manchuk yax yahlon*	
I speak to the world	in order not to stumble [...]	
K'alal yax laj,	*ya ka'be smahtan te bahlumilal,*	*ya ka'be te tomut*
When this is done,	I give the world its **present**,	I give it **the egg**,
ya ka'be sok te trawo,	*ya ka'be te yuch'* [...]	*ya ka'be te pom* ...
I also give it **alcohol**,	I give it its **drink** [...]	I give it **the incense**

(Interview with the San Sebastián kabinal chief, 1996)

We see in San Sebastián's festival a sociability structured around the same actions as Carnival—the meals, dancing in the *yax na* ("green shelters"), visits between authorities and the kabinal, exchanging of food—albeit sometimes in a scaled-down version, with a "nod and wink" to the upcoming ritual and with certain notable differences: for example, the chocolate beverage offered around at Saint Sebastian presages the cocoa beans distributed at Carnival by the kabinal chief to the authorities after the new captains have been sworn in. Similarly, one sequence in which food is prepared for the kabinal is lengthy and unusual, both in terms of content and cooking methods, with all ingredients meticulously chosen for their contrasting and complementary qualities.[4] This food preparation process is unique at the festival. It foreshadows the kinds of food that will appear at the Carnival banquet held for the kabinal, their animal-spirit pelts, and their musical instruments to coax and assuage them for the year ahead (Monod Becquelin and Breton 2003).

There is one final (private and nocturnal) ritual that begins "when the sun dies," before the expedition into the forest leaves. Through an act of mating between the wild men and the captains, the roles and functions of these two main groups are assigned. The ritual simulates copulation (which is expressed by the term *kuch*, used to denote both "carrying [or bearing] something" and "coupling" regarding animals) by incorporating the act into a dance (*ahk'ot*) (figure 8.3). Later at Carnival, this dance will be civilized and transformed into dances between kabinal and women from the captain group. As we will see, the act of mating consecrates the ontological alterity of the kabinal in various spatial and interactional dimensions. It renders the kabinal's essential function in the construction of ancestral identity explicit through references to condensed temporalities calculated according to a logic of patrilineal filiation.

The kabinal are invited into the house after the initial dialogue beyond the threshold, whereupon they seize the captains with an immediacy and force reminiscent of a kidnapping, or of animals mating. *Ja' te kapitan . . . ya skuchik ta ahk'ot* (The captain . . . the *kabinal* carry him [or copulate with him] during the dance), the kabinal chief explained straightforwardly. During the *kuch kapitan*, the captains are carried around the main room of the house, thirteen circles, quickly or slowly depending on the carriers and the musicians, in front of the principales, the women, the captain's relatives, and other visitors. The musical din of the kabinal, the small, jerking steps transferring the captain from one back to another without letting him touch the ground of his own house, these are preliminaries, suffused with both tension and laughter, to an even more intimate event. The pregnant man is feminized with traditional women's clothing (skirt and belt) before being laid down on the domestic couch. The kabinal chief then proceeds to massage his or her abdomen, and feels the pulse on both wrists, as a midwife would do (figure 8.4).

Then, he summons his main assistant to carry out the same procedure, after which the two discuss this unnatural pregnancy and the diagnosis that they should come to. The kabinal assembled in the adjoining room listen to the two men's jokes and laugh. The kabinal chief then returns to the main room, where the principal asks after the subject with an anxious smile. The kabinal chief offers an uncertain

Figure 8.3. The *kabinal* "carrying the captains" (photographs by Monod Becquelin, 1994)

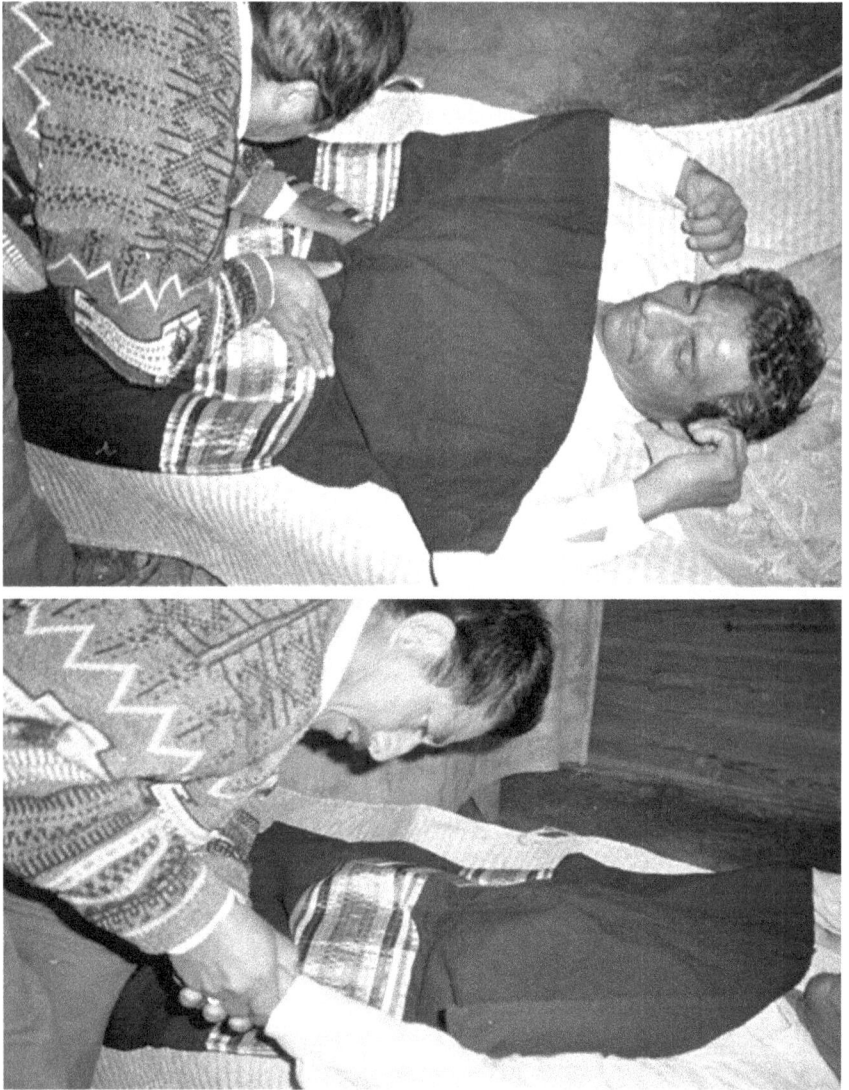

Figure 8.4. (a) The *kabinal* chief massages the "pregnant" captain's stomach . . . (b) then takes his pulse (photographs by Monod Becquelin, 1994)

diagnosis, full of troubling possibilities, like birthing a monstrous creature, in punishment perhaps for some past misbehavior; at the same time, he gives advice to the expectant "mother" and confirms the due date, which always corresponds to the return date of the expedition into the forest.[5]

Concerns and doubts are raised about when the pregnancy will end (neither too soon nor too late), parentage (who is the father, who is the mother?), and how many and what kind of beings will result from it.

> KABINAL CHIEF: Between now and the 16th February, we'll see how it is [the foetus], and if it arrives on its due date. What will it be? A man or a woman? [...]
> CAPTAIN: I can already feel it kicking. Perhaps it will come early. [...]
> KABINAL CHIEF: A boy, and a girl. We'll see. The man will have three testicles [laughter] ... and the women will have three breasts [...]
> Let's see if it looks like me, if we'll look the same!
> OTHER KABINAL: But it's not due yet, there's still some time to go.
> KABINAL CHIEF: If it doesn't look like me, someone must have double-crossed me.
> If that's the case, no matter, even an older brother.
> It's the same thing, never mind: it's the same name. (San Sebastián 1993)

The new captain is effectively named *snich'an te kabinal* (child of the kabinal). He will be born as an infant at the start of Carnival, at which time he will take his oath.

It is not just the presence of the same actors and the announcement during Saint Sebastian of the series of ritual actions that will occur at the forthcoming Carnival that allow us to connect these two rituals as parts of the same whole. It quickly becomes apparent that the ritual dialogues exchanged during these two events possess distinguishing features that make them both different from other types or subgenres and similar to one another. To show this, we will briefly revisit the specificity of this pair of rituals relative to other ritual dialogues in Bachajon's oral tradition and compare certain features of the ritual speeches in question with those of a healing ritual.[6] Only the most audible and striking contrasts will be highlighted. Later, we will examine in more detail the nature of the close link between the Saint Sebastian and Carnival dialogues, which are so particular as to afford this sequence an exceptional meaning.

THE *PAT'O'TAN* OF SAINT SEBASTIAN AND CARNIVAL: A SUBGENRE WITHIN RITUAL ORAL TRADITION

The pat'o'tan (ritual dialogues) of Saint Sebastian and Carnival festivals present characteristics different from all the other pat'o'tan. For the sake of space, we will focus on the three contrasting linguistic and rhetorical strategies that we consider the most relevant to this analysis: the use of personal pronouns, the use of parallelism, and the use of inventories.

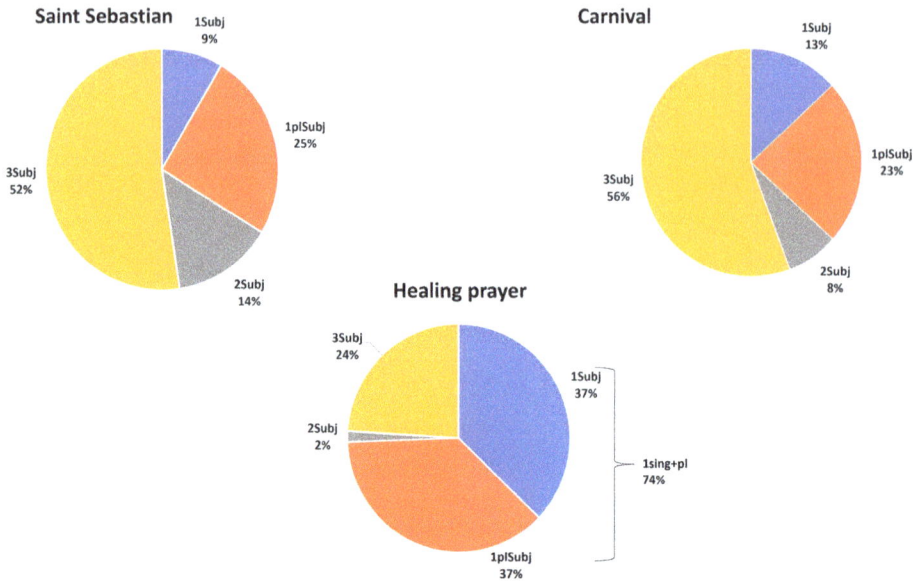

Figure 8.5. Frequency and use of person markers in the Saint Sebastian and Carnival *pat'o'tan* compared with a healing prayer

The use and distribution of subject person markers provide an initial contrast between the construction of ritual dialogues at Saint Sebastian and Carnival on the one hand, and a healing discourse on the other.[7] During the latter, the first person, singular or plural, is predominant (74%). It is primarily used to index the presiding shaman, alone or in co-activity with the *ajaw*,[8] assisting him. In contrast, at Saint Sebastian and Carnival, the third-person singular predominates (figure 8.5), despite almost never being referenced or named in lexical terms. The dialogical nature of the discourse is also more apparent in the feast day speech. While the use of the second person during the healing prayer is practically negligible (2%), second-person markers, albeit still a minority, make up 8 percent and 14 percent, respectively, of those used at Saint Sebastian and Carnival.

There is also a marked contrast in the distribution of lexical pairs in parallel association (figure 8.6)—parallelism is a common configuration in Mayan oral tradition. First, the healer's discourse is structured based on a small set of three ubiquitous pairs, with one repeated up to fifty-nine times in the extract analyzed (*ihk'/sak*, black/white). This distribution may be explained by the fact that this "healing" measure refers, through the recurring interrogation *ihk'bal/sakbal* (is it ominous? / is it auspicious?), to the names of places and objects that occur only

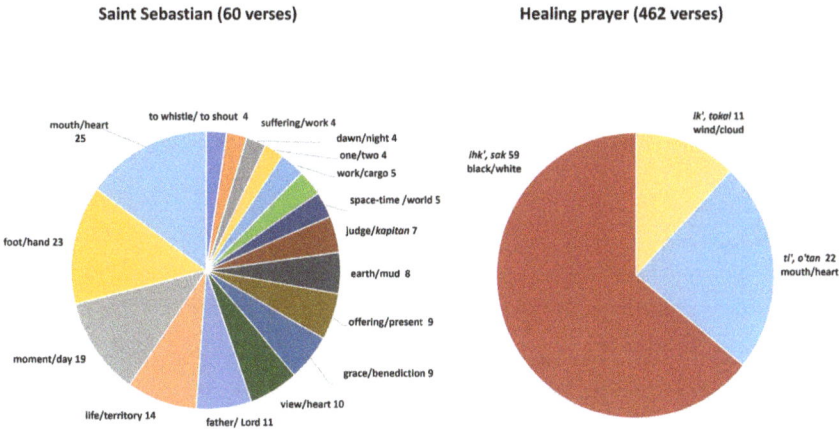

Figure 8.6. Comparative diagrams of parallelism in Carnival and healing prayers

once in the speech, so marking a progression of the shaman on the figurative path, sign, and symbol of a natural ecogeography. Meanwhile, the two other predominant pairs, *ik'/tokal* (wind/cloud) and *ti'/o'tan* (mouth/heart), refer respectively to the vectors of the illness and the pronouncement of the healing words. The thirty-three pairs that occur only once are distributed along the circuit evoked in the prayer. Conversely, the discourses of Saint Sebastian and Carnival involve a greater diversity of frequently used pairs, revealing the speakers' inventiveness in the formation of parallelisms. The pairs refer explicitly to the feast day itself (*ora/k'ahk'al*, moment/day; *maytines/ahk'abal*, dawn/dusk), or more metaphorically (*nichim/buhts'an*, flowering/pleasant: a typical pair for festivals); to its actors (*ok/k'ab*, feet/hands, referring to the group as a whole; *jwes/kapitan*, judges/captains, or *tat/ajaw*, father/master); and to the space in which the ritual unfolds (*kuxlejal/tehlumal*, life/territory; *lum/bahlumilal*, earth/world, etc.). Certain pairs also refer to the ritual activity in general, such as *k'eluj/k'abuj* (to see / to observe), which evokes the obligation to watch; *a'tel/patan* (work/responsibility), and *wokol/trabajo* (suffering/obligations) or *mahtan/obol* (offering/gift), relating to the execution of a traditional office. Nevertheless, despite the variability of the specific pairs used by each ritual speaker, the impressive repetition of such a rich parallelistic ensemble restricted to the semantic field of the instauration ritual creates a typified description, which conceptualizes the ritual process and freezes actions through the use of co-implicit terms uncovering shared knowledge.

A final point on this comparison: the rhetorical feature of parallelism always allows for the introduction of inventories, that is, lists of things that diverge from the rigorous parallelistic dual organization. In the healing prayer, for example, we observe all manner of creatures, toponyms, and other features of the land (pairs) counted in groups of thirteen (context)—an important number for the Maya.

[. . .] ya jmajanbat te yik'alil	I will borrow for you his wind
Ya jmajanbat te tokalil	I will borrow for you his cloud
Oxlajuneb me ho'bin nabil	thirteen of the lake's caves
Oxlajuneb sjololil kabinal	thirteen of the hair of kabinal
Oxlajuneb sjoyil nabil	thirteen of the lake's whirlpools
Oxlajuneb pamlej nabil	thirteen of the lake's eddies
Oxlajuneb yahl pech	thirteen (places where) the ducks go to water [. . .]
[. . .] ya ts'ujulin lok'el	I will cast out (the sickness) with droplets

Or elements questioned as auspicious or bad:

[. . .] Ihk'bal koko	is the coconut black?
Sakbal koko	is the coconut white?
Ihk'bal kobre	is the copper coin black?
Sakbal kobre	is the copper coin white?
Ihkbal lula	is the rue black (sp. "ruda")?
Sakbal lula [. . .]	is the rue white?

Examples from a healing prayer, 1996

The discourses of Saint Sebastian and Carnival include landscape features and inventories of various living species of animals and plants, such as *max* (spider monkey), *bats* (howler monkey), *inatan* (iguana), and *periko* (parrot), as well as various forest fowls such as *nako* (the thicket tinamou), *isul* (the great curassow), and *tabul* (the crested guan), and so forth. Generic nouns such as *wankululil* (animals of the land) and *xililul* (animals of the forest) are also found. Other contrasting parallel inventories invoke a number of saints preceded by the titles "Our Father" or "Our Mother," including San Fernando, San Lucas, San Joaquín, San Martín, San Barsin, San Sebastián, San Miguel, Santa Ana, and the Virgen de Natividad.

However, the use of inventories has a different function depending on the subgenre. Those found in the healing ritual relate to the collective of beings that the shaman summons as he retraces the patient's footsteps in search of where the latter lost one of his or her souls. The healing discourse abounds with highly performative words, since they describe actions carried out with the intention of inciting their interlocutors to cooperate and various linguistic measures are employed to anchor the ritual in the situation: agents declare their intention, whether concretely or symbolically, for example, by addressing the interlocutors, stating aloud the sequences of action, or evoking the local context (Becquey 2016). In contrast, none of these characteristics are found in the Saint Sebastian and Carnival discourses surrounding handovers of authority. The effectiveness of the instauration ritual relies on the diversity and repetition of its pairings. Significant for example is a certain discrepancy in the use of place names: the healing prayer refers to a common, everyday space, while the instauration ritual evokes the path of tradition.

THE *PAT'O'TAN* OF BOTH FESTIVALS PRESENT
THE SAME CHARACTERISTICS

Certain mechanisms in the way *pat'o'tan* are constructed reveal the specificity of the dialogues performed at Saint Sebastian and Carnival alike, in contrast with all the other forms of ritual discourses.

The first mechanism is a disanchoring from the speech situation. This process involves various grammatical devices: the prevalence of third-person markers without any explicit referent (figure 8.5); enunciative distantiation deliberately achieved through discursive strategies intended to limit agency: use of the passive without explicit agent (*ts'upts'up-tay-**bil***, "he was whistled to" [by whom?]); rendering transitive verbs intransitive (*x-k'el-u-j-uk*; "may he be an observer" [of what?]) or as nominals (*ni me patan-ij*, "in offer/ing" [who and what to whom?]); use of a reflexive form with a transfer of agency (***ak'a*** *choht-an-ik **s-ba** te mesa*, "may the tables set by themselves" [alone?]); inclusion of unspecified and unnamed beneficiary (*ya j-majan-**be-**tik y-o'tan*, "we borrowed" [whose heart? from who? for whom?]). In short, an array of tactics is used to transpose the enunciative tinge of the discourse to another level, that of the ancestors, legitimized permanent roles, actions that are not carried out on the spot but embedded to ensure that *ma' me lajin te kostumbre* (tradition does not end), a touching and recurring theme encouraged by the principales and other authorities.

The second mechanism concerns verbal morphology and the modal particle *wan*: the two instauration rituals show the same occurrent hierarchy in the distribution of aspect and mood markers (completive>incomplete>irrealis>perfective> imperative). As with all Mayan languages, temporality in Tseltal is obligatorily expressed by a paradigm of verbal aspect markers that emphasizes the configuration of an action, rather than by tense in the morphological sense. An action can be considered as a nonfinite state (incomplete) or in its entirety from beginning to end (completive). One may also describe the course of the action with the progressive or else use the rich modal set to signal its virtuality, counterfactuality, probability, or possibility. The verb phrases, regardless of their aspect markers, may refer to past, future, or present (though, normally, an action considered in its completed totality will denote a past event; Polian 2013). Yet, we observe a tendency to introduce the epistemic *wan*, akin to "maybe" and indicating uncertainty, applied quite frequently to both complete and incomplete actions, regardless of the type of knowledge (old or new) and what is being said.

The modal *wan* is found far more often in the *pat'o'tan* than in the healing prayer (there are 2 *wan* in the prayer, 31 in Carnival based on the same sample size). The persistent use of this particle of uncertainty casts doubts on planned actions as well as on the description of already completed actions which, because this is an aspectual and not a tense system, may potentially be in the past, present, or future. The action in itself, in its completeness, is called into question: will it be accepted? Did it really happen that way? Is it definitely over?

*laj **wan** ak 'an oxeb bentisyon*	you **may** have wanted three blessings
*laj **wan** j-pas-tik-ix jun lunes*	we **may** have already celebrated one Monday
*[...] ya **wan** j-mohl-ix bah-tik*	we **may** already go and meet ...
*ya **wan** a-kanantay-ix nichimalil k'ahk'al*	probably, we protect already the flowering day

The pervasive presence of *wan* throughout these dialogues would imply that nothing is given: the positive receipt of deeds and offerings is not assured; the declaration of actions to be performed is tempered by troubling contingencies. Saint Sebastian is a time of fear in the face of an uncertain future; the *wayeb* exists in worlds of darkness, chaos, and doubt, what Octavio Paz neatly described as "this bath of chaos" (Paz 1950), until such time as the ritual acts of sacrifice, exchange, and pacification give way—it is hoped—to a demonstrable change, with the return of the sun and the birth of a new year.

The third and last mechanism we would like to draw attention to concerns the lexical semantics of the Saint Sebastian discourses in particular. Here, one sees a strong emphasis on actions of traversing space and time, performed to remember and protect the territory (*tehlumal*) and lives (*kuxlejal*) of the community (an intent that does not preclude the doubt surrounding the result), for these actions are essential to the restoration of temporal cycles. In this way, the verb *behentay* (to wander) is used with specific spaces expressed as an inventory (*wits*, mountain; *nahbil*, lake; etc.), or the generic pair *k'inal/bahlumilal* (territory/world). Yet the journeys evoked here have a different function and purpose from the healer's precisely mapped geography. In San Sebastian speech, *behentay* seems to refer to the territory in its entirety, as can be inferred from its use to express the space to which the invoked being is called in order to exercise its power (*amakil sit*, space of its vision; *amakil yo'tan*, space of its heart; *amakil ch'ul ajaw*, space of the sacred master). The same verb, *behentay*, is also used in the context of moving through time, for example, with the pair *ora/kahk'al* (moment/day).

The recurrence of pairs used to establish the genealogy of spirits, ancestors, and the new captains is another feature of these discourses, in which the following are frequently repeated:

te'/ch'ajan	*antiwo/costumbre*	*nich'an/untikil*	*tat/me*
tree/vine	former/custom	man's child / lineage	father/mother
karibyo/tat	*tat/nich'an*	*pasado/jach*	
caribio/father	father / man's child	past/new	

There is also an obsessive insistence on the need to gather "in the eyes of" the principales, the ancestors, and the ajaw, as if to induce, through the meeting of minds, the co-presence and co-activity of the groups of actors involved, human and nonhuman alike. This is seen in the frequent repetition of certain position or action verbs, such as *kulatay -ba* (to visit each other), *jokin -ba* (to keep each other company), *tsak -ba* (to come together), *tsobol* (to be gathered), and *molol* (to be joined). At the same time, the ubiquity of the pair *mesa/banko* (table/bench) refers directly to the understanding of the essentially communal responsibilities of the newly appointed figures.[9]

There is one last interesting aspect to this study: we have not found any meaningful sign of a formal shift in the relation between the request and its fulfillment. Instead, the consistent distribution of aspect and modal markers, the repetition of the parallelistic formulas, are the same from the beginning to the end of the two rituals until exhaustive studies of the *pat'o'tan* corpus may be achieved.

THE DIALOGUES OF THE *KUCH KAPITAN* AND THE INTRUSION OF TEMPORALITIES

The features described thus far—inventories, evocation of genericized actions, modality of uncertainty—present us with worlds whose parameters we must define.

But to properly scrutinize the transition from a seemingly disembodied discursive world to a present of socio-ritual restoration—our hypothesis—we must first divert our attention to a dialogue specific to Saint Sebastian.

We struggled to find a better translation than "mock *pat'o'tan*" to characterize the spontaneous, unregulated, performative, pragmatic back-and-forth between the kabinal chief, his assistants, and the captain during the diagnosis sequence, a repartee that undermines the rules of social interactions. As mentioned above in our description of the night-time "captain-carrying" ceremony, the exchange relates a male pregnancy, detailing multiple inseminations and proffering troubling disabilities of the future child(ren). Texts, exegeses, and glosses show that this essential evocation triggers de facto the recognition of several timelines linked to the proclamation of forthcoming scheduled events: duration of the pregnancy, duration of the kabinal expedition, duration of Carnival over the five dark days of the Mayan calendar (the "lost days," *ch'ay.k'in*). But these different timelines represent more than just twisted adherences to the calendar.

The *pat'o'tan* depict abstract relationships where spaces, times, and conceptions of the ritual acts are typified (unrelated to acts in progress) and abstract (poorly embodied in the ritual), with a common understanding of their ancestral and traditional basis (co-implicit shared knowledge).

In contrast, the dialogues during the visit to the pregnant captain relate directly to what is happening: frequent use of the second person; actions corresponding to what is being said, specific to the co-activity of the moment; a performance that can change depending on the situation; and the almost prophetic allusions to *ch'ay.k'in*, the primordial darkness to come if the ritual is not achieved. The mock *pat'o'tan* twists the meaning of the words (for example, the ostensibly "natural" world in the kabinal inventories becomes a reference to the mythohistorical referential world). These exchanges re-anchor the meaning of the instauration *pat'o'tan* in a global ceremonial performativity, beyond the moment itself, that is, in the cycle of the request, its acknowledgment, and the realization of a revival—in short, in the estimated timeframe of the ritual's effectiveness.

HOW SAINT SEBASTIAN RITUAL RECONCILES
ASPECT AND TIME: PRELIMINARY REMARKS

Our analysis has outlined only three categories of referentials: enunciative, cosmohistorical, and rhetorical.[10] These are explored below through the lexical or grammatical elements particular to each.

The "enunciative" referential is characterized by its adequacy to the external referential—that of the cosmic phenomenological temporality—and is the one in which an enunciator produces a discourse in which he or she is more or less involved. For example, the mention of days (*sabaro*, Saturday; *dominko*, Sunday; *nichimal k'ahk'al*, day in flower; etc.) or parts of the day (*sakal k'inal*, dawn; *mahl k'ahk'al*, dusk; *ch'ul ahkabal*, sacred night) corresponding to the ritual's progression.

The "cosmo-historical" referential manifests temporalities in several ways: first, in the form of simple lexical inventories; forest fare brought back (or not) by the kabinal, recalling the lowlands, the ancestors, and chthonic beings, especially the *ajaw bahlumilal* ("Master of the World"); lists of saints commemorating the building of the church; references to "exemplary" actions, to describe the kabinal in the lowlands, while the captains' actions are described in terms of men and women's *ok k'ab* (literally, "feet and hands"), efforts to guarantee "life and the territory" (*kuxlejal tehlumal*); the instrumental music of the kabinal, made up of conch shells, tortoise shells, drums, flutes (dating back centuries, as evidenced by the Classic era murals at Bonampak), that plays over, indeed drowns out, the captains' own orchestra of violins and guitars; the voices of the spirits and their imitation—*awtay ts'uts'uptay* (to shout at [or whistle at])—that counter the captains' total silence. The pair *uhnin chajan muk'ul te'* (tender shrub / large tree), is another way to allude to the course of time in a captain's career: young incoming captain / former outgoing captain. Altogether, these multimodal signs form a vast, magnificent forest of clues, in which humans and nonhumans alike are presented with an ensemble of paraphernalia, music, fine foods, and all manner of objects resulting from the sacrifices of the community and the mediation of the kabinal with the *ajaw bahlumilal*.

In what we have termed the "rhetorical" frame of reference, the dialogical narrative of the *pat'o'tan*, when less contextualized, is more abstract and evasive; the referents are more roles than individuals (kabinal, ancestors, traditions, ajaw, life); the action verbs are generic (go, come, work, see), and, when they do allude to actions specific to Carnival (bathing in the dust, whistling), these are verbs referring to actions that are magnified, transformed, and linked to detached realities; interpretation rests on evocation and inferences; uncertainty *and* rupture with the lived present partially unveil an unconscious collective historical memory as guarantor. Disanchoring devices are numerous and the rhetorical frame of reference is that of the possible and the counterfactual. One more sign is that the directional verbs are not used as progressive predicates as in ordinary conversation, which reinforces the eviction of the agent. The *pat'o'tan* rhetorical level could be qualified as the manifestation of a narrative whose performance shapes the ritual itself, which cannot be realized without this particular dimension. Within the dialogical narrative's internal framework, the strands of multiple temporalities interweave (lexical allusions, grammar, or rhetorical devices used for different references, summarized in figure 8.7). It is the expression of these different levels of references that is at work in this multivocal ritual ensemble of instauration. Diverse scenarios create timelines that are both restrictive and disturbing, such as the pregnancy and the anticipated birth that follows, the expedition into the forest and the return of the kabinal endowed with animated pelts, or ancestors that must be imitated even if not remembered, including the skeleton of K'inichil winik playing the flute and the drum in the original myth. It is an aspectual language describing the texture of the action as one that creates "fragments of time," periods, "far away" anchor points in different worlds, just as night and day inaugurated time in the past from obscurity; a crucial factor at stake is the conversion of the past year into the new, the darkness into light. Coitus is the irruption of the primordial, threatening darkness (Galinier 2011), before time, constantly unconsciously or consciously encrusted in the memory, reminded of (Monod Becquelin and Chosson 2020). Pregnancy is a calendrical phenomenon that can be evaluated; a nycthemeron has been created and can be counted (*ahtay*) in lunations as women do. Childbirth is a social, lineal, and patrilineal phenomenon. The new masters are the "tender/young fruit" descendant of the joined *me'il/tatil* and the kabinal.

We might also hypothesize a configuration whereby the collective consciousness does not actively commemorate historical events from the distant past yet continues to perpetuate itself nonetheless through "deference," as Bloch (2004) might say. Or perhaps it continues instead by a necessary adjustment to the past, unrelated to remembrance, having to do with this vital connection to "the way of tradition," and the perpetuation of this symbolic path through space and time: *yokel* (footsteps, tradition). This adjustment to the past represents what Mayanists interpret as the double orientation of Mayan thought, folding the past and the future onto one another. As such, the feast of Saint Sebastian sets three separate elements in motion: (1) the kabinal and, by extension, the spirit-masters that accompany them; (2) the new actors, namely the captains, responsible for tradition continuity; (3) and time, with its parallel structures of anticipation, in particular a birth and a restoration of the solar cycle (*k'in*) from out of the primordial darkness (*ihk'al*). The passage from a fetus to a child and from a child to a leader is based on the transformation of a nonexistent (lost) space-time in and by a ritual whose function is to construct a strict chronological support based on a disengagement of the language performers in the ritual dialogues. The ritual, having for its function the multiplication of temporalities for the construction of time, the topological analysis of aspects and voices, illustrates a case where the acted ritual gives its meaning to an asemantic language.

The distribution of devices in the ritual language combined with the introduction of new temporal worlds through language *and* ritual are what makes it possible to transition from a temporally disanchored aspectual world (neither hic nor nunc) to the creation of time by pointing multiple temporalities: the gestation ritual and the specific form of its associated discourses; the numerous actualizers of the multiple temporalities; the mock *pat'o'tan* (indexical anchoring)—all enable the possible instauration of time and the renewal of those various cycles of such importance to humankind. The Carnival exhibits aspect, mode, and lexical temporal semantics.

Linguistic expressions

Verbs denoting typified and generic actions

Co-implicit

Completive

Genealogies

Shouting (*ajaw* language)

Uncertainty, doubt

Incompletive

Epistemic modalities

Calendar references

Rhetorical figures

Inventories (lists)

Temporal specifications (now, yore)

Linguistic re-enactment of tradition

Referentials

Enunciative referentials
(calendar, natural time, daytime)

Cosmo-historical referentials
(*ajaw* genealogies, saints, ancestors
and cosmology)

Rhetorical referentials
(pat'o'tan narrativity)

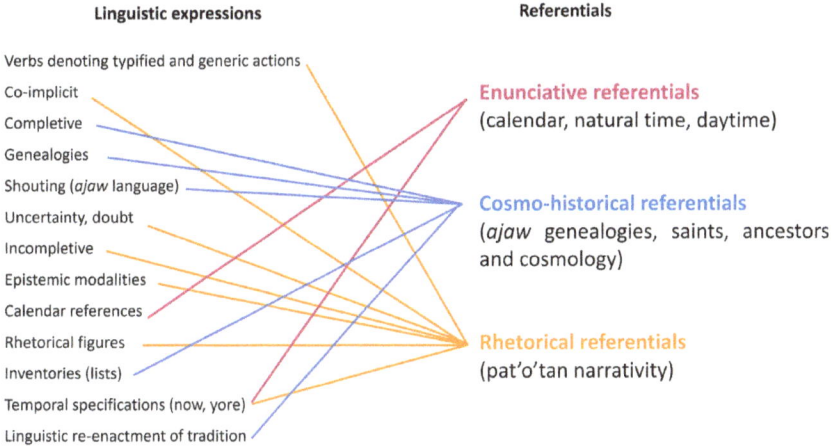

Figure 8.7. Linguistic expressions and three major temporalities' referentials

We propose the hypothesis that the junction of the multiple worlds evoked in the *pat'o'tan* inaugurates, through this double ritual, an axis of time emerging from atemporal chaos (*wayeb*), which carries chronology (from conception to birth), genealogy (from ancestors to descendants), and succession (reflected in the lexicon). This new temporal axis imposes itself as much on the natural world as on the social one. As a manifestation of a new potential based on a calendar and the calculation of time, the double ritual formed by the San Sebastian and the Carnival recalls the ancient Mayan practice of recording history on stelae. Far from mere "decorative" oral references to a bygone age, other forms of performativity are induced here, expected to provide a way out of the disruptive, inescapable chaos of the *wayeb*. And we must emphasize the discriminant function of the kabinal, men of disorder, without which genders, social roles, and rules cannot be reinstaurated.

NOTES

1. For other descriptions of Carnivals, see Zinacantán (Bricker 1973), Tenejapa (Medina Hernández 1965), Chamula (Gossen 1986), Chenalhó and Polhó (Martínez González 2013).

2. A Tseltal term derived from the Nahuatl *calpulli*, "big house."

3. Spelled today "Lakma," a name thought to derive from a river in the Lacandon forest, Lakam.ha', "river of Lakam."

4. Huge tortillas fried in lard and cauldrons filled with green papayas (cold foods), counted in *tsontle* (in quantities of 400) and served with honey and molasses (hot ingredients).

5. It is the return from the forest marking the end of the captain's pregnancy that confirms that this period is not based on any chronological sequence or fixed calendar, and that the kabinal are in fact the masters of time here.

6. This prayer was recorded in Bachajon in 1996 (another healing prayer was published in Breton and Becquelin Monod 1989).

7. Briefly, in Tseltal—an ergative language—ergative prefixes (Series A) are attached to transitive verbs, while absolutive suffixes are attached to intransitive verbs and nonverbal predicates.

8. Spirits and other nonhuman entities that are part of everyday Tseltal life.

9. As Cuturi (2000) seamlessly demonstrated in her study of a handover ritual among the Huave, the use of inclusive/exclusive grammatical forms, or of associated concepts, like those expressed in the Tseltal pairings mentioned here, is essential for the ritual to be accepted by the community.

10. We adopt the definition of the referentials proposed by Desclés n.d., chapters 9 and 10.

REFERENCES

Becquey, Cédric. 2016. "Rituel d'inauguration de maison chez les Chol: Une étude ethnolinguistique." In *(Re)fonder: Les modalités du (re)commencement dans le temps et dans l'espace*, edited by Philippe Gervais-Lambony, Fréderic Hurlet, and Isabelle Rivoal, 243–57. Paris: De Boccard.

Bloch, Maurice. 2004. "Ritual and Deference." In *Ritual and Memory: Toward a Comparative Anthropology of Religion*, edited by Harvey Whitehouse and James Laidlaw, 65–78. Walnut Creek: Altamira Press.

Breton, Alain. 1979. *Les Tzeltal de Bachajon*. Nanterre: Laboratoire d'ethnologie.

Breton, Alain. 1988. "En los confines del norte chiapaneco, una región llamada 'Bulujib: Itinerario y enseñanzas de una visita en el 'país chol' (1737–1738) y otros textos." *Estudios de Cultura Maya* 18: 295–355.

Breton, Alain, and Aurore Becquelin Monod. 1989. *Mais j'ai transmis l'espérance: Étude d'une prière de guérison tzeltal (Maya du Chiapas, Mexique)*. Paris: Association d'ethnolinguistique amérindienne.

Bricker, Victoria R. 1973. *Ritual Humor in Highland Chiapas*. Austin: University of Texas Press.

Cuturi, Flavia. 2000. "'Tal vez estamos aquí': Autoridad, responsabilidad y 'antideíctico' en las interacciones dialógicas rituales huave." In *Les Rituels du dialogue: Promenades ethno-linguistiques en terres amérindiennes*, edited by Aurore Monod Becquelin and Philippe Erikson, 401–30. Nanterre: Société d'ethnologie.

Desclés, Jean-Pierre. N.d. "Ch. 9: Référentiel énonciatif et repérage temporal" and "Ch. 10: Autres référentiels." Unpublished manuscript.

de Vos, Jan. 1980. *La paz de dios y del rey: La conquista de la Selva Lacandona, 1522–1821*. Tuxtla Gutiérrez: Gobierno del Estado de Chiapas.

Galinier, Jacques. 2011. *Une Nuit d'épouvante: Les Indiens Otomis dans l'obscurité*. Nanterre: Société d'ethnologie.

Gossen, Gary H. 1986. "The Chamula Festival of Games: Microanalysis and Social Commentary in a Maya Carnival." In *Symbol and Meaning beyond the Closed Community: Essays in Mesoamerican Ideas*, edited by Gary H. Gossen, 227–55. Albany: State University at New York.

Hellmuth, Nicholas M. 1972. "Progreso y notas sobre la investigación etnohistórica de las tierras bajas de los siglos XVI a XIX." *América Indígena* 32 (1): 179–244.

Martínez González, Rocío Noemi Martha. 2013. "K'in tajimol: Danse, musique, gestes et parole comme mémoire rituelle. Une analyse du carnaval maya-tsotsil à San Pedro Chenalhó et Polhó, Chiapas, Mexique." PhD diss., EHESS, Paris.

Medina Hernández, Andrés. 1965. "El carnaval de Tenejapa." *Anales del Museo Nacional de México* 17: 323–41.

Monod Becquelin, Aurore, and Alain Breton. 2002. *La "guerre rouge," ou, Une politique maya du sacré: Un carnaval tzeltal au Chiapas, Mexique*. Paris: CNRS Éditions.

Monod Becquelin, Aurore, and Alain Breton. 2003. "¿Cuál espacio para los *kabinal* de Bachajón?" In *Espacios mayas: Usos, representaciones, creencias*, edited by Alain Breton, Aurore Monod Becquelin, and Mario Humberto Ruz, 327–62. Mexico City: Universidad Nacional Autónoma de México / Centre d'Études Mexicaines et Centraméricaines.

Monod Becquelin, Aurore, and Marie Chosson. 2020. "La nocturnité au quotidien chez les Tseltal." In *Alors vint la nuit . . .*, edited by Aurore Monod Becquelin et Jacques Galinier, 115–69. Nanterre: Société d'ethnologie.

Paz, Octavio. 1950. *El Laberinto de la soledad*. Mexico City: Fondo de Cultura Económica.

Polian, Gilles. 2013. *Gramática del tseltal de Oxchuc*. Mexico City: CIESAS.

Thompson, J. Eric S. 1976. *Maya History and Religion*. Norman: University of Oklahoma Press.

Ximénez, Francisco Fr. 1930–31. *Historia de la Provincia de San Vicente de Chiapa y Guatemala, 1666–1722*. 3 vols. Guatemala: Sociedad de Geografía e Historia.

PART III
Ritual Temporalities and Their Material and Sensorial Dimensions

9

The Materialities of Ritual Practices

An Archaeology of Traces of Stylized Events

ROSEMARY A. JOYCE

INTRODUCTION

This chapter builds on a sustained investigation of deposits excavated in sites in Honduras dating to the Formative Period (1500–500 BC) and Late to Terminal Classic Period (AD 500–1000) to illuminate a theoretical framing of the materiality of ritual practice. In some ways, this departs from the main approach of Mesoamerican archaeology to similar deposits. Where this community of scholars has employed the assumptions of Americanist culture history to support projecting present-day meanings of materially similar practices into the past (a method labeled the "direct historic approach" in the 1930s), the work I am considering instead adopts an anthropological perspective rooted in the contemporary anthropology of religion, material cultural studies, and posthumanism.

The key terms I want to clarify include *event, ritualization*, and *trace*. I am concerned here with the event as used in particular by Lisa Johnson in her doctoral research on Palenque (Johnson 2018). This work also draws on the concept of ritualization from the work of religious studies scholar Catherine Bell (1992). In archaeology, the use of ritualization has been advocated most centrally by Richard Bradley (2003, 2005). The concept of trace that I employ is one that I have been developing in ongoing work (Joyce 2006, 2012, 2015). The advantage of this vocabulary is that it is not anchored in any way to a presumed use for archaeological cases that would preclude its use in ethnographic settings; these concepts are intended to be used for understanding the practices of living humans, whether witnessed directly or

https://doi.org/10.5876/9781646426829.c009

inferred indirectly from the study of the material participants in ritual action that survive beyond the human lifespan. Because event and ritualization have both been subject to more discussion in archaeology, it is in my discussion of trace that I make the broadest arguments, which are necessary in order to connect this archaeological work to approaches from other fields.

Ultimately, this theoretical perspective calls into question the way archaeologists and ethnographers are accustomed to thinking about time, as an unfolding, unidirectional flow along which moments can be placed and separated from each other. If we take materiality seriously, my analysis suggests that we need instead to understand time as reversible, its effects witnessed at spatial scales from the micro- to the landscape in the congealment of traces that always connect what we attempt to separate as past and present, past and future. This then introduces the futurity of ritual temporalities and materialities as critical to their composition.

EVENT

In her study of a series of material deposits she excavated in Group IV at Palenque, Lisa Johnson (2018) approached the formation of the sequence using the concept of "event." Building on and refining proposals by William Sewell (2005) and William Connolly (2013), Johnson defines events not as ruptures or breaks in routine practice but as "heightened moments, whose outcomes or effects may differ: they can prompt change to those moments that follow or not" (Johnson 2018, 14). Johnson notes that this idea of the event as emergent and active distinguishes it from previous scholarly uses of the term. Quoting Sewell (1996, 3), she writes "social theorists did not consider historical events as context-specific, or even accidental, but rather, often treated them as the inevitable outcome of an inherent logic of social development. The 'event' was a manifestation of that logic. The event was not attributed to anything concrete but rather, to abstract 'transhistorical processes leading to some future historical state'" (Johnson 2018, 13).

It is worth underlining that this classical conception of events attached them firmly to the present and the past but ignored their relationship to a future. In the final section of this paper, I will argue that events, including ritual events, when seen as emergent, are also as much future-oriented as they are past-oriented.

Johnson demonstrates that even more recent approaches to event, including those familiar from the Annales school, the practice theory of Marshall Sahlins, the structuration theory of Anthony Giddens, and Victor Turner's "ritual process," frame events as the outcomes of exercise of human agency. For a posthumanist anthropology that seeks to understand the animacy of things, and for archaeology, whose primary observed subjects are nonhumans, this is a serious limitation.

That is, while nonhumans can include a variety of entities, including ancestors and supernatural forces, sometimes imagined in anthropomorphic form, archaeology as a practice does not allow direct observation of people; it does not allow dialogue about humans' understanding of entities like ancestors, the dead, or supernatural forces. Instead, archaeology is fundamentally a practice engaging with nonhumans in the forms sometimes characterized as artifacts, objects, or things. Thus, an archaeology of nonhumans in events is always a contribution to an understanding of the agential capacity of things, objects, and artifacts.

Taking the animacy (Chen 2012) or vibrancy (Bennett 2004, 2010) of matter seriously, Johnson argues that nonhumans can be equally effective in creating events, understanding an event as "a moment, in a series of moments that stands apart . . . because it *punctures* stretches of stability." This leads her to propose that we can see events in material configurations that puncture the field of materiality. The event as such is not solely the actions humans undertook; it includes the activity of materials that were acting along with, or even without, human agency.

An example comes from my own work in Honduras at the site of Cerro Palenque, which grew from a Late Classic small center to the largest known site in the lower Ulua valley in the Terminal Classic period (Hendon 2010; Joyce 1991). In two spaces within this site, archaeologists encountered an assemblage of things consisting of two matched valves of a spiny oyster (*Spondylus* sp.) and a piece of worked green stone. In one of these assemblages, the green stone was a roughly spherical bead placed between the valves, the whole then plastered onto a surface of a small platform (Joyce 1991, 50–52, 113–15). In the other, the green stone was a fragment from the corner of a square green marble vessel, placed with the two valves under a ceramic bowl, buried in an architectural terrace (Hendon 2010, 114–18). The first of these deposits dates roughly to the seventh century AD; the second, between AD 950 and 1050. Julia Hendon and I view these two deposits as evidence of historically reproduced practices of emplacing ritual offerings. In this analysis, the earlier one (with the jade bead contained in the shell, laid on the surface of a central platform in an exclusive residential compound) is the precedent for the later one (the two valves and green marble fragment buried in the expanded terrace of an exclusive residential building, contained under an inverted bowl).

We can interpret this as evidence of a repeated ritual practice, like one seen at sites in the same valley such as Travesia, and also known at the closest Classic Maya site, Copan, from as early as AD 400–600 (Longyear 1952; Stone 1941). These in turn could be linked to other examples reported from Belize, the Peten, and Highland Guatemala (Andrews 1969; Feldman 1974; Pendergast 1979; Thompson 1939). We might trace the practice of burying *Spondylus* shells containing jade beads even farther, linking Guatemala, Belize, and Honduras to Teotihuacan (Borhegyi

1966). This is the culture-historical approach familiar in Mesoamerican archaeology. Implicitly, it suggests that the deposits in all these areas are evidence of similar motivations, similar intentions, and similar meanings, regardless of the very different social and political circumstances in which they took place.

Alternatively, we can treat the two assemblages from Cerro Palenque as events, each distinct, which work to create ritualized space and time in their own historical relationship. As eventful, we cannot collapse the two together. They demonstrably stand in what science and technology studies scholar Karen Barad (2003) labels material-discursive intra-action with each other via the recurrence to *Spondylus* and green stone. Yet their differences matter as much as their similarities. The use of a complete bead in the earlier event, and of a fragment from a vessel in the later event, distinguishes them relationally. The bead/vessel contrast cannot be ignored; the former is a personal ornament, the latter a container gesturing toward shared meals. What we are called to attend to in their eventfulness is the specific work each does punctuating the space and time where it is located.

In the space and time of AD 650, the shell and jade bead punctuate what had been a continuous sequence of quite different events. For this, we need to return closer to the phenomenon, to the original description of the excavated context with all its detail (Joyce 1985, 156–59). This began with digging a pit into marl bedrock, depositing eight small pebbles and a single obsidian blade in the pit, smoothing the reburied marl, covering it, then placing an obsidian biface in one corner of a small square enclosure with low walls built around the mouth of the pit, and paving over the space enclosed with flat stones. It ended with the plastering that incorporated the oyster and jade bead. Each materially produced assemblage in this sequence is a moment that differs from what preceded it and what follows, each an event that punctures the flow of time. The effect produced is to saturate the otherwise modest platform produced by these deposits with ritualized temporality.

In the space and time of AD 1050, the shell and green marble act quite differently (Hendon 2010). There are no earlier or later ritualized events to which they gesture at the location to which they contribute materiality. This is a platform that supported a residential structure, and the terrace in which this deposit was placed is similar to others used as work spaces around residential buildings. If the *Spondylus* and green stone assemblage were not present, acting at this site, we today would have no clue to understand that expanding the building required and was facilitated by ritual action. The event these things are part of is spatial more than historical. It is worth noting that other building terraces in this place contained quite different buried materials in fill over architectural extensions. These include human long bones, encountered along with a ceramic effigy of a bone bundle that once formed part of an incense burning vessel (Hendon 2010, 184–86). Multiple events, again made active by different material participants but, in these instances, contributing to ritualizing spatial contexts of everyday life rather than distinguishing a particular location as a place of ritual.

The concentration of events in the later building does different work than the concentration of events in which the first assemblage described takes part. That earlier assemblage marked a final point in a series of ritualized events that succeeded each other over time in the same place. The later assemblage was part of the expansion in space of a residential structure and its terraces, enabling ongoing activity. Where the earlier assemblage forms the capstone for a platform that was centrally located within an encircling group of buildings, the later one is peripherally placed on a terrace extending outward from a building that formed part of the perimeter of the patio of a residential compound. Despite both being evidence of ritual in residential confines, these are eventful deposits with different consequences.

To identify an archaeologically detected assemblage as an event, and in particular, as a ritual event, is to recognize it as an interruption in ongoingness, something that marks space-time as not uniform. This is also one of the effects of ritualization as described by Catherine Bell (1992).

RITUALIZATION

Johnson (2018) links the event to ritualization, through the common feature of making memorable what would otherwise be repetitive, achieved through intensification of affect. The concept of ritualization she uses is derived from the work of Catherine Bell (1992), widely popularized in archaeology of ritual by Richard Bradley (2003, 2005). Bell, a religious studies scholar, offered the term *ritualization* for "a way of acting that is designed and orchestrated to distinguish and privilege that which is being done in comparison to other, usually more quotidian, activities" (1992, 74). Ritualization, consequently, "specifically establishes a privileged contrast, differentiating itself as more important or powerful" (90). Like events, ritualization can only be identified through the difference it makes.

There are serious problems for an archaeology of active materials presented by the original discussion of ritualization. Bradley (2005, 34) redefined ritualization for archaeological purposes as a "process by which certain parts of life are selected and provided with added emphasis." While this reformulation of the concept has been very productive in archaeology, it is worth noting that ritualization is often employed by archaeologists within a paradigm that separates ritual and religion, which was not part of Bell's original proposal (see Joyce 2017).

Bell (1992, 98) saw the outcome of ritual, "that which it does not see itself doing," as "the production of a 'ritualized body,'" linking ritualization to human subjects in an essential way. By incorporating a more contemporary understanding of non-human materials as active, as agential in the way specified in Barad's (2003) "agential realism," we can see ritualization not just as a project of human subjects employing passive objects but as an emergent property of certain kinds of assemblages of non-humans, whether acting with humans or independently.

My own demonstration of the utility of the concept of ritualization as originally formulated by Bell in an archaeological analysis was based on my excavations at Puerto Escondido, an Early to Middle Formative village in Honduras (Joyce 2017). I showed that ritualization began there with burial of objects indexing and thus ritualizing pragmatic actions of everyday life. In one example, two deposits buried under a house platform contained separate white and black assemblages of objects. The white assemblage took the form of multiple marine shell ornaments, pierced and strung together in the manner of a belt, wrapped into a bundle. The black assemblage was marked in the excavation by a group of unworked obsidian nodules, which probably also were originally bundled together.

The placement of these assemblages below the ancient ground surface, in a pre-pared pit, bundled, resulted in the ritualization of what otherwise were objects of use in everyday life, punctuating their existence in the event of their burial. Obsidian nodules like those placed in one of these assemblages were employed at the site in a bipolar reduction industry producing flakes used as tools to process a wide range of plants used for food, medicinal purposes, and other ends (Joyce et al. 2004; Morell-Hart et al. 2019). These nodules were derived from deposits in the surrounding mountains, where they occurred along with ignimbrite rocks that provided tempering material, and near sources of marble used for stone vessels (Joyce 2021, 2022; Luke, Tycot, and Scott 2006). In ordinary circumstances, these obsidian nodules flowed into the village from the mountains and were held until processed for relatively expedient, informal tool use. Placing unworked nodules in a bundle under the house floor could have been seen as simply the creation of a pragmatic store for future use.

The proximity of the second bundle makes that an untenable proposition. In this case, marine shells left otherwise almost unworked were drilled for suspension, and from their position on excavation, had been threaded together before burial. Abundant evidence of shell working in the contemporary site supports the idea that like the obsidian nodules, the shells flowed into the village for pragmatic uses, in this case, from the northern Caribbean coast (Joyce and Henderson 2003). The string of shells can be seen as itself a ritually active assemblage, which when worn would have enabled specific kinds of contact with the cosmological watery realm. Rather than being inactive, waiting to be activated, the shell belt was agential.

The juxtaposition of the two assemblages ritualized aspects of everyday life, placing them into a dialogue in which each reflected on the other, a dialogue evident as well in their colors. In the early village of Puerto Escondido, black and white contrasts were produced on ceramic vessels used to serve cacao through techniques of control of firing atmospheres (Joyce and Henderson 2003, 2007). The emphasis on black and white as significant, contrasting colors continued within the ensuing historical tradition, expressed in the preference for white marble for fine carved stone (Luke 2012; compare Joyce 2022). Events like those in which the black obsidian nodules and white marine shells were agential ritualized these material contrasts within a local history and a spatial frame that extended from the ocean to the mountains.

Ritualization at Puerto Escondido also employed another spatial tactic, the construction of visible marks on the landscape in the form of raised earthen platforms (Joyce 2007; Joyce and Henderson 2001, 10; Joyce and Henderson 2003). These provided visibly marked locations where buried assemblages were put in place. The first such platform built at Puerto Escondido contained a series of at least five buried vessels, of a kind that analysis shows contained cacao-based beverages (Joyce and Henderson 2007). That these complete vessels indexed the pragmatic everyday action of drinking was further marked by an extraordinary aspect of this event. The base of the new platform began with a deposit consisting of a bed of broken pieces of pottery vessels covered by the collapsed burned walls of a building, products of conflagration and demolition converted into part of the history of the platform.

Johnson (2018, 12) notes that Bradley redefined ritualization slightly as both "a way of acting which reveals some of the dominant concerns of society, and a process by which certain parts of life are selected and provided with an added emphasis" (Bradley 2003, 12). The "added emphasis" at Puerto Escondido was produced by the activities of burial and burning, both of which continued as part of practices of ritualization in later centuries. These practices produced deposits that are more than things assembled in space through human intentions, however: they are congealments of traces of actions (Joyce 2021). Composed of pragmatic tools employed in actions and residues of actions carried out, their preservation is a way to stylize what would otherwise be relatively ephemeral experiences, turning them into punctuated ruptures of temporality, or events.

Once existing, ritualized assemblages were active in ways that exceeded any reasonable proposal that their activity was caused by the original intentions of the humans who were present at their initiation. Later pits dug into preceding deposits at Puerto Escondido encountered at least one of the complete vessels that were part of the congealment of a raised platform as a space for ritual practices, including human burial (Joyce 2011). While digging those later pits does not exhibit any obvious evidence of ritual intentions, the encounter with the buried pot initiated a ritualized event. The broken pieces of the older, agentive pot were regathered and reburied. Similarly, in the process of burying another of the pots, the bed of broken vessels was apparently encountered, and a base sherd from that deposit was added to the later pot as a lid, linking these two ritualized events.

These incidents, and other instances in which older materials were re-encountered and then incorporated into new marked events and ritualized deposits, suggest that there was a form of historicity immanent in ritualized deposits. That temporality, I argue, is a product of the status of all the materials involved as traces.

TRACE

The concept of trace that I employ (Joyce 2015) is rooted in two distinct theoretical or philosophical lineages. One comes from Tim Ingold's anthropological work where he defines a trace as "any enduring mark left in or on a solid surface by a continuous movement" (Ingold 2007, 43). One of Ingold's points of reference for the trace is Michel de Certeau's (1984, 120–21) discussion of medieval maps and their replacement by discontinuous spatial representations.

A second genealogy of trace would lead us to Walter Benjamin's concept of aura and its relation to the trace, which Carlo Salzoni (2007, 181) tells us

> comes from the unique existence of an object "that bears the mark of the history to which the work has been subject" [. . .] aura is thus the result of the transmission of traces as an instance of tradition. Benjamin, however, explicitly counterposes the two. In an entry to *The Arcades Project* he writes: "Trace and aura. The trace is appearance of a nearness, however far removed the thing that left it behind may be. The aura is the appearance of a distance, however close the thing that calls it forth. In the trace, we gain possession of the thing; in the aura, it takes possession of us." *The problem revolves around the concept of a tradition, its conservation, cancellation, or rewriting, and our relation with it.* (emphasis added)

Salzoni (2007, 177) quotes Benjamin: "To dwell means to leave traces," linking this phrase (a commentary on modern consumption) to his concept of the work of the detective: "Personal traces thus become incriminating clues, dangerous evidence in the hands of the detective-as-spy" (180). Salzoni (182) continues, "the detective, whose job it is to follow traces, becomes in this context a possible instance for reconstructing the condition of production from the collection of evidence or traces of social relations in commodities. *Benjamin's detective becomes thus an archaeologist*" (emphasis added).

If we treat materialities as an accumulation of traces of actions, "our attention should be directed to the ways archaeologists rematerialize traces of practices in the past, traces of materialities that in their time themselves materialized practice" (Joyce 2012, 121). This calls for treating every materially perceptible difference as a potential trace. Insofar as ritualization has been defined as the creation of differences, and archaeological ritualization has been described as detectable through contrasts, what we are involved in is a narration of traces as processes of formation of marked differences.

There is a tension in much of archaeology between those things understood to be significant due to external hierarchies of value (the monumental) and traces (Joyce 2006). When we treat phenomena as traces, "recording and analysis are transformed from a description of products of unexamined action to sequences of action that can be recognized as traditional or innovative, intentional or unreflective. This is a shift from a simple referential model of archaeological language to a more complex semiotic one" (Joyce and Lopiparo 2005, 369). "Referential" here is aligned with what John Barrett (1994, 87–90) calls "representational" approaches, in which traces are "simple residues of events," "mere traces of a past in the past" (Joyce 2001, 12).

The alternative, antirepresentational view aligns the concept of trace I am employing with the work of Karen Barad, in particular her ideas about the material-discursive nature of phenomena. "Matter," Barad (2003, 822) writes, "does not refer to a fixed substance; rather, *matter is substance in its intra-active becoming—not a thing, but a doing, a congealing of agency. Matter is a stabilizing and destabilizing process of iterative intra-activity*" (emphasis original). Barad (2003, 817–18) marks the agential possibility of substance by adopting the word "mattering," which "acquires meaning and form in the realization of different agential possibilities. Temporality and spatiality emerge in this processual historicity."

Trace thus captures the sense that what we are interested in is more than the thing itself, while reminding us that the thing itself is *part* of what interests us. An emphasis on "materials as traces" leads us to attend as much to the rare and particular as to the typological and uniform. I have suggested that in archaeology, "the trace we recognize is a sign of history, not a thing recaptured from a past lived experience and revived in our present circumstances" (Joyce 2012). Traces bind different temporalities together. Traces are, in this sense, active.

I can exemplify the concept of ritual deposition as traces of events that punctuated temporalities, with the extremely complex sequence of material assemblages that were excavated at the Late Classic to Terminal Classic site of Mantecales, in the lower Ulua Valley (Henderson and Joyce 2005). I argued that these should be viewed as examples of structured deposition (Pollard 2001; Richards and Thomas 1984), a concept also employed by Richard Bradley in the same studies where he argues for a specifically archaeological version of ritualization. Structured deposition, stylized, marked as different from other deposition, is ritualized deposition.

That certainly continues to be a useful way to think about things that otherwise can simply be treated as exotica. But it does not completely encompass how deposits that we can recognize by their structure as ritualized actually accomplish things. If we instead treat them as material traces of the events through which ritualization happened, we can do more, including address the somewhat problematic humanism embedded in Bell's concept of ritualization and its intended product, the ritualized person.

The Mantecales deposits consist of a series of layers containing burned material and multiple incense-burning vessels, arranged around a focal point provided by the interment of jar necks (Joyce and Pollard 2010, 299–303). Ultimately, as a result of a repeated history of use, the stack reaches a total of seven jar necks. Contained within the deposit in the jar necks are the only pieces of serving vessels in these deposits, fragments of bowls and cylinders with polychrome painting. These are never complete, always simply parts of the vessel. Also included inside the jar neck are fragments of figural musical instruments. Some of the incense-burning vessels were shaped in the form of living beings, felines and humans, materially presenting them as active agents in familiar ways. All of these things, whether figural or not, should be understood as agential, as actively making and remaking time, space, and ritual.

Treated as traces, the assemblages point to a series of actions: eating and drinking, playing musical instruments, and burning incense, probably resins. These actions become marked events, punctuated interruptions to ongoing time, in part through the construction of structured deposits of their residues. Those deposits themselves are traces not just of the ephemeral activities but of the events as such, the inflections of temporality. They ritualize those events through their conversion into unusual forms, which gain force by their repetition over time in a series and their concentration in a space occupied for related events of incense burning.

The sequence of deposits from Mantecales are like the first assemblage I discussed from Cerro Palenque in their constitution as a series in place. Yet instead of being a disjunctive event that ended a series, the deposits at Mantecales reiterate the same pragmatic actions over and over. It is as if the *Spondylus* and green stone bead at Cerro Palenque were part of a series of shell and green stone deposits. What is at issue here are different temporal positions: the one at Cerro Palenque looking back at a past and firmly ending it in a final event, the one at Mantecales continuing to look forward to a future.

FUTURITY

My argument is that for a concept of posthumanist ritualization, the product of ritualization is not a human body, and not a body at all; it is a temporality. Different temporalities are produced through ritualization. This implies that what is at issue for thinking about ritual, and especially ritual continuity uniting archaeological deposits and more recently witnessed living actions, is a conception of time that involves framing connections between phenomena with various kinds of material extensions, in which some may persist over long periods relatively unchanged, while others are subject to shorter temporalities of material cycling.

Archaeologists are accustomed to think about time as an unfolding, unidirectional flow along which moments can be placed and separated from each other, exemplified by chronological charts. If we take materiality seriously, my analysis suggests that we need instead to contemplate time as reversible, temporalities produced through ritualization evident at spatial scales, from the micro scale to the landscape scale, in the congealment of traces. Traces always connect what we attempt to separate as past and present, past and future. This then introduces the futurity of ritual temporalities and materialities as critical to their composition. Temporality is framed from the present with a view toward a future; what we recognize as a temporal span is not merely given by the passage of time in a closed prior moment.

Thus, Barad (in Dolphijn and van der Tuin 2012, 66–67) argues that "time is not given [. . .] time is articulated and re-synchronized through various material practices. [. . .] its sedimenting effects, its trace, can not be erased. The memory of its materializing effects is written into the world." In a similar vein, feminist theorist Sara Ahmed (2010) writes that "if we were simply to 'look at' the object we face, then we would be erasing the 'signs' of history. We would apprehend the object as simply there, as given in its sensuous certainty, rather than as 'having got here,' *an arrival which is how objects are binding*, and how they assume a social form" (Ahmed 2010, 241; emphasis added). Ahmed (2010, 241) adds, "what passes through history is not only the work done by generations but the 'sedimentation' of that work as the condition of arrival for future generations." It is the binding between humans and nonhumans that is accomplished by the ritualization of traces, and the definition of boundaries around such bindings, that we recognize as temporalities.

Futurity is implicit in ritualization. Deposits like those that were created over time through the repeated use of the same location at Mantecales in a linked sequence of incense-burning rituals are not simply commemorative of activities. They are creative of events which separate what preceded not just from what happened in the moment of the event but from a future which is the implicit product of the event.

In concrete terms, when after two generations of use a new group of petitioners returned to the same spot and placed two more jar necks on top of the initial visible earth-opening, they were not just acting as their predecessors had expected when they buried previous jar necks. They were acting as the material assemblage both facilitated and demanded. They were the future that the previous events called into being. For reasons we do not know, the later visitors decided to surround the earth opening with rectangular stone walls on three sides. Doing so, they participated in a new ritualized event, punctuating the history of production of temporalities with a sharper break than before. Whether intended or not, one product of this new spatial-material configuration, a response to its material-discursive existence, came in the next episode of activity here. This was the complete pavement of the outlined space, covering the earth-opening, making it no longer visible as a creative agent encouraging the kinds of ritual events it previously witnessed.

A new ritualized event took place on this surface. In it, a solid layer of broken food-serving vessels was laid down on the pavement, surrounding and covering a single, partly broken, green marble vase. While the original earth opening was no longer visible on the surface where these things were left in place, the green marble vase re-created a ritualized central axis, a spatial orientation transmitted as much through the definition of the boundaries over the buried deposits as through any intentions of the people who were co-participants with the things that created this new ritual time and place.

DISCUSSION

I have argued here for reconsidering ritual materialities as productive of events, in part through their generative capacity as traces. Ritualization, I suggest, can be rethought from a position that takes the agential capacity of nonhumans seriously. Ritualization does inflect some phenomena in contrast to others; but it does more. It inflects those phenomena as events, as breaks in temporality. While archaeologists, looking at material deposits as a kind of fixed register of a past, have emphasized the commemorative capacity they have, this aspect of commemoration is a product of temporal standpoint. For the human participants in the eventful acts of structured deposition that are the least ambiguous material traces of ritualization we can define archaeologically, the acts to which they were committed were equally oriented to futures. Those futures were created when the material event punctured time, giving a pause to ongoingness. Those events, the pauses in time, the ruptures they created, link what appears to be past to the present and its future, placing archaeological ritualization in historical relation to ethnographically witnessed acts of ritual.

Acknowledgments. All Honduran fieldwork took place under permit from the Instituto Hondureño de Antropología e Historia. Fieldwork at Puerto Escondido was co-directed by John S. Henderson of Cornell University and supported by grants from the Heinz Foundation, Wenner-Gren Foundation, and the National Science Foundation. Work at Mantecales was also codirected. Both codirected projects also had support from our respective institutions (University of California, Berkeley, and Cornell University). The discussion of traces reuses previously published material (Joyce 2015) with permission.

REFERENCES

Ahmed, Sara. 2010. "Orientations Matter." In *New Materialisms: Ontology, Agency, and Politics*, edited by Diana Coole and Samantha Frost, 234–57. Durham, NC: Duke University Press.

Andrews, E. Wyllys, IV. 1969. *The Archaeological Use and Distribution of Mollusca in the Maya Lowlands*. New Orleans: Tulane University, Middle American Research Institute.

Barad, Karen. 2003. "Posthumanist Performativity: Toward an Understanding of How Matter Comes to Matter." *Signs: Journal of Women in Culture and Society* 28: 801–831.

Barrett, John. 1994. "Defining Domestic Space in the Bronze Age of Southern Britain." In *Architecture and Order: Approaches to Social Space*, edited by Michael P. Pearson and Colin Richards, 87–97. London: Routledge.

Bell, Catherine. 1992. *Ritual Theory, Ritual Practice*. New York: Oxford University Press.

Bennett, Jane. 2004. "The Force of Things: Steps toward an Ecology of Matter." *Political Theory* 32: 347–72.

Bennett, Jane. 2010. *Vibrant Matter: A Political Ecology of Things*. Durham, NC: Duke University.

Borhegyi, Stephan F. de. 1966. "Shell Offerings and the Use of Shell Motifs at Lake Amatitlan, Guatemala, and Teotihuacan, Mexico." *XXXVI Congreso Internacional de Americanistas, Sevilla* 1: 355–371.

Bradley, Richard. 2003. "A Life Less Ordinary: The Ritualization of the Domestic Sphere in Later Prehistoric Europe." *Cambridge Archaeological Journal* 13: 5–23.

Bradley, Richard. 2005. *Ritual and Domestic Life in Prehistoric Europe*. London: Routledge.

Certeau, Michel de. 1984. *The Practice of Everyday Life*. Berkeley: University of California.

Chen, Mel. 2012. *Animacies: Biopolitics, Racial Mattering, and Queer Affect*. Durham, NC: Duke University Press.

Connolly, William E. 2013. "The 'New Materialism' and the Fragility of Things." *Millenium—Journal of International Studies* 41: 399–412.

Dolphijn, Rick, and Iris van der Tuin. 2012. *New Materialism: Interviews and Cartographies*. Ann Arbor, MI: Open Humanities Press.

Feldman, Lawrence. 1974. "Shells from Afar: Panamic Molluscs in Mayan Sites." In *Mesoamerican Archaeology: New Approaches*, edited by Norman Hammond, 129–34. Austin: University of Texas Press.

Henderson, John S., and Rosemary A. Joyce. 2005. "Structured Deposition and Commemoration at Classic Period Mantecales, Honduras." Paper presented in the Archeology Division invited session The Archaeology of Ritual, Memory, and Materiality (Barbara Mills and William Walker, organizers). Annual Meeting of the American Anthropological Association, Washington, DC.

Hendon, Julia A. 2010. *Houses in a Landscape: Memory and Everyday Life in Mesoamerica*. Durham, NC: Duke University Press.

Ingold, Tim. 2007. *Lines: A Brief History*. London: Routledge.

Johnson, Lisa M. 2018. "Tracing the Ritual 'Event' at the Classic Maya City of Palenque, Mexico." PhD diss., University of California, Berkeley.

Joyce, Rosemary A. 1985. "Cerro Palenque, Valle del Ulua, Honduras: Terminal Classic Interaction on the Southern Mesoamerican Periphery." PhD diss., University of Illinois.

Joyce, Rosemary A. 1991. *Cerro Palenque: Power and Identity on the Maya Periphery*. Austin: University of Texas Press.

Joyce, Rosemary A. 2001. "Burying the Dead at Tlatilco: Social Memory and Social Identities." In *New Perspectives on Mortuary Analysis*, edited by Meredith Chesson, 12–26. Arlington, VA: American Anthropological Association.

Joyce, Rosemary A. 2006. "The Monumental and the Trace: Archaeological Conservation and the Materiality of the Past." In *Of the Past, for the Future: Integrating Archaeology and Conservation*, edited by Neville Agnew and Janet Bridgland, 13–18. Los Angeles: Getty Conservation Institute.

Joyce, Rosemary A. 2007. "Building Houses: The Materialization of Lasting Identity in Formative Mesoamerica." In *The Durable House: House Society Models in Archaeology*, edited by Robin Beck, 53–72. Carbondale: Center for Archaeological Investigations, Southern Illinois University.

Joyce, Rosemary A. 2011. "In the Beginning: The Experience of Residential Burial in Pre-Hispanic Honduras." In *Residential Burial: A Multiregional Exploration*, edited by Ron L. Adams and Stacie King, 33–43. Arlington, VA: American Anthropological Association.

Joyce, Rosemary A. 2012. "Life with Things: Archaeology and Materiality." In *Archaeology and Anthropology: Past, Present and Future*, edited by David Shankland, 119–32. Oxford: Berg.

Joyce, Rosemary A. 2015. "Transforming Archaeology, Transforming Materiality." In *The Materiality of Everyday Life*, edited by Lisa Overholtzer and Cynthia Robin, 181–91. Arlington, VA: American Anthropological Association.

Joyce, Rosemary A. 2017. "Religion in a Material World." In *Beyond Integration: Religion and Politics in the Precolumbian Americas*, edited by Sarah Barber and Arthur Joyce, 141–64. New York: Routledge.

Joyce, Rosemary A. 2021. "Flows of Clay and Site Ontologies: Towards a Realist Archaeology of Congealment and Emergence." *World Archaeology* 53 (1): 94–103.

Joyce, Rosemary A. 2022. "An Alchemy of Medieval Honduras." *Postmedieval: A Journal of Medieval Cultural Studies* 13 (1). https://doi.org/10.1057/s41280-022-00228-0.

Joyce, Rosemary A., and John S. Henderson. 2001. "Beginnings of Village Life in Eastern Mesoamerica." *Latin American Antiquity* 12 (1): 5–24.

Joyce, Rosemary A., and John S. Henderson. 2003. "Investigaciones recientes de la Arqueología del periodo Formativo en Honduras: Nuevos datos según el intercambio y cerámica Pan-mesoamericana (o estilo 'olmeca')." In *XVI Simposio de Investigaciones Arqueológicas en Guatemala, 2002*, edited by Juan Pedro Laporte, Barbara Arroyo, Hector Escobedo, and Hector Mejía, 819–32. Guatemala: Museo Nacional de Arqueología y Etnología and Asociación Tikal.

Joyce, Rosemary A., and John S. Henderson. 2007. "From Feasting to Cuisine: Implications of Archaeological Research in an Early Honduran Village." *American Anthropologist* 109 (4): 642–53.

Joyce, Rosemary A., and Jeanne Lopiparo. 2005. "Doing Agency in Archaeology." *Journal of Archaeological Method and Theory* 12: 365–74.

Joyce, Rosemary A., and Joshua Pollard. 2010. "Archaeological Assemblages and Practices of Deposition." In *Oxford Handbook of Material Culture Studies*, edited by Dan Hicks and Mary Beaudry, 289–304. Oxford: Oxford University Press.

Joyce, Rosemary A., M. Steven Shackley, Kenneth McCandless, and Russell Sheptak. 2004. "Resultados preliminares de una investigación con EDXRF de obsidiana de Puerto Escondido." In *Memoria del VII Seminario de Antropología de Honduras*, edited by Kevin Aválos, 115–29. Tegucigalpa: Instituto Hondureño de Antropología e Historia.

Longyear, John M., III. 1952. *Copan Ceramics: A Study of Southeastern Maya Pottery*. Washington, DC: Carnegie Institution of Washington.

Luke, Christina. 2012. "Materiality and Sacred Landscapes: Ulúa Style Marble Vases in Honduras." *Archaeological Papers of the American Anthropological Association* 21 (1): 114–29.

Luke, Christina, Robert H. Tykot, and Robert W. Scott. 2006. "Petrographic and Stable Isotope Analyses of Late Classic Ulúa Marble Vases and Potential Sources." *Archaeometry* 48 (1): 13–29.

Morell-Hart, Shanti, Rosemary A. Joyce, John S. Henderson, and Rachel Kramer. 2019. "Ethnoecology in Pre-Hispanic Central America: Foodways and Human-Plant Interfaces." *Ancient Mesoamerica* 30 (3): 535–53.

Pendergast, David. 1979. *Excavations at Altun Ha, Belize, 1964–1970*. Vol. 1. Toronto: Royal Ontario Museum.

Pollard, Joshua. 2001. "The Aesthetics of Depositional Practice." *World Archaeology* 33 (2): 315–33.

Richards, Colin, and Julian Thomas. 1984. "Ritual Activity and Structured Deposition in Later Neolithic Wessex." In *Neolithic Studies: A Review of Some Current Research*, edited by Richard Bradley and Julie Gardiner, 189–218. Oxford: BAR.

Salzoni, Carlo. 2007. "The City as Crime Scene: Walter Benjamin and the Traces of the Detective." *New German Critique* 34: 165–87.

Sewell, William H., Jr. 1996. "Three Temporalities: Toward an Eventful Sociology." In *The Historic Turn in the Human Sciences*, edited by Terrence J. McDonald, 245–80. Ann Arbor: University of Michigan Press.

Sewell, William H., Jr. 2005. *Logics of History: Social Theory and Social Transformation*. Chicago: University of Chicago Press.

Stone, Doris Z. 1941. *Archaeology of the North Coast of Honduras*. Cambridge: Peabody Museum of Archaeology and Ethnology.

Thompson, J. Eric S. 1939. *Excavations at San Jose, British Honduras*. Washington, DC: Carnegie Institution of Washington.

10

Recreating the Memory of the Origins

Sociocultural Meanings of "Graphic Symbols" in Land Titles

TSUBASA OKOSHI

INTRODUCTION

Among the colonial Maya documents that have survived to our days, a group of clearly distinguishable documents is characterized by using specific graphic symbols, such as periods, commas, colons, semicolons, dashes, and equal signs throughout the texts. For instance, every page of the Chilam Balam of Chumayel exhibits a constant use of colons, as shown in folio 4v (figure 10.1). Similarly, the Libro de los cantares de Dzitbalché includes dashes separating words (figure 10.2).

These symbols were not exclusive to documents created for the internal use of Indigenous communities, such as the two mentioned above. They were also seen in administrative and legal documents. I refer to the Maní and Calkiní land titles, in which the Indigenous scribes frequently used to separate words and sentences. For instance, the constant use of full stops on the first folio of the Maní Land Title included in the Maní Chronicle[1] (figure 10.3). Likewise, dashes and equal signs are seen in the Códice de Calkiní (figure 10.4).

Despite these graphic symbols' constant and explicit use in colonial Maya documents, most scholars have ignored them in their editions and analysis. The only exception here is Alfredo Barrera Vásquez, who studied the Libro de los cantares de Dzitbalché and called attention to the "abusive" use of dashes along its pages which separate one word from another, but sometimes in an arbitrary manner (Barrera Vásquez 1965, 14). This lack of interest is quite understandable, since scholars were more concerned with using such documents to reconstruct

https://doi.org/10.5876/9781646426829.c010

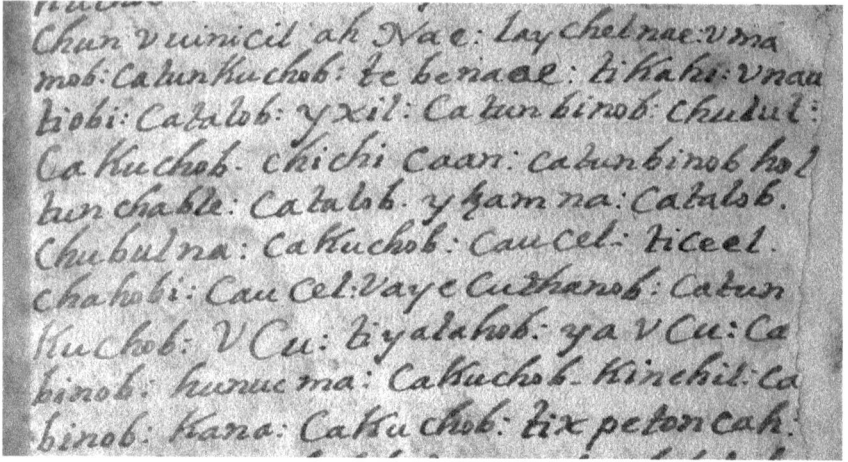

Figure 10.1. Part of folio 4v of the Chilam Balam of Chumayel, Princeton Mesoamerican Manuscripts, no. 4, Manuscripts Division, Dept. of Rare Books and Special Collections, Princeton University Library. http://pudl.princeton.edu/viewer.php?obj=0z708w51x #page/6/mode/1up

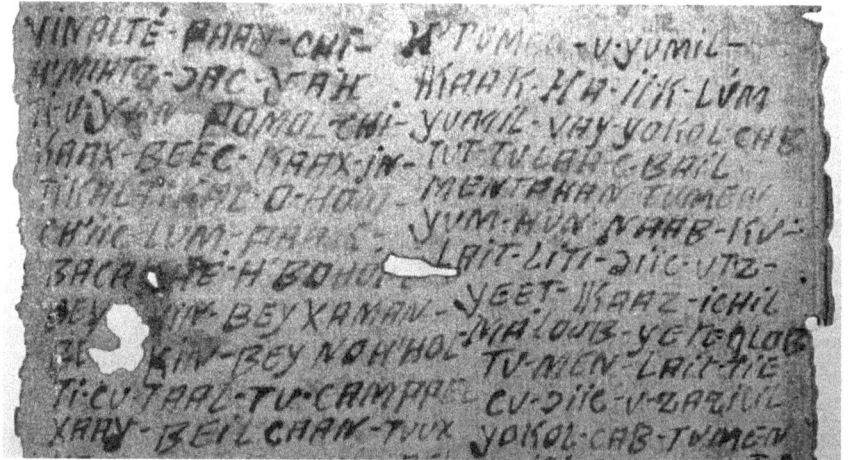

Figure 10.2. Part of the Libro de los cantares de Dzitbalché (Barrera Vásquez 1965, 57)

the history of the pre-Columbian Maya society or to analyze their discursive and rhetorical style.

This chapter explores, therefore, the possible meaning and sociocultural implications of these graphic elements to understand the performative aspects of the colonial Maya land titles. I will first discuss the presence of such graphic symbols

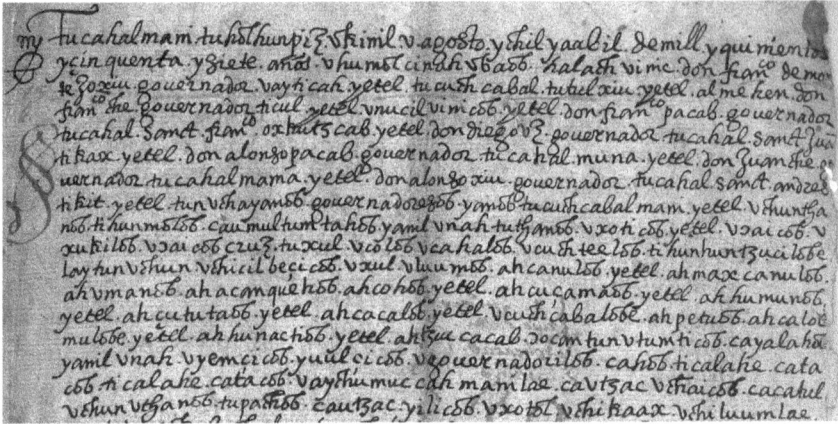

Figure 10.3. Part of the folio 1r of the Maní Chronicle (Crónica de Maní 1557–1813, 1r). Courtesy of the Latin American Library, Tulane University

Figure 10.4. Part of page 23 of the Códice de Calkiní (Okoshi Harada 2009, 18, modified by S. Éliès)

in the Maní and Calkiní land titles as tools to indicate pauses in speech when reading them aloud. Then I will analyze how the foundation history of the pueblos or Indigenous villages was reproduced in these titles. Its rhetorical style was closely related to orality, whereas reading them aloud produced a sense of legitimacy in the listeners' minds that recreated and reaffirmed their community identity. In this sphere of action, these graphic symbols played a relevant role. They were instruments "of silence," that is, pause markers, providing nuances of sound, which offer a rich performative expression to every meaning of the text. Finally, in the last part of this chapter, I will examine the sociocultural implications of reading the titles in situ, that is, at the boundaries in dispute.

GRAPHIC SYMBOLS AS A DISCURSIVE TOOL

Like their Spanish counterparts, colonial Maya documents were written in continuous lines, indicating only changes of paragraph or subject. In 1949, Barrera Vásquez and Morley presented an "urtext" based on comparative study of the three slightly different "chronicles" contained in the books of Chilam Balam of Maní, Tizimin, and Chumayel. In its work, the text was presented with lines divided into verses highlighting the differences and similarities among chronicles (Barrera Vásquez and Morley 1949).

In the 1980s, several colonial Maya documents with versified texts were published, offering a basis for the detection, analysis, and identification of rhetorical figures (e.g., Arzápalo Marín 1987; Barrera Vásquez 1984; Breton 1994; Bricker and Miram 2002; Edmonson 1982, 1986; Okoshi Harada 2009; Quezada and Okoshi Harada 2001; Tedlock 2003). An example of a passage from the Calkini Land Title is as follows:

6.	*Bay xan he ca hunmolhi cah*	Likewise when they gathered in the town,
7.	*uay Calkini lae*	here in Calkini,
8.	*yan ua u canob*	they deliberated.
9.	*ca ti huli*	Then he came,
10.	*Ah Tzab Euan*	Ah Tzab Euan,
11.	*u batabob*	*batab*
12.	*ah mopilaob*	of the people of Mopilá,
13.	*u cante*	[to] talk,
14.	*u canob*	[to] negotiate
15.	*ti Naa Chan Canul*	with Na Chan Canul,
16.	*u batabob*	*batab*
17.	*ah calkini*	of the people of Calkini,
18.	*caix tu nuchcantahob*	and they arranged
19.	*yetel yet batabil*	with their fellow *batabob*
20.	*ua tab uchac u colob*	where they would [cultivate] the milpas (cornfields)
21.	*u cahalob*	for each town.

(Okoshi Harada 2009, 60)

As seen above, there is a clear presence of parallelisms in lines 10–12 and 14–16, which were characteristic of Maya oral literature (Burns 1983, 28; Edmonson and

Bricker 1985, 59; Hanks 2010, 160–61), as well as rhymes with the pluralizing suffix *-ob*. In addition, most dashes and equal signs match the versification and reveal a deliberate use of literary devices in the text.

Let us see another example from the Maní Land Title (Crónica de Maní 1557–1813, 2r):

1.	Lay hab yan.	It was the year
2.	*de mill y quinientos 88 años.*	1588
3.	yan ca ti hunmolhob	when got together
4.	almehenob.	the nobles:
5.	*don* Melchor Coba.	don Melchor Cobá
6.	yetel u chun thanob.	and his *chun thanes*
7.	yetel *don* Alonso Xiu.	as well as don Alonso Xiu
8.	tal P'uztunich	who came from P'uztunich
9.	yetel u chun thanob.	with his *chun thanes*.
10.	ti hunmolob.	They got together
11.	uay yokol. akal. Yiba lae	here, at the *aguada* (pond) of Yibá.

In this passage, we see periods instead of dashes. Still, most of them also occur at the division of lines into verses and allow for the highlighting of literary devices, specifically the anaphora from the repetition of the conjunction *yetel*, and the *-ob* suffix rhyme used in the text.

The presence of these rhetorical elements has been explained a result of the transcription made from the "oral reading" of glyphic texts due to the fear of losing the pre-Columbian traditions after the Spanish conquest (Christensen 2016, 106, 108, 215; Edmonson and Bricker 1985, 58; Hanks 2010). This hypothesis allows us to assume that the graphic symbols indicate "pauses" used by those who read the texts aloud and were indeed part of an embedded "performative process" sought by the scribe. However, they may also indicate specific ways to read aloud the texts, that is, graphic elements were visual discursive aids used by the Maya scribes to represent the pauses and silences in their future reading.

According to Allan Burns, "in the performance of Mayan stories (pauses and silences) are oral features which give rhythm and style to the material" (1983, 24). In addition, those who read the texts drew on other theatrical resources, such as gestures, to reinforce the transmission of contents beyond written words, like recitation (Nájera Coronado 2007, 11). These performative and theatrical characteristics in reading the texts allowed for the conspicuous incorporation of two different times: primordial and present. The former refers to the origin myth and territory, while the latter refers to the moment of reading. "Their sound effects did engage and interact with the receivers' five senses." Thus, the receivers felt "involved" by the conjugation of both periods and conferred a temporal depth to every landmark or boundary stone described in land titles, the base of their identity, whenever a dispute came to light. Hence, it is not a coincidence that the "Memoria de la distribución de los montes" starts with the Mayan expression *kahlay*,[2] which stands for "refreshing the memory by some means to make the past recorded in the memory, come back to life in the present time" (Okoshi Harada 2017a, 26). The means or vehicle to bring it back was undoubtedly the "Memoria" or land title, and its expression determined a constant of two periods of time interacting upon reading. This function is emphasized at the end of the "Memoria" in a passage that points out its future use in times to come (Quezada and Okoshi Harada 2001, 65). The graphic symbols in land titles served as a fundamental discursive tool to give reading aloud an emotional and temporal dimension and confirm "the present" by asserting "our rights" to the land in these documents.

In the following section, I will focus on the "past" described in the land titles. Specifically, I will briefly describe the historical context in which these legal texts were written and their internal structure, as it is necessary for us to know how and which "past" is referred to in the documents. Then, I will discuss in section 4 the effect their reading produced and their sociocultural meaning for the "present."

RECOUNTED "PAST," CREATION OF A NEW ORDER (*TZOL*), AND LAND TITLES

In 1552, when the congregation policy was implemented at the Gobernación de Yucatán, don Juan Cocom (Na Chi Cocom) realized he needed to register his domain under the Hispanic colonial regime. And shortly before 1557, he set the limits of his lordship as *halach uinic* (supreme ruler) without the consent of neighboring lords. This egocentric measurement caused disagreement among many bordering towns, resulting in boundary disputes throughout the colonial period (Okoshi Harada 2017c, 221–22; Roys 1939).

In this circumstance, don Francisco de Montejo Xiu, the last *halach uinic* of the *cúuchcabal* of Maní, rectified the boundary lines with Sotuta in 1557 and set the limits of his lordship by a collective agreement with all the neighboring towns (Quezada and Okoshi Harada 2001, 55–58). The text lists the names of the participating lords, highlighting the attendance of this *halach uinic* as supreme ruler of the Indigenous world who gave authenticity and legitimacy to the agreed-upon landmarks and boundaries. Besides, he is also described as the giver of luxury goods from Honduras and Guatemala, such as cacao beans, a necklace of red beads and of jade, and so forth, to the lords of the neighboring towns (Crónica de Maní 1557–1813, 1r; Quezada and Okoshi Harada 2001, 57–58). It was another aspect of don Francisco de Montejo Xiu's undeniable power and prestige. However, these discursive elements served as a sociocultural code, understandable within the Indigenous world by its members.

The act of creating a territory limited by a boundary is described with the Maya word *tzol*: "he hop'anil u tzol. utial ah maniob. ah mamaob. ah kitob [Then it was put in order for the people of Maní, the people of Mama, the people of Tekit]" (Crónica de Maní 1557–1813, 1v). According to the Calepino Maya de Motul, *tzol* means "in order, orderly, put in order, organize" (Acuña 2001, 166). In this case, Montejo Xiu and the other lords negotiated the reorganization of the lands where their people used to cultivate their milpas in an interlaced and widely dispersed way. Their goal was to create a continuous territory for each town as a primary space for their everyday life. From the Spanish Crown's perspective, the Maya intended to live *en policía* (with civility), another meaning implied by the term *tzol* (Hanks 2010). Consequently, Montejo Xiu, the supreme authority in the Indigenous world, was credited as a founder of a new space order (tzol), one of the significant attributes of his title, in addition to his landmarks validation role.

Don Francisco de Montejo Xiu's death in the 1560s led to the loss of his lordship and the disappearance of the cúuchcabal of Maní of pre-Columbian origin. The Maní Land Title became a primary document for those who wanted to consult their boundaries as agreed upon by the participating towns in 1557. Since they did not depend on the *halach uinic*'s protection anymore, they saw the need for legal documents to preserve their territories. Consequently, in the next decade, the Indigenous *cabildos* or town councils made several copies of the Title to draw up their own, which served as instruments of paramount importance to defend their ancestral rights on their lands (Okoshi Harada 2009; 2017a, 289). Thus, the Maní Land Title became the most reliable and legitimate document or urtext during the colonial period, even after Mexican Independence in the nineteenth century (Okoshi Harada 2009, 92–93).

One of the main features of the Maní Land Title sets it apart from other towns' titles: the whole text is written in the third person, without offering a particular point of view, a discursive style that is characteristic of the pre-Columbian period (Hanks 1989, 109). The Maya scribe who wrote the Title was fully aware of this "neutrality" and included a passage at the end of it where he pointed out the possibility of this document being consulted and copied by interested parties in the future (Quezada y Okoshi Harada 2001, 65). This neutrality may be the very reason why the scribes did not write down facts for the benefit of interests or individual towns and also why this document, as discussed in the following section, was consulted for many centuries as an invaluable source of tzol, or sociopolitical order realized by "setting limits and landmarks." Even after being copied several times and remaining in the Maní archive during the colonial period, the Title was not subject to any modification to its content, which was the only way to keep its neutrality.[3]

In contrast to the Maní Land Title, the titles of other towns are based on a translation of the Title and do not maintain a constant discursive neutrality. For example, the Maní Chronicle version explains how the boundaries were laid out in the third person. Still, then the scribe moves away from this discursive style and introduces the first-person plural to describe the scene of the deliberation:

1.	dzocan tun **u tumticob**.	Then **they met to deliberate**
2.	**ca yalahob**.	[and] **they said**
3.	yanil u nah.	that it was necessary
4.	u yemçicob.	[to] make them come down
5.	yuulçicob.	[to] make them arrive,
6.	u *governadorilob*.	the governors
7.	cahob.	of the towns.
8.	**ti c alahe**.	**Then we told them**
9.	ca tacob.	[to] come.
10.	**ti c alahe**.	**Then we told them**
11.	ca tacob.	[to] come
12.	uay chumuc cah Maní lae.[4]	here to the center of the town of Maní

(Crónica de Maní 1557–1813, 1r)

The insertion suddenly introduces the first-person plural "we" as a participating agent in the conversation, which conveys into the listener's mind two separate temporal dimensions. The first corresponds to the year 1557, when the Title was written down under don Francisco de Montejo Xiu. The second refers to the time of reading. In other words, it conjugates both "past" and "present," with the latter related to a "reality" marked by the people's "particular interests or needs" (Okoshi Harada 2018, 321–23).

This title belonged to the town of Nohcacab, and its authorities used it in a dispute in 1800 (Okoshi Harada 2009, xxix–xxv) to evidence their long-standing occupation of the territory. The first-person plural insertion was a literary device applied by the scribe to create the illusion that their ancestors took part in the 1557 deliberation, when the "current" colonial Indigenous world of 1800 was founded. In other words, its reading aloud gave legitimacy to the Nohcacab's reclamation, in clear contrast with the original Maní Land Title, characterized by its discourse neutrality.

Another example of a particular title is the Calkini Land Title in the Códice de Calkiní. In 1565, due to the congregation policy, the Franciscans gathered six towns in Calkini, a number that grew up to eight towns seventeen years later (Quezada 1993, 89–93, 96). This massive concentration of towns caused problems, because Calkini did not have enough land to feed a growing population. On April 1579, the *batab* (local headman) of Mopilá, Ah Tzab Euán, met with his counterpart, Na Chan Canul of Calkini, to ask him where his people could cultivate their corn-fields (Okoshi Harada 2009, 60–68). The Códice de Calkiní describes the conversation between the two lords as follows (Okoshi Harada 2009, 60–61):

13.	caix yalah	Then he said,
14.	u batab	the *batab*
15.	ah calkini—	of the people of Calkini:
16.	ua bin dzococ u banal	"When they finally get together,
17.	ca lakob—	our brothers,
18.	tzucentzuc ti cahob—	[from] every town
19.	u[a]y Calkini lae	here at Calkini,
20.	te u binel—	they will move
21.	u colob—	their cornfields
22.	tan dzelil [tzelil]	somewhere else,
23.	ti [no]hol—	down to the south,
24.	tal ti uitze—	heading to the hills.
25.	uaix bin u kat—	[And] if they ask,
26.	tex xane	you too,
27.	teex tun a uohel—	then you would know
28.	ua uchac a dzaicex—	whether you let them cultivate
29.	u colob—	their cornfields
30.	tu yam a colexe	among yours.
31.	heuac tu canil u talel	But [this] will depend on the deal
32.	ca bin a bel texxe	you make with them."
33.	ca tun u katah—	Then he asked,
34.	Ah Tzaab Euan—	Ah Tzab Euán,
35.	u batab—	*batab*
36.	ah mopila—	of the people of Mopilá:
37.	ua tab yan	"Where is

38.	u dzail kax	the land given
39.	te ti xaman lae	to the north,
40.	uaix tab yan—	and what is
41.	u xul u kax	the extent of the forest
42.	ah becalob xane	of the people of Bécal?"

(Okoshi Harada 2009, 63)

This is a direct quote of the conversation between the two lords, reproducing the original speech's style and texture. According to Hanks (Hanks 2000, 148–49), this kind of quotation is interpreted initially concerning the original context of its utterance, not its reading, which offers the receptor a better understanding of the speech. In other words, the Calkini Land Title is intended to be read aloud and to reproduce vividly and somehow dramatically the meeting and the landscapes where the boundary stones were located. All of this was reinforced by the specific use of literary devices.[5]

In sum, the titles of the towns differ from the Maní Land Title in both their content level and their discursive level: they refer to the territory of a single town and introduce first-person and second-person sentences to describe how boundaries were set. In addition, the third person is used to explicitly talk about the history of the town's foundation, the lord's ruling house, and a list of the toponyms where the boundary stones were laid.

In addition, the graphic symbols that indicated pauses in land titles and rhetorical figures helped the performance of reading aloud to improve the listeners' re-creation of the scene and reaffirm their physical and emotional ties to the space-territory of their hometown. "Graphic marks" also took listeners into a time between a space-founding past and a living present. In the following section, I will discuss this issue within the context of land disputes and their sociocultural meaning for the Indigenous colonial world.

INTERACTING "PRESENT": SOCIOCULTURAL MEANING OF "GRAPHIC SYMBOLS" IN LAND TITLES

Before the Juzgado de indios (Court of Indians) foundation at the Gobernación de Yucatán (1592), boundary disputes among towns were settled orally. Usually, the two parties involved met in situ at the boundary in dispute to agree. For instance, in 1588, Ticul came into conflict with P'ustunich, and the governors and *principales* or council officers from both towns met at the water pond of Yibá. After long deliberation, the town scribe of Ticul recorded the agreement on paper, and all participants put their signatures (Crónica de Maní 1557–1813, 2r–2v).

After 1592, the legal procedures set forth by the Juzgado de Indios required every complainant and defendant town to provide "maps and papers" in support of their claims. Consequently, all the supporting documents had to be reviewed and examined against the observable reality on the ground. Thus, in 1800, when the authorities of Nohcacab accused the town of Calkini, claiming that since 1791 their land had been illegally taken away from their people, the Juzgado ordered both representatives to submit "book, map, and other files" (Crónica de Maní 1557–1813, 15r, 41v). Accordingly, Nohcacab put forward their title and related papers,[6] and Calkini submitted a land title now known as Códice de Calkiní. After examining all the documents, commissioned judge Pedro Ignacio Manzanilla set off for a nine-day inspection to check out the disputed landmarks and boundaries in situ together with the rulers and other council members of the involved towns (Crónica de Maní 1557–1813, 18v–25v).

During this process, they compared it against the documents they carried, to rectify and correct its location every time they went by a key or misplaced landmark. Yet, the "ancient book and map of the distribution of the lands made by don Francisco Montejo Xiu in the year 1557" (Crónica de Maní 1557–1813, 18v) brought by the representative of the Maní town council[7] was always consulted as the most reliable source of information about the boundaries, not only by the local Indigenous community but also by the authorities of the Yucatan government.

We may ask who read the titles to confirm or rectify the boundaries of the disputed lands (*kaxob*). Ignacio Manzanilla never mentioned it in his inspection report, because it might be an ordinary legal procedure in land disputes. It is very likely, however, that Indigenous council scribes, the only ones capable of drafting legal documents in Latin characters, were responsible for reading the titles aloud. They read the land title in front of other town councilors, who listened and checked out the maps where the key landmarks were represented. At the same time, assistant witness interpreters translated for the commissioned judge.

I have not found any data in colonial documents of the Yucatan government to support this hypothetical interpretation. Nevertheless, several contemporary ethnographic notes from towns in Guatemala and the Central Mexican Highlands have revealed the existence of such a tradition, in which community officers read the land titles aloud to their people. They even walk along the boundaries at least once a year (Wood 2003, 61; 2014, 287n58; Rafael Flores, personal communication, August 2017; Raquel Güereca, personal communication, February 2014; Alberto Sarmiento, personal communication, August 2018).

Societies where orality prevails, such as the Maya, did not conceive words in their written form but rather as concrete images, that is, sound reflections of objects, feelings, and ideas (Craveri Slaviero 2004, 97; Ong 2005, 32–33). Thus, the reading was marked through rhetorical figures, specific rhythm, intonation, and highly performative elements, such as gestures and facial expressions (Johansson 2004, 58–59). However, the "spoken word" was not isolated from its context. The in situ performative reading of land titles at the boundaries made receivers focus on the observed reality and the feelings involved by a (re)created and (re)affirmed collective identity. All this, perceived through the five human senses, provided a more intimate and vivid understanding of the content. For the Maya, their land was the space where every shared feeling and memory of the past (*kahlay*) joined together and was reenacted by a performative reading in the "now," or present moment.

The Maya did not consider the land allocated by the colonial authorities to be just a physical territory but rather a social and sacred space (Restall 1997, 289). The land titles contain several passages that evidence the performance of ritual acts, such as choosing the right day to lay out the boundaries (Martínez Hernández 1928, 33), drinking chocolate and balché during a deliberation (Okoshi Harada 2009, 60–61), or drinking Spanish wine (Crónica de Maní 1557–1813, 1r). For example, don Francisco de Montejo Xiu offered two thousand beans of cacao, five pieces of cotton cloth, a necklace of red shells (*Spondylus*), and two hundred threaded jade beads to the lords of the neighboring towns of the cúuchcabal of Maní (Quezada and Okoshi Harada 2001, 57–58). This was to show them his "generosity" as *halach uinic* or supreme ruler and as the legitimate authority of the cúuchcabal of Maní within the Indigenous colonial world. In addition, the boundary lines were initially laid out at a site located in the northern end, from which they were moved south counterclockwise following a pre-Columbian traditional ritual movement (Barrera Vásquez 1984; Crónica de Maní 1557–1813, 1r–2v; Martínez Hernández 1928; Quezada and Okoshi Harada 2001, 59–65). All these acts were supported by a ritual code related to the fundamental and integral conception of the world that only the Maya conceived and shared collectively. The scribe's voice followed the rhythm and intonation of words and symbols written on the land titles, and it became an appealing performative vehicle to guide its receivers through an imaginary journey between the past and the present time, revealing the social and ritual meanings of the town's territory where the Maya lived.

With the figure of don Francisco de Montejo Xiu as the supreme authority and neutral legitimator, the Maní Land Title kept the neutrality unchanged, despite being copied several times during the colonial period. Maya and colonial authorities knew of its existence as "a truthful land document," which inscribes the archetypical order (tzol) for the former region of the cúuchcabal of Maní.

On the contrary, the town's particular land title stresses the invocation of the past in the moment of its reading. For example, the "Nohcacab Title," included in the Maní Chronicle, contains a direct quote insertion of a first-person plural voice going back as far as 1557, when the boundaries were laid out under the direction of don Francisco de Montejo Xiu.[8] This "modification" of a passage taken from the Maní Land Title was typical of a common practice among many colonial Indigenous towns to "update" their titles, which aimed to authenticate the "here" (the town's territory) and "now" (the time of a dispute) through the past. In other words, the Indigenous scribes added specific changes to the core text of the Maní Land Title (1557) according to the town's interests and need (Okoshi Harada 2017a, 2017b).

The Calkini Land Title has a slightly different discourse style, because it was not based on the Maní Land Title. In this title, rhetorical devices vividly reproduced the deliberation scene between the lords of Calkini and Mopilá, and pauses and silences indicated by dashes. Its performative or theatrical reading added value to the recreation of the past "here (in Calkini) and now (present time)," and it reinforced and reaffirmed the *ah calkini* (inhabitant of Calkini) identity, which was constantly expressed along the document (Okoshi Harada 2009). The pride of being an "inhabitant of Calkini" was so intense that on January 10, 1801, when a commissioned judge was engaged in reviewing the boundaries in dispute between Nohcacab and Calkini, he wrote down in his report that everything was going well except the issue with the lord of Calkini, who "despite being convinced, as it was previously noted, he still (lord of Calkini) wanted to quarrel, followed in this by a great number of proud natives who came with him, and claimed that, since his map was ignored during the measurement in what was written on it, he would leave under protest in the exercise of his rights" (Crónica de Maní 1557–1813, 22v). This passage shows the lord of Calkini's disagreement with the decision of the other towns (Muna, Becal, and Maní) for having ignored his "map," that is, the "title" of his town, the source of his pride.

This "pride" was in every sense a synonym of community identity and shared by all representatives of Calkini. This sensus communis was a consequent notion in which the following three elements participated: (1) reading aloud the titles, (2) where it was done, and (3) the past and present times. In other words, reading the land titles in situ took the audience's personal and collective feelings into an acoustic and imaginary ritual journey from the past to reset the present sociocultural order (tzol).

FINAL REMARKS

Using specific graphic symbols in colonial Maya documents did not obey an arbitrary decision. On the contrary, they were carefully applied by the Maya scribes to achieve efficiency through rhetorical devices, taking into consideration both contemporary and future purposes (Quezada and Okoshi Harada 2001, 65). Reading the land titles aloud at the Indigenous councils or the disputes over boundaries served as a way for the audience, members of these colonial institutions, to (re)create and (re)affirm their sensus communis, that is, their belonging to a community where their everyday life took place. In other words, the land titles legitimated not only the town's space-territory, but they were also primarily written, sacred sources for the community's affection and identity, endowed with a temporal depth.

The temporality revealed through constantly going back and forth between past and present is expressed by the Maya term *kahlay* (memory). The past, that is, the history of establishing the town's boundary-territory described in the land titles, was acknowledged as a sacred archetypical ruling order (tzol) over the town's territory. These space-territories founded in primordial times through ritual acts had been considered sacred. The present was a current reality that had to be modified by this "past," that is, "order [tzol]." Thus, the constant turning back to the past may also be understood as a ritual journey through time. The graphic elements used in land titles to separate words and sentences were, therefore, a visual system to efficiently convey the "meaning" contained in the texts. The Maya scribes were quite conscious of their role and reproduced them faithfully, and we can appreciate this in the documents that are currently in our hands.

The Indigenous communities constantly struggled during the colonial period to keep their towns' territory "in order [tzol]," and the land titles were a valuable instrument to support their claims. Such order (tzol) applied and referred not only to a physical territory but also to the stable sociocultural order meant by the term "*policía* (civility)" (Hanks 2010). For example, in 1802, Agustin Crespo, protector of the natives, wrote down that "the people of Kalkini (Calkini) have always tried through government commissioners to revive and maintain the ancient landmarks" (Crónica de Maní 1557–1813, 42r). This statement helps us understand that the colonial Maya put a great deal of effort into preserving their lands, the source of their identity, based on their land titles. Consequently, land titles were conceived and treated as sacred books, because they showed how to restore order in the present as a prelude for the future. Thus, reading aloud was an essential performative act where graphic marks functioned as vehicles to transmit affective messages to the audience.

NOTES

1. There are four different known versions of the Maní Land Title, originally written in 1557. The most important version is called "Memoria de la distribución de los montes," and it is included in the *Papeles de los Xiu de Yaxá, Yucatán* (Quezada and Okoshi Harada 2001, 55–65). A second version is a text embedded in the Maní Chronicle (1557–1813, 1r–2v), a version based on a *traslado* (copy) of the title kept in Ticul by the mid-sixteenth century, which is in turn a copy of the Maní Land Title held in the Maní archives (Crónica de Maní 1557–1813, 1r; Okoshi Harada 2017a, 22–23). Roys published a critical English translation under the title "Land Treaty of Maní" (Roys 1943, 173–94). Here I will refer to the original base document from 1557 as the Maní Land Title, and to the particular versions with their own titles (as in the case of the "Memoria") or the title of the containing document (such as the Maní Chronicle).

2. *U kahlay thoxci kaax* (Memory of the lands distribution) is the starting sentence of the "Memoria de la distribución de los montes" (Quezada and Okoshi Harada 2001, 55).

3. The "Memoria de la distribución de los montes" is the last copy available to us (Quezada and Okoshi Harada 2001, 55–65).

4. See literary resources such as rhymes (*-ob* in lines 1, 2, 4, 5, 6, 7) and parallelisms or repetition of the same phrase in lines 8–9 and 10–11 (*ti c alahe ca tacob*).

5. Literary devices such as rhymes (*-ob* in lines 17, 18, 20; *-ex* in lines 27, 29, 31), anaphora (*t* + vocal in 20–23, 25 and 26; *ca* in 31 and 32), and parallelisms in 36 and 38–39, among others.

6. As I mentioned in note 1 above, the Maní Chronicle begins with a document that is nothing less than a version based on a copy of don Francisco de Montejo Xiu's Maní Land Title.

7. The "Memoria de la distribución de los montes" was the Title brought by the representatives of Maní.

8. See second passage cited in this chapter's section "Recounted 'Past,' Creation of a New Order (*Tzol*), and Land Titles."

REFERENCES

Acuña, René, ed. 2001. *Calepino maya de Motul*. Mexico City: Plaza y Valdés Editores, S.A. de C.V.

Arzápalo Marín, Ramón. 1987. *El ritual de los Bacabes*. Fuentes para el estudio de la cultura maya. Vol. 5. Mexico City: Centro de Estudios Mayas / Instituto de Investigaciones Filológicas / Universidad Nacional Autónoma de México.

Barrera Vásquez, Alfredo. 1965. *El libro de los cantares de Dzitbalché*. Mexico City: Instituto Nacional de Antropología e Historia.

Barrera Vásquez, Alfredo. 1984. *Documento n. 1 del deslinde de tierras en Yaxkukul, Yuc.* Mexico City: Centro Regional del Sureste / Instituto Nacional de Antropología e Historia.

Barrera Vásquez, Alfredo, and Sylvanus G. Morley. 1949. *The Maya Chronicles.* Contributions to American Anthropology and History. Washington, DC: Carnegie Institution of Washington.

Breton, Alain. 1994. *Rabinal Achi: Un drame dynastique maya du quinzième siècle. Édition établie d'après le Manuscrit Pérez.* Nanterre: Société des américanistes and Société d'ethnologie.

Bricker, Victoria R., and Helga-Maria Miram. 2002. *An Encounter of Two Worlds: The Book of Chilam Balam of Kaua.* New Orleans: Middle American Research Institute / Tulane University.

Burns, Allan F. 1983. *An Epoch of Miracles: Oral Literature of the Yucatec Maya.* Austin: University of Texas Press.

Christensen, Mark Z. 2016. *The Teabo Manuscript: Maya Christian Copybooks, Chilam Balams, and Native Text Production in Yucatán.* Austin: University of Texas Press.

Craveri Slaviero, Michela. 2004. "La boca y el ojo en la comunicación oral: Lenguaje e imágenes del Rabinal Achí." In *La palabra florida: La tradición retórica indígena y novo-hispana,* edited by Helena Beristáin and Gerardo Ramírez Vidal, 95–106. Mexico City: Universidad Nacional Autónoma de México.

Crónica de Maní. 1557–1813. Maní Land Treaty (L. 497.2051 M278), Folder 1, Box 1, Yucatan Collection 1557–1880, Manuscript Collection 26, Special Collections, Latin American Library, Tulane University, New Orleans.

Edmonson, Munro S. 1982. *The Ancient Future of the Itza: The Book of Chilam Balam of Tizimin.* Austin: University of Texas Press.

Edmonson, Munro S. 1986. *Heaven Born Merida and Its Destiny: The Book of Chilam Balam of Chumayel.* Austin: University of Texas Press.

Edmonson, Munro S., and Victoria R. Bricker. 1985. "Yucatecan Mayan Literature." In *Supplement to the Handbook of Middle American Indians,* vol. 3, edited by Victoria R. Bricker, 44–63. Austin: University of Texas Press.

Hanks, William F. 1989. "Elements of Maya Style." In *Word and Image in Maya Culture: Explorations in Language, Writing, and Representation,* edited by William F. Hanks and Don S. Rice, 92–111. Salt Lake City: University of Utah Press.

Hanks, William F. 2000. "Discourse Genres in a Theory of Practice." In *Intertexts: Writings on Language, Utterance, and Context,* edited by William F. Hanks, 133–164. Lanham: Rowman and Littlefield.

Hanks, William F. 2010. *Converting Words: Maya in the Age of the Cross.* Berkeley: University of California Press.

Johansson, Patrick. 2004. "Retórica náhuatl o la teatralidad del verbo." In *La palabra florida: La tradición retórica indígena y novohispana*, edited by Helena Beristáin and Gerardo Ramírez Vidal, 57–72. México City: Universidad Nacional Autónoma de México.

Martínez Hernández, Juan. 1928. *Crónica de Yaxkukul*. Mérida: Talleres de la Compañía Tipográfica Yucateca, S.A.

Nájera Coronado, Martha Ilia. 2007. *Los cantares de Dzitbalché en la tradición religiosa mesoamericana*. Mexico City: Centro de Estudios Mayas / Instituto de Investigaciones Filológicas / Universidad Nacional Autónoma de México.

Okoshi Harada, Tsubasa. 2009. *Códice de Calkiní*. Fuentes para el estudio de la cultura maya. Vol. 20. Mexico City: Centro de Estudios Mayas / Instituto de Investigaciones Filológicas / Universidad Nacional Autónoma de México.

Okoshi Harada, Tsubasa. 2017a. "Espacio, tiempo y escritos: Los títulos de tierras y la red de comunicación entre los pueblos de indios de Yucatán." *Indiana* 34 (2): 15–33.

Okoshi Harada, Tsubasa. 2017b. "Los 'títulos de tierras' en Yucatán, siglo XVI: Análisis de los documentos de Sotuta y de Maní." In *Piedras y papeles, vestigios del pasado: Temas de arqueología y etnohistoria de Mesoamérica*, edited by Raymundo C. Martínez García and Miguel Ángel Ruz Barrio, 159–85. Mexico City: El Colegio Mexiquense, A.C.

Okoshi Harada, Tsubasa. 2017c. "Tiempo vivido y tiempo recordado de don Francisco de Montejo Xiu: 'Título de tierras de Maní' en la historia." Special issue, *Journal de la Société des Américanistes*: 219–38.

Okoshi Harada, Tsubasa. 2018. "Construcción del 'futuro pasado': Una reflexión sobre la elaboración y traslado de los títulos de tierras mayas colonials." *Cuadernos de Lingüística de El Colegio de México* 5 (1): 286–330.

Ong, Walter J. 2005. *Orality and Literacy: The Technologizing of the Word*. New York: Routledge / Tayler and Francis e-Library.

Quezada, Sergio. 1993. *Pueblos y caciques yucatecos, 1550–1580*. Mexico City: El Colegio de México.

Quezada, Sergio, and Tsubasa Okoshi Harada. 2001. *Papeles de los Xiu de Yaxá, Yucatán*. Fuentes para el estudio de la cultura maya. Vol. 15. Mexico City: Centro de Estudios Mayas / Instituto de Investigaciones Filológicas / Universidad Nacional Autónoma de México.

Restall, Mathew. 1997. *The Maya World: Yucatec Culture and Society, 1550–1850*. Stanford, CA: Stanford University Press.

Roys, Ralph L. 1939. *The Titles of Ebtun*. Washington, DC: Carnegie Institution of Washington.

Roys, Ralph L. 1943. *The Indian Background of Colonial Yucatan*. Washington, DC: Carnegie Institution of Washington.

Tedlock, Dennis. 2003. *Rabinal Achi: A Mayan Drama of War and Sacrifice*. New York: Oxford University Press.

Wood, Stephanie. 2003. *Transcending Conquest: Nahua Views of Spanish Colonial Mexico*. Norman: University of Oklahoma Press.

Wood, Stephanie. 2014. "8. Nahua Christian Worriers in the Mapa of Cuahuhtlantzinco, Cholula Parish." In *Indian Conquistadors: Indigenous Allies in the Conquest of Mesoamerica*, edited by Laura E. Mathew and Michel R. Oudijk, 254–87. Norman: University of Oklahoma Press.

11

Substances, Subjects, and Senses

Temporality of Perception in Nahua Rituals

ALESSANDRO LUPO

INTRODUCTION

Rituals consist of multiple actions, objects, and substances whose properties reach our senses in different ways. An incredible array of diverse circumstances and phenomena thus take shape, which in anthropology are traditionally documented through the collection of audiovisual material, as well as—when possible—the transcription and interpretation of the various forms of speech that accompany them. Despite the fact that rituals incorporate a profusion of olfactory, tactile, and gustatory stimuli as well as visual and acoustic ones, anthropological analysis seldom pays enough attention to such sensorial dimension. The values and meanings it embodies are thus often overlooked, although it can provide precious glimpses into native conceptions of the different temporalities in which human and extra-human beings are immersed: in fact, for the latter it appears to be somehow discontinuous (in the sense that the time windows in which sensorial aspects can interact with humans are concentrated mainly in some moments of the day, week and year), more expanded (for some disembodied beings, an earthly year equals a day), and at the same time not embarrassed and slowed down by the "heaviness" of the body (the perception and appropriation of the goods offered by humans occurs only through some of the senses, less related to materiality). Furthermore, the Nahuas conceive the person as a combination of components (body, soul, shadow, alter ego; see below), each subjected to a temporality that partially differs from that of the others. This implies that the subject's sensorial experiences can also unfold (and

https://doi.org/10.5876/9781646426829.c011

multiply) on a variety of timescales: what they perceive through the body has a different immediacy compared to what they feel in a dream when the shadow moves elsewhere, either in the animal double or in ontologically "other" spaces (see Lupo 2012). Depending on the components of the person (whose lifespan is temporally uneven), the duration and intensity in perceiving the heat, scent, flavor, appearance, color, and sound of things and beings that they happen to encounter also vary, which also determines a multivocal ambiguity of these perceptions.

In this contribution, therefore, I shall advance some reflections on the meanings attributed to the sensory qualities of ritual objects and actions. I will take into consideration their variations over the time span of ritual performances, to bring to light what they can tell us about the subjects (human, nonhuman, and extrahuman) that interact within the setting and timeframe of the ritual, as well as any intended outcomes. My analysis will be centered on domestic rituals, considered in their variety so as to attempt—comparatively—to grasp their underlying logic. Hopefully, combining attention to the sensorium with that to the temporal sequence of ritual actions will provide us with appropriate analytical keys to disentangle the use of the senses in ritual. I am indeed led to believe that the attention paid by performers to the sensorial dimension enables more effective communication and interaction with their ritual interlocutors, at least in the Nahua ethnographic context. The extrahuman entities are in fact endowed with radically different "corporealities" and, accordingly, perceptive faculties.

The majority of the ethnographic data I draw upon was collected over a long period of time among the Nahuas of Cuetzalan (Puebla),[1] before I could consciously embrace the methodologies that would later be recommended by the advocates of "sensorial ethnography." This consists in "taking as its starting point the multisensoriality of experience, perception, knowing and practice. [. . .] a process [. . .] that accounts for how this multisensoriality is integral both to the lives of people who participate in our research *and* to how we ethnographers practice our craft" (Pink 2009, 1). Nonetheless, as I set out to reframe and examine my ethnographic data in an anthropological-sensorial key, I have to acknowledge my debt to the founding fathers of the branch of the discipline known as the "anthropology of the senses": mainly D. Howes and C. Classen, A. Corbin, S. Feld, A. Gell, and P. Stoller.[2]

As far as the Mesoamerican area is concerned, a number of significant studies on sensoriality focus on the pre-Hispanic past (Dupey 2013, 2019; Houston, Stuart, and Taube 2006; Houston and Taube 2000); unfortunately, they ignore most of the contributions and suggestions of the authors mentioned before. As for current ethnographic studies in the region, save for an article of Pitarch (2022) and a few others focusing on individual senses—such as taste (Cuturi 2002, 2009), smell

(Enríquez 2014; Galinier 2009)—the ritual dimension does not seem to have been systematically addressed (see Lupo 2012).

TO PERCEIVE AND BE PERCEIVED

A first observation to be made from the analysis of domestic Nahua rituals concerns the central role played by the evocation of extrahuman entities or forces, which are summoned at the scene of the ritual in order to establish forms of communication, negotiation, or exchange (quid pro quo). The purpose of the ritual can also be to control, manipulate, or command them, in order to vicariously influence practical aspects of reality upon which an individual's or a group's health, prosperity, and well-being depend. A striking quality of such forces and entities is that they inhabit a space and temporality that differ from those of human, everyday existence, originating in an ontologically distinct dimension, such that human senses—sight, touch, and hearing, above all—find it difficult to apprehend them. The Nahuas themselves call such dimension, in Spanish, "espiritual." However, it would be inaccurate to describe it as fully "immaterial," as frequently there are clues to some form of materiality—only that its materiality is impalpable, subtler, or "lighter" and therefore hard to grasp by our sense organs (López Austin 1994).

A key quality of such forces and entities is therefore their being incorporeal (Galinier 2009), that is, lacking a "heavy" material fabric that would make them fully perceptible by humans. On the one hand, this explains their being "transparent" to our senses; on the other hand, their incorporeality ensures that they have nonhuman perceptive capacities. In other words, this is the notion that lacking a body, in one way, empowers, while, in another, it constrains certain sensory faculties, orienting them in peculiar ways. Therefore, these entities not only escape human beings' perception, but they also—in turn—possess an altogether different sensoriality to the human one, which expresses itself in the modes of interaction found in ritual settings. Drawing inspiration from recent theoretical debates around Amerindian perspectivism,[3] one could argue that the subjects' perceptual faculties change in accordance with the transformations of their nature, in a sort of "perceptual perspectivism."[4]

As for the materiality of certain perceptual functions, the Nahuas are well aware that these rely on sense organs located in the body. Nevertheless, they situate what could be called "sentient subjectivity" among the spiritual components of the person. These are in part located inside the boundaries of our bodies, in part outside of them. The "immortal soul" (*yolo*) is found in the heart, with which it is terminologically identified and joined until death. The "shadow" (*ecahuil*)[5] represents a person's liveliness, resistance, and center of agency, and it is normally found in our blood and head but can detach itself from the body: spontaneously (in one's sleep; see Lupo 2022a) as well as because of external intervention (fright, witchcraft, and so on). Finally, we should mention the alter ego (*tonal*), which resides within a parallel and separate dimension and is thus largely unbeknown to the subject whose temperaments, strengths, and destinies are, however, determined by its animal species (Lupo 1995, 2012, 2013; Signorini and Lupo 1989). The ontological diversity between the human body and the alter ego (which despite having a material consistency is still a soul component) determines a temporal asymmetry in their lifespan: while the death of the alter ego immediately determines that of the human counterpart, if the human dies first, the animal alter ego will die with some delay, no longer receiving the energy supply transmitted to it by the human body (Signorini and Lupo 1989, 72). As for the duration of the other components of the person, the soul (*yolo*) is born simultaneously with the body, like the "double," but has no end; the "shadow" (*ecahuil*) enters the body only at the moment of birth and usually survives it for some time, especially if a violent death unexpectedly "shortens" the duration of life established by God (Signorini and Lupo 1989, 71–74).

Some forms of thought and memory are associated with specific organs, such as the heart or soul with *talnamiquiliz* /recollection, memory/, in Spanish *sentido*; and the head with *tanemililiz* /capacity to deliberate/, in Spanish *pensamiento*, which would more appropriately correspond with the ability to act consciously and responsibly (agency) and is directly associated with the shadow (see Lupo 2013, 63–90). In other words, deliberative processes can be inspired by the heart-soul and then perfected by the head-shadow. And since the shadow can temporarily leave the body during one's sleep and extracorporeal journeys, here the persistence of perceptive activities during sleep is explained by the projection into other spaces of the spiritual component in charge of our sensorial perceptions:

> Think of the body as if it was a radio with a tape recorder. If it doesn't have batteries, then it doesn't work. [. . .] It does work, but thanks to the spirit [*ecahuil*]. [. . .] The spirit never rests: the body does. Then the spirit goes out, goes about. [. . .] The energy keeps working. If you turn off a radio, even if you see that it is turned off, [. . .] it's as if it was resting, but the energy keeps working. Only if you remove the batteries, then it no longer works. [. . .] Just as our spirit. [. . .] My shadow is what comes out. [. . .] Because thought lasts, it is alive, it is working [. . .] like a clock. [. . .] But if it doesn't have batteries, it won't work. [. . .] The spirit comes back again [into the body], works again, works well. But if four, five days go by without you putting the batteries in, the device will malfunction. [. . .] The same goes for our body: [if] it doesn't have the spirit, it doesn't work. (Miguel Cruz,[6] interview, July 7, 2009)

The subject's perceptual capacity, therefore, "never rests." It wanders in space, sometimes remaining in one's body—in the wakeful state—sometimes going "elsewhere." Pathological conditions caused by the loss of the shadow can point to the locations of the spiritual component and to what entity is responsible for its expulsion (Lupo 2022a). Such "loss" happens when a fright leads the shadow to "fall" and to be captured by the Earth or other extrahuman entities. Thus, a sick person's sensations reveal where the spiritual component is retained: if the fright occurred in the water, she will feel a sensation of cold; in the case of a "fire" fright, she will be prey to burning fevers (Signorini and Lupo 1989, 119–21).

According to this "dividual" conception (Lupo 2013, 63 ff.; Strathern 1988), the person is not simply made up of a plurality of components existing both within and without the body, but these also shift over time, move in space, and sometimes join, or interfere with, other people's components. Accordingly, some senses are given an "active" role, as they are believed to convey a person's affective impulses, which are emanated into the bodies of others. Such is the case for the sense of sight, which is also believed to endow those who have powerful alter egos with the power to actively project something onto the subjects of their gaze (Signorini and Lupo 1989, 157–68).

One of the most serious spiritual ailments is fright (*nemouhtil*), and it is thought to be caused by the loss of the shadow. In this case, ritual healing revolves entirely around the retrieval of this spiritual substance, which escapes ordinary sensory perceptions. Therefore, knowledge of the subject's condition is gained through divinatory techniques which strengthen and extend the ritual specialists' perceptive faculties. Some healers formulate their diagnosis by relying on processes of spiritual spatiotemporal transfer in order to determine the ultimate causes of the illness: in their dreams, they believe, their shadow travels and locates the patient's. In that parallel dimension—which brings together different temporalities and ontological spaces—it is possible to see the condition of the lost spiritual components, as well as the outcome of the ritual practice (Lupo 2022a).

FEED THE EARTH AND RECOVER THE SHADOWS

The retrieval of a shadow takes place through ritual acts that rely on various sensory spheres, which in turn reveal a hierarchy of senses within the Nahua sensorium. The extrahuman antagonists, unlike the Christian devil, are seen not as intrinsically evil but rather as greedy entities inherently predisposed to capture and swallow all that "falls" within their reach. In other words, these bodiless entities feel an appetite for the vital essence that animates earthly beings and tend to appropriate it whenever possible, even aggressively, when humans do not bestow

Figure 11.1. The healer Miguel Cruz praying to treat a patient suffering from "fright," just before calling his "shadow," Zuapilaco, 4 May 2013 (photo by Alessandro Lupo)

it to them spontaneously through ritual offerings. In order to make them deliver a shadow they may have captured, they have to be persuaded that the request is legitimate and righteous. Hence long and articulate invocations are recited, in Nahuatl (see Lupo 1995, 2013, 2022b; Signorini and Lupo 1989). Afterward, the favor of extrahuman entities has to be gained through considerable offerings, all to some extent providing energy—"heat." This is expressed through the colors and scents of flowers,[7] and the light, heat, and aromas of candles and incense, as well as the "power" of Catholic prayers in Spanish; the latter repeated as many times as the circumstances and relative "heat" of their content demand (see Signorini and Lupo 1989; Lupo 1995, 2013, 2022b).

However, in order to persuade the extrahuman entities to return the stolen shadow, it is above all necessary to compensate them with a "payment" (*taxtahuil*) or a "replacement" (*iixpatca*), which may consist of coins or a chicken. The animal thus provides actual meat nourishment in lieu of the ethereal one.

Once the transaction is concluded, the ritual moves to the next stage, the call of the shadow (figure 11.1), which consists in invoking the patient's name, instructing them to get up and "go home" and the Earth to release them (see Lupo 1995, 128–52; Signorini and Lupo 1989, 124–29). After using polite, courteous blandishments and exhortations, the specialist passes to verbal and physical coercion through forms of tactile solicitation: Miguel Cruz used to strike the ground with a wand and summon the patient's shadow to get up and follow him on the way home; he also ordered the Earth to release them. Francisco Tejero[8] more respectfully brushed the ground with a rosary.

Lastly are those healers who, at the end of the "call" stage, turn to additional operations that are aimed at effectively reinstating the lost spiritual component into its bodily receptacle. After concluding his "calls," José Morales[9] had the patient drink water from a glass that contained the "payment" coin, based on the idea that water also held the patient's shadow (Lupo 1995, 128–52).

Hence, we can identify a sequence akin to a crescendo of materiality in this therapeutic ritual. At the outset are those senses less involved with material reality, which are in turn associated with the summoned incorporeal entities: sight, hearing, and smell (with sacred furnishings on the altar and words of devotion and supplication). At a later stage, we find instead taste and touch, senses "of proximity" expressed in the material offering of the coin dropped into water or in the burial of a chicken before the altar. This latter stage is also characterized by a great deal of ritual speech—Catholic prayers—delivered in series (as if praying rosary beads), and repeated in quantities corresponding to their "thermal" properties (perceived through touch), which are believed to produce essentially performative effects (see Lupo 1995; 2013, 135–56; 2022b). The "call" coincides with the ritual's climax, as the healer establishes physical contact with his interlocutors, including the Earth and the shadow itself. In this phase, the ground is either violently struck with a stick or delicately touched with a rosary. Here words are akin to lashes: commands whose recipients are supposed to have no chance of evading. Finally, the patient is compelled to drink the glass of water in which the healer has trapped their shadow: a confirmation of the greater efficacy attached to senses "of proximity," as the patient is offered a very concrete and gustatory experience of the definitive reinstatement of their spiritual component. The latter is among the few ritual actions capable of concretely inducing the patient's "sensory awareness" by shaking them out of apathy and exhaustion, thus helping to trigger eventual endogenous responses (see Desjarlais 1996, 157–58).

Table 11.1 illustrates the temporal sequence of the ritual recovering of a shadow. Notable is the gradual transition from the senses "of distance" (sight, smell, and hearing) to those "of proximity" (taste and touch). I believe this successfully conveys an increasing desire to coerce the entities involved, and the greater efficacy of actions that concretely influence bodies. Indicative examples are introjection or swallowing (coin, chicken, and water with the shadow) and the blows, or touch (with a stick or rosary). In my opinion, Nahua ritual healers' confidence in the possibility of achieving forms of "co-activity" with extrahuman beings, and the positive outcome of their rituals, relies precisely on this: their capacity to adjust their operations to the supposed disembodied sensoriality of the extrahuman beings whose help they require (Pitrou 2016).

TABLE 11.1. Senses in the treatment of a fright

Sequence	Duration[a]	Action	Extrahuman entities' senses involved		Patient's senses involved
			Saints	Earth	
1	A few minutes	Setting up of the altar with flowers, candles, and incense	Sight + Smell		–
2	Up to half an hour	Invocation in Nahuatl	Hearing		–
3	Five to several tens of minutes	Offering of Catholic prayers in Spanish	Hearing + Touch		(Hearing + Touch[b])
4	A few seconds or minutes	Payment (coin in the glass) or "replacement" (chicken)	–	Smell + Touch + Taste	–
5	A few minutes	Call (with wand or rosary)	–	Hearing + Touch	(Hearing + Touch)
6	A few seconds	Reinstatement (drinking water from glass)	–		Touch + Taste + Smell + Sight

a. Although the healing rite can take place in different times, most specialists prefer to perform it at night (but not at midnight, when evil forces circulate).

b. In brackets, I indicate the outcomes that gestures and words addressed at extrahuman entities are meant to produce, as they also invest the patient's body and especially their lost "shadow." The latter is thought to benefit from the prayers' energy—"heat"—and to be supporting their "weight" (see Lupo 2013, 149–50; 2022b; Signorini and Lupo 1989, 128–29).

OBJECTS, SUBSTANCES, AND SENSORIAL PROPERTIES

Let us now turn to another aspect of the sensorial dimensions of rituals: the offerings to extrahuman entities and the dead's souls: two categories that—despite clear differences in nature and powers—are equally unable to rely on human means for obtaining the vital energy they still require, although free from the bodily needs of the beings that populate the earth's surface. M.-N. Chamoux (2011) has showed how vital energy (*nemiliz*), or strength (*chicahualiz*), is a hallmark of the entities endowed with "animacy." This energy-strength is usually represented through the metaphor of "heat" (*tonalli*). Found in every substance and living creature, it manifests itself in various sensorial modalities but is always identifiable with what life feeds on: hence it coincides with the nourishment that edible plants and domestic animals supply. But it can also reside in the color, scent, and beauty of flowers;

in the fragrance and warmth of incense; in the warm and perfumed brightness of votive candles; in the polychromy and shapes of paper decorations; in the sonorities and harmonious richness of songs and music; in the dynamism, coordination, and daring of choreutic practices; and in the devotion and illocutionary and persuasive strength of ritual supplications and Catholic prayers (see Lupo 2022b). These outward, perceptible manifestations of ritual offerings have in common the human protagonists' intent, dedication, effort, and sacrifice, sometimes summarized through the metaphor of "sweat" (*neton*). This purposefulness is the key ingredient for the offerings to be well received and for the ritual itself to succeed. Without it, the most copious and expensive offerings could be displeasing; poor and inconspicuous ones, on the other hand, are well accepted, and harbingers of good things to come, if *neton* is present:

> It is a form of devotion that you are manifesting to the dead: [. . .] you put it on the altar, you offer it to the deceased. *This is the most valuable thing: purpose—that's it—one's purpose.* (José María Flores,[10] interview, September 14, 2018; emphasis added)

Offerings are needed to furnish incorporeal entities with vital energies to ingratiate, nourish, support, invigorate, and allow them to perform well what humans request. Such exchange has to take into consideration their peculiar perceptive faculties, which to a great extent do not match the "earthly," human ones "of proximity" (touch and taste), whose exercise entails consumption and material destruction of what is being perceived. The interlocutors and incorporeal recipients of a ritual are not incapable of "eating" what is offered, but they do so in other forms:

> They see, but not with the body, [. . .] spiritually. [. . .] At the same time they touch, but it is not with the hand. [. . .] Material things cannot be taken away; they could take them away in spirit. (Celina Martínez,[11] interview, September 15, 2018)

> They take it away like bread, the same. They take it away to the sky as if it was powder. (Francisco Landero,[12] interview, September 18, 2018)

RITUAL TEMPORALITY AND THE SENSES

I will now turn my attention to the perceptive sphere of the actors involved in ritual performances, and to their variations over time. I will do so by focusing on ritual offerings' sensorial properties, particularly of those intended for the souls of the deceased during Todos los Santos.

It is widely known that the numerous Mexican Indigenous communities consider this feast the main family celebration in the liturgical year. It is valued for keeping the loved ones' memory alive as well as for propitiating the souls of the dead as mediators and intercessors with the main actors of the extrahuman world (the Holy Trinity and the saints). In addition, this celebration is an opportunity to strengthen—through ceremonial exchanges within the community—bonds of solidarity and alliance (see Lok 1991; Lupo 2019; Nutini 1988; Signorini 2008). Plenty of visual records can testify to the profusion, variety, and polychromy of the decorations and ritual offerings displayed in Indigenous villages during Todos los Santos. Firsthand experience is, however, incomparably richer, more complex and composite, thanks to its multitude of synesthetic stimulations. Besides sight and hearing, the vast array of flowers, ritual fumes, and foods envelop one's nasal membranes with their scents; one comes into contact with substances and dishes that stimulate diverse configurations of touch through their consistency, temperature, and variable softness or roughness of surfaces; finally, taste buds are awakened by the remarkable assortment of flavors and beverages laid on altars and tombstones.

Yet it would be a mistake to claim that we perceive that reality exhaustively, in its multitude of stimuli, experiences, and meanings. What is more, the very assumption that—as nonindigenous observers—we could share the natives' sensations is naive and misleading, as it disregards how sensorialities are historically and culturally situated. A fundamental tenet of the whole ritual structure of Todos los Santos is that its participants are endowed with diverse perceptive faculties and evaluation models. The incorporeal nature of the dead prevents them from exercising the senses of touch and taste the way living humans do. Their surviving kin left on earth must therefore supply ritual offerings, whose qualities respond to specific perceptive and appropriative faculties. Indeed, since the loss of their bodies made the dead unable to acquire vital energy autonomously, they must be supplied with food and substances by their living survivors. The display of these offerings thus takes into consideration the *ánimas*'s diverse sensorial abilities. For example, the deceased's preferences are considered when dishes and drinks are prepared and placed on the altar, and toys for children, or cigarettes and alcoholic beverages, are chosen.

At the outset, a clear temporal variation of the offerings follows the age of the deceased. Dead children are believed to lead the way and are the first to reach their relatives' homes, on October 31; the adult dead arrive later, on November 1, while those who died of sudden death arrive in the following days.

In order to accommodate children's preferences, portions are scaled down (five tortillas, fruits, etc.—instead of seven, as for adults), and spicy as well as "heavy" dishes are avoided, opting instead for sweet and "tender" ones (see Lok 1991; Lupo 2019). The following day, however, the adult dead are presented with dishes suitable to a more "mature" taste: meat and spicy sauce tamales, dark beans, and, above all,

Figure 11.2. The offering for the dead on the altar of the Tacuapan therapist José Morales, November 2, 1988; note the *panes* on top of the coffee cups and the turkey cooked with the beak (photo by Alessandro Lupo)

turkey with mole sauce. Remarkably, the dead birds are cooked whole, including spurs, claws, and beak (figure 11.2). They thus carry into the afterlife the ability to scratch about and feed themselves. Similarly, coffee, alcoholic drinks, and cigarettes are often placed on the altars for the dead to consume.

In addition to such remarkable assortment of foods and drinks, particular attention is paid to their temperature and to the timing of their being placed on the altars: indeed, it is believed that the dead arrive at their former homes at noon sharp. It is extremely important that the offerings are placed on the altar still very hot, just moments before the stroke of twelve (the rapidity with which the fire cooks the dishes is followed by their slow cooling, which allows the deceased to consume their impalpable essence for a few tens of minutes): the fragrances, scents, and the "smoke" they emanate as they are removed from the heat can thus be appropriated by the incorporeal senses of the dead, since they would not be able to consume food that has already cooled, as heat and its emanations are precisely what is identified with vital energies:

> [The offering is placed on the altar] as soon as it is removed from the fire [...] as soon
> as the tamales have come out [of the pot], when they are nicely hot. [...] Then, they say,
> the steam will reach the dead. Yes, they pull the tamal [from the pot] hot, that's why the

steam comes out. They put it there hot so the smoke comes out, the steam; this is what goes to the dead, the smell. (José María Flores, interview, September 14, 2018)

They come to eat *poctzin* /smoke/. You have to put the tamales there; they already have the *poctzin*, [they] eat it. And then put it all there and if they take this *poctzin* away to the sky, it's enough for the whole year.[13] [...] *Quicua yon niahuyahcayot, poctzin, inetontzin de Dios* /They eat that perfume, that Smoke, the Sweat of God/. (Francisco Landero, interview, September 18, 2018)

Placing *pan de muertos* on top of a cup of hot coffee can be explained with the need to make it consumable by the dead: else its energy content, or "smoke"—that is, a food's fragrance—could not be appropriated, as it is the only substance they can perceive.

The passage of the dead goes unnoticed by the living's sight and hearing, but it can be detected through other senses: it is indeed believed that food taken off the altars, to be exchanged and consumed by godparents and compadres, is irreparably insipid, and reheating it would be to no avail: "[The deceased] took the flavor up there. [...] If you place [a plate of food] on the altar, the flavor goes away. Because the *ánimas* take it away" (Miguel Cruz, interview, September 14, 2017). Smell and taste can thus reveal to the living the lack of the essence that the deceased came to "eat" from the afterlife.

However, if food removed from the altar is believed to be depleted of its taste, why do the living eat it? Some of the dishes have anthropomorphic qualities, in accordance with their identification with the dead to whom they are offered (Lupo 2019). This is true in particular for *pan de muertos*, *hojaldras*, and meat tamales, thought of as envelopes, receptacles, coatings through which the dead can be present on the scene of the ritual. Not unlike the way edible images of the divinities represented their *ixiptlahhuan* /faces-covers/ in pre-Hispanic times (Dehouve 2016, 5; López Austin [1980] 1984, 1:433; [1973] 1989, 118 ff., 151–53), foods with such qualities make it possible for the dead to be present within the sphere of human action and for their characteristics to be appropriated via ritual ingestion. The *ánimas* therefore do more than merely "touching" the food offered: they strip it of its essence and temporarily embed themselves inside its "body" coating. Thus embodied, they become present on the ritual scene, "bringing life to [their] coverings, and becoming agents capable of action" in the world (Dehouve 2016, 8). Hence when the living consume food that hosted the dead's souls as they visited the altars, are they not committing something akin to anthropophagy? Moreover, those dead would be their own ancestors and close relatives (a form of "endo-cannibalism," or food incest). An "eso-phagic" preference indirectly confirms this interpretation, as suggested by the practice of gifting one's offerings to spiritual kin, so that each family eats another family's offerings (Lok 1991; Signorini 2008).

At any rate, why eat the dead's "leftovers"? Being insipid, they are energetically "depleted" and, to some extent, still bear traces of the dead's visitation. Otherwise, people would have no reason to avoid consuming food offered to their dead kin. Doubtless, offerings are eaten because of the dead's intrinsic semidivine qualities, bestowed in the ethereal afterlife where God and the saints reside, and also because the deceased have at least partially atoned for their sins and are therefore purified. A ritual specialist clarifies it well:

> [People offer bread loaves] because [the dead] come: a sign of this, [...] *so that we know it's true [that] they come, that's why they bake the panes.* [...] [The shadow] is what comes, but one does not see it. Their Shadow comes from the skies. There it is seen as alive as here we are speaking. [...] And they put [food] there on the altar. And after a while they remove it. Then one can eat it, *by now the [deceased] have blessed it*; there is no more *poctzin* /smoke/, *there is nothing left.* [...] Because they come, [the offerings] *are now clean, good. They bring blessings from God.* (Francisco Landero, interview, September 18, 2018; emphasis added)

The desirableness of the dead's ephemeral presence[14] in food was indirectly confirmed by another ritual specialist, as he commented upon the fleeting duration of such "embodiment" of souls within food, evocatively equated to Christ's presence in the consecrated host:

> [Once the deceased have gone,] *the scent has been taken away.* The aroma, they took it away, now *what you eat is only bread and that's it.* It is like the priest says: *when the host is not consecrated, it's only wheat. It has nothing, there's nothing,* [you] can eat it, [...] it's clean, it's simple. But once it's consecrated, now not everyone can eat it. [After some time] *the dead aren't there anymore, there's nobody.* The scent is gone, the aroma is gone now. After you put [the food on offer], ten minutes later the aroma is gone. In twenty minutes at most. After an hour you can already eat bread, *it has nothing left.* Now they've touched the *panes*, they've already taken them away. (Miguel Cruz, interview, September 14, 2017; emphasis added)

Although we cannot perceive these propitious entities through our senses, their passage (they "touch" the *panes*) leaves a trail that has positive effects on the whole body-and-soul complex of those who eat the foods offered on the altars, as these foods are believed to convey the "blessing of God" that the deceased bring down from their celestial realms in exchange for the offerings that they receive.

FINAL CONSIDERATIONS

I hope to have shown the significance of investigating Nahua rituals on a sensorial level, drawing on the handful of cases I have presented. The variations sensorial stimuli undergo within the ritual timeframes are revelatory of local ideas around the qualities of the actors involved. These, as we have seen, are endowed with perceptive faculties that adjust to the presence/absence of a bodily medium. It is no coincidence that one of the functions of several ritual objects seems to be that of "bringing into presence," to the scene of the ritual, entities whose friendly intervention they try to summon. A similar role is played elsewhere by paper cuttings fed with the blood of sacrificial animals, or by lithic and wooden effigies (the Otomi *antiguas*) to be regularly dressed and nourished.[15] The representation of incorporeal entities through effigies often has the purpose of "bringing the spirits into the physical world" in order "to mimetically gain control over the mirror-image of physical reality" (Taussig 1993, 105). Likewise, I believe Nahua rituals succeed in evoking these disincarnate entities and bringing them into presence through the conscious use of a rich array of sensory stimulations. They do so despite displaying a scarcity of iconic representations, when compared with other areas of the Sierra and the Huasteca. Even though the dead are not visible or audible by those who are awaiting at the stroke of noon, their presence is revealed through the motions the living address at their peculiar perceptual abilities: it is indeed the natives' dedication in placing very hot and fragrant offerings on the altar that indicates the desired presence of the *ánimas*. The offerings' incorporeal essence can in fact be absorbed through the sense of smell only when at the apex of thermal-aromatic emanations. The adoption of peculiar modes of serving, such as placing loaves on hot coffee cups, is consistent with this interpretation. Once the ritual is over, it is indeed an absence that validates the dead's visitation: that of the offerings' scent and taste, taken into the dead's realm, where its transience is compensated by an extended timeframe (1 year = 1 day).

In other words, I find an analogy between the role of sensoriality in the Nahua rituals and the qualities that Carlo Severi (2018) assigns to "chimerical" images: rather than performing a visual representation of the portrayed thing, these "bring out a presence that is neither physically embedded on the painted surface nor in the sculpted object." The aim is to generate a mental space within which the observers can perform an act of "projection": "A chimera [. . .] is a set of visual indexes in which what one sees inevitably recalls the interpretation of something implicit. This hidden feature of an image is wholly generated within a mental space, on the basis of specific indexes" (Severi 2018, 109). In the case at hand—rather than focusing solely on the iconic dimension—we have ventured to consider the perceptual spheres of smell, taste, and touch-heat, for which "the invisible takes precedence over the visible and appears to provide its context" (Severi 2018, 221). In my view, they also facilitate the ritual actors' task of bringing into presence, and activity, the entities summoned through the senses. For a subject to have a projective experience, it is necessary that what inspires their "act of belief" remains "incomplete, [since] this incompleteness is the very condition for the attribution of subjectivity and for the projective actions of which it becomes the support" (Severi 2018, 337). In view of the above, it seems that the dead's incorporeal and silent nature, as well as the extraction of flavors from the food they are offered, represent perceptive "gaps" filled with purpose and sense: they provide the impalpable mental space required to project the desired presence of the natives' incorporeal interlocutors, and gift the latter with the ability to act in this world. Thus, the range of different stimuli and sensory perceptions that follow one another during the Nahua rituals allow those who examine them carefully to understand which actors are present on the scene; in what sequence, with what roles, and through what kind of actions they perform; and what are the desired consequences of such actions. And the temporality of the sensory indexes clearly contributes to revealing the conceptions and meanings that the actors attribute to their ritual endeavor.

NOTES

1. Ethnographic data has been collected in Cuetzalan del Progreso (Puebla), where I have been carrying out fieldwork since 1984 within the Italian Ethnological Mission in Mexico. My work has been possible thanks to the continual support of the Italian Ministry of Foreign Affairs and the Sapienza University of Rome.

2. With regard to the vast literature on the theme by the authors mentioned, see, at least, Boccara and Rey-Hulman (1998), Candau (2000), Classen (1993, 1997, 1999), Classen, Howes and Synnott (1994), Corbin (1982, 1990), Feld (1982), Gell (1977, 2006), Howes (1991, 2003, 2005), Howes and Classen (2013), Le Breton (2006), Méchin, Bianquis, and Le Breton (1998), Stoller (1989, 1997).

3. I do not deal here with the issue of whether analytical models developed from Amazonian ethnographies are pertinent to the Mesoamerican context (see Descola 2005; Viveiros 1998). I will only point out how, sometimes, the desire to validate potential reversals of humans' predatory behavior toward animals can lead to disregarding the huge role played for over four millennia by intensive maize farming among Mesoamerican populations, and the consequent hegemony of plant metaphors in their conceptions of humans and their relationship with the cosmos and the beings that populate it (see López Austin 1994; Lupo 1995).

4. Common narratives in which a person happens to visit the dead's world despite being still alive provide an example of this. The perception of time is enormously dilated there

(one day corresponds to an earthly year), and food that is inedible for the human visitor is consumed and to the deceased it is identical to what they once ate on earth: ash buns are maize tortillas, insects are beans, etc. (see López Austin 1984, 1, 382; Lupo 2019).

5. Literal translations of Nahuatl terms are written between two slash bars (/ . . . /), free translations between oriented single high quotation marks ('. . .'). In the Nahuatl of Cuetzalan the phoneme /tl/ is replaced by the allophone [t]; however, I will follow each author's spelling of specific terms.

6. Miguel Cruz (1928–2022) was a renowned traditional healer who earned a living from his profession, which he practiced in his home in Zuapilaco and in Cuetzalan (see Lupo 1995, 64–67).

7. For an in-depth diachronic examination of the Nahuatl linguistic expressions that link flowers to the spirit world, see Hill (1992).

8. Francisco Tejero (1905–1999), from Cuauhtapanaloyan, until about sixty years of age made a living from his crops, undertaking his career as a healer only following a serious illness. In his eighties, he moved to Yancuictlalpan to live with his daughter. He boasted of an uncommon endurance in reciting Catholic prayers for therapeutic purposes (see Lupo 1995, 69–71; 2022b).

9. Farmer from Tacuapan and admired musician in a Cuezalime dance group, José Morales (1926?–2002) learned his trade as a healer from a paternal great-uncle and practiced it until his death (see Lupo 1995, 67–69).

10. José María Flores is a retired eighty-year-old farmer from Yancuictlalpan; he has an in-depth indirect knowledge of ritual practices, having witnessed the performances of both his father and his father-in-law, who lived in his home for years.

11. Celina Martínez is a pious widow in her seventies, residing in Zuapilaco; she supplements the state subsidy with domestic help at the second home of a family from Mexico City.

12. Francisco Landero (1924–2019) was a farmer and a renowned ritual specialist and healer; originally from Tacuapan, he later moved to Xiloxochico, where he died.

13. The Nahua hold the deep-rooted belief that different timeframes pertain to the world of the living and that of the dead, so that an earthly year equals one day in the afterlife (see Lupo 2019).

14. However, it should be remembered that—while it is possible to touch and eat the food-receptacles after the passage of the *ánimas*—it is strongly forbidden to do so while they are present on the altar and are consuming them, as direct contact—which means "at the same time," both temporalities in presence—with the dead is lethal (see Lupo 2019, 245).

15. On paper cuttings, see Dow (1986), Galinier (1990), Sandstrom and Effrein (1986); on the statuettes whose clothes are changed, see Baez Cubero (2012), Dow (1986), Galinier (1990).

REFERENCES

Baez Cubero, Lourdes. 2012. "'Vistiendo Santitos': La acción ritual para vestir a los 'antiguas' entre los otomíes de Hidalgo." *Estudios de Cultura Otopame* 8: 237–56.

Boccara, Michel, and Diana Rey-Hulman, eds. 1998. *Odeurs du monde*. Paris: L'Harmattan.

Candau, Joël. 2000. *Mémoire et Expériences Olfactives: Anthropologie d'un savoir-faire sensoriel*. Paris: Presses Universitaires de France.

Chamoux, Marie-Noëlle. 2011. "Persona, animacidad, fuerza." In *La noción de vida en Mesoamérica*, edited by Perig Pitrou, María del Carmen Valverde Valdés, and Johannes Neurath, 155–80. Mexico City: Centro de Estudios Mexicanos y Centroamericanos / Universidad Nacional Autónoma de México.

Classen, Constance. 1993. *Worlds of Sense: Exploring the Senses in History and across Cultures*. London: Routledge.

Classen, Constance. 1997. "Foundations for an Anthropology of the Senses." *International Social Science Journal* 153: 401–12.

Classen, Constance. 1999. "Other Ways to Wisdom: Learning through the Senses across Cultures." *International Review of Education* 45 (3/4): 269–80.

Classen, Constance, David Howes, and Anthony Synnott. 1994. *Aroma: The Cultural History of Smell*. London: Routledge.

Corbin, Alain. 1982. *Le miasme et la jonquille*. Paris: Aubier.

Corbin, Alain. 1990. "Histoire et anthropologie sensorielle." *Anthropologie et Sociétés* 14 (2): 13–24.

Cuturi, Flavia. 2002. "Il sapere dei sapori." In *Saperi e sapori mediterranei*, edited by Domenico Silvestri, Antonietta Marra, and Immacolata Pinto, 245–80. Napoli: Università degli Studi di Napoli "L'Orientale."

Cuturi, Flavia. 2009. *Comida ikoots de San Mateo del Mar: Conocimientos y preparación*. Mexico City: Instituto Nacional de Lenguas Indígenas.

Dehouve, Danièle. 2016. "El papel de la vestimenta en los rituales mexicas de 'personificación.'" *Nuevo Mundo Mundos Nuevos, Colloques*. http://nuevomundo.revues.org/69305.

Descola, Philippe. 2005. *Par-delà nature et culture*. Paris: Gallimard.

Desjarlais, Robert R. 1996. "Presence." In *The Performance of Healing*, edited by Carol Laderman and Marina Roseman, 143–64. New York: Routledge.

Dow, James. 1986. *The Shaman's Touch: Otomí Indian Symbolic Healing*. Salt Lake City: University of Utah Press.

Dupey García, Elodie. 2013. "De pieles hediondas y perfumes florales: La reactualización del mito de creación de las flores en las fiestas de las veintenas de los antiguos nahuas." *Estudios de Cultura Náhuatl* 45: 7–36.

Dupey García, Elodie. 2019. "Lo que el viento se lleva: Ofrendas odoríferas y sonoras en la ritualidad náhuatl prehispánica." In *De olfato: Aproximaciones a los olores en la historia de México*, edited by Elodie Dupey García and Guadalupe Pinzón Ríos, 83–131. Mexico City: Secretaría de Cultura / Fondo de Cultura Económica.

Enríquez Andrade, Héctor M. 2014. *Olor, cultura y sociedad*. Mexico City: Instituto Nacional de Antropología e Historia.

Feld, Steven. 1982. *Sound and Sentiment*. Philadelphia: University of Pennsylvania Press.

Galinier, Jacques. 1990. *La mitad del mundo: Cuerpo y cosmos en los rituales otomíes*. Mexico City: Universidad Nacional Autónoma de México / Centro de Estudios Mexicanos y Centroamericanos / Instituto Nacional Indigenista.

Galinier, Jacques. 2009. *El espejo otomí: De la etnografía a la antropología psicoanalítica*. Mexico City: Instituto Nacional de Antropología e Historia / Centro Nacional para el Desarrollo de los Pueblos Indígenas / Centro de Estudios Mexicanos y Centroamericanos.

Gell, Alfred. 1977. "Magic, Perfume, Dream." In *Symbols and Sentiments*, edited by Ioan Lewis, 25–38. London: Academic Press.

Gell, Alfred. 2006. "Parfum, symbolisme et enchantement." *Terrain* 47: 19–34.

Hill, Jane H. 1992. "The Flower World of Old Uto-Aztecan." *Journal of Anthropological Research* 48 (2): 117–44.

Houston, Stephen, David Stuart, and Karl Taube. 2006. *The Memory of Bones*. Austin: University of Texas Press.

Houston, Stephen, and Karl Taube. 2000. "An Archaeology of the Senses: Perception and Cultural Expression in Ancient Mesoamerica." *Cambridge Archaeological Journal* 10 (2): 261–94.

Howes, David, ed. 1991. *The Varieties of Sensory Experience: A Sourcebook in the Anthropology of the Senses*. Toronto: University of Toronto Press.

Howes, David. 2003. *Sensual Relations: Engaging the Senses in Culture and Social Theory*. Ann Arbor: University of Michigan Press.

Howes, David, ed. 2005. *Empire of the Senses: The Sensual Culture Reader*. Oxford: Berg.

Howes, David, and Constance Classen. 2013. *Ways of Sensing: Understanding the Senses in Society*. New York: Routledge.

Le Breton, David. 2006. *La saveur du monde*. Paris: Métailié.

Lok, Rossana. 1991. *Gifts to the Dead and the Living: Forms of Exchange in San Miguel Tzinacapan, Sierra Norte de Puebla, Mexico*. Leiden: Centre of Non Western Studies, Leiden University.

López Austin, Alfredo. (1980) 1984. *Cuerpo humano e ideología: Las concepciones de los antiguos nahuas*. 2 vols. Mexico City: Universidad Nacional Autónoma de México.

López Austin, Alfredo. (1973) 1989. *Hombre-dios: Religión y política en el mundo náhuatl.* Mexico City: Universidad Nacional Autónoma de México.

López Austin, Alfredo. 1994. *Tamoanchan y Tlalocan.* Mexico City: Fondo de Cultura Económica.

Lupo, Alessandro. 1995. *La tierra nos escucha: La cosmología de los nahuas a través de las súplicas rituales.* Mexico City: Instituto Nacional Indigenista / Conaculta.

Lupo, Alessandro. 2012. *Corpi freddi e ombre perdute: La medicina indigena messicana ieri e oggi.* Roma: CISU.

Lupo, Alessandro. 2013. *El maíz en la cruz: Prácticas y dinámicas religiosas en el México indígena.* Xalapa: Instituto Veracruzano de la Cultura / Conaculta.

Lupo, Alessandro. 2019. "Comer (con) los difuntos: Las ofrendas comestibles de Todos los Santos y las lógicas de la comensalía entre vivos y muertos en la Sierra de Puebla." *Estudios de Cultura Náhuatl* 58: 223–64.

Lupo, Alessandro. 2022a. "*Tlacochitta*, ver cosas durmiendo: Enunciados y reflexiones sobre las prácticas oníricas de los nahuas." *Estudios de Cultura Náhuatl* 63: 157–92.

Lupo, Alessandro. 2022b. "Heaps of Prayers: The Materiality of Catholic Prayers, Their Temporal Dimension and Ritual Effectiveness within Nahua Ritual Discourse." In *Materializing Ritual Practices*, edited by Lisa M. Johnson and Rosemary A. Joyce, 162–91. Louisville: University Press of Colorado.

Méchin, Colette, Isabelle Bianquis, and David Le Breton, eds. 1998. *Anthropologie du sensoriel.* Paris: L'Harmattan.

Nutini, Hugo G. 1988. *Todos Santos in Rural Tlaxcala.* Princeton, NJ: Princeton University Press.

Pink, Sarah. 2009. *Doing Sensory Ethnography.* London: Sage.

Pitarch, Pedro. 2022. "Sinestesia ontológica: Fragmentos de una etnografía de la comunicación sensorial en el chamanismo tseltal." In *Volver al chamanismo: La oscuridad, el silencio y la ausencia*, edited by Laura Romero, 57–83. México: Universidad Iberoamericana.

Pitrou, Perig. 2016. "Co-activity in Mesoamerica and in the Andes." *Journal of Anthropological Research* 72 (4): 465–82.

Sandstrom, Alan R., and Pamela Effrein Sandstrom. 1986. *Traditional Papermaking and Cult Figures of Mexico.* Norman: University of Oklahoma Press.

Severi, Carlo. 2018. *L'oggetto-persona: Rito Memoria Immagine; Un'antropologia della memoria.* Torino: Einaudi.

Signorini, Italo. 2008. "El regreso de los difuntos en el mundo indígena mesoamericano contemporáneo." In *Morir para vivir en Mesoamérica*, edited by Lourdes Baez Cubero and Catalina Rodríguez Lascano, 249–58. Veracruz: Consejo Veracruzano de Arte Popular.

Signorini, Italo, and Alessandro Lupo. 1989. *Los tres ejes de la vida: Almas, cuerpo, enferme-dad entre los nahuas de la Sierra de Puebla*. Xalapa: Universidad Veracruzana.

Stoller, Paul. 1989. *The Taste of Ethnographic Things*. Philadelphia: University of Pennsylvania Press.

Stoller, Paul. 1997. *Sensuous Scholarship*. Philadelphia: University of Pennsylvania Press.

Strathern, Marilyn. 1988. *The Gender of the Gift*. Berkeley: University of California Press.

Taussig, Michael. 1993. *Mimesis and Alterity*. London: Routledge.

Viveiros de Castro, Eduardo. 1998. "Cosmological Deixis and Amerindian Perspectivism." *Journal of the Royal Anthropological Institute* 4 (3): 469–88.

PART IV

Ritual Temporalities in the Longue Durée

12

Rituals of Inauguration

Temporalities and Spatialities in the Maya Area and Mesoamerica

MARIE CHOSSON, JOHANN BEGEL, AND CÉDRIC BECQUEY

INTRODUCTION

Among contemporary Mesoamerican groups, the inauguration[1] of buildings implies the setting up of ritual protocols that have been broadly described in the ethnography since the beginning of the twentieth century (among others, Chapman 1985; Lok 1987; Vogt 1979). The review of this literature and its comparison with archaeological data allows us not only to extract and put forward some common threads largely shared today in Mesoamerica, especially in the Maya area, but also to establish some parallels with the past practices and even to hypothesize the existence of continuities over time in these rituals. In order to re-evaluate the specificity given to house inauguration ceremonies, it seems necessary to compare them with ritual protocols related to the use of spaces for other activities. In the ethnographic record, all these rituals are often classified in different categories such as construction, domestic, or agricultural ceremonies. By comparing them, we will question both the possible variety of intentions and expectations sustaining them, and the existence of a single conceptual paradigm encompassing all the ceremonies of occupation of space.[2] As these rituals are periodically renewed, a special focus will be made on their time spans. A time span is here defined as a period between two ritual events, or a duration marked by the continuation of a particular process. This analysis will tend to demonstrate that the past and present inauguration rituals analyzed here share a common logic that translates into similar ritual protocols coinciding with goals and comparable cosmovision.

https://doi.org/10.5876/9781646426829.c012

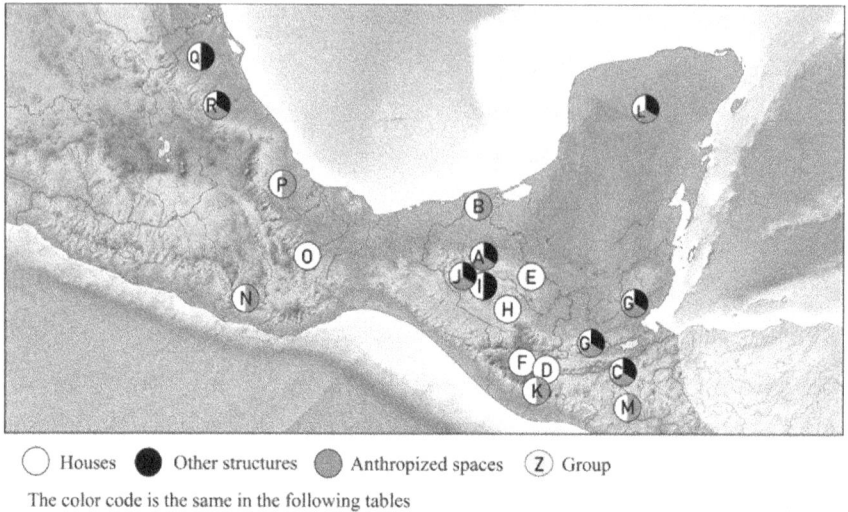

Houses ○   Other structures ● (black)   Anthropized spaces ● (gray)   Group (Z)
The color code is the same in the following tables

Figure 12.1. Spatial distribution of the rituals of the corpus

HOUSE INAUGURATION RITUALS

In a previous study (Begel, Chosson, and Becquey 2022), we compared the modalities and local exegesis of 35 contemporary house inauguration rituals, highlighting the existence of strong convergences between them. The present analysis extends the study to 48 ceremonies in Mesoamerica (figure 12.1; table 12.1). Among the most common features, these rituals are performed at the four corners of a building, following a path circumscribing the space to be occupied, before ending in the center of the house. The different sequences of these ritual actions located at the four corners and the center of the house draw a quintipartite diagram reminiscent of the Mesoamerican cosmogram.[3] This circuit performed by the ritual specialist is most often levorotatory, beginning either at the east pole or at the domestic altar placed toward this cardinal point associated with the direction of sunrise. These paths or ritual gestures may take different forms, either circular or cross-shaped; however, they must never end in the west, which connotes death. Peripheral ritual actions most often involve sprinkling of liquids—animal blood, holy water, alcohol, broth—and may also include buried deposits. The focal point is the center of the house, where a buried deposit is always made. A pit dug for the occasion, into which the blood of the sacrificial victims—usually one or more birds or the juice of the dish prepared with them—can be poured when they are not deposited in whole. More detailed descriptions also inform us that the content is sometimes spatially organized in different strata or levels (Becquey 2017, 253; see also various

TABLE 12.1. Corpus of rituals by categories

Ethnic group	Letter on the map	House	Other structures	Anthropized spaces	Total
MAYA AREA					
Chol	A	3	2	2	7
Chontal	B	3		2	5
Chorti	C	2	1	4	7
Kiche'	D	4			4
Lacandon	E	1			1
Popti'	F	1			1
Q'eqchi'	G	2	3	2	7
Tojolabal	H	1			1
Tseltal	I	6	2		8
Tzotzil	J	12	2	3	17
Tz'utujil	K	1		1	2
Yucatec	L	4	1	7	12
MESOAMERICA					
Lenca	M	2		4	6
Mixe	N	1		1	2
Mixtec	O	1			1
Nahua	P	1		4	5
Teenek	Q	1	1		2
Totonac	R	2	4	2	8
Total		48	16	32	96

Mesoamerican examples in the special issue edited by Ariel de Vidas, Hémond, and van 't Hooft 2014). Finally, this device can also be supplemented by additional items placed on or in front of the domestic altar.[4] All of these acts are accompanied by ritual speeches addressed to various nonhuman entities. The inauguration rite is usually concluded with a collective meal and a celebration, sometimes accompanied by music and dance. Many similar ceremonies are documented beyond the Maya area. This is the case for houses under construction among the Nahuas (Lok 1987, 213–19), Mixes (Lipp 1991, 73), or Mixtecs (Monaghan 1998, 47–50) or for new houses among the Lencas (Chapman 1985, 149) or Totonacs (Ichon 1969, 265).

These rituals are generally meant to be repeated on a regular basis: depending on the case, annually, biannually, or over longer time intervals. Some circumstances also require a repetition of the ritual protocol: when a space changes in function or organization (for instance, for an extension of the occupied space; Becquey 2017, 256), when a new member joins the household (Guiteras Holmes 1961, 144–45), or as soon as disorders such as diseases appear (Becquey 2017, 256; Nash 1970, 17; Pitarch Ramón 1996, 103).

Both the content of the ritual discourses and the exegesis of these ceremonies by their actors reveal that they are organized to respond to two major concerns. On the one hand, these rituals are conceived as a way to ask for forgiveness and to compensate the entities or forces related to the earth, following the nuisances caused by construction work. On the other hand, these apotropaic rituals are an opportunity to address a petition to other entities (saints, God, etc) for the protection of the circumscribed space. Indeed, it is essential to protect the house against the entry of harmful entities, curses, and other inconveniences, in order to guarantee a peaceful life for its inhabitants. It should be noted that, among the large corpus considered here, only Vogt's survey (Vogt 1979, 1998) mentions that the main objective of this ritual intends to confer a soul to the house.[5] By extending the framework of the study to the rituals of delimitation and inauguration of other types of buildings and spaces (churches, mills, fields, pens, etc.), it appears, however, that their protocols are quite comparable.

We have also put the description of the contemporary rituals of house inauguration into perspective with archaeological data on caches. This confrontation reveals a number of material similarities that allow us to infer certain parallels in the system of thought that structures the ritual protocol, despite the centuries that separate the two sets of rituals (Begel, Chosson, and Becquey 2022). The ceremonies of the Preclassic and Classic periods show a particularly notable continuity despite a temporality spread over centuries. They are evidenced by caches installed at each stage of the architectural history of the building (construction, occupation, abandonment) and sometimes respect the spatial cruciform logic of the cosmogram (for example, in Aoyama et al. 2017). Moreover, the convergences between contemporary and pre-Hispanic rituals are not foreign to archaeologists, who have willingly interpreted these ancient ceremonies as rituals for animating structures, drawing inspiration from the aforementioned ethnographic work by Vogt (Boteler-Mock 1998).

It is, therefore, above all through the study of special deposits that archaeology can question rituals. William Coe classified Tikal caches into recurring patterns now called cache ritual complexes, based on a similarity of content, a particular spatial arrangement of the artifacts, and their context of discovery (Moholy-Nagy and Coe 2008, 18–21). This typology was recently revisited and expanded (Begel 2020,

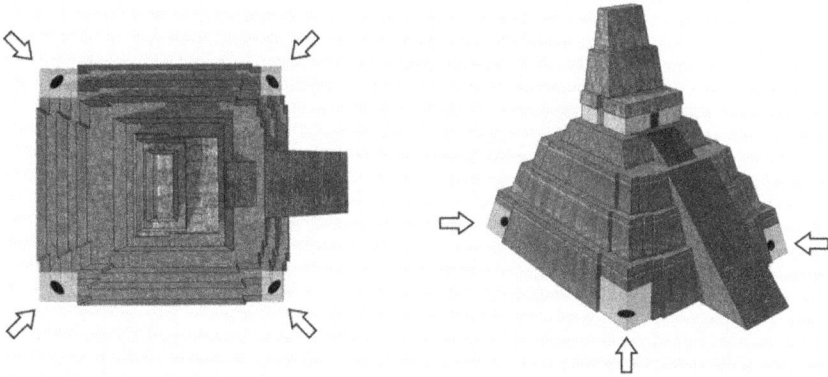

Figure 12.2. Position of caches of the Xik A cache complex in Tikal's Temple II (from the 3D model by Krzysio drawn with SketchUp)

n.d.). According to Begel's new analysis, the cache complexes could constitute "recipes" reused repeatedly over time, with similar content, in identical architectural or monumental contexts. Among many other examples, a *Bool* ritual complex presents a similar association of chert eccentrics, incised obsidians, pottery vessels, and sometimes lithic debitage or human remains found specifically under Late Classic stelae in Tikal. In this site, cache complexes appear as early as the Late Middle Preclassic (600–350 BC) and multiply during the Early Classic (AD 250–554). Until the end of this period, their use does not always seem to be governed by immutable rules. Although they are linked to specific stratigraphic categories (periods of construction, occupation, abandonment) and to specific types of structures (temples, houses, stelae, etc.), some of them are rather multipurpose and can be used in different contexts: inside buildings, in outdoor rituals, or for monument dedication, for instance. In the Late Classic (AD 554–869), cache complexes become standardized, as if specific ceremonies were required for each circumstance, such as the construction or reconstruction of a temple, a plaza, or a platform or the dedication of a stela.

In some cases, several caches can delimit a space (figure 12.2) as the Xik A cache complex in Tikal (Begel 2020, n.d.), while in others, some authors argue, a microcosmic staging may have been concentrated in a single pit, similar to the stratified deposits of the Templo Mayor of Tenochtitlán (Baudez 2002[6]; Calligeris 1999). As for modern rituals, these ancient deposits could indicate a circumscription or concentration, in other words, a figurative centralization of space.

Since there are a large number of different cache complexes in Tikal (23 in total, 10 of which were divided into 27 variants for a total of 327 caches on 337 sufficiently documented; Begel n.d.), their original meanings were probably extremely varied and not restricted to the sole development and occupation of the buildings. Other petitions of a significantly different nature must have been carried by these rituals (Begel 2020). It is therefore necessary to distinguish the various cache complexes or even their variants, which were actually linked to the building actions or inaugurations. This can only be done in future research by means of a more complete corpus of caches than the sole case of Tikal.

INAUGURATION AND PROTECTION OF BUILDINGS

The archaeological data seems to point to the existence of some recurrent cache complexes clearly associated with the construction of ceremonial structures. In residential areas, the situation is different in that caches are scarcer. This is partly due to a sampling bias, since domestic patios were less excavated in the past, but recent excavations confirm this trend, in Naachtun for instance (Nondédéo et al. 2010–23). For the Classic period, the focus is therefore clearly on the temples and public spaces. What about the ethnographic data? Are there any ritual protocols comparable to those for the inauguration of a house that would be performed in other contexts? Sixteen contemporary rituals of this kind have indeed been recorded, as represented on the map (figure 12.1, tables 12.1–12.3).

Among these examples, Laughlin (1969, 307) mentions the organization of a ritual for the inauguration of a sugar mill among the Teenek of Tantoyuca. The performance involves the sacrifice of a chicken, whose heart is buried near the machinery in the center of the building and sprinkled with alcohol, as are the four corners of the building. Among the Q'eqchi', Cabarrús's (1979, 117) and Thompson's (1930, 70) informants explicitly specify that the rituals organized during the construction of piggeries or henhouses are identical to those performed for the house.

Cabarrús (1979, 121) also reports the proceedings of a Q'eqchi' ritual for the building of a small chapel in Cahabón. In this performance, although the path and location of the ritual deposits are identical to the ones made for the house, the material content of the "recipes" varies in size, and probably in value, according to the importance of the building. Pigs, rather than chickens, were sacrificed. The animal's blood was buried in the center of the church, its head placed at the doorway, and its body divided into four pieces buried in the four corners of the building. Figuerola Pujol (2010, 537) indicates that the Tseltal inhabitants of Cancuc consider that the solidity of different structures such as churches, administrative buildings, and even highway bridge piers can be explained by the presence of human bodies buried in their foundations.

In Chol's land, henhouses, kitchens, offices, and shops may also be the object of a ritual protocol comparable to that of the house inauguration. As Becquey's field data suggest, this ritual is, ideally, reiterated annually. The repetition strengthens

TABLE 12.2. Characteristics of nondomestic Mayan inauguration rituals (twentieth and twenty-first centuries)

Group	Reference	Space	Ritual performances				Deposits						Goals			Ritual meal
			Four corners	Center	Altar	Speech	Sacrifice	Incense	Candles	Holy water	Alcohol	Others	Animation	Protection	Permission or forgiveness	
Chol	Becquey 2017	Corral	X		X	X	X	X	X	X	X	X		X	X	X
		Corral	X	X	X	X	X	X	X	X	X	X		X	X	X
		Office	X	X	X	X	X	X	X	X	X	X		X	X	X
		Henhouse	X	X	X	X	X	X	X	X	X	X		X	X	X
Chontal	Becquey 2016	Milpa x2	X	X		X	X	X	X			X				X
Chorti	Wisdom 1940	Milpa	X	X	?		X		X					X	X	X
		Milpa (rain)	X	X		X	X		X					X	X	X
	Fought 1972	House-plot	X	X		X	X	X	X					X	?	X
		Milpa	X	X		X	X	X	X					X	?	X
		Granary	X	X		?	X					X		X	?	
Q'eqchi'	Cabarrús 1979	Chapel	X	X		X	X							X	X	X
		Milpa	X	X		X	X	X	X					X	X	X
	Thompson 1930	Henhouse	X	X		X		X	X			X		X	X	X
		Piggery	X	X		X		X	X			X		X	X	X
		Milpa	X	X		?		X						X	X	X
Tseltal	Nash 1970	Milpa	?	?		X	?		X					?	?	?
	Groark 1997	Temazcal x2		X			X					X	X	X	X	X
Tzotzil	Vogt 1979, 1998	Milpa	X	X	X	X		X	X		X	X		X	X	X
	Guiteras Holmes 1961	Milpa x2		X		X		X	X			X		X	?	X
	Groark 1997	Temazcal x2	X	X		X	X	X	X			X	X	X	X	X
Tz'utujil	Christenson 2010	Milpa	X	X		?	X							?	X	X
Yucatec	Ramos-Perez 2019	Milpa	X	X	X	X	X			X	X	X		X	X	X
		Village	X	X		X	X			X	X	X		X		X
	Pierrebourg and Ruz 2014	Solar	X	X	X	?	X				X	X		X	X	X
		Village	X	X	?	?	?	?	?	?	?	?		?	?	?
	Redfield and Villa Rojas 1934	Village	X	X	X	X	X				X	X		X	?	X
		Corral		X	X	X	X	?	X	?	X	?		X	?	X
		Beehives	?	X	X	X	X	?	X	?	X	?		X	?	X
		Milpa	X	X	X	X								X	X	X

TABLE 12.3. Characteristics of nondomestic Mesoamerican inauguration rituals (twentieth and twenty-first centuries)

Group	Reference	Space	Four corners	Center	Altar	Speech	Sacrifice	Incense	Candles	Holy water	Alcohol	Others	Animation	Protection	Permission or forgiveness	Ritual meal
			Ritual performances				*Deposits*						*Goals*			
Lenca	Chapman 1985	Milpa	X	X	X	X	X	X	X		X	X	X	X		X
		Coffee plantation	X	X	X	X	X	X	X	X	X	X	X	X		X
		Clay's quarry	?	X	X	X	X	X	X		X	X	X	X		X
		Laundry area (spring)	?	?	X	X	X	X	X			X	X	X		X
Mixe	Lipp 1991	Milpa	X	X		X	X	?	?	?	?	?	X	?		X
Nahua	Lupo 1995	Milpa x2		X		X				X	X		X	X		
	García de León 1969	Milpa x2	X	X		X		X					X	?		
Teenek	Laughlin 1969	Sugar mill	X	X		?	X	?	?	?	X	?	?	?		?
Totonac	Ichon 1969	Town hall	X			?	X	?	?	?	?	?	X	?		X
		Jail	X			?	X	?	?	?	?	?	X	?		X
		Church	X			?	X	?	?	?	?	?	X	?		X
		Cure	X			?	X	?	?	?	?	?	X	?		X
		Village	X			?	X	?	?	?	?	?	X	?		X
		Milpa	X	X		?	X	?	?	?	?	?	X	?		X

the protection of the place, as was clearly expressed by one of the ritual specialists: "That is how the blessings [of these spaces] are, they are very strong, it is so that their blessings serve and establish themselves for one year."[7] When several buildings belong to the same owner, it is not uncommon for several rituals to be organized concurrently, as Becquey observed it in Tyoki Pa', Salto de Agua, in 2016. The first part of the day was dedicated to a henhouse ritual, which resembled a minimalist version of a house inauguration. In fact, it shared all its main characteristics, that is, a buried deposit containing the same elements and in the same order as in the house, the presence of candles, the sprinkling of holy water and alcohol in the four directions and in the passageways (door), and, finally, a ritual speech respecting the same structure as the one pronounced for the house. The second part of the day aimed at reiterating the petition to the entities for the protection of the house attached to this henhouse. Since the house had recently been converted into a shop, a reiteration of the ritual was thus necessary. The house had already been consecrated when constructed: the center of the cement floor (*piso firme*) had collapsed, revealing a earlier buried deposit's pit. While the ceremony in the henhouse endorsed the delimitation of a new space, the ritual reiterated in the house was performed to renegotiate the protection requested on the occasion of a change in the function of the building. It corresponded, therefore, to an extension of the effective time span of the initial rite, the validity of which seems to be called into question by a change of use. In addition to presenting two distinct objectives and implying two different temporalities (inauguration and reiteration), both ceremonies were performed on the same day, sharing some ritual sequences such as the opening and closing ritual speeches. It is also noteworthy that, on a material level, the content of the deposits in the henhouse and in the house came from the same broth cooked with the flesh of the same sacrificial victims. Similar ritual protocols are also found outside the Maya area. Among the Totonac people, Ichon (1969, 255) mentions that the same ceremony is performed for either a town hall, a jail, or a church. On the other margins of Mesoamerica, Chapman (1985, 130, 154–55) describes *composturas* ceremonies for coffee plantations, clay quarries, and springs where the laundry takes place. The practice of caches is also attested to during the colonial period, showing a continuity of these rituals, although there is less known evidence of them for these centuries. For instance, in Lamanai, Pendergast (1998, 60) reports that various caches and even a stela were installed in the nave of an abandoned chapel.

For all the studied present-day populations, the erection of new human constructions—from large buildings such as churches up to small installations such as beehives—requires the implementation of the same type of ritual protocol. The importance given in these rituals to negotiations with the nonhuman entities in order to occupy a defined space, and especially the need to protect this space from various evils, is not limited to the construction of houses alone. These convergences, in terms of ritual modalities and expected objectives, is found not only for any kind of buildings but also for other anthropic spaces.

CULTIVATED FIELDS AND ANTHROPIZED SPACES

As seen in the previous section, inauguration rituals may be performed for every used space, even a plot or an entire village (6 rituals; figure 12.1, tables 12.1–12.3).

In theory, these rituals are supposed to be renewed cyclically to extend the time span of the protection agreement sealed with the entities. In Yucatán, it has been reported that the future repetition of rituals aiming at circumscribing and protecting domestic lands called *solares* should be announced as early as the initial ritual, although this is often forgotten (Pierrebourg and Ruz 2014, 179). Indeed, as in other Maya regions and as in the case of houses, these ceremonies are generally reiterated only in times of crisis: when people or animals fall sick or when the hives are not productive enough, that is to say, when the protection of the space conferred by the ritual actions no longer seems effective enough. Here, the repetition of the ritual explicitly corresponds to a compromise between humans and entities. The latter become accustomed to receiving offerings, sacrifices, food, and drink and threaten to be less benevolent in case of omission (Vapnarsky 2022; Vapnarsky and Le Guen 2011). Redfield and Villa Rojas (1934, 134), along with Ramos-Perez (2019), also signal that similar kinds of rituals, also called *hetz lum* or *looh* (*jeets' lu'um* or *looj*, using the modern Maya orthography), are performed on a much larger scale, that of the inhabited territory of the village. Tania Ramos-Perez (2019) states that it is a matter of both closing the space against the influence of evil winds and keeping it open to human traffic.

A parallel can be established between the pre-Hispanic patios around which ancient Maya domestic groups were organized in the residential areas and contemporary *solares*. At Chunchucmil in northwestern Yucatán, domestic groups are delimited by drystone walls (*albarradas*) and separated from each other by paths (Hutson, Magnoni, and Stanton 2008, 200). However, it is difficult to postulate the systematic existence of this kind of delimitations, since such spaces may not have been physically circumscribed or marked off by organic devices. Considering the extent of the excavations that would be necessary to provide evidence, it seems unrealistic to establish an excavation protocol in order to locate possible caches or traces of rituals delineating these patios, and even more illusory at the scale of the city.

We also find, in the Mesoamerican ethnographic record, the existence of the same inauguration ritual protocol for the delimitation of spaces, outside the residential areas (27 rituals; figure 12.1, tables 12.1–3). This is especially the case for rituals organized for crop fields, enclosures (unbuilt), and pastures. They too are supposed to signal the change of use of these spaces to the entities, but also to protect the animals or crops as well as the farmers. In Chol's lands, two examples are documented for spaces dedicated to cattle breeding. They are both very similar and present features highly convergent with those of the inauguration of the henhouse. The ritual is divided into three distinct phases. A first sequence takes place on an altar located in the house, a second in the corral, and a third, again on the altar of the house. This division of the ritual into several stages can be explained by different factors. The three ceremonies all begin with a ritual discourse addressed to the celestial entities. This sequence is always performed in the house or the church. The communication with these entities is reinforced by the presence of their representations (icons) on the altars. In a second stage, the ritual action occurs on the specific place to be protected, although it must be concluded in front of the altar in order to close the sequences of direct communication with the entities.

The same procedure is observed for the cultivated fields during the first rituals of the agricultural calendar that accompany the clearing or sowing of the milpa. Among the Ch'orti', for example, Wisdom (1940, 441–42) notes two successive sequences. The first one takes place in the field itself. Deposits are buried at the four corners, followed by the sacrifice of four turkeys and then another deposit made at the center. The second sequence is performed in the farmer's house; it involves the offering of candles on the domestic altar followed by a meal shared with the whole village.

Thompson (1930, 45) provides an excerpt from the prayer of the ritual he attended in Yucatán:

> Hey God! My mother! My father! Saint Mountain! Saint Hok! Saint Forest! [. . .]
> Well, I'm letting you know that I am bothering you. [. . .]. I am about to damage
> you [plural], I am about to work you [plural] for my existence. But I do not wish to
> be pursued by those among the wild animals, let it be snakes, whether scorpions, or
> wasps, that they make me suffer; let it be trees that fall upon me, whether the axes or
> the machetes that hit me. With all my heart, I'm about to work you.[8]

The owner of the milpa turns successively to the four cardinal directions while uttering his oration. His words address the recipients of the offerings by their name, including the Masters of Earth, which is warned of the nuisance that the coming agricultural work will cause. The ritual speech also sets out the various petitions from the owner of the field, who asks for protection against potentially hostile wildlife and the accidents inherent to field work. In contrast, Redfield and Villa Rojas (1934, 132) state that in Chan Kom, Yucatán, the *k'uilob k'áaxob* (deities of the forest), whose protection is invoked, are not thanked when a new square of land is cleared or an old one is recultivated but later, at harvest time. It is also worth noticing that because ethnographers have integrated and categorized these rituals as sequences within a broad cycle, that of the agricultural ritual calendar, they have tended to leave aside their prominent function as inaugurations of spaces to be used by humans.

For a long time, the identification of pre-Columbian fields has been a problem for archaeologists. However, various studies in the past, notably in Caracol but also the still ongoing Pacunam LiDAR Initiative project, have identified numerous hillside terraces or raised field systems served by canals in seasonal swamps (Canuto et al. 2018). The identification of milpas is more problematic. We have currently no knowledge of ancient agricultural ritual linked to the circumscription of the area to be cleared or recultivated.

DISCUSSION

The mirroring of the ethnographic data related to inauguration rituals in various Maya regions highlights the great operational similarity of the rites linked to the occupation of space in Mesoamerica (see tables 12.2–3). It appears that in each of the ethnic groups documented, a single ritual protocol with similar patterns and objectives has been implemented for the occupation and human use of different types of spaces. In some cases, the rituals even bear the same name as *looj* in Yucatán (Redfield and Villa Rojas 1934) and *compostura* among the Lencas (Chapman 1985). The analogy between both spaces (house and fields) is revealed by the words of a Chol ritual specialist: "It is this blessing that is realized today, this is how it is done for the house, this is how it is done for the pastures."[9] In fact, whereas Western thought tends to consider the administration of territory as a set of property rights over land, in Mesoamerica, the occupation of space requires, above all, to reach an agreement with nonhuman entities. These are, in fact, the real guardians or even, in some cases, the personifications of these spaces, with whom it is essential to come to terms during inauguration rituals. Traditionally, this cohabitation, and even codependence, requires constant negotiation between the different actors, human and nonhuman, beginning with this first ritual. First of all, an attempt must be made to establish a temporary authorization for the usufruct of this land on which a new human activity is established, and then to extend this agreement.

These rituals are often referred to as foundation or dedication rituals. With regard to rituals linked to the house, we had already avoided this categorization by using the term *inauguration* (Begel, Chosson, and Becquey 2022). The extension of the study to new spaces leads us today to new considerations. These rituals can be used to mark a change in the use of a space, as in the case of the construction of a new building or the delimitation, by clearing, of a new plot of land for cultivation. But they are also performed in the case of a change in the modalities of occupation, such as the arrival of a new member in the home (Guiteras Holmes 1961, 144–45), which extends their scope and time span beyond the inauguration. From this point of view, one of the examples encountered seems particularly noteworthy. Becquey (2017) reports a Chol ritual organized during the setting up of an office in a long since built and previously occupied apartment in the modern city of Palenque. This ritual scrupulously follows the same pattern as the one performed in the village during the construction of a house. Indeed, if, in most of the cases described, the first occurrence of these rituals corresponds to the construction of a new building, the Palenque ritual, among others, offers an example not of the inauguration of a new building but of the inauguration of a new modality of occupation. Today, most of the time, the abandonment of an occupied space is done without any ritual precautions, contrary to what archaeology seems to reveal to us for the Classic period (see Begel 2024). In these cases, rituals are unavoidable temporal milestones performed to (re)negotiate the conditions of the cohabitation between humans and nonhumans in the same space. Thus, as soon as one of the parties ceases to occupy a space, the ritual interaction no longer persists (Becquey and Chosson 2022).

In the corpus, it is possible to distinguish two different patterns that contrast the rituals for the residential area versus the remote spaces, with one exception, the Chol henhouse mentioned above. On the one hand, in our sample, rituals taking place in the "residential" area of the village only require a single ceremony performed within the space in need of protection. On the other hand, those performed outside this area, such as the delimitation and protection of pastures and milpas, imply a sequence of two or three ritual performances considered as complementary: the first on the altar of the house or the church—sometimes at the beginning and again at the end of the sequence—and the second within the place to be protected. The temporal sequence of the ritual thus shows a variation between those performed in the residential area and the others performed in different places through a multistage process.

In any of these cases, this ritual protocol is expected to be repeated cyclically. The inauguration ritual aims, above all, to anticipate repercussions deemed inevitable, linked to the dissatisfaction of nonhuman entities. Humans thus attempt to project into the future not only the existence of a new mode of use but also its protection, for an estimated time span of one to two years, depending on the ritual protocol concerned. However, this performative duration could be qualified as an "ideal" expectation, which has an eminently preventive, prophylactic role. In practice, most of the time, different factors imply an anticipated reiteration of the ritual, with a curative purpose.

Even more, the most common behavior is to wait for a problem to occur, such as illness, a witchcraft attack, a lack of productivity—when the imbalance in the relationship between humans and nonhumans is sufficiently manifest and harmful—to urge the reiteration of the ritual. In Yucatan, verification procedures at the end of rituals such as the *loj kaaj*, which aims at protecting the whole locality, may occur. Thanks to his *sáastun* (divinatory crystals), the ritual specialist gets visual indexes of the good progress and the effectiveness of the ritual, which also help him formulate a recommendation relative to when it should be repeated, for instance, every year or every two years (see Ramos-Perez 2019, 35). The first ritual is here seen as a commitment; the entities get used to it and wait for precise dates, the repetition of performances, deposits, and sacrifices. But even in this case, we have no evidence that this recommendation is being followed, and the setting of a ritual is frequently subject to the hazards of what is possible and of what suddenly becomes an urgent necessity (especially following illnesses). Moreover, the Yucatec (Fabienne de Pierrebourg, personal communication, 2018) and others consider that all land has, in absolute terms, already been used one day and that the ancient inhabitants had accustomed the entities to receive drinks and meals (Vapnarsky 2022; Vapnarsky and Le Guen 2011). For the inauguration of *temazcals* among the Tzotzil and Tseltal, there is even a specific ceremony, a variant of the inauguration rite, in case the latter had failed, meaning if diseases appear or if the fireplace does not heat up sufficiently for good sweating (Groark 1997).

With regard to the use and occupation of space by humans or their herds, in most cases, it would therefore seem that the repetition of these rituals depends essentially on the gap observed between the expected and the effective time spans. Thus, relations with entities are more generally marked by uncertainty: the negative consequences are almost certain, while the effectiveness of countermeasures remains undetermined. In Chol ritual discourses, for instance, the only words associated with the future—indicated by the sequence of words "tomorrow, the day after tomorrow, in three days," a list that can extend to "in five days"—are entirely made up of petitions that are all marked by volition, wish, or hope but never by certainty (Becquey 2017).

The rituals made for the milpa scrupulously respect the agricultural calendar, being systematically renewed following the duration of the life cycle of the crops concerned. Since the ritual also aims to protect the seeds and guarantee their good growth, it is of no surprise that it must be repeated at each new planting.

CONCLUSION

Within the diversity of Mesoamerican cosmovisions, humans are often called to live together with a great number of nonhuman entities of different kinds. In order to ensure a good life, the former may multiply the rituals according to modalities (temporal, spatial, protocol, etc.) that vary according to the entities solicited and the objectives (good harvest, protection, auspices, favors, etc.). Among these, the rituals linked to the more or less permanent occupation of a space are worthy of interest.

Some specific rituals are directed to various buildings and spaces, such as houses, mills, milpas, and even entire villages, and are repeated according to cyclical time spans or more circumstantial events. All of them are linked to a new occupation or a change of use of a space by humans or to the need for renegotiation with nonhuman entities. These similar patterns, both in the ritual protocol in its material translation and the metadiscourses that makes them explicit, lead to the assertion of the existence of a broader emic category encompassing all the rituals linked to the human occupation of space. Lacking access to the native's metadiscourses, this hypothesis could be of greater interest for archaeologists who find at each excavation campaign new caches for which it is not always easy to propose a meaning. The effectiveness of the initial ritual is presumed to extend only for an estimated duration. In the end, only one meaningful variation of the modern rituals was highlighted: the one concerning space inside versus outside the urban area. In the first case, the ritual takes place only in the new building. For remote places, the protocol is composed of several sequences performed, in the field or pasture to be protected and in the house of its owner or in the church or both.

The cross-referencing of data allowed us to highlight similarities in rituals that, until now, have only been studied in a separate way. The review of ethnographic data has revealed similarities in rituals that were once studied in isolation. Despite spatial variations, our examination of these rituals, both materially and conceptually, leads to considering them as forming a single paradigm. This result allows us to open up new interpretations of archaeological data, especially by taking into consideration their similarities of content, layout, and maybe intent, among them and with ethnographic data. The hypothesis that most rituals related to space share a similar paradigm (declined in time and space) would be reinforced by the collection of a larger corpus, and gain from being complemented by the analysis of emic categorizations. In any case, the substantial corpus studied in this chapter, and the particularly marked convergence of modern ritual protocols and metadiscourse that we observed, confirms the existence of a common base for Mesoamerican inauguration rituals.

NOTES

1. We use the expression "inauguration" of spaces throughout the text, to distinguish this ritual action from "instauration" and from what is commonly considered as "foundation" by archaeologists, in opposition to abandonment deposits (Begel, Chosson, and Becquey 2022). The term *inauguration* seems better-suited to describe various rituals marking the new use of a space, the focus of our chapter, whereas "instauration" as used in Breton, Chosson, and Monod Becquelin (this volume) refers to the broader process of creating and setting up a new space-time throughout a more encompassing cosmo-historical ritual.

2. The expression "occupation of space" marks the difference here with other uses of space in the forest, for example hunting or collecting firewood, which are not subject to the same ritual precautions.

3. The quintipartite cosmogram is particularly illustrated in the iconography since the Preclassic until the Post-Classic (Mathews and Garber 2004, 49).

4. See Begel, Chosson, and Becquey (2022) for an extended discussion about this ritual materiality.

5. It is worth, however, distinguishing between the living character of the house (a conception shared by some groups in the Mayan highlands) and animation ritually conveyed (see Begel, Chosson, and Becquey 2022).

6. This assumption is based on three caches of the Muul complex in Tikal, which in fact are not stratified. Nevertheless, the cosmogram is clearly visible in Tikal's newly identified ritual complex, Sak B; see Begel 2020.

7. "*Che' b'ahche' añ ibendisyoñ, weñ tsäts, cha'añ mi'k'äñ tyi chuñtyäl tyi hump'e hab' hihiñ ibendisyoñi*" (Becquey 2008).

8. This literal translation has been revised by C. Becquey, based on Thompson's transcript: "*Ay Díos, in na, in yum, Santo Witz, Santo Hoq, Santo Txe. [. . .]. Alebe tan in tzek a welte tan in tuksik a wol. [. . .]. Bel in kah in qaskun-tetx, bel in kah in meya-tetx tial in kuxlebal. Pero ma in qati ka u t'ul-en maxqui ti baaltxeil, maaxtowa kun, maaxtowa sinaan, maaxtowa xux ka u yakunten, maaxtowa txe ka u putxen, maaxtowa baat, maaxtowa maska ka u txuken. Etel tulakal in wol bel in kah in meya tetx.*"

9. "*Hiñi bendisyoni mubä ik'ähñe wa'liyi, che' mi'mehle cha'añ otyoty, // che' mi'mehle cha'añ potrero*" (Becquey 2008).

REFERENCES

Aoyama, Kazuo, Takeshi Inomata, Flory Pinzón, and Juan Manuel Palomo. 2017. "Polished Greenstone Celt Caches from Ceibal: The Development of Maya Public Rituals." *Antiquity* 91: 701–17.

Ariel de Vidas, Anath, Aline Hémond, and Anuschka van 't Hooft. 2014. "Dar de comer para convivir." *Anthropology of Food*, special number S9. http://journals.openedition.org/aof/7643.

Baudez, Claude-François. 2002. *Une histoire de la religion des Mayas*. Paris: Albin Michel.

Becquey, Cédric. 2008. Fieldnotes among the Choles. Unpublished notes.

Becquey, Cédric. 2016. Fieldnotes among the Chontales. Unpublished notes.

Becquey, Cédric. 2017. "Rituel d'inauguration de maison chez les Chols: Une étude ethnolinguistique." In *(Re)Fonder: Les modalités du (re)commencement dans le temps et dans l'espace*, edited by P. Gervais-Lambony, F. Hurlet, and I. Rivoal, 243–58. Nanterre: Editions de Boccard.

Becquey, Cédric, and Marie Chosson. 2022. "Deserted Ruins? Maya Tseltal and Ch'ol Engagement with Salient Spaces." In *Living Ruins: Native Engagements with Past*

Materialities in Mesoamérica, Amazonia and the Andes, edited by P. Erikson and V. Vapnarsky, 104–23. Louisville: University Press of Colorado.

Begel, Johann. 2020. "Dépôts rituels mayas et séquences architecturales dans l'Acropole Nord de Tikal aux périodes préclassique et classique." PhD diss., University Paris I–Panthéon Sorbonne, Paris.

Begel, Johann. 2024. "Characterizing and Classifying Mayan Ritual Deposits." *Estudios de Cultura Maya* 64 (Autumn–Winter): 97–128.

Begel, Johann. N.d. *Special Deposits and Ritual Complexes in Tikal: Caches, Fires, Feasts and Termination*. Forthcoming Tikal Report No. 35A. Philadelphia: University of Pennsylvania Museum.

Begel, Johann, Marie Chosson, and Cédric Becquey. 2022. "Materiality and Agentivity of Structure Building Rituals: An Ethno-Archaeological Approach." In *Materializing Ritual Practices*, edited by R. Joyce and L. Johnson, 144–61. Boulder: University Press of Colorado.

Boteler-Mock, Shirley, ed. 1998. *The Sowing and the Dawning: Termination, Dedication, and Transformation in the Archaeological and Ethnographic Record of Mesoamerica*. Albuquerque: University of New Mexico Press.

Cabarrús, Carlos Rafael. 1979. *La cosmovisión k'ekchí en proceso de cambio*. El Salvador: UCA Editores.

Calligeris, Catherine. 1999. "Fonction et signification des dépôts de fondation mayas, dans les basses terres, à la période classique." PhD diss., Paris I–Panthéon Sorbonne, Paris.

Canuto, Marcello, Francisco Estrada-Belli, Thomas G. Garrison, Stephen D. Houston, Mary Jane Acuña, Milan Kováč, et al. 2018. "Ancient Lowland Maya Complexity as Revealed by Airborne Laser Scanning of Northern Guatemala." *Science* 361 (6409). https://doi.org/10.1126/science.aau0137.

Chapman, Anne. 1985. *Ritos agrarios y tradición oral de los lencas de Honduras*. Los Hijos del copal y la candela, vol. 1. Mexico City: Universidad Nacional Autónoma de México.

Christenson, Allen. 2010. "Maize Was Their Flesh: Ritual Feasting in the Maya Highlands." In *Pre-Columbian Foodways: Interdisciplinary Approaches to Food, Culture, and Markets in Ancient Mesoamerica*, edited by John Staller and Michael Carrasco, 577–600. New York: Springer.

Figuerola Pujol, Helios. 2010. "De Sacrificio y Sacrificios en la comunidad Tzeltal de San Juan Evangelista Cancuc." In *El Sacrificio humano en la tradición religiosa mesoamericana*, edited by L. López Luján and G. Olivier, 536–46. Mexico City: Instituto Nacional de Antropología e Historia, Instituto de Investigaciones Históricas / Universidad Nacional Autónoma de México.

Fought, John. 1972. *Chorti (Mayan) Texts*. Vol. 1. Edited by Sarah Fought. Philadelphia: University of Pennsylvania Press.

García de León G., Antonio. 1969. *El universo de lo sobrenatural entre los nahuas de Pajapan, Veracruz*. Estudios de cultura Nahuatl VIII. Mexico: Instituto de Investigaciones Historicas, Universidad Nacional Autónoma de México.

Groark, Kevin. 1997. "To Warm the Blood, to Warm the Flesh: The Role of the Steambath in Highland Maya (Tzeltal-Tzotzil) Ethnomedicine." *Journal of Latin American Lore* 20 (1): 3–96.

Guiteras Holmes, Calixta. 1961. *Los peligros del alma: Visión del mundo de un Tzotzil*. Mexico City: Fondo de Cultura Económica.

Hutson, Scott, Aline Magnoni, and Travis Stanton. 2008. "Landscape Transformations and Changing Perceptions at Chunchucmil, Yucatán." In *Ruins of the Past: The Use and Perception of Abandoned Structures in the Maya Lowlands*, edited by A. Magnoni and T. Stanton, 193–222. Boulder: University Press of Colorado.

Ichon, Alain. 1969. *La Religion des Totonaques de la Sierra*. Paris: Éditions du Centre National de la Recherche Scientifique.

Laughlin, Robert. 1969. "The Huastec." In *Handbook of Middle American Indians*, vol. 7, edited by R. Wauchope, 298–311. Austin: University of Texas Press.

Lipp, Frank. 1991. *The Mixe of Oaxaca: Religion, Ritual, and Healing*. Austin: University of Texas Press.

Lok, Rossana. 1987. "The House as a Microcosm. Some Cosmic Representations in a Mexican Indian Village." In *The Leiden Tradition in Structural Anthropology: Essays in Honor of P. E. de Josselin de Jong*, edited by R. de Ridder and J. A. J. Karremans, 211–33. Leiden: Brill.

Lupo, Alessandro. 1995. *La tierra nos escucha: La cosmología de los nahuas a través de las súplicas rituales*. Mexico City: Dirección General de Publicaciones del Consejo Nacional para la Cultura y las Artes / Instituto Nacional Indigenista.

Mathews, Jennifer, and James Garber. 2004. "Models of Cosmic Order: Physical Expression of Sacred Space among the Ancient Maya." *Ancient Mesoamerica* 15: 49–59.

Moholy-Nagy, Hattula, and William Coe. 2008. *Tikal Report No. 27a: The Artifacts of Tikal: Ornamental and Ceremonial Artifacts and Unworked Material*. Philadelphia: University of Pennsylvania Museum of Archaeology and Anthropology.

Monaghan, John. 1998. "Dedication: Ritual or Production?" In *The Sowing and the Dawning*, edited by S. Boteler-Mock, 47–53. Albuquerque: University of New Mexico Press.

Nash, June. 1970. *In the Eyes of the Ancestors: Belief and Behavior in a Maya Community*. New Haven, CT: Yale University Press.

Nondédéo, Philippe, et al., eds. 2010–23. *Informes del Proyecto Petén Norte—Naachtun*. 12 vols. Guatemala City: Instituto De Antropología E Historia de Guatemala.

Pendergast, David. 1998. "Intercessions with the Gods: Caches and Their Significance at Altun Ha and Lamanai, Belize." In *The Sowing and the Dawning*, edited by S. Boteler-Mock, 54–63. Albuquerque: University of New Mexico Press.

Pierrebourg, Fabienne de, and Mario Humberto Ruz, eds. 2014. *Nah, otoch: Concepción, factura y atributos de la morada maya*. Mérida: Universidad Nacional Autónoma de México / Instituto de Investigaciones Filológicas.

Pitarch Ramón, Pedro. 1996. *Ch'ulel: Una etnografía de las almas tzeltales*. Mexico City: Fondo de Cultura Económica.

Ramos-Perez, Tania. 2019. "El giro: Cerrar y abrir el cuerpo y el espacio, una etnografía del movimiento en un pueblo maya de Quintana Roo, México." Master's thesis, Universidad Nacional Autónoma de México, Mexico City.

Redfield, Robert, and Alfonso Villa Rojas. 1934. *Chan Kom: A Maya Village*. Washington, DC: Carnegie Institution of Washington.

Thompson, Eric. 1930. *Ethnology of the Mayas of Southern and Central British Honduras*. Chicago: Field Museum of Natural History.

Vapnarsky, Valentina. 2022. "Maya Living Ruins: The Hidden Places of Interlocking Temporalities." In *Living Ruins: Native Engagements with Past Materialities in Mesoamérica, Amazonia and the Andes*, edited by Philippe Erikson and Valentina Vapnarsky, 74–103. Boulder: University Press of Colorado.

Vapnarsky, Valentina, and Olivier Le Guen. 2011. "The Guardians of Space and History: Understanding Ecological and Historical Relations of the Contemporary Yucatec Maya to Their Landscape." In *Ecology, Power, and Religion in Maya Landscapes*, edited by C. Isendahl and B. Liljefors Persson, 191–206. Markt Schwaben, Germany: Verlag Anton Saurwein.

Vogt, Evon. 1979. *Ofrendas para los dioses: Análisis simbólico de rituales zinacantecos*. Mexico City: Fondo de Cultura Económica.

Vogt, Evon. 1998. "Zinacanteco Dedication and Termination Rituals." In *The Sowing and the Dawning*, edited by S. Boteler-Mock, 21–30. Albuquerque: University of New Mexico Press.

Wisdom, Charles. 1940. *The Chorti Indians of Guatemala*. Chicago: University of Chicago Press.

13

Monuments and Mounds as Time

A Brief Argument for the Isthmo-Colombian Area

ALEXANDER GEURDS

This chapter provides a discussion on ritual spaces in the Isthmo-Colombian Area and the possible relation to the human awareness of time, highlighting, for example, the importance of the long-lasting character of monumental spaces of earth and stone, and how periodic communal ritual may have helped assure regional integration. Using the two examples of stone sculpture and mounded sites, I argue that the human past in the Isthmo-Colombian Area shows evidence for ritual action that establishes relationships with the inherently unpredictable features of the surrounding world. Ritual actions help order time and space, producing a lasting material legacy that provides a sense of past and present.

The area is connected to the edges of the Mesoamerican culture area and several regions of cultural practices that merge in parts of Colombia and western Venezuela. In relative contrast to Mesoamerican studies, archaeological scholarship here has entertained a significant debate on how to conceptually understand the area, a discussion not repeated here (for overviews, see Geurds 2018; Hoopes and Fonseca 2003; Sheets 1992). Earlier archaeological syntheses of the area have tended to draw qualitative developmental comparisons to both Mesoamerica and the central Andes, resulting in the signaling of differences in societal complexity, and the apparently fragmented connectedness within the area overall. Often sketched from the neighboring perspective of Mesoamerican studies, such comparisons defined the area as culturally static and merely a receiver of Mesoamerican cultural traits.

https://doi.org/10.5876/9781646426829.c013

Mesoamerican patterns of interregional interaction link into southern Central America from the Middle Formative period onward and become more sustained from the Epiclassic period onward (Geurds 2023), featuring the movement of groups from central Mexico into Pacific coastal regions of present-day Nicaragua and Costa Rica. Equally, along the coastlines of the Caribbean Sea, merchants— including (Putún?) Maya—traveled up and down in canoes, exchanging materials and objects.

Overall, the many regions and subregions of the Isthmo-Colombian Area describe a mix of particular and shared histories, going back to the Terminal Pleistocene and Early Holocene periods. What seems to be a general pattern across the area is the long-lasting trajectories of organizing social life through villages and other forms of small-scale settlements. Traces of urbanism are completely absent, but energy investments in monumentally built structures are certainly not. Equally, developed writing systems are absent, but figurative and abstract carvings on rock are widespread, providing semiotic signposting of geographical features of various kinds. Subsistence strategies vary, describing a mixed agriculture based on root crops and palm nut combined by corn but seemingly less intensive than Mesoamerican examples of raised fields, and retention terraces. Forms of leadership seem to concentrate around itinerant chiefly behavior, including ritualized contests with surrounding communities. Another contrast with Mesoamerica is the dearth of historical sources on the Indigenous societies as well as the starker disintegration of Indigenous presence. These factors, combined with the irregular coverage of archaeological research across the area, make discussions on Indigenous timekeeping practices incidental at best, and this study may be one of the first to discuss it more centrally.

FRAMING RITUAL IN THE ISTHMO-COLOMBIAN AREA

In drawing on Renfrew's definition, ritual is understood as describing those actions and practices that address the forces and energy of the surrounding world (Renfrew 2007). The understanding of ritual contexts is the preferred template on which to reconstruct how people, animals, landscapes, and materials cohabited. When we look at how ritual is discussed in scholarship, an emphasis on political ideology and worldview is apparent, with an intensified focus for the period from the start of the first millennium AD up to the arrival of the Spanish in the early sixteenth century.

Following Rappaport, the group experience of a ritual is one of its key components (Rappaport 1999), and it is also important that those witnessing it will be impacted accordingly, thereby representing a window of opportunity for political agents. However, ritual practices are also a holistic aspect of society, one that political leadership is likely to collectively reflect rather than exclusively administrate. Rituals also include a confirmation of the awareness surrounding the passage of time (Bloch 1977; Lucas 2004). As rich and fruitful as it has proven to use ritual contexts and objects as a means for recognizing ideology, doing so bypasses viewing ritual as an active practice.

This emphasis on the historicity of the ritual process is important here, as it acknowledges the informative potential of archaeological materials and the—sometimes unexpected—ways in which societies encounter their surrounding world. Reflecting processes of learning and experimenting, it is in the confrontation with the world that intelligent understandings are created, thereby inviting ritual practices to moderate the challenges encountered in pre-Hispanic life. I would argue that this is what archaeology recovers the material traces of: the sedimented history of attempts at enabling cyclical continuity or the preventing of undesirable transformations.

In part, this approach to ritual acknowledges the Durkheimian tradition of regarding ritual as a codifying mechanism to provide and ensure moral order (Durkheim [1915] 1965), but it also argues to see ritual as a process of making sense of time, rather than merely a method to reinforce societal norms. Developing over the long term in human history, ritual structures take up an active and central position in how people relate to their surrounding world. This active role is also echoed in archaeological work on ritual elsewhere (Bradley 2005; Joyce 2008). Seen as such, ritualization becomes central to making sense of time and "setting apart" some actions in daily life from others, awarding them special status (Bell 1992; Joyce, this volume).

Following recent work by Keane, ritual can be considered a semiotic technology in service of a moral order in society (Keane 2016, 200–202). Such an order will indeed involve politics and leadership, but it would be shortsighted to equate politics with morality. Rather, we can understand ritual to create and reinforce communal awareness. Such rituals lead to what Webb Keane refers to as a "historical object," characterized by a certain amount of persistence and durability and capable of serving as a long-term referent to the passage of time. This is of interest to an archaeology that attempts to understand ritual process through material traces. Such historical objects, Keane explains, may exist along different scales; they can be a single thing (e.g., a sculpture), entail a spatial location (e.g., a communal space), or define an entire cultural landscape. Along all these scales, Keane's historical objects are capable of indexically referencing the moral order, and doing so through their different affordances. Over time, these historical objects may then allow for radically different views and ideas.

Their indexical properties make such historical objects prime candidates for communities to interrogate and criticize them, and for a collective awareness of the deep and more recent past to be cultivated through ritual action. This action, in turn, needs to be flexible to the extent of being able to join elements of foundational understandings of ahistorical primordial times, with the historical actors involved in the ritual at any given moment.

Awareness of time and ways of timekeeping are codependent on social practices in communities, which in turn are formed by the constraining potential of surrounding landscapes (Gosden 1994). This means that time awareness stands in relation to landscape affordances. In other words, how people engaged with environments codetermines their notions of temporality, thereby linking the particularities of lived surroundings and the understanding of time. This corresponds to ideas of how Isthmo-Colombian societies understood the world to work, in its broadest ontological definition.

These ontological matters are complex to grasp through archaeology, but we cannot bypass the features of surrounding environments that seem "animate" even to Western eyes. This animism awards landscapes a certain delicacy, to which human responses must be purposeful, appropriate, and timely. If we accept the premise that landscapes consist of animate features, in line with many Indigenous ontologies, then it is reasonable to assume that most Isthmo-Colombian societies engaged with those environments not through a set of static, orthodox rituals but by acknowledging the contingent and unpredictable causal relation between their intentionality and these animate surroundings (see also Ferrero Acosta 1981).

TIME IN RITUAL, AUTHORITY, AND ART

Variations in later pre-Hispanic history are plentiful, as is the geographical diversity that splits between more wet tropical forests, Pacific savannas, and various other regional ecologies. Indeed, it is perilous to generalize about this area of the Americas. Studies are often focused around two extremes, one being the small-scale focus, to highlight subsistence strategies and the economic potential of a given microregion, and the other arguing for an area-wide shared cultural ontology, often through semiotic object analysis and largely disconnected from physical surroundings.

One of the problems, then, of discussing time in the pre-Hispanic past of this area is the tidy scholarly disconnect between these different scales of study—one in which patterns are highlighted and processes are left in shadows. These scales were, of course, not separated, and lived lives were experienced on a day-to-day basis, reflecting on the past and considering the future (see Bintliff 1991, in particular Braudel's Annales School approach for archaeology). Such daily work and action translated into traditions and practices, and those, in turn, were partially preserved over generations.

When considering how long-term awareness was instilled in people, then, stone objects are lingering protagonists. The pronounced focus on stone sculptures in this part of the Americas allows us to see their long-term relevance and societal role, which lasts up to the present day, enmeshed in heritage narratives (Geurds 2011). What would such a process look like, however, when explored for the decidedly nonliterary Isthmo-Colombian communities prior to—or in some cases, well beyond—the arrival of Spanish colonizers?

Widely distributed across this research area are numerous notational practices, including semiotic strategies revolving around motifs that are pecked, carved, painted, and sculpted across a range of media. Nothing, however, seems to constitute anything close to the registering of history. Did the absence of materialized historical recordings somehow impact the way time and space were viewed by local groups? For example, does material culture reflect in some way how knowledge is preserved and transferred between humans? If we accept that objects have such mediating and generative powers to shape human experience (in the sense of Gell 1998; Gosden 2005), then what does the patterning mean recognized in, for example, the highly complex and ambiguous forms and motifs on material culture across this area?

Sources of Authority

An indication of personalized political power are forms of social valuables, prominently including, but not restricted to, gold, polished stone, ground stone objects, and specialized forms of pottery (Quilter and Hoopes 2003). Practices of social valuables are often invoked in discussions on ritual. These rare objects, coming from far-off places, are then deemed to have served as prestige items in the hands of knowledgeable political leaders (Helms 1979). Arguments around personal wealth are also mobilized in these discussions (Lange 1992).

How individual ritual specialists related to presumed political agents, or if indeed they are societal roles united in one single individual, is less often discussed (but see Hoopes 2005, 31–32). Part of the problem in discerning different forms of Indigenous authority resides in the blanket use of the term *cacique* by the Spanish colonial administration to recognize Indigenous persons having some form of authority. It is quite likely that different individuals, male and female, shared aspects of communal authority across the area, as work by Eugenia Ibarra has also argued convincingly (see Ibarra 2003, 384).

Historic-era descriptions among the Talamanca in southern Costa Rica suggest that magical knowledge was acquired through undergoing prolonged training to demonstrate skills and taxonomic knowledge (Ibarra 2003, 396–97). For the early Colonial period, this relationship of specialized knowledge and authority has also been argued for parts of Caribbean Panama, as shown in Helms's study on the societal structure of the Cuna (central Panama) using ethnohistoric, ethnographic, and archaeological data (Helms 1979, 104–28). Such authority, then, seems to have been based on experience and expertise, perhaps combined with proven courage and success in specific tasks. What these studies show is that detailed knowledge of regional physical surroundings, either based on experience, kinship ties, or an innate gift, was a key source of authority.

Based on the writings of the Spanish chroniclers Fernández de Oviedo y Valdéz and Andagoya, we see that individuals trained in such ontological expertise would develop into roles of either prognosticators or healers (Howe 1974, 224–29). They were regarded as expertly suited to reflect on matters affecting a community more widely. Such individuals were charged with responsibilities such as predicting weather patterns and the availability of game for hunting, based on their intimate knowledge to interpret local landscapes.

For the late pre-Hispanic period, relations between the dispersed communities were defined by both cooperation and competition and conflict, as is shown by a combination of settlement pattern data, early colonial historic reference, and an iconographic emphasis on headhunting (Hoopes 2007). Spanish chroniclers shared their surprise when observing this, at first glance, odd combination of working together and ceremonial warring, defying late Medieval European under-standings of societal relations and diplomacy (e.g., Fernández Guardia 1908). Not unlike parts of Classic and Postclassic Mesoamerica, however, warring and raiding were forms of temporally structured and ritualized engagement, and a key aspect of social organization to defuse or settle conflicts or competitions. Iconography alludes frequently to this, but archaeological traces lack in detail to properly appreciate local dynamics.

One ethnographic example, echoing such intercommunity ritual competition, is the description of the *balsería* event taking place among the Ngäbe currently living at the national frontier of Caribbean Costa Rica and Panama. A biannual intercommunity festival with pre-Hispanic roots, the *balsería* centers on ritualized actions to demonstrate physical strength by prolonged whacking of one's opponent with a stick of balsa wood (figure 13.1). These multiday events included the preparation of food for visitors, who come in from far and wide, and the organiza-tion of games where participants demonstrate strength and agility. While these competitive events are occasions to accrue individual prestige, it is important to bear in mind that this is mostly an egalitarian society with a dispersed settlement pattern (Young 1971, 1976).

Figure 13.1. Photograph, taken by Samuel K. Lothrop (1948–1953), of the *balsería* ceremonial contest among the Guaymí (Caribbean Panama), showing the moment in which a man aims at the legs of an opponent (courtesy of the Peabody Museum of Archaeology and Ethnology, Harvard University, 2004.1.398.35).

TIME IN OBJECTS

Associated to these social valuables is an additional source of information on temporal awareness, channeled through iconographic studies. Such work stresses the importance of ritual specialists engaging in shamanic practices, often found represented in various stages of abstraction on pottery, metal, and stonework and revolving around animistic human-animal relationships.

From AD 300 onward, various developments in form and motifs are documented for individual regions of this part of the Americas, with the best stylistic granularity in central Panama, but also extending across the poorly named Darien Gap into present-day Colombia (see Bray 1984). Despite stylistic development, a constricted range of animals often features on these materials (Cooke 1984), which leads to understandings of such art as being indicative of commonalities of ideas related to worldview and ritual. This is also why I consider a concept such as "art" suitable for the objects in question here, as they have a capacity to visually impact beholders in a range of ways. In other words, how this art is *received* is a central concern, wherein such visually impressive objects are either informative of ritual knowledge, related to kinship systems, or can simply be seen as offering the affordance to be appreciated in quite different ways.

This visible presence of metal and metalworking practices made it a central feature of people's lives, one not easily summarized by equating, for example, gold pendants to icons of identity or power (see also Briggs 1989). This form of art is not associated to a presumed people, in contrast to how perhaps "Maya art" is used in scholarship. The notion of "Chibchan culture" was put forward in the formative period of culture area thinking, alongside that of Mesoamerican culture (Kirchhoff 1943), but it remains difficult to consider how that can be understood through social practices.[1]

The combination of a wide range of diachronic and synchronic stylistic connections (see Fonseca 1998), and the lack of a larger sociopolitical unity, has given rise to interpretations that argue for intermediate coherence (for a critical overview, see Sheets 1992). In such area debates, a particular position is taken up by the idea of a "diffuse unity." Hoopes and Fonseca argue that "[iconographic] themes persisted for more than fifteen hundred years in some parts of the region. While it is difficult to attach specific meanings to these themes, and it is important to keep in mind that similarities in form may not signal similarities in meaning, this thematic focus in gold work and other media suggests a considerable ideological coherence of thought in the area" (Hoopes and Fonseca 2003, 64).

Hoopes and Fonseca identify six themes, cross-cutting across forms of material culture. Themes including the "Meditative Shaman," the "double-headed saurian," or the "Crocodile Man" are argued to be linked to past oral history, perhaps also spoken about in ritual settings or as ritual action (Hoopes and Fonseca 2003) (figure 13.2). As such, these objects and their forms and motifs are viewed to help sustain and recall primordial narratives, perhaps in combination with public display, and ritual actions such as singing and dancing. Beyond singular iconographic identification, a concern could also be the ambiguous stylistic nature of these objects, and the abovementioned sensory triggers entailed in their handling and display.

The core of objects featuring in discussions on Isthmo-Colombian ritual is relatively circumscribed, invariably appearing in exhibition catalogues, but where this core fades into its edges is more difficult to discuss. What constitutes an object as forming part of the "iconographic context" of prehistoric Central America is not easily determined. This is equally true for the material in which these objects are made. While clay, stone, and metalwork might be central and most voluminous, shell, sperm whale teeth, wood, and textile also participated. And these also are the product of earlier historical legacies of Western collecting and appreciations of aesthetics. The historical nature of what is seen as iconic here is, therefore, defined by

Figure 13.2. Gold pendant (Caribbean Costa Rica) of a frontally depicted anthropomorphic figure. Note the internal symmetry of the top and bottom brackets, showing double-headed saurians (courtesy Metropolitan Museum of Art).

contestable boundaries; a feature which is not unique to the archaeology of Central America.

The question of time is also activated in Isthmo-Colombian art, through the visual appreciation of these objects. This is often far from direct, indeed sometimes following a visual trajectory. There is a sensory negotiation in these objects that balances between what is separated in form, or perhaps better perceived as joined, as well as 3D objects, such as the flying-panel metates that simply do not allow for instantaneous appreciation (figure 13.3). Such visually complex objects also may be considered magical in terms of the effect on the beholder, harboring "technology of enchantment" (Garrow and Gosden 2012, 25–26, following Gell).

One could argue that this renders these objects as process; they offer the beholder different affordances, thereby simultaneously generating both identification and

Figure 13.3. Ceremonial grinding stone (Caribbean Costa Rica), showing internal visual complexity of interwoven themes and the potential for "enchantment" (courtesy Metropolitan Museum of Art, photograph taken by Kim Richter)

ambiguity. While some themes predominate, a straightforward iconography is not the entire story with these artistic objects. Following Keane's notion on historical objects, there are indeed rules of iconography, through certain explicit features, but they are also "historical" in that they are likely to have been subjected to revision and debate, perhaps led by ritual specialists.

Most arguments are derived from portable materials, many of which were deposited in funerary contexts. Exceptions are studies focusing on the volcanic landscape of western Panama or studies on procession in the Arenal region of Costa Rica (Sheets 2011).[2] There are reliable ethnographic references to animistic beliefs referencing natural features and phenomena, including mountains, volcanoes, lakes and rivers, rock formations, and tropical forest animals particular to the Isthmo-Colombian Area (Halbmayer 2020). How these beliefs result in regional notions of sacred landscape still merits further study, however. Quite rare are studies observing ritual action based on static archaeological features, prominently, rock art and monumental stonework.

Holmberg's emphasis on rock art makes the point that the stone traces of past ritual action are resistant and, in a way, physically immutable (Holmberg 2005). Interestingly, cases where rock art is intentionally altered in prehistory are extremely rare. This, I think, is meaningful, as it speaks to the continued, if muted, presence of such past traces in the landscapes of Central America (for an overview on regional rock art, see Künne and Strecker 2004).

Rock art is an apt avenue for discussing the human-environment links, and to consider the role of time and change among the diverse communities in Central America. Ritualized "marking" through rock art may have been one element in leaving permanent marks in a landscape, but there is a more long-term concern that needs attention as well. The human engagement with the tropical forest– and savannah-type geographies of Central America (to be sure, difficult to lump together) took form from the early Holocene onward, gradually creating dependencies between plants, animals, and humans on a range of often small-scale and complex ecosystems, managed through knowledge on temporality and expressed through ritual actions.

This long-term presence points also to a spatially stable emergence of historical ecological relations in this area. Indigenous societies shaped changing environments to accommodate agricultural production, but also engaged with, and were conscious of, the delicate reliance on environmental events, including tornadoes, river flooding, volcanic eruptions, and tectonic events. The insights gleaned from the different temporal scales of human-environment relations, from seasonal to sporadic but disastrous sudden changes, were integrated in preventative ritual practices.

These mitigating practices center largely around arguments stressing animistic beliefs and the negotiations of the relations to the wider world along cosmological principles, which in turn are the domain of shamanic ritual specialists. Largely precluded in such discussions are the instances in which places such as El Gavilán and Aguas Buenas are gradually created, where knowledge of the past is recollected and where cultural memories are thus created, in large part also through the bodily practices involved in sculpting, dragging, and heaping (in the sense of Bradley 2002; van Dyke and Alcock 2003).

DRAGGING AND HEAPING: TWO EXAMPLES OF MONUMENTAL WORK

Stone sculpture has a noticeable presence across the area. Obviously, this is partly due to the durable nature of stone. Density and mass help to keep it in place. But that may not be the only reason for the sculptural frequency. Occurring from the Bay Islands of Honduras down to parts of central and southern Colombia, practices of crafting stone sculpture and using unworked monoliths are ubiquitous (for overviews, see Bruhns 1992; Haberland 1973). In the central lowlands of Caribbean Nicaragua, one such location, El Gavilán, urges a consideration of the human work involved in the creation of such ceremonial sites centering on stone, enquiring into its societal use and long-term presence (figure 13.4). Approximately 70 kilometers

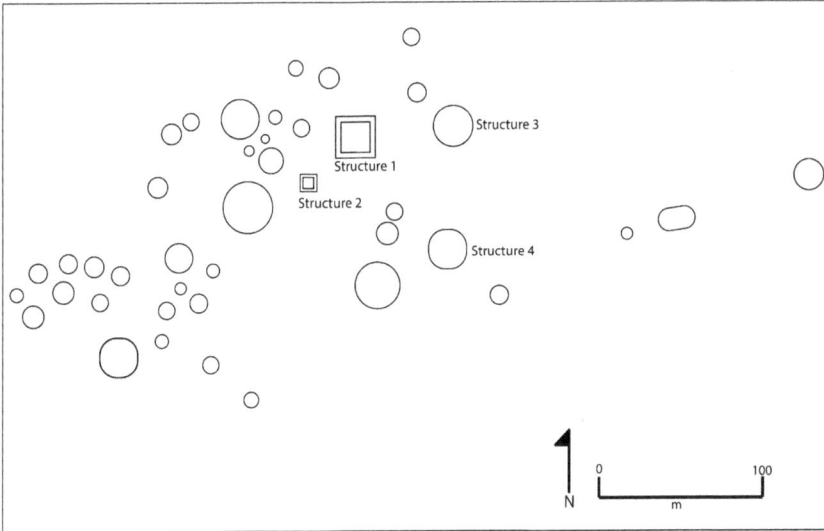

Figure 13.4. The El Gavilán site (central Nicaragua), showing indicative distribution of circular mounds and rectangular platforms (map by the author)

southwest of El Gavilán, a second expression of public ceremonial space is found at Aguas Buenas, in the neighboring Chontales region. Very different in composition and size, Aguas Buenas provides a further example of a public location, consisting of many low mounds created to form internal and external concentric circles (Auziņa 2018; Geurds and Terpstra 2017) (figure 13.5). This is not the place to provide much detail on either of these sites, but, for the present purpose, suffice it to say that the two sites' values are that they illustrate the interplay of long-term continuity in ritual use, and their capacity to create (inter)communal histories.

RITUAL EFFORTS AT EL GAVILÁN

El Gavilán is situated on the western extremities of the Caribbean region of Nicaragua, on a low elevation at the confluence of the Siquia river (a major artery draining into the Caribbean Sea) and its Nawawas tributary (figure 13.6). The site is a small yet dense complex of mounds and platforms and includes 56 individual monoliths, of which at least 23 are carved in low relief to depict anthropomorphic figures. Some of these were associated to organic materials dated to between AD 650 and 700. These large and narrow stones—complete specimens averaging 1.5 meters in length—are situated in and between 36 mounded surface structures, with the overwhelming majority clustered around two large and square stone-built platforms (Geurds 2021).

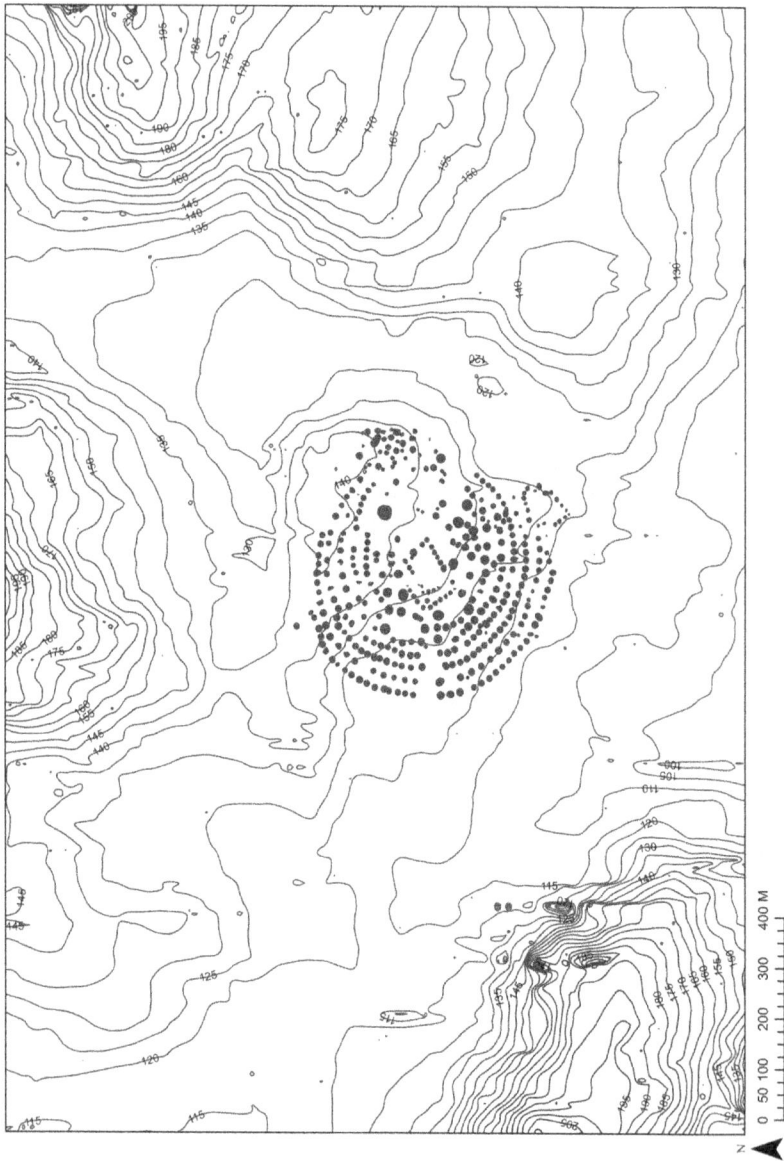

Figure 13.5. The Aguas Buenas site in central Nicaragua (map by Dita Auziņa)

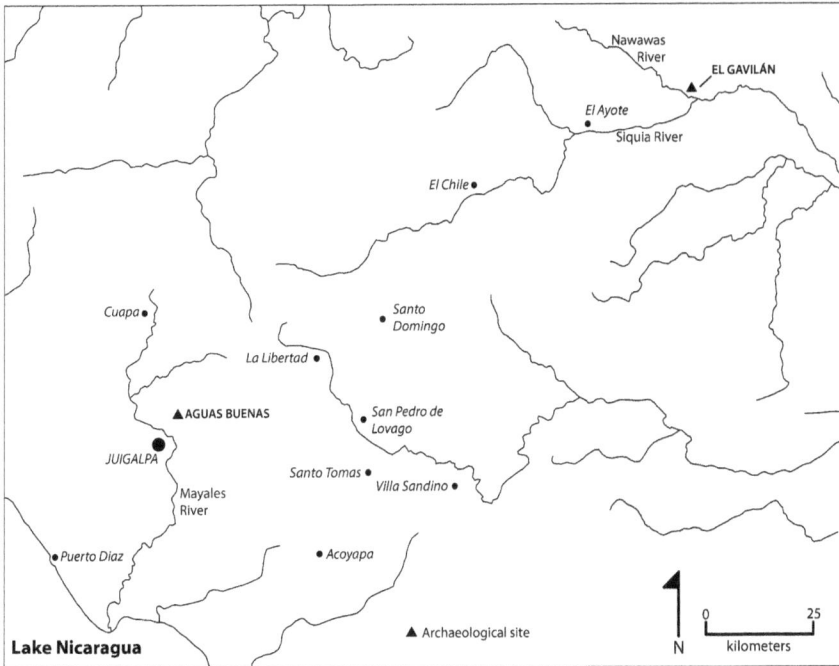

Figure 13.6. Central Nicaragua, showing sites mentioned in the text (map by the author)

Most sculptures are associated to these two larger structures, with additional monoliths semi-interred, protruding horizontally from the stepped sides of the larger of the two structures (figure 13.7). Several dozen small mounds are also found nearby or at the perimeter of the site. The mounded structures are either constructed entirely from the reddish clay sediment that predominates in the region, or are assembled from uncut stones harvested from exposed sections of bedrock surrounding the site. While the two central square platforms likely served a public ceremonial function, the smaller mounds may be traces of residential places, possibly temporary huts, but this remains inconclusive for now. More typical remains of domestic settings feature a circular configuration and a low platform, often lined by a row of foundational stones. Such traces were not documented here, and ethnographic data point instead to a regional preference for locating settlements in proximity to riverbanks. In all, El Gavilán appears to exemplify a location where periodic ritual action took place, through deposition and placement of stone sculptures and monoliths.

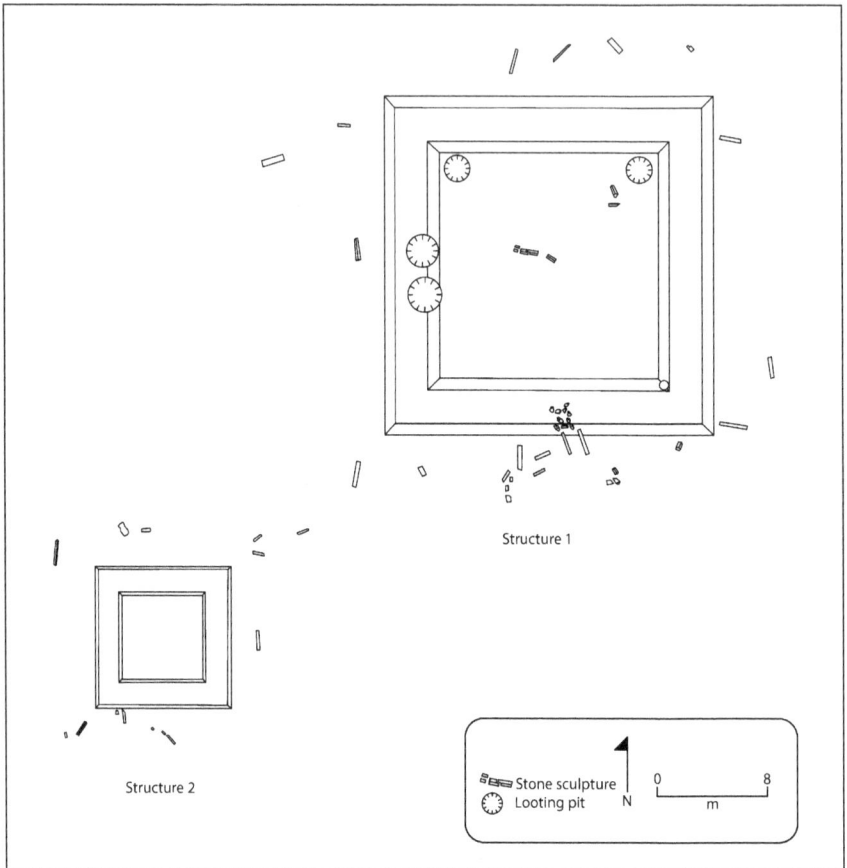

Figure 13.7. Detailed map of El Gavilán, showing the two principal rectangular platforms and associated stone sculptures (map by the author)

While specific geomorphological and climatic conditions prevent establishing a high-resolution chronology of human activity at the site, it remains central to consider why, in an area as restricted as this site, we find such a high number of individual and stylistically quite distinct sculpted monoliths.[3] The repetition of actions is never identical in its result, always leading to slightly different sculptural renderings, but the set of actions is nonetheless likely to have followed strict procedure. When one considers the origin of the individual stones, sourced at multiple kilometers' distance, and their weight of between several hundred and a thousand kilograms, then strict practices are likely to have been observed.

How can we think of ways in which the stones would have been transported to the site? The tempo at which these objects were moved must have been low and well-considered. Perhaps this added to a certain mood and experience for those involved in the carefully planned operational steps. The temporal rhythm of these actions—how often they took place, how much time elapsed between these ritual episodes—remains elusive to archaeology, but the nature of the materials and surroundings involved do have a capacity to be traced.

El Gavilán appears to be the product of repeated collective human action to expand and add to the appearance of this ceremonial location (Geurds 2021). When viewing the repeated formal actions of adding to the sculptural corpus that would become the El Gavilán site, we are describing a consequential social process, creating a form of local or intercommunal history.

In such a practice-oriented view on actions in the past, one can think about the conceptualization of time in prehistory (following Gosden and Lock 1998, 3) and ask what was intended to be represented or displayed and how this possibly reinforced a certain understanding of the past by what would have been the Ulwa Indigenous people living in the central parts of the Caribbean lowlands. The high number of sculptures, coming from different rock outcrops, points to repeated visiting of the site, and renewing or repeating ritual actions such as the erecting of a sculpture.[4] Who or what these sculptures represented is speculative, but ethnographic analogy from the Araucanians offers an interpretation perhaps relating to re-establishing contact with community ancestors (Dillehay 2007). Over time, weathering processes on the igneous rock, discoloration from bright white and pink to typical grays showed the "aging" of earlier sculptures, providing sensorial cues that signal the passage of time. It is interesting to consider that perhaps this was paralleled by the different process of deterioration of wooden sculptures, although no traces of those are known from El Gavilán.

Apart from the site configuration, its strategic location at the confluence of the Siquia and Nawawas Rivers, removed from settlements but central in terms of access, attests to a specific perception of ritual and landscape. The uncommon geographic feature of a river confluence raises ideas of directionality (in river flows) and centrality, creating a cultural or sacred environment of value, resonating with archaeological work that stresses the creation of cultural landscapes (Bradley 2000; Nieves Zedeño and Bowser 2009; Thomas 2001). Access to the site itself may have been restricted in terms of period and ritual knowledge, with navigators on the rivers being conscious of approaching and passing the site on their day-to-day travels. For now, El Gavilán remains but one regionally isolated site, but it is unlikely to be an exception for anything other than lack of regional research.

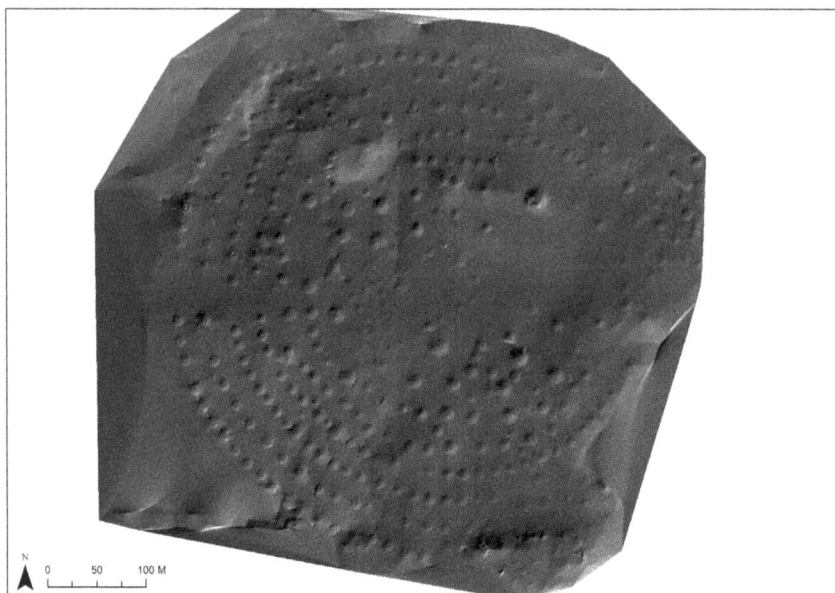

Figure 13.8. Digital elevation model of Aguas Buenas (courtesy of Dita Auziņa)

REPETITION AT AGUAS BUENAS

Expanding through repetition is also a key facet of the Aguas Buenas site. Several concentrically aligned arcs of mounds define this largest of ceremonial sites known in Nicaragua (figure 13.8), marking a powerful central place in the central region of the country, wedged in between the central mountain ranges and Lake Nicaragua (Arteaga 2017; Donner 2020; Geurds and Auziņa, n.d.). The earliest traces currently date to around AD 400 (Donner and Geurds 2018, 2020), and the overall construction techniques recorded at the site, in building the close to 400 mounds, point to a periodic enlargement of the site, following the concentric pattern in many instances but also adhering to surrounding landscape affordances. Aguas Buenas is not a socially liminal space, with other small settlements and isolated domestic clusters in proximity (Donner et al. 2018). The site is largely composed of small mounds, most of them consisting in assembled piles of uncut rock. Generally, these mounds do not exceed 1.5 m in height (from present surface), and their diameter is predominantly between 10 and 14 m (Auziņa 2018).

The purpose of each individual mound is challenging to determine. Excavated cases revealed very limited amounts of material culture, except for occasional caches in the form of flint objects or ceramic vessels. It is unclear whether such caches were placed at the time of original construction, or whether these are the result of return visits to the site. A purpose as domestic platforms is unlikely due to the small diameter in relation to the curvature of the mound. These are very clearly not platforms but intentionally built convex structures.

With residential and depository purposes ruled out as primary functions, it may well be that the act of construction, and its periodic repetition, formed the goal of these mounds. This would have required a wider collective effort and helped develop an integrating dynamic among local villages. This would have entailed regular return to the site, carrying out coordinated construction activities involving complex tasks of procuring, preparing, and transporting building materials, as well as the expertise involved in setting out mound locations and their individual construction steps. This process was likely completed sometime between AD 900 and 1250. Additionally, a range of maintenance tasks were also needed to manage vegetation, remove accumulating soil, and so forth.

Much remains unclear and controversial about Aguas Buenas. That is unescapable until research progresses more at this site. But the construction of this monumental ritual landscape does provide some urgent considerations and, in the process, also generates new questions. The current form of Aguas Buenas appears to underline an overall continuity in form. This apparent linear development, however, is questionable, given the periodic enlargement of the site and the subtle differences in construction technique employed between several of the rings of mounds and the later, more visually disruptive, alterations in its northeast sector (Donner and Geurds 2020).

From the surrounding landscape filled with traces of contemporary domestic structures (Arteaga 2017; Donner et al. 2018), Aguas Buenas would have appeared stabile, perhaps even timeless, when compared to the surrounding eventfulness of daily life. What we can see is that Aguas Buenas develops and changes over time, and that such changes are spatially integrated in the growth of the site. This, in turn, results in a built environment that recalls a long and deep past. As such, Aguas Buenas provides compelling evidence for prehistoric ritualization, marked by forms of social action that were evidently highly valued over time.

An additional question is why these two sites are apparently so different. It may well be that these variations developed out of the space of possibilities ("Handlungsraum") from which they emerged (in the sense of Pollock 2013, 148). One example could be the abovementioned stone sculpture tradition of central Nicaragua: in a relatively restricted region, we witness the emergence of a range of figurative expression through large columnar stone blocks, sculpted in low relief to depict human traits, often mixed with supernatural features. While working with stone is noticeable in various parts of the area, the concentration found in central Nicaragua is much higher than elsewhere (Geurds 2021). Similarly, the concentric configuration may loosely recall other sites in the region and beyond, but its precision and scale of work is like nothing else currently known.

One possible answer is that these two practices developed a sense of momentum, resulting in increasing numbers of stone sculptures being fashioned, perhaps at an increasingly faster rate. The latter is hard to confirm for now, as the chronological control of El Gavilán needs more work. A similar spurt of sculpting activity may have occurred in the Alto Magdalena region of Colombia (Duque Gómez and Cubillos Chaparro 1979). Whatever the specific trajectory of this form of material culture, what stands out is the endurance of both monoliths and mounds, stretching across human generations and indeed outlasting memories and meanings.

While different in many ways, these two sites are both expressions of long-lasting landscape modification, using stone and mounded accumulations of earth. In terms of their features, they may be quite unique, for now, in Isthmo-Colombian archaeology, but they also form part of wider patterns of building public ceremonial spaces that is seen across the area (for a comparative discussion, see Frost and Quilter 2012). In their various forms, these public ritual spaces open a range of questions, including reflection on how time was perceived through and in such locations.

CONCLUSION

We have indications that Isthmo-Colombian societies were finely attuned to the affordances of the landscapes in which they made their living, and the installment of ritual practices is a key piece of evidence for such a sensitive engagement with the environment. Such an engagement seems more to echo ideas on dynamic engagement with material surroundings than on rigid separations of human/animal or even also on the manipulative potential of ritual for aggrandizing chiefly individuals.

Ethnohistoric sources allude to Indigenous engagement with such temporal rhythms, principally through early Colonial-period observations by Spanish colonizers. Beyond ethnohistory, ethnography in the Isthmo-Colombian Area offers a richer body of materials but is invariably localized in focus. This chapter argued that archaeological evidence for timekeeping is available in this area of the Americas if, crucially, studies go beyond functionalist perspectives and appreciate, for example, archaeological features that use stone, either as a canvas on which to engrave rock art, or as a material to be quarried, transported, and build with.

From the available evidence, concerns emerge focused on safeguarding livelihoods and coming to terms with the surrounding world: features that allow for both contrast and comparison to Mesoamerican societies.

Understanding of collective rituals in this area remains sparse, partly due to the fragmentary and often site-based archaeological work in the region, but what indications there are point to a social landscape in which dispersed villages used both central and decentralized ritual sites for periodic ritual actions. Aguas Buenas and El Gavilán are examples of the former and the latter. They included certain monumental environments, particular key geographic locations, or even liminal natural spaces. This may have featured pilgrimages to intercommunal ceremonies, perhaps not unlike the ritual competition noted for the Ngäbe of southern Costa Rica and northern Panama. These ritualized environments would have provided some space for individual performance and perhaps allowed for distilling a level of community status from this, but it is likely that ritual life was neither controlled by a select few, nor was it the sole avenue for a career in individual political power.

Societies in prehistory are continually shaped by, and to some degree always in friction with, the irregular or unpredicted consequences of being entangled with a surrounding wider world. In other words, events invade societies, even those with a high degree of structure. Such a structure is helped by ritualized action and events, helping to order time and space. But this ritual is primarily also needed to interpret and navigate said events.

In this regard, the varied prehistories in this area of the Americas, from AD 0 onward, demonstrate some success in gradually developing a regular, yet flexible, set of ritual practices. The introduced examples of stone sculpture and ceremonial mounded sites illustrate, if with crude brevity, how the human work on durable materials resulted (intentionally or not) in the creation of a sense of past, present, and future time, reinforced by the repetitive acts of enlarging, expanding, increasing, or maintenance of these special places.

NOTES

1. Why this association never happened may be related to a combination of linguistic patterns, diverse geography, and the small sociopolitical units that are induced for the region.

2. One urgent avenue of research is to investigate human travel across regional landscapes to periodically visit special places. Such pilgrim movement, it is argued (van Dyke 2018), puts the emphasis on the journey, alongside the importance of places.

3. While El Gavilán has a high number of in situ large stone sculptures, there are certainly also other locations where figurative anthropomorphic stone sculpture and monoliths were recorded in numbers (Duque Gómez and Cubillos Chaparro 1979; Hartman 1901; Mayo and Mayo 2010).

4. These sculptures may show a hybrid mix of entities, possibly a combination of ancestral figures and metaphysical beings, alluding to Sahlins's "metapersons" (Sahlins 2017).

REFERENCES

Arteaga, Alejandro. 2017. "Reconstrucción del paisaje social prehispánico en la microcuenca del río Mayales, Chontales, Nicaragua." Master's thesis, Universidad Nacional Autónoma de México, Mexico City.

Auziņa, Dita. 2018. "Monumentality by Communities: Mapping the Spatial Logic of the Pre-Hispanic Aguas Buenas Site (AD 400–1600) in Central Nicaragua." Master's thesis, University of Leiden, Leiden.

Bell, Catherine. 1992. *Ritual Theory, Ritual Practice*. Oxford: Oxford University Press.

Bintliff, John, ed. 1991. *The Annales School and Archaeology*. Leicester: Leicester University Press.

Bloch, Maurice. 1977. "The Past and the Present in the Present." *Man* 12 (2): 278–92.

Bradley, Richard. 2000. *An Archaeology of Natural Places*. London: Routledge.

Bradley, Richard. 2002. *The Past in Prehistoric Societies*. London: Routledge.

Bradley, Richard. 2005. *Ritual and Domestic Life in Prehistoric Europe*. London: Routledge.

Bray, Warwick. 1984. "Across the Darién Gap: A Colombian View of Isthmian Archaeology." In *The Archaeology of Lower Central America*, edited by Frederick W. Lange and Doris Z. Stone, 303–38. Albuquerque: School of American Research.

Briggs, Peter S. 1989. *Art, Death and Social Order: The Mortuary Arts of Pre-Conquest Central Panama*. Oxford: British Archaeological Reports.

Bruhns, Karen Olsen. 1992. "Monumental Sculpture as Evidence for Hierarchical Societies." In *Wealth and Hierarchy in the Intermediate Area*, edited by Frederick W. Lange, 331–56. Washington, DC: Dumbarton Oaks Research Library and Collection.

Cooke, Richard G. 1984. "Birds and Men in Prehistoric Central Panama." In *Recent Developments in Isthmian Archaeology*, edited by Frederick W. Lange, 243–81. Oxford: British Archaeological Reports.

Dillehay, Tom D. 2007. *Monuments, Empires, and Resistance: The Auracanian Polity and Ritual Narratives*. Cambridge: Cambridge University Press.

Donner, Natalia R. 2020. *The Potters' Perspectives: A Vibrant Chronology of Ceramic Manufacturing Practices in the Valley of Juigalpa, Chontales, Nicaragua (cal 400 CE–Present)*. Leiden: Leiden University Press.

Donner, Natalia R., Alejandro Arteaga, Alexander Geurds, and Kaz van Dijk. 2018. "Caracterización inicial de los sitios arqueológicos en la subcuenca del río Mayales, Departamento de Chontales, Nicaragua." *Cuadernos de Antropología* 28 (1): 1–26.

Donner, Natalia R., and Alexander Geurds. 2018. "The Valley of Juigalpa, Mayales River Subbasin Microregion (Chontales, Nicaragua) Date List I." *Radiocarbon* 60 (2): 717–26.

Donner, Natalia R., and Alexander Geurds. 2020. "The Valley of Juigalpa, Mayales River Subbasin Microregion (Chontales, Nicaragua) Date List II." *Radiocarbon* 62 (3): 1503–14.

Duque Gómez, Luis, and Julio César Cubillos Chaparro. 1979. *Arqueología de San Agustín. Alto de los Ídolos: Montículos y tumbas.* Bogota: Banco de la República.

Durkheim, Émile. (1915) 1965. *The Elementary Forms of the Religious Life: A Study in Religious Sociology.* New York: Free Press.

Fernández Guardia, Ricardo. 1908. *Cartas de Juan Vázquez de Coronado.* Barcelona: Imprenta de lavinda de Luís Tasso.

Ferrero Acosta, Luis. 1981. "Ethnohistory and Ethnography in the Central Highlands-Atlantic Watershed and Diquís." In *Between Continents / Between Seas: Precolumbian Art of Costa Rica,* edited by Elizabeth P. Benson, 93–103. New York: Abrams.

Fonseca, Oscar. 1998. "El espacio histórico de los amerindios de filiación Chibcha: El Área Histórica Chibcha." In *Historia general de Centroamérica: Historia Antigua,* edited by Robert M. Carmack, 217–82. San José: Ediciones Siruela.

Frost, Jeffrey R., and Jeffrey Quilter. 2012. "Monumental Architecture and Social Complexity in the Intermediate Area." In *Early New World Monumentality,* edited by Richard L. Burger and Robert M. Rosenswig, 231–52. Gainesville: University Press of Florida.

Garrow, Duncan, and Chris Gosden. 2012. *Technologies of Enchantment? Exploring Celtic Art: 400 BC to AD 100.* Oxford: Oxford University Press.

Gell, Alfred. 1998. *Art and Agency.* Oxford: Oxford University Press.

Geurds, Alexander. 2011. "Dual or Dualistic Collaboration? Competing Imaginings of Archaeological Heritage in Central Nicaragua." *Archaeological Review from Cambridge* 26 (2): 87–104.

Geurds, Alexander. 2018. "Prehistory of Southern Central America." In *Encyclopedia of Global Archaeology,* edited by Claire Smith, 1–20. Boston: Springer.

Geurds, Alexander. 2021. "Monumental Stone Sculpture in Central Nicaragua." *Pre-Columbian Central America, Colombia, and Ecuador: Toward an Integrated Approach,* edited by Colin McEwan and John W. Hoopes, 149–63. Washington, DC: Dumbarton Oaks Research Library and Collection.

Geurds, Alexander. 2023. "Understanding Greater Nicoya: Epiclassic and Early Postclassic Extended Relations in Southern Mesoamerica." In *East to West: Chichen Itza, Tula, and the Postclassic Mesoamerican World,* edited by Travis Stanton, Karl Taube, and Jeremy Coltman, 635–50. Oxford: British Archaeological Reports.

Geurds, Alexander, and Dita Auziņa. N.d. "Aguas Buenas: An a-Typical Form of Pre-Columbian Monumentalism in Central Nicaragua." Unpublished manuscript.

Geurds, Alexander, and Denise Terpstra. 2017. "Circular Reasoning in Mound Building? Large-Scale Planned Construction Patterns at the Aguas Buenas Site (AD 400–1525)." In *War and Peace: Conflict and Resolution in Archaeology; Proceedings of the 45th Annual Chacmool Archaeology Conference,* edited by Adam K. Benfer, 47–59. Calgary: University of Calgary.

Gosden, Chris. 1994. *Social Being and Time*. Oxford: Blackwell.

Gosden, Chris. 2005. "What Do Objects Want?" *Journal of Archaeological Method and Theory* 12 (3): 193–211.

Gosden, Chris, and Gary Lock. 1998. "Prehistoric Histories." *World Archaeology* 30 (1): 2–12.

Haberland, Wolfgang. 1973. "Stone Sculpture from Southern Central America." In *The Iconography of Middle American Sculpture*, edited by Dudley T. Easby, 134–52. New York: Metropolitan Museum of Art.

Halbmayer, Ernst, ed. 2020. *Amerindian Socio-Cosmologies between the Andes, Amazonia and Mesoamerica: Toward an Anthropological Understanding of the Isthmo-Colombian Area*. Abingdon: Routledge.

Hartman, Carl V. 1901. *Archaeological Researches in Costa Rica*. Stockholm: Royal Ethnological Museum.

Helms, Mary W. 1979. *Ancient Panama: Chiefs in Search of Power*. Austin: University of Texas Press.

Holmberg, Karen. 2005. "The Voices of Stone: Unthinkable Materiality in the Volcanic Context of Western Panamá." In *Archaeologies of Materiality*, edited by Lynn Meskell, 190–211. Oxford: Blackwell.

Hoopes, John W. 2005. "The Emergence of Social Complexity in the Chibchan World of Southern Central America and Northern Colombia, AD 300–600." *Journal of Archaeological Research* 13: 1–47.

Hoopes, John W. 2007. "Sorcery and the Taking of Trophy Heads in Ancient Costa Rica." In *The Taking and Displaying of Human Body Parts as Trophies by Amerindians*, edited by Richard J. Chacon and David H. Dye, 444–80. Boston: Springer.

Hoopes, John W., and Oscar Fonseca. 2003. "Goldwork and Chibchan Identity." In *Gold and Power in Ancient Costa Rica, Panama and Colombia*, edited by Jeffrey Quilter and John W. Hoopes, 49–89. Washington, DC: Dumbarton Oaks Research Library and Collection.

Howe, James. 1974. "Village Political Organization among the San Blas Cuna." PhD diss., University of Pennsylvania, Philadelphia.

Ibarra, Eugenia. 2003. "Gold in the Everyday Lives of Indigenous People of Sixteenth-Century Southern Central America." In *Gold and Power in Ancient Costa Rica, Panama and Colombia*, edited by Jeffrey Quilter and John W. Hoopes, 383–420. Washington, DC: Dumbarton Oaks Research Library and Collection.

Johnson, Frederick. 1948. "The Caribbean Lowland Tribes, the Talamanca Division." In *The Circum-Caribbean Tribes*, vol. 4 of *Handbook of South American Indians*, edited by Julian H. Steward, 231–52. Washington, DC: Bureau of American Ethnology.

Joyce, Rosemary A. 2008. "Practice in and as Deposition." In *Memory Work: Archaeologies of Material Practices*, edited by Barbara J. Mills and William H. Walker, 25–40. Santa Fe, NM: School of American Research Press.

Keane, Webb. 2016. *Ethical Life: Its Natural and Social Histories*. Princeton, NJ: Princeton University Press.

Kirchhoff, Paul. 1943. "Mesoamérica." *Acta Americana* 1 (1): 92–107.

Künne, Martin, and Matthias Strecker. 2004. *Arte rupestre de Mexico oriental y Centro América*. Berlin: Mann Verlag.

Lange, Frederick W., ed. 1992. *Wealth and Hierarchy in the Intermediate Area*. Washington, DC: Dumbarton Oaks Research Library and Collection.

Lucas, Gavin. 2004. *The Archaeology of Time*. London: Routledge.

Mayo, Julia, and Carlos Mayo. 2010. "La escultura precolombina del Área Intermedia: Aproximación al studio estilístico, iconográfico y especial del grupo escultórico de El Caño." In *Producción de bienes de prestigio ornamentales y votivos de la América Antigua*, edited by Emiliano Melgar Tísoc, Reyna Solís Ciriaco, and Ernesto González Licón, 12–21. Miami: Syllaba Press.

Nieves Zedeño, María, and Brenda J. Bowser. 2009. "The Archaeology of Meaningful Places." In *the Archaeology of Meaningful Places*, edited by Brenda J. Bowser and María Nieves Zedeño, 1–14. Salt Lake City: University of Utah Press.

Pollock, Susan. 2013. "Commensality, Public Spheres and *Handlungsräume* in Ancient Mesopotamia." In *Big Histories, Human Lives*, edited by John Robb and Timothy R. Pauketat, 145–70. Santa Fe, NM: School of American Research.

Quilter, Jeffrey, and John W. Hoopes, eds. 2003. *Gold and Power in Ancient Costa Rica, Panama and Colombia*. Washington, DC: Dumbarton Oaks Research Library and Collection.

Rappaport, Roy. 1999. *Ritual and Religion in the Making of Humanity*. Cambridge: Cambridge University Press.

Renfew, Colin. 2007. "The Archaeology of Ritual, of Cult, and of Religion." In *The Archaeology of Ritual*, edited by Evangelos Kyriakidis, 109–22. Los Angeles: Cotsen Institute of Archaeology.

Sahlins, Marshall. 2017. "The Original Political Society." *Hau: Journal of Ethnographic Theory* 7 (2): 91–128.

Sheets, Payson. 1992. "The Pervasive Pejorative in Intermediate Area Studies." In *Wealth and Hierarchy in the Intermediate Area*, edited by Frederick W. Lange, 15–42. Washington, DC: Dumbarton Oaks Research Library and Collection.

Sheets, Payson. 2011. "Pilgrimages and Persistent Social Memory in spite of Volcanic Disasters in the Arenal Area, Costa Rica." *Ancient Mesoamerica* 22 (2): 425–35.

Thomas, Julian. 2001. "Archaeologies of Place and Landscape." In *Archaeology Theory Today*, edited by Hodder, 165–86. Malden, MA: Polity Press.

van Dyke, Ruth M. 2018. "From Enchantment to Agencement: Archaeological Engagements with Pilgrimage." *Journal of Social Archaeology* 18 (3): 348–59.

van Dyke, Ruth M., and Susan E. Alcock, eds. 2003. *Archaeologies of Memory*. London: John Wiley.

Young, Philip. 1971. *Ngawbe: Tradition and Change among the Western Guaymí of Panama*. Urbana: University of Illinois Press.

Young, Philip. 1976. "The Expression of Harmony and Discord in a Guaymí Ritual: The Symbolic Meaning of Some Aspects of the Balsería." In *Frontier Adaptations in Lower Central America*, edited by Mary W. Helms and Franklin O. Loveland, 37–53. Philadelphia: Institute for the Study of Human Issues.

14

The End of the Long Dynastic Time in the Southern Maya Lowlands

(750–810 CE)

M. CHARLOTTE ARNAULD AND CHLOÉ ANDRIEU

INTRODUCTION

What is generally called the "Maya collapse" of the end of the Classic period (ninth to tenth centuries CE) designates the end of royal dynasties and disintegration of the Maya Lowlands city system, later relocated in the Northern Lowlands and around the southern lakes (figures 14.1a and 14.1b). Some scholarly consensus is now forming on an intricate causality web implying an abrupt political change, globalization or "mesoamericanization," and climatic droughts. Although it is useful to roughly situate the phenomenon, such a triangular causality web still needs to be refined and validated. We need to specify the chronology of events and processes, along with the perception the actors had of them, the way they acted, and the mechanisms of their coordination at different spatiotemporal scales. But at the least, it now appears that the most critical events had already taken place as early as 750–810 CE, even before "the Terminal Classic," a period traditionally dated 830–950 CE (Arnauld, Andrieu, and Forné 2017; Demarest, Rice, and Rice 2004; Houston and Inomata 2009).

The research project entitled Transition et Prédiction is currently developed in the framework of RITMO exchanges and meetings. RITMO investigates how the modalities of ritual actions and their temporal inscription bring up the creation, destruction, or transformation of objects or entities in the Mesoamerican present and past (see the introduction to this volume). In this perspective, Transition et Prédiction (hereafter TP) raises an ambitious issue: what specificities and dynamics

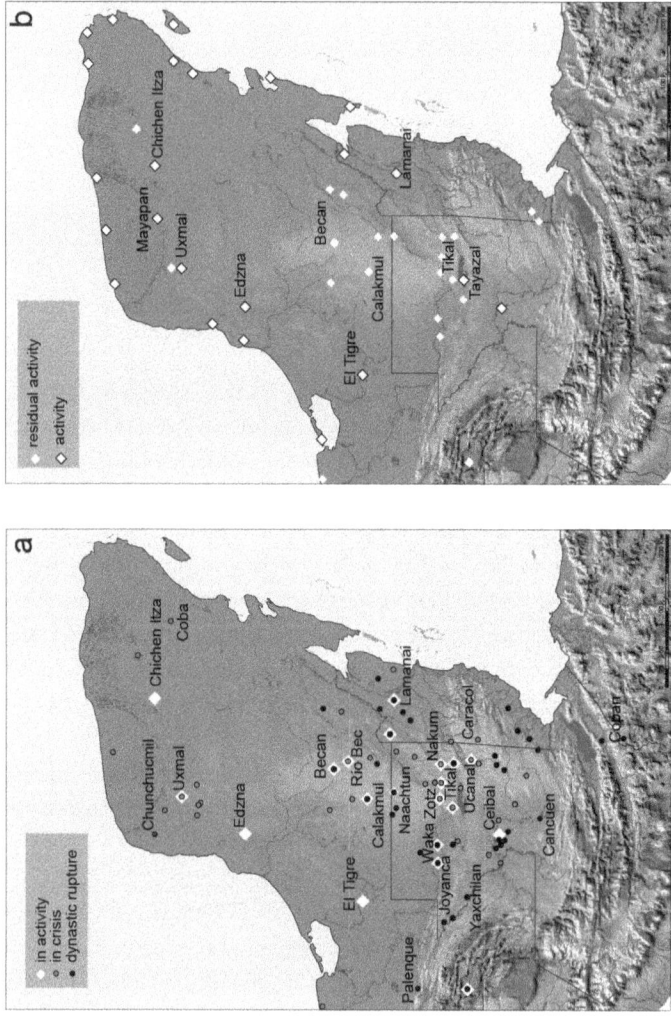

Figure 14.1. (a) Impact of the political collapse on the urban system in the Maya Lowlands during the Terminal Classic (800–900 CE): sites in black lost their dynasties before 830; sites in gray lost them later on, sites with white quadrangle retained some degree of activity (drafted by M. Charlotte Arnauld and Sylvie Eliès, Archam UMR 8096, CNRS); (b) impact of the political collapse on the urban system in the Maya Lowlands during the Early Postclassic period (900–1200 CE); most settlements relocated along the sea coasts (drafted by M. Charlotte Arnauld and Elliot Mathieu, Archam UMR8096, CNRS).

in Maya political rituals during the Terminal Classic period could have brought up the destruction of objects and entities and their transformation into their Postclassic counterparts throughout the collapse process? The issue is raised only if one admits that, for the most part, determinant collective and individual agency of Maya political elites have left traces and that, also for the most part, such traces were the effects of political rituals. If so, the study of those traces of rituals—mainly epigraphic and iconographic, but also archaeological—informs us about political actions, since the rituals had direct effects well beyond what can be expected in propagandistic or formalist (ritualistic vs. real) politics. We take the position that this efficiency lay precisely in the fact that political rituals instantiated several temporalities, inscribing action in historical frames of the past, contingent perceptions of the present, and prospective models of the future, all of great significance for Maya actors.

One specific issue raised is whether repetition, anticipation, and prediction might have had a part in the chain of ritual actions and their contexts, which can be reconstructed for the Terminal Classic period. Guided by the works of a number of scholars on Maya historicity and time concepts (Bricker 1981; Bricker and Miriam 2002; Farris 1995; Hanks 2017; Knowlton 2010; Sullivan 1989; Vapnarsky 2017; among others), in the TP research project, we attempt to articulate paths toward answers to this question through a multidisciplinary approach on the ninth century CE, in search for conceptual comparison with Postclassic, colonial, postcolonial, and contemporaneous episodes. Some rituals that in particular founded the exercise of Classic Maya kingship show a remarkable duration through even late colonial and present times (e.g., Arnauld 1996, 2016b; Dehouve 2006; Olivier 2015).

The present chapter will focus on a limited aspect of late Maya political rituals in their capacity of configuring a geopolitical institution that covered the Southern Lowlands (vs. the Northern Lowlands, i.e., including the Central Lowlands). In particular we suggest that the Classic Maya historicity regime (Hartog 2003) can shed light on the Terminal Classic elites' chain of action. The first, second, and third parts of the chapter concentrate on the specific link to be retrieved between historicist inscriptions and the supra-regional organization of kingdoms, by analyzing some of the temporalities articulated in political rituals. The fourth part discusses the idea that repetition, anticipation, and prediction of historical and mythical schemes that were enacted in political rituals may have modeled and coordinated elitist strategies during the late eighth and early ninth centuries CE.

THREE COLLAPSES

It is well known that political claims inscribed in glyphs on Classic Maya stone stelae, altars, panels, and steps indirectly registered events through the ritual acts and discourses that Maya political agents performed on those occasions (e.g., Munson and Macri 2009; Munson et al. 2016). Except for texts painted on ceramic cylinder vases, other categories of records are lost for us. In other words, we have only those records made and waived in ritual circumstances—stone monuments, also ceramic vases.[1] The primary (etic) diagnostic of the Maya collapse is the cessation of ritual erections of such stone monuments with inscriptions dated in the Long Count calendric notation system, along with changes in architecture and royal images (including on ceramics) during troubled times (e.g., Ebert, Prufer, and Kennett 2014; Schwartz 2006). Within the triangular causalities mentioned above, so far only one quantitative correlation is being explored and dated, that is, the frequency of inscribed-dated monuments, recorded wars, and climatic droughts (e.g., Kennett et al. 2012, figure 2). The number of inscriptions abruptly decreased by 775 CE, war narratives increased during the 760–790 years, while dry years punctuated the eighth- to ninth-century transition, then later came in tremendously long and continuous sequences from 1020 to 1150 CE, or Early Postclassic times (Hoggarth et al. 2015, 2017). The latter period was when subsistence was most radically affected, as was probably also Lowland population demography. It is important to note that, even though the early dry years might have impacted Maya societies, the most severe droughts developed long after the political rupture marked by warfare and epigraphic-iconographic changes. We are left with the issues of this early political rupture, its associated wars, and the expression of both on stone monuments and archaeological evidence.

Inscriptions on stone publicly validated the hierarchical status of kings and dynasties duly situated in calendric times and Lowland places (rather than territories; Martin 2020; Martin and Grube 1995, 2008). In late years (780–880 CE), the king was less frequently represented alone, as he rather appeared surrounded by other dignitaries; also calendar dates were noted in the Short Count (counting 13 *katuns* of 20 vague solar years each), and the Long Count rapidly ceased to be used. This is considered to have been the end of the Classic canonic kingship, replaced by aristocratic regimes (e.g., Chase and Chase 2006; Ringle 2004). Likely, the latest dated inscription in any one site indicates the local end of dynastic authority (Ebert, Prufer, and Kennett 2014), although the exceptionally detailed sequence of events at Ceibal mitigates this interpretation (Bazy and Inomata 2017; Inomata et al. 2017; Martin 2020, 280–81). In many sites, episodes of hiatus, reappraisal, or emergence of erection rituals rather point to quite intricate ninth-century scenarios of demise, founding, and restoration. Empirical evidence on the moment of royal palace abandonment is not available in all cases. However, if the pan-Lowland hierarchy of kingdoms is considered (Martin and Grube 2008), it is clear that most if not all highest-rank old dynasties had abruptly disappeared before 810–820 CE (including

Calakmul and Dos Pilas even earlier, Tikal, Copan, Caracol, and many other sites; Martin 2020; Okoshi et al. 2021). Furthermore, in most of the cases, the latest dated inscription does not coincide with the desertion of the corresponding city. The gradual urban exodus lasted at least until 950–1000 CE (with relocation of settlements only much later), a chronology suggesting that with or without the trappings of the old dynasties, new authorities had been installed after their demise. Our TP archaeological database on urban activity[2] indicates that the urban collapse lasted longer than the political collapse and had a partly distinct causal system (Arnauld et al., n.d.). Then, during the Early Postclassic (after 1000 CE), a relative absence of settlement and land-use evidence across the Southern Lowlands suggests that the long eleventh-century drought might have resulted in a severe demographic crisis of local societies (Andrews, Andrews, and Castellanos 2003; Hoggarth et al. 2015).

Thus, three sequent political, urban, and demographic collapses must be distinguished. Most issues bearing on political rituals have obviously to do with the first one, the abrupt political collapse. The link the rituals maintained with geopolitics should be investigated mainly for the same period, of the late eighth and early ninth centuries. Our preliminary time-space analysis of archaeological data-set distributions detects marked dynamics in the supra-regional organization that was based on the hierarchy of old dynasties and their subordinates; the entire geopolitical system was disintegrating, segmenting, and transforming. Statistics limited to dates of last monument erection across a hundred sites (Ebert, Prufer, and Kennett 2014) also allowed scholars to detect the dynamics of kingdom networks matching to a certain extent the networks obtained on the basis of the TP surveys. But before dealing with the ritual-geopolitic link, the crucial issue of political rituals articulating multiple time dimensions must be assessed.

CLASSIC MAYA RITUALS OF TIME-CYCLE COMPLETION

According to the Classic Maya system of Long Count notation, 830 CE was the closing date of the Ninth Cycle (400-year baktuns, counting from the mythological 3114 BCE origin date; figure 14.2). On the basis of chrono-ceramic analyses and radiocarbon dating, until recently Mayanist archaeologists used this 830 date as the end of the Late Classic and the beginning of the Terminal Classic—a limit now moved back to 800, although contested by Demarest with some reasons (see Okoshi et al. 2021). Archaeologists assign dates to processes in a probabilistic way with an uncertainty margin, whereas Classic sophisticated calendars allowed recording precise histories that represented an effective political resource of primary importance structuring collective action. Dates of performed political rituals were inscribed on stone monuments localized on urban plazas, publicly proclaiming information

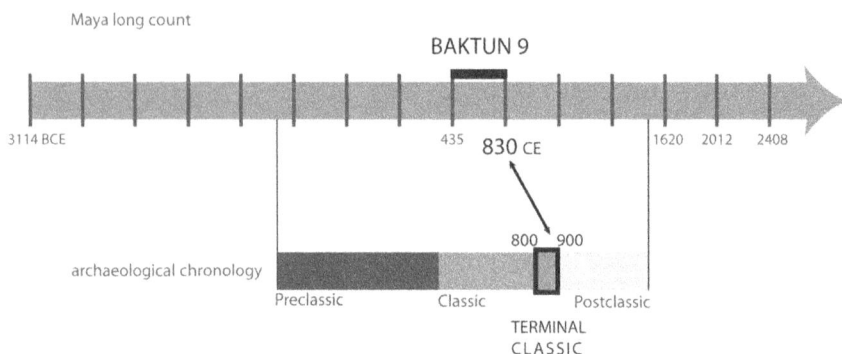

Figure 14.2. Correlation of the Classic Maya Long Count of 400-year cycles with the archaeological chronology of the Maya Lowlands, as currently assessed (drafted by Sylvie Eliès, ArchAm, CNRS UMR 8096)

(event, ritual, performer, and patron) of great geopolitical significance for members of the Southern Lowland kingdom hierarchy. Instead of the date of their occurrence, political events or actions were ritually correlated with the end of their calendric period (baktun, katun, half-katun, etc.); both dates were recorded, or only the second one as it counted more than the date of the event or action itself. This time gap between the "true" date and the ending date means that the Maya not only perceived the contingent timeframe in which they acted through the calendar system, along with the historicist schemes it perpetuated, but also that the shift from one period to another was conceived as a binding of events and actions properly ending a time cycle, then opening the next one. According to Stuart (2011a), the "completion" moment should be understood as equivalent to the gathering of a crop in agriculture, simultaneously opening a new cycle of production (see also the *tz'ak* concept of wholeness and completeness in Maya languages; e.g., Stuart 2005, 2024).

Stuart has presented two epigraphic illustrations of time completion (2011a, 274–82). At Copan, Altar Q (figure 14.3), a squared stone block carved in 776 CE, depicts all sixteen kings of the local dynasty in sequence, placing four of them on each side of the square, equivalent to a quarter (100 years) of the ninth baktun opened by the founder king. This first king is figured transmitting the ceremonial bar to the sixteenth king, the one commissioning the monument and thus closing the series. A later, similarly squared monument, Altar L (circa 816), depicts the *last* king transmitting the bar to his successor, opening a new series of kings in inverse order. But as the Copan dynasty was ended by 820, the sculpture was never finished (see also the case of the late Stela 11; Guenter 2020). The second example is analogous since Palenque also had a dynastic sequence of 16 kings covering Cycle 9.

Figure 14.3. Altar Q, Copan: (a) the geometry of a quadripartite dynastic sequence on a four-sided stone altar; (b) scenarizes the final encounter of the founder with the sixteenth and last ruler (photos by Jean-Pierre Courau)

From the seventh century on (if not earlier), the kings received names according to their ancestors, following an order such as the sixteenth king was named after the founder, effectively closing the list. We ignore what formula of continuity was created at Palenque to bypass such a projected dynastic end. In any case, the Palenque dynasty collapsed by 820 CE. Both examples point to a quite long anticipation of the 830 CE completion. The future was anticipated through a reschematization of the past (dynastic lists). The ritual practices involved in formulating the content of the inscription, in calculating the correct (desired) dates to be inscribed, in materially carving, and in ceremoniously dedicating monuments, all these instantiated royal authority in history. We can surmise that the shift in date notation from the Long Count to the Short Count, which occurred during the Terminal Classic, must have been the consequence of deeply significant changes in authority practices (Arnauld et al. 2018; Knowlton 2010, 20).

Archaeology provides us with other illustrations of completion anticipating the future through binding (wrapping up) the past, although they are more difficult to interpret. Massive deposits of ceramics and other artifacts, either buried or inserted in artificial caves located in epicenters, have been found and interpreted as effectively closing and opening periods, thus ritually "making" political transitions between places, people, or both (Galván Bernal, Bey, and Ciau 2017, at Kiuic; Ichon and Arnauld 1985, 65, at La Lagunita, Quiché, Guatemala, see figure 14.4; Schieber de Lavarreda 2002, 2003, at Takalik Abaj). Similarly, yet on a less collective, more domestic scale, termination rituals left on domestic floors many kinds of daily remains, mixed with ashes from domestic hearths, barring entrances and stairways (although many of those deposits appear more scattered than bundled). Those on-floor remains clearly showed to everybody passing by that the house was abandoned and definitely closed by its occupants as they had departed to another

Figure 14.4. Massive Deposit C-48 in an artificial cave under Plaza A at La Lagunita, Quiché, Guatemala (circa 350 CE; Ichon and Arnauld 1985; photo by Alain Ichon, Fond Alain Ichon, ArchAM, UMR 8096 CNRS)

life place. Completion rituals articulate time periods to create the effect of a transition opening a new order through an accumulation of kings or things, which were in some way "cropped" and wrapped up out of the past by means of some calendric, or historicist, scheme. Such a scheme is therefore crucial for understanding the Maya historicity regime, where future and past were analyzed through this narrative of time.

GEOPOLITICS OF CYCLE-COMPLETING RITUALS

Most of the Classic glyphic inscriptions contain references to ritual completion of time periods. Stone altars and stelae erected on plazas publicly proclaimed the accomplishment of such rituals as either a local expression of sovereignty or a subordinate action carried out under the patronage of some higher-rank dynast, resulting in Late Classic Lowland geopolitics forming a weakly institutionalized network of hierarchical affiliations maintained among dynasties (Martin 2020, 237–76, 303–19; Martin and Grube 1995, 2008). Instead of a grand territorial pattern, this hierarchy of subordinated individuals literally mapped the kingdoms and their geopolitics, thus structured by many ranked status distinctions above and below the king node.

Those distinctions corresponded to "highly personal charts of affiliation" (Grube 2000), dictated not only by kinship positions and ties but also by loyalty links and interpersonal obligations. Among other series of individual titles, specific numbered *tzuk* titles tended to be shared by kings of cities located within spatially contiguous areas in the Southern Lowlands (mainly east of Lake Petén Itza; Beliaev 2000; Helmke et al. 2015, 26; Tokovinine 2013). Frequently associated with the numerals seven, thirteen, or nine, *tzuk* would have the meaning of "partition" or "province." All rulers bearing one of those titles would have been vassals to a paramount dynasty—Seven-*tzuk* under Motul de San José, Thirteen-*tzuk* under Tikal, Nine-*tzuk* under some northern Belize site, perhaps Naranjo. Another geopolitical collectivity would have assembled twenty-eight dynasties under the sovereignty of Tikal, yet its mentions (late eighth century) would only make sense in relation with one much earlier Tikal inscription, to which we will return (Tokovinine 2013, 113–15).

These numeral-*tzuk* titles would perhaps afford the first clue of some late Late Classic "territorial organization" in what would have been the Central and Eastern Lowlands. Although perhaps also prevalent in occasions of alliance-making and warfare, this was a (sociopolitically) hierarchical scheme mainly enacted in ritual circumstances in which dynasts gathered at some particular dates. The Thirteen-*tzuk* network has been particularly discussed by several epigraphists due to its mention in an inscription at Naranjo (on Stela 30, dated 714 CE) and on the recently discovered Altar 3 of Altar de los Reyes in Southern Campeche (800 CE), the latter extending the list of kingdoms beyond the Central-Eastern Lowlands to Palenque to the west, and Edzna to the north (see Tokovinine 2013, 102–10). As Altar 3 is circular, and the mentioned thirteen (emblem glyph) dynastic titles are carved around its side, Houston, Stuart, and Taube (2006, 89–97) interpret the inscription in the context of a widespread Lowland representation of a king as an *ajaw* day name of the katun time cycle on circular altars (like on the well-known Tonina examples; Stuart 2011a, 256–60), thus equating the Altar de los Reyes circular list to a "katun wheel." In the Postclassic. this was a key political space-time concept (linked to the twenty-year cycle along with its gods) well documented in a number of colonial sources (e.g., Avendaño de Loyola 1987) and also linked to a particular iconography of Classic-Postclassic turtle sculptures (the turtle shell figuring the katun wheel; Taube 1988; see also Martin 2020, 147–49). It may have been that Late Classic Lowland geopolitics were enacted in historicist times by calendric rituals, a conclusion that Tokovinine cautiously restricts to the idea of "a landscape divided in space and time between thirteen royal dynasties and possibly between thirteen deities, with an implication that one polity may claim a supreme status that *would not likely last*" (2013, 108; emphasis added). The scheme would thus imply that supremacy was bounded in time as in space.

Obviously such ritual geopolitics should not be equated to any administrative, state-like, imperial, or colonial institution. Instead, they should be referred to the old model of galactic polities (Demarest 1992; Inomata 2006; Tambiah 1977), in which the capital would have been an exemplary center replicated by satellite centers in a global scheme maintained by ritual cohesion (e.g., Coe 1965; Mathews and Garber 2004; see also Arnauld 2016b; Grube 2000), with likely space-time dimensions which would have made these geopolitics "cosmocentric" (in the sense of Descola 2005, 288–307). What we now propose to explore is whether those cosmocentric geopolitics, as structured by time-cycle completion rituals, would have been liable to broad, rapid movements reversing the cosmos by way of calendric projections.[3]

THE TIKAL ORDER

One plausible example of such swinging past-future movements can be viewed in a famous episode of the Central Lowland Classic history. In 445 CE, ten years after the opening of Cycle 9 (a 400-year baktun), and 67 years after the CE 378 entrada of a Teotihuacan powerful leader into the Maya Lowlands, Tikal erected Stela 31. This monument bears one of the longest Classic Maya texts, in which the new local dynasty, which had been abruptly installed by the intruder, claims hegemony on 28 provinces (Stuart 2000, 2011b). The 378 entrada was registered in inscriptions of at least ten cities of the Central Lowlands at the turn of the fourth-fifth centuries, or later on (e.g., Nondédéo, García Gallo, and Cases Martín 2019). The production of Stela 31 required 67 years that elapsed after the real event, so as to situate its erection ritual within the opening Cycle 9, and thus to ritually create a temporality that Tikal authorities probably wanted to project in the future. This was well before any military dominance was effectively achieved by the dynasty, even though a few cities had already submitted (through their early recording of the entrada). An uncontroverted momentum in the Lowland status quo, the 378 rupture was not ritually created until 445 CE so as to open the temporality of the four hundred years to come. To retake Tokovinine's proposition, the 28 provinces emerged as a landscape in which "one polity [Tikal] may claim a supreme status that would not likely last" (2013, 108; yet, the 28 entities of Stela 31 are *pet*, not *tzuk*; see Carter 2014, 205–6).

The 67-years gap likely involved a sequence of intellectual and material practices in preparing and carrying out the ritual that was to open the new times and order. In all probability, scribes who were also astronomers, calendar specialists, and mathematicians oversaw the Stela 31 production (see Bricker, Aveni, and Bricker 2014; Saturno et al. 2012, for one later case at Xultun, 780 CE). In this way, the practices of geopolitics would have been in the hands of specialists subordinated to the king.

But still, one of the most important aspects of this Teotihuacan entrada relevant to the ritual geopolitics and their temporalities lay in the creation of specific investiture (or accession) rites for high-rank Maya kings bearing the Teotihuacan *kaloomte* title (Martin 2020, 77–85). Those rites were in part performed at a mythical place, called Wite' Naah in Maya languages, or Wiinte' Naah, hypothetically identified as the platform appended to the Sun Pyramid at Teotihuacan (Fash and Fash 2006; Fash, Tokovinine, and Fash 2009; Stuart 2004; Taube 2004; Tokovinine 2020). Originally the ritual referred to the investiture of the new king of Tikal (whom the Teotihuacan intruder had placed on the throne), who had traveled to the great city to receive the ritual investiture at some moment between 378 and 445 CE. On his return to his city, the displacement of his physical person (which either really occurred or was symbolically arranged in some place of the Maya Lowlands) and the established bondage of sovereignty to Teotihuacan made the Tikal king a "stranger king" in the local context (Graeber and Sahlins 2017; Sahlins 1985). A stranger king whose son, the king centrally represented on Stela 31 in 445 CE, is nevertheless said to be the sixteenth king of Tikal (Marcus 2020, 59), a plausible analog to the royal counts mentioned above for Copan and Palenque.

This is the "mythohistoric" scheme, enacted in the Wiinte' Naah investiture rituals, that all or most high-rank Lowland kings attempted to reproduce for themselves—the case of Copan being the most precisely documented, through several detailed glyphic inscriptions, including the long trip to Teotihuacan. The displacement to Wiinte' Naah was still operating several centuries after Teotihuacan had fallen and ceased to be the political capital of Mesoamerica. According to Tokovinine (2020, 265), "the very last Tikal inscribed stela (Stela 11: C14) evokes Wiinte' Naah (Jones and Satterthwaite 1982, figure 16)" (Stela 11 is dated 869 CE). Beyond Tikal and Copan, it has been registered in inscriptions of Late Classic Calakmul, La Corona, Naranjo, Yaxchilan, and Piedras Negras, as well as Terminal Classic inscriptions of Machaquila-Tres Islas, Ukanal, Pusilha, and perhaps Ixtutz (Fash, Tokovinine, and Fash 2009; Stuart 2000; Tokovinine 2013, 94, 115). The Terminal Classic and Early Postclassic investiture rituals performed at the Chichen Itza capital were also related to the same scheme (Ringle 2004, 2009; Wren 1989). Still, several features of the grand ritual were repeated during the Late Postclassic in Maya Highland kingdoms, with a reference to a Mesoamerican primate city that was no longer Teotihuacan but Tollan, that is, successively Tula, Chichen Itza, then Mayapan, and eventually Tenochtitlan. Highland kings even traveled to Madrid by 1550 CE (Arnauld 1996; see historical context as explained in Romero, this volume). Displacement to a superordinate city to receive ritual investiture produced a hierarchy of kings, which seems to have been basic to the Classic Lowland geopolitics.

In the operation of those geopolitics, another aspect of the investiture ritual imported from Teotihuacan likely had a lasting impact on the Lowlands. Rituals of royal creation prescribed the practice of royal wars waged to obtain captives for sacrifice. This refers to an ideology, or religion, that Stuart (2012) and Taube (2000) see metaphorized by the figure of Waxaclajuun Ubaah Kan, or the "Teotihuacan War Serpent Deity" (Martin 2020, 159). This aspect has been, and still is currently, the object of several independent investigations by epigraphists and iconologists in the Southern Lowlands (see Grube and Schele 1994; Inomata and Triadan 2009, 70–71; Scherer and Golden 2014; Stone 1989; also Arnauld 2016a). A number of Late Classic war narratives appear in stelae inscriptions dated close to the accession of the local king, indicating that "the duty of battle captive-taking came to be personified within the local [. . .] dynasty" (Stuart 2005, figure 11.8).[4] Yet, royal warfare for sacrifice inspired from Teotihuacan is poorly known, in particular its effective role in Maya geopolitical dynamics. A few raids launched by young kings were not necessarily wars of conquest, but taking a royal captive certainly modified hierarchies (Martin 2020, 204–6, 232). What should be tentatively explored is that both practices (war, sacrifice) under the aegis of the War Serpent deity operated and constructed continuity through time changes during the critical moments of royal succession (López Austin and López Luján 1991; among others).

Therefore, the Tikal-Teotihuacan political link helps envision that political rituals, mainly royal investitures, combined at least five distinct temporalities:

- the temporality of monument production, that is, formulating inscriptions, calculating calendar dates, preparing speeches of rulers bound to participate in joint rituals, or building an edifice to be dedicated, also materially carving and erecting the stela;
- the inner temporality of the ritual itself, which in some cases could span months or years, including travels and warring episodes (Martin 2020, 111);
- the (linear) temporality opened by the public claim made on stone monuments erected for no less than eternity, and dated in the Long Count (from 3114 BCE)— by contrast, Late Postclassic stelae were periodically re-stuccoed and re-painted and were not meant to bear eternal information (Martin and Grube 2008, 228);
- the (cyclical) temporality of royal political action assigned to a specific series of calendric cycles and their divine "masters," reenacting mythohistorical episodes like the Wiinte' Naah "temporalization" (a 400-year baktun) likely imposed on the Southern Lowlands by the Tikal dynasty;
- and the (cyclical) temporality of every ruler's life (proximate to the 20-year katun), deemed to provoke succession crises with risk of dynastic change.

To weave such complex time threads into rituals required well-coordinated and strictly controlled activities among courtiers (Saturno et al. 2012), and these activities likely covered most of what we call "governance" in our current-day political sphere. It is no surprise that practices like stone inscriptions, stela erection, and Long Count notation (more difficult to calculate) were abandoned soon after the demise of the old dynasties. Specialists, royal court institutions, and probably the conflation of military, sociopolitical, and religious roles in the kingly person were assets of the Classic regimes that became intolerable to a number of subordinated individuals and groups.

The Tikal-Teotihuacan 378 CE encounter should not have been the only "swinging event" that might have anticipated completion rituals by means of the Wiinte' Naah mythohistorical scheme. The end of the powerful Kaan dynasty of Calakmul, brought up by two military Tikal victories (695, then 736 CE), seems to have had extremely serious consequences on the geopolitical scale (Martin and Grube 2008[5]). Historically, the 736 CE victory opened the way to the empowerment of several cities eager to emancipate and emerge as new powers (e.g., Martin 2020, 313, 318). From this date to 775 and even later, the increase in war narratives is so marked (Grube 2021; but see Martin 2020, 218; Tokovinine 2019, 87–91) that one wonders whether a good part of those conflicts did not originate in royal accession rituals of formerly subordinated dynasties attempting to emancipate by emulating the Wiinte' Naah scheme of investiture. In so doing, those dynasts intended to claim a direct connection to the early Teotihuacan sovereignty, obtaining the *kaloomte* title that would have placed them at the apex of the Lowland hierarchy, thus challenging the Tikal primacy. This idea has some likeliness, since political accession rituals are by far the most frequent ones referred to in Late Classic inscriptions (Munson et al. 2016), and *chuk* actions of captive-taking are the most frequently narrated war types from 550 CE on (see Grube 2021; also Tokovinine 2019). It is also consistent with the sudden distribution of kingly *kaloomte* titles previously restricted to Tikal and a few dynasties, and with the high number of cities that erected their first stela during the ninth century (e.g., Martin 2020, 81, 280).

DISCUSSION

It is in the framework of the particular time-completion geopolitics of the Classic Maya Southern Lowlands that the agency of ninth-century rulers and their successors should be investigated, through epigraphic, iconographic, and also archaeological evidence. The preliminary data series we have obtained in the TP project already point to a remarkable degree of spatial similarity in the way elites acted in or reacted to the crisis across configurations of kingdom networks. An "archaeology of the political collapse" may bring forth a Lowland geopolitical organization entering into segmentation, reorganization, and transformation (see also Ebert, Prufer,

Kennett 2014). Whereas the "cosmocentric structure" of the Lowlands disintegrated before 810 CE, some degree of reactivation might have developed during the ninth century around Ceibal, and there are indications of strong vitality across a northwest crescent-shaped sector open toward the rest of Mesoamerica—geographically, the Postclassic Acalan region, the Petén lakes, Río Bec, and Edzna (Arnauld et al., n.d.). Joint rituals known to have been held at Ceibal (849 CE) and previously at Altar de los Reyes (800 CE) would reflect reactivated and newly formed configurations, which, however, seem to have failed soon—at least by 890 CE, when Uxmal and Chichen Itza rapidly emerged as capitals in the Northern Lowlands. Yet, this archaeology would require that archaeological signals be improved, and assigned to fifty-year time spans within the Terminal Classic.

Pending more archaeological evidence, the geopolitics of time-completion rituals as sketched in this chapter suggest a likely chain of perceptions and conscious elitist agency throughout the 750–810 CE time lapse. A preliminary model would consist of the following sequence:

    a. local emancipation through many ritualized investiture rites including royal wars, occasioned in formerly subordinated cities by the Tikal 695–736 CE victory against Calakmul; likely the fall of the Kaan dynasty came to form a new scheme to be projected in the future;

    b. expectancy and anticipation of the completion moment attached to the 830 CE date ending the Ninth Cycle, with probably distinct moods and hues associated with each of the 770–790, 790–810, and 810–830 katuns (katuns punctuated by dry years; Hoggarth et al. 2017);

    c. projection into an uncertain post-830 future, through prospectivist or predictive discourses, of the Tikal hegemony mythohistorical scheme linked to the Teotihuacan entrada that had occurred at the opening of the same four-hundred-year cycle now to be completed;

    d. coordination of numerous actors (engaged in a, b, and c) through chains of rituals in order to create the conditions of a swinging moment of time completion that could properly close the old period and open the new one; this is when new alliances were forged and old dynasties destroyed (750–810 CE);

    e. and competition among numerous new actors seeking the best position for themselves in the reorganizing geopolitics, and in an emerging calendar "science" promoting shorter time cycles for political action (see Arnauld et al. 2018).

In each of those sequent moments, royal investiture rituals would have involved the five distinct temporalities (see above). Even though possibly articulated by the operation of the War Serpent ideology (war and sacrifice during succession crises, see above), our model remains too simplistic to allow us to explore such mechanisms. At the least, the model elucidates the abruptness and rapidity of the political collapse in a sequence integrating apparently contradictory actions. Foremost among the latter is the sudden increase of royal war narratives by the years 760–790. In the meantime, the old hegemonic dynasties were unable to counter the anticipation trends that they themselves possibly perceived well before 830 CE (as seen in the dynastic schemes of Copan and Palenque briefly mentioned in this chapter); also, new rulers emerged still in the full exercise of canonic kingship, even including the use of old Teotihuacan references (e.g., the *kaloomte* title), while attempts were made at reorganizing the Southern Lowland geopolitics repeating old schemes, and the notation of calendric dates changed from the Long Count (linear time) to the Short Count (cyclical time).

The projected Tikal-Teotihuacan scheme that was meant to open the Tenth Cycle from 830 CE would be reflected by new relationships linking the Mexican Highlands and Veracruz Lowlands with the Maya Lowlands, by Terminal Classic times on a Mesoamerican scale (this has been widely documented; e.g., Lacadena 2010; López Austin and López Luján 1999; Martin 2020, 294–99; Pascual Soto and Velásquez 2012; Ringle 2004; Ringle, Gallareta Negron, and Bey 1998). Since Tula was accepted as the heir of Teotihuacan, the ancestral Teotihuacan-Tikal bind would have been consciously replicated by the Tula-Chichen Itza bind. By then, new "stranger kings" had already emerged in the Northern Lowlands, as they had at Tikal four hundred years before (Ringle, Gallareta Negron, and Bey 2021). This order of Tollan was to become the Postclassic order until the Spanish intrusion.

CONCLUDING WORDS

We do not mean that expectancy in the decades preceding the end of the ninth baktun should be considered more causative of the political collapse than dry years and wars in the same katuns. But in view of the rapid and generalized processes that developed before 810–820 CE, we raise the issue of the agency modes of elites possibly obsessed by history, calendrics, and mythical schemes more than dry years and warfare output per se. After 810–820, there are several clues of an irreversible change, such as the sudden silence in inscriptions on war narratives (Grube 2021), the extreme decrease in stela erection, alliance shifts, formerly exclusive royal titles distributed among lower-rank dynasties, and joint rituals held in newly emerging capitals (synthetized in Arnauld, Andrieu, and Forné 2017). Among others, these very deep (revolutionary) changes in political rituals must be interpreted on the basis of what had happened in the preceding katuns, yet taking into account, as we propose to do in this chapter, the specific ways through which multiple-temporality rituals structured strategies, coordinated collective action, and, as such, truly constituted governance.

The model we formulate and the question we raise have a number of implications bearing on how historicist schemes were related to the anticipation of future times in Maya Classic societies, how the past helped define the future, or, instead, how expectancy of the future was used to reschematize the past and create innovative repetitions. Although qualifying and quantifying the many kinds of Terminal Classic agency are critically needed, these questions cannot be solved solely through archaeological evidence and good chronologies. Epigraphy, ethnohistory, and ethnolinguistics should contribute to explore, in given situations, "mechanisms" in political agency, rituals, and written and discursive expressions of Classic, Postclassic, and later Maya societies.

Acknowledgments. The Transition et Prédiction project has benefited from funds from Maison d'Archéologie et d'Ethnologie de Nanterre. We would have been unable to develop the entire research without the intellectual stimulation of the international RITMO network, the interdisciplinary perspectives it opened, and the exchanges we had on many occasions. We are much in debt to Julien Hiquet, Jennifer Saumur, and Juliette Taieb, who carried up the task of settling the database in its early phase (then University of Paris 1 doctoral students). Special thanks are due to Valentina Vapnarsky for her dedication and precise coordination work of the RITMO network.

NOTES

1. This raises the issues of how written transcripts relate to rituals performed, and how an effective ritual performance related to the event which supposedly occurred. The research by Munson and Macri (2009) and Munson et al. (2016) tackles both, but these are very complex issues (see also Stuart 2005). Preliminary statistics (Munson et al. 2016) correlate sites preserving the highest number of inscriptions with the highest lexical diversity bearing on rites. Although somewhat simplistic, this might be interpreted as, locally, the largest scribal communities (measured by their production) determining the most diverse ritualistic traditions (and lexical referents). At the least, this offers one approach (among others) to the issue of the mechanisms by which written political records helped configure Classic geopolitics.

2. Two surveys of the abundant Maya Terminal Classic literature, including fieldwork reports, were carried out on the following data sets: political rituals, urban activities, population movements, climate-related subsistence crises, warfare, trade activities, mesoamericanization (Arnauld et al., n.d.).

3. The idea is not so different from our modern "revolution," except that movements were not so much those of social or political human groups as those of duly integrated time

and space categories: periodic "turning of the cosmos on its axis and repetition of the past in the future" (*retournement périodique du cosmos sur son axe et répétition du passé dans l'avenir*) (Descola 2005, 379; authors' translation).

4. The complete quote is as follows: "Lintel 25 is perhaps the most explicit statement of the ideological underpinnings of Maya warfare, where the duty of battle captive-taking came to be personified within the local Yaxchilan dynasty" (Stuart 2005, figure 11.8).

5. Indeed the iconography of Structure 5D-57 in the Central Acropolis royal palace suggests that the 695 victory was itself reframed into the Teotihuacan-Tikal mythohistoric scheme (Miller 1978, figures 3 and 4).

REFERENCES

Andrews, Anthony P., E. Wyllys Andrews, and Fernando Robles Castellanos. 2003. "The Northern Maya Collapse and Its Aftermath." *Ancient Mesoamerica* 14 (1): 151–56.

Arnauld, M. Charlotte. 1996. "De Nacxit a Rabinal Achi: Estados territoriales en formación en las tierras altas mayas (Postclásico)." In *Investigadores de la Cultura Maya* 3, 231–68. Campeche: Publicaciones de la Universidad de Campeche.

Arnauld, M. Charlotte. 2016a. "Rituales de victoria: Investidura de reyes guerreros." Paper presented at El tiempo en recomposiciones: Enfoques interdisciplinarios sobre los rituales mesoamericanos (RITMO, organizers). Colloquium RITMO, Rome.

Arnauld, M. Charlotte. 2016b. "Agua-cerro, ideología y realidades en el área maya." *Americae Altepetl* 1. Accessed October 2019. https://americae.fr/dossiers/altepetl/agua-cerro-ideologia-realidades-area-maya/.

Arnauld M. Charlotte, Chloé Andrieu, and Mélanie Forné. 2017. "'In the Days of My Life': The Maya Lowlands from Classic to Early Postclassic Times (CE 780–920) (the Long Ninth Century)." *Journal de la Société des Américanistes*, online special issue, *Maya Times*. https://doi.org/10.4000/jsa.15362.

Arnauld, M. Charlotte, Chloé Andrieu, Julien Hiquet, Jennifer Saumur, and Juliette Taieb. 2018. "Changement dans la prédiction politique au IXe siècle apr. J.-C. dans les royaumes mayas." In *La composition du temps? Prédictions, événements, narrations historiques*, edited by Chloé Andrieu and Sophie Houdart, 39–49. Paris: De Boccard.

Arnauld, M. Charlotte, Chloé Andrieu, Julien Hiquet, Jennifer Saumur, and Juliette Taieb. N.d. "An Archaeology of the Maya Collapse: Classic-to-Postclassic Transition."

Avendaño de Loyola, Andrés. 1987. *Relation of Two Trips to Peten: Made for the Conversion of the Heathen Ytzaex and Cehaches (1696)*. Edited by Frank E. Comparato and translated by Charles P. Bowditch and Guillermo Rivera. Culver City: Labryrinthos.

Bazy, Damien, and Takeshi Inomata. 2017. "Multiple Waves of Political Disintegration in the Classic Maya Collapse: New Insights from the Excavation of Group D, Ceibal, Guatemala." *Journal of Field Archaeology* 42: 82–96.

Beliaev, Dimitri D. 2000. "Wuk Tsuk and Oxlahun Tsuk: Naranjo and Tikal in the Late Classic." In *The Sacred and the Profane: Architecture and Identity in the Maya Lowlands*, edited by Pierre Robert Colas, 63–81. A. Saurwein: Markt Schwaben.

Bricker, Victoria. 1981. *The Indian Christ, the Indian King: The Historical Substrate of Maya Myth and Ritual.* Austin: University of Texas Press.

Bricker, Victoria R., Anthony F. Aveni, and Harvey M. Bricker. 2014. "Deciphering the Handwriting on the Wall: Some Astronomical Interpretations of the Recent Discoveries at Xultun, Guatemala." *Latin American Antiquity* 25 (2): 152–69.

Bricker, Victoria R., and Helga M. Miram, eds. 2002. *An Encounter of Two Worlds: The Book of Chilam Balam of Kaua.* New Orleans: Tulane University.

Carter, Nicholas. 2014. "Kinghip and Collapse: Inequality and Identity in the Terminal Classic Southern Maya Lowlands." PhD diss., Brown University, Providence.

Chase, Diane Z., and Arlen F. Chase. 2006. "Framing the Maya Collapse: Continuity, Discontinuity, Method and Practice in the Classic to Postclassic Southern Maya Lowlands." In *After Collapse: The Regeneration of Complex Societies*, edited by Glenn M. Schwartz and John J. Nichols, 168–87. Tucson: University of Arizona Press.

Coe, Michael D. 1965. "A Model of Ancient Community Structure in the Maya Lowlands." *Southwestern Journal of Anthropology* 21 (2): 97–114.

Dehouve, Danièle. 2006. *Essai sur la Royauté sacrée en République mexicaine.* Paris: CNRS.

Demarest, Arthur A. 1992. "Ideology and Ancient Maya Cultural Evolution." In *Ideology and Precolumbian Civilizations*, edited by Arthur A. Demarest and Geoffrey W. Conrad, 135–57. Santa Fe, NM: School of American Research Press.

Demarest, Arthur A., Prudence M. Rice, and Don S. Rice. 2004. *The Terminal Classic in the Maya Lowlands: Collapse, Transition, and Transformation.* Boulder: University Press of Colorado.

Descola, Philippe. 2005. *Par-delà nature et culture.* Paris: Gallimard.

Ebert, Claire E., Keith M. Prufer, and Douglas J. Kennett. 2014. "Maya Monuments and Spatial Statistics: A GIS-Based Examination of the Terminal Classic Period Maya Collapse." *Ancient Mesoamerica* 25 (2): 337–56.

Farriss, Nancy M. 1995. "Remembering the Future, Anticipating the Past: History, Time, and Cosmology among the Maya of Yucatan." In *Time: Histories and Ethnologies*, edited by Diane Owen Hughes and Thomas R. Trautmann, 107–38. Ann Arbor: University of Michigan Press.

Fash, William L., and Barbara W. Fash. 2006. "Ritos de fundación en una ciudad pluri-étnica: Cuevas y lugares sagrados lejanos en la reinvidicación del pasado en Copán." In

Nuevas Ciudades, nuevas patrias: Fundación, refundación y relocalización de las ciudades en Mesoamérica y el Mediterraneo antiguo: una perspectiva desde la antigüedad, edited by Ma Josefa Iglesias Ponce de Leon, Rogelio Valencia Rivera, and Andres Ciudad Ruiz, 105–30. Madrid: Sociedad Española de Estudios Mayas.

Fash, William L., Alexander Tokovinine, and Barbara W. Fash. 2009. "The House of New Fire at Teotihuacan and Its Legacy in Mesoamerica." In *The Art of Urbanism, How Mesoamerican Kingdoms Represented Themselves in Architecture and Imagery*, edited by W. L. Fash and Leonardo Lopez Luján, 201–29. Washington, DC: Dumbarton Oaks Research Library and Collection.

Galván Bernal, Melissa, George J. Bey III, and Rossana May Ciau. 2017. "From Temple to Trash: Analysis and Interpretation of a Dismantled Stucco Façade and Its Deposit from Kiuic, Yucatán." In *Recent Investigations in the Puuc Region of Yucatán*, edited by Meghan Rubenstein, 39–58. Oxford: Archaeopress.

Graeber, David, and Marshall Sahlins. 2017. *On Kings*. Chicago: Hau Books.

Grube, Nikolai. 2000. "The City-States of the Maya." In *A Comparative Study of Thirty City-State Cultures*, edited by Mogens Herman Hansen, 547–66. Copenhagen: Royal Danish Academy of Sciences and Letters.

Grube, Nikolai. 2021. "Nostalgic Kings: The Rhetoric of Terminal Classic Maya Inscriptions." In *Rupture and Transformation of Maya Kingship: From Classic to Postclassic Times*, edited by Tsubasa Okoshi, Arlen F. Chase, Philippe Nondédéo, and M. Charlotte Arnauld, 1–18. Gainesville: University Press of Florida.

Grube, Nikolai, and Linda Schele. 1994. "*Kuy*, the Owl of Omen and War." *Mexicon* 16 (1): 10–16.

Guenter, Stanley. 2020. "On Copan Stele 11 and the Origins of the Ill Omen of Katun 8 Ahau." In *A Forest of History: The Maya after the Emergence of Maya Kingship*, edited by Travis W. Stanton and M. Kathryn Brown, 236–60. Boulder: University Press of Colorado.

Hanks, William F. 2017. "The Plurality of Temporal Reckoning among the Maya." *Journal de la Société des Américanistes*, online special issue, *Maya Times*, 497–520. https://doi .org/10.4000/jsa.15294.

Hartog, François. 2003. *Régimes d'historicité, présentisme et expériences du temps*. Paris: Seuil.

Helmke, Christophe, James A. Awe, Shawn G. Morton, and Gyles Iannone. 2015. "The Text and Context of the Cuychen Vase, Macal Valley, Belize." *Maya Archaeology* 3: 8–29.

Hoggarth Julie A., Sebastian F. M. Breitenbach, Brendan J. Culleton, Claire E. Ebert, Marilyn A. Masson, and Douglas J. Kennett. 2015. "The Political Collapse of Chichén Itzá in Climatic and Cultural Context." *Global and Planetary Change* 138: 25–42.

Hoggarth, Julie A., Matthew Restall, James W. Wood, and Douglas J. Kennett. 2017. "Drought and Its Demographic Effects in the Maya Lowlands." *Current Anthropology* 58 (1): 82–113.

Houston, Stephen D., and Takeshi Inomata. 2009. *The Classic Maya*. Cambridge: Cambridge University Press.

Houston, Stephen D., David Stuart, and Karl A. Taube. 2006. *The Memory of Bones: Body, Being, and Experience among the Classic Maya*. Austin: University of Texas Press.

Ichon, Alain, and M. Charlotte Arnauld. 1985. *Le Protoclassique à La Lagunita, El Quiché, Guatemala*. Paris, Guatemala: Institut d'Ethnologie / CNRS-RCP 294 y 500 / Piedra Santa.

Inomata, Takeshi. 2006. "Plazas, Performers, and Spectators: Political Theaters of the Classic Maya." *Current Anthropology* 47 (5): 805–42.

Inomata, Takeshi, and Daniela Triadan. 2009. "Culture and Practice of War in Maya Society." In *Warfare in Cultural Context: Practice, Agency and the Archaeology of Violence*, edited by Axel E. Nielsen and William H. Walker, 56–83. Tucson: University of Arizona Press.

Inomata, Takeshi, Daniela Triadan, Jessica MacLellana, Melissa Burhama, Kazuo Aoyama, Juan Manuel Palomoa, Hitoshi Yonenobu, Flory Pinzónd, and Hiroo Nasu. 2017. "High-Precision Radiocarbon Dating of Political Collapse and Dynastic Origins at the Maya Site of Ceibal, Guatemala." *Proceedings of the National Academy of Sciences* 114 (6): 1293–98. https://doi.org/10.1073/pnas.1618022114.

Jones, Christopher, and Linton Satterthwaite. 1982. *The Monuments and Inscriptions of Tikal: The Carved Monuments*. Philadelphia: University Museum, University of Pennsylvania.

Kennett, Douglas J., Sebastian F. M. Breitenbach, Valorie V. Aquino, Yemane Asmerom, Jaime Awe, James U. L. Baldini, Patrick Bartlein, Brendan J. Culleton, Claire Ebert, Christopher Jazwa, Martha J. Macri, Norbert Marwan, Victor Polyak, Keith M. Prufer, Harriet E. Ridley, Harald Sodemann, Bruce Winterhalder, and Gerald H. Haug. 2012. "Development and Disintegration of Maya Political Systems in Response to Climate Change." *Science* 338: 788–91.

Knowlton, Timothy. 2010. *Maya Creation Myths: Words and Worlds of the Chilam Balam*. Boulder: University Press of Colorado.

Lacadena García-Gallo, Alfonso. 2010. "Highland Mexican and Maya Intellectual Exchange in the Late Postclassic: Some Thoughts on the Origin of Shared Elements and Methods of Interaction." In *Astronomers, Scribes, and Priests Intellectual Interchange between the Northern Maya Lowlands and Highland Mexico in the Late Postclassic Period*, edited by Gabrielle Vail and Christine Hernandez, 383–406. Washington, DC: Dumbarton Oaks.

López Austin, Alfredo, and Leonardo López Luján. 1991. "The Temple of Quetzalcoatl at Teotihuacan: Its Possible Ideological Significance." *Ancient Mesoamerica* 2: 93–105.

López Austin, Alfredo, and Leonardo López Luján. 1999. *Mito y realidad de Zuyua: Serpiente Emplumada y las transformaciones mesoamericanas del Clásico al Posclásico*. Mexico City: El Colegio de México / Fideicomiso Historia de las Américas / Fondo de Cultura Económica.

Marcus, Joyce. 2020. "Maya Usurpers." In *A Forest of History: The Maya after the Emergence of Maya Kingship*, edited by Travis W. Stanton and M. Kathryn Brown, 49–66. Boulder: University Press of Colorado.

Martin, Simon. 2020. *Ancient Maya Politics: A Political Anthropology of Classic Period 150–900 CE*. Cambridge: Cambridge University Press.

Martin, Simon, and Nikolai Grube. 1995. "Maya Superstates." *Archaeology* 48: 41–46.

Martin, Simon, and Nikolai Grube. 2008. *Chronicles of the Maya Kings and Queens: Deciphering the Dynasties of the Ancient Maya*. London: Thames and Hudson.

Mathews, Jennifer P., and James F. Garber. 2004. "Models of Cosmic Order: Physical Expression of Sacred Space among the Ancient Maya." *Ancient Mesoamerica* 15: 49–59.

Miller, Arthur. 1978. "A Brief Outline of the Artistic Evidence for Cultural Contact between the Maya Lowlands and the Central Mexican Highlands." In *Middle Classic Mesoamerica: A.D. 400–700*, edited by Esther Pasztory, 63–70. New York: Columbia University Press.

Munson, Jessica L., and Martha J. Macri. 2009. "Sociopolitical Network Interactions: A Case Study of the Classic Maya." *Journal of Anthropological Archaeology* 28: 424–38.

Munson, Jessica, Jonathan Scholnick, Matthew Looper, Yuriy Polyukhovych, and Martha J. Macri. 2016. "Ritual Diversity and Divergence of Classic Maya Dynastic Traditions: A Lexical Perspective on Within-Group Cultural Variation." *Latin American Antiquity* 27 (1): 74–95.

Nondédéo, Philippe, Alfonso Lacadena García Gallo, and Juan Ignacio Cases Martín. 2019. "Teotihuacanos y mayas en la 'entrada' de 11 Eb' (378 d. C.): Nuevos datos de Naachtun, Petén, Guatemala." Special issue, *Revista Española de Antropología Americana* 49: 53–75.

Okoshi, Tsubasa, Arlen F. Chase, Philippe Nondédéo, and M. Charlotte Arnauld, eds. 2021. *Rupture and Transformation of Maya Kingship: From Classic to Postclassic Times*. Gainesville: University Press of Florida.

Olivier, Guilhem. 2015. *Cacería, sacrificio y poder en Mesoamérica*. Mexico City: IIH-UNAM / Fondo de Cultura Económica / CEMCA.

Pascual Soto, Arturo, and Erik Velásquez García. 2012. "Relaciones y estrategias políticas entre El Tajin y diversas entidades mayas durante el siglo ix d.C." In *Maya Political Relations and Strategies*, edited by Jaroslaw Zralka, Wieslaw Koszkul, and Beata Golinska, 205–30. Krakow: Jagiellonina university and Wayeb / Proceedings of the 14th European Maya Conference.

Ringle, William M. 2004. "On the Political Organization of Chichen Itza." *Ancient Mesoamerica* 15: 167–218.

Ringle, William M. 2009. "The Art of War: Imagery of the Upper Temple of the Jaguars, Chichen Itza." *Ancient Mesoamerica* 20: 15–44.

Ringle, William, Tomas Gallareta Negron, and George J. Bey. 1998. "The Return of Quetzalcoatl: Evidence for the Spread of a World Religion during the Epiclassic Period." *Ancient Mesoamerica* 9: 183–232.

Ringle, William, Tomas Gallareta Negron, and George J. Bey. 2021. "Stranger Kings in Northern Yucatan." In *Rupture and Transformation of Maya Kingship: From Classic to Postclassic Times*, edited by Tsubasa Okoshi, Arlen F. Chase, Philippe Nondédéo, and M. Charlotte Arnauld, 249–68. Gainesville: University Press of Florida.

Sahlins, Marshall. 1985. *Islands of History*. Chicago: University of Chicago Press.

Saturno, William A., David Stuart, Anton F. Aveni, and Franco D. Rossi. 2012. "Ancient Maya Astronomical Tables from Xultun, Guatemala." *Science* 336 (6082): 714–17.

Scherer, Andrews K., and Charles Golden. 2014. "War in the West: History, Landscape, and Classic Maya Conflict." In *Embattled Bodies, Embattled Places: Wars in Precolumbian Mesoamerica and the Andes*, edited by Andrew K. Scherer and John W. Verano, 57–92. Washington, DC: Dumbarton Oaks.

Schieber de Lavarreda, Christa. 2002. "La ofrenda de Tak'alik Ab'aj (antes Abaj Takalik)." In *XV Simposio de Investigaciones Arqueológicas en Guatemala, 2001*, edited by Juan Pablo Laporte, Hector Escobedo, and Barbara Arroyo, 399–412. Guatemala: Museo Nacional de Arqueología y Etnología.

Schieber de Lavarreda, Christa. 2003. "Una nueva ofrenda en Tak'alik Ab'aj (antes Abaj Takalik): El Entierro 1." In *XVI Simposio de Investigaciones Arqueológicas en Guatemala, 2002*, edited by Juan Pablo Laporte, Barbara Arroyo, Hector Escobedo, and Hector Mejía, 784–92. Guatemala: Museo Nacional de Arqueología y Etnología.

Schwartz, Glenn M. 2006. "From Collapse to Regeneration." In *After Collapse: The Regeneration of Complex Societies*, edited by Glenn M. Schwartz and John J. Nichols, 3–17. Tucson: University of Arizona Press.

Stone, Andrea. 1989. "Disconnection, Foreign Insignia, and Political Expansion: Teotihuacan and the Warrior Stelae of Piedras Negras." In *Mesoamerica and the Decline of Teotihuacan. A.D. 700–900*, edited by Richard A. Diehl and Janet C. Berlo, 153–72. Washington, DC: Dumbarton Oaks.

Stuart, David. 2000. "The Arrival of Strangers." In *Mesoamerica's Classic Heritage: From Teotihuacan to the Aztecs*, edited by Davíd Carrasco, Lindsay Jones, and John S. Sessions, 465–513. Boulder: University Press of Colorado.

Stuart, David. 2004. "The Beginnings of the Copan Dynasty: A Review of the Hieroglyphic and Historical Evidence." In *Understanding Early Classic Copan*, edited by

Ellen E. Bell, Marcello A. Canuto, and R. J. Sharer, 215–48. Philadelphia: University of Pennsylvania Museum of Archaeology and Anthropology.

Stuart, David. 2005. "Ideology and Classic Maya Kingship." In *A Catalyst for Ideas: Anthropology and Archaeology and the Legacy of Douglas Schwartz*, edited by Vernon Scarborough, 287–86. Santa Fe, NM: Seminar of Advanced Research, School of American Research Press.

Stuart, David. 2011a. *The Order of Days: Unlocking the Secrets of the Ancient Maya*. New York: Three River Press.

Stuart, David. 2011b. "Some Working Notes on the Text of Tikal Stela 31." www.mesoweb .com/stuart/notes/Tikal.pdf.

Stuart, David. 2012. "Notes on a New Text from La Corona." deciphermentworldpress.com /2012/06/30.

Stuart, David. 2024. "La replantación de los años: Metáfora agrícola en las ceremonias del calendario maya clásico y en la ideología política." Paper presented at the Coloquio internacional de la red RITMO Ciclos e historia en el discurso en idiomas mayas y de Mesoamérica. Casa Herrera, La Antigua, Guatemala, July 22–23, 2024.

Sullivan, Paul. 1989. *Unfinished Conversations: Maya and Foreigners between Two Wars*. Berkeley: University of California Press.

Tambiah, Stanley J. 1977. "The Galactic Polity: The Structure of Traditional Kingdoms in Southeast Asia." *Annals of the New York Academy of Sciences* 293: 69–97.

Taube, Karl A. 1988. "A Pre-Hispanic Katun Wheel." *Journal of Anthropological Research* 44 (2): 183–203.

Taube, Karl A. 2000. "The Turquoise Hearth: Fire, Self-Sacrifice, and the Central Mexican Cult of War." In *Mesoamerica's Classic Heritage: From Teotihuacan to the Aztecs*, edited by David Carrasco, Lindsay Jones, and Scott Sessions, 269–340. Boulder: University Press of Colorado.

Taube, Karl A. 2004. "Structure 10L-16 and Its Early Classic Antecedents: Fire Shrines and the Evocation and Resurrection of K'inich Yax K'uk' Mo." In *Early Classic Copan*, edited by Ellen E. Bell, Marcello A Canuto, and Robert J. Sharer, 265–95. Philadelphia: University of Pennsylvania Museum of Archaeology and Anthropology.

Tokovinine, Alex. 2013. *Place and Identity in Classic Maya Narratives*. Washington, DC: Dumbarton Oaks.

Tokovinine, Alex. 2019. "Fire in the Land. Landscapes of War in Classic Maya Narratives." In *Seeking Conflict in Mesoamerica: Operational, Cognitive, and Experiential Approaches*, edited by Shawn G. Morton and Meaghan M. Peuramaki-Brown, 77–100. Boulder: University Press of Colorado.

Tokovinine, Alex. 2020. "Distance and Power in Classic Maya Texts." In *Reinventing the World: Debates on Mesoamerican Colonial Cosmologies*, edited by Ana Díaz, 251–81. Boulder: University Press of Colorado.

Vapnarsky, Valentina. 2017. "Futuros en contrapunto: Proyección, predicción y deseo en maya yucateco." *Journal de la Société des Américanistes*, special online issue, *Maya Times*, 129–72. https://doi.org/10.4000/jsa.15387.

Wren, Linnea H. 1989. "Ceremonialism in the Reliefs of the North Temple, Chichén Itzá." In *Seventh Palenque Round Table*, edited by Virginia Miller and Merle Greene Robertson, 25–31. San Francisco: Pre-Columbian Art Research Institute.

PART V

Ritual Temporalities in Confrontation

15

To Figure, to Condense, and to Stretch

Temporalities and Gestures in the Colonial Catechisms of Mexico

BÉRÉNICE GAILLEMIN

Several pictorial catechisms were made in colonial Mexico over the period from the end of the sixteenth into the nineteenth centuries. At present, about twenty-five such manuscripts are extant, held by Mexican, European, and US institutions.[1] In these pocket-sized notebooks, the primary ritual texts of Catholicism (i.e., Christian doctrine) were transcribed as hundreds of images that we might consider signs denoting words.[2] Written in this way, texts that had to be memorized include the Sign of the Cross, the Our Father, the Hail Mary, and the Creed, along with several lists, for example the Ten Commandments. The group of manuscripts discussed in this study are from the seventeenth and the first half of the eighteenth centuries.[3]

Since the iconographies of Europe and Mesoamerica gradually intermingled, enriching each other, analyzing only the style or the iconography of these unsigned manuscripts does not provide sufficient reliable evidence to assert their authorship. As we will see, however, we can analyze the authors' strategies when it came to transferring Christian concepts into images—and, in particular, those that refer to time. Trying to approach more closely both the knowledge base and environment of the painters, I will highlight a few noteworthy features of how Catholic faith and its rites spread almost surreptitiously, thereby creating a new relationship to time and ritual temporalities.

To introduce this type of pictorial transcription, I begin by commenting on several pictures used to transcribe the Five Church Commandments[4] (figure 15.1), one

https://doi.org/10.5876/9781646426829.c015

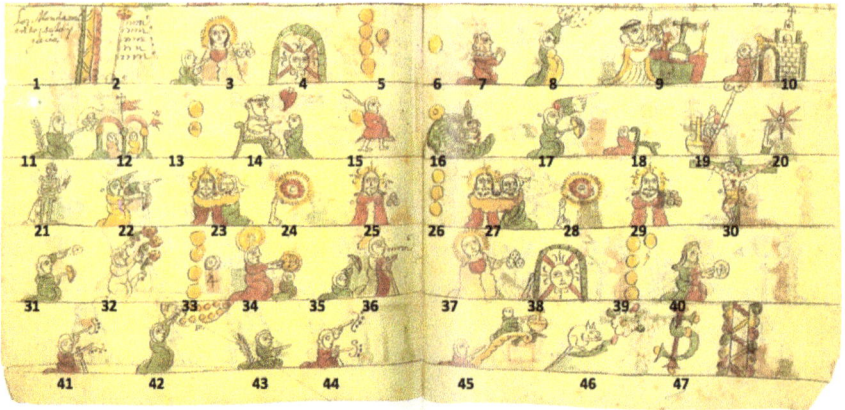

Figure 15.1. Pictorial transcription of the Five Church Commandments, no. 809, folios 5v–6r, detail

of several examples discussed herein that come from a manuscript preserved in the Bibliothèque Nationale de France in Paris.

The title ("Los Mandamientos de la yglecia") here appears in Spanish and with alphabetical characters (1). Then, the reading order of the manuscript, from left to right across two following pages, follows the number of each commandment as represented by a series of yellow circles numbering one to five and beginning at boldface number six—hereafter (6)—in figure 15.1, after the total is depicted in (5).

This pictorial text corresponds to the following text, which is a translation from the basic list of the Five Church Commandments. This text has been stable through time and, in this case, can be understood in several languages, meaning that even the translations into Indigenous languages have some correspondence in terms of number of words and syntax:

> The commandments (2) of Our Holy Mother (3) the Church (4) are five (5); **First (6)**, to hear (7) and see (8) a Mass (9) on Sundays (10) and (11) feasts (12); **Second (13)**, to confess (14) once (15) a year (16) or when (17) one is expecting (18) the coming (19) of a danger (20) of death (21) or when (22) one communes (23) with the flesh (24) of our Lord (25); **Third (26)**, to commune (27) with the flesh (28) of our Lord (29) Jesus Christ (30) during (31) flowery Easter (32); **Fourth (33)**, to fast (34) when (35) commanded (36) by our Holy Mother (37) the Church (38); **Fifth (39)**, to pay (40) the (41) tithes (42) and (43) the (44) first fruits (45); So be it (46), [amen] Jesus (47).

Many figures beyond the "main characters" assigned to primary actions appear among these images; we refer to these figures as "guides" or "narrators." They appear standing and with extended fingers (see figure 15.1, images no. 3, 10, 11, 17, 22, 31, 35, and 41 to 45) and the depiction of just one hand can signify their presence (see figure 15.1, images no. 20, 21, 24, 28, and 38). These guides' function is to accompany the reader through the visual text and to mark important passages: they organize the material and fulfill a role that is emphatic more than semantic. Guide figures are thus comparable to manicules, the ubiquitous small pointing hands that appear in the margins of manuscripts and printed books from the twelfth to the eighteenth centuries and that were produced both for and by readers (Sherman 2008, 2).

The Church Commandments pages bring together a plethora of ideas, words, and details. Of course, the more than 20 pages and 600 complex pictures that constitute the whole manuscript are even richer than this small sample, but even this restricted visual text allows us to focus on time, ritual, and their articulation in pictures. Indeed, it is not only the symbols but also the representations of gestures and postures that refer to adverbs, verbs, or substantives related to time or actions inscribed in precise temporalities. Looking for a classification depending on the relation existing between the picture and time, I will highlight images corresponding to the figuration of temporal adverbs. I will then turn to a comparison between two types of images that allude to different Catholic rites and daily acts. To do so, I present some images that seem to narrow or condense time and others that, in contrast, are intended to stretch it.

FIGURING NOTIONS OF TIME

One of the functions of the symbols we will describe here is that of "figuring" terms related to time—that is, illustrating a temporal term by means of an image to transcribe certain deictic values (i.e., past, present, future) or adverbs, (e.g., now, tomorrow, yesterday, when). Other images are used to refer to units of time measurement (e.g., day, month, year, eternity) or terms indicating a sequential temporal relationship (e.g., before/after, start/end, first/last).

To make these transcriptions from word to image, painters used a variety of procedures and referenced (a) natural phenomena and spatial organization (e.g., the vertical axis), (b) the human body, and (c) objects and buildings.

Natural Phenomena and Spatial Organization
The Moon

The temporal relator "when" was transcribed as a sort of arc (see figure 15.1, images no. 17, 22, 31, and 35) that, I propose, depicts a stylized crescent moon. The celestial body refers to the idea of a temporal moment; the observation of changing natural

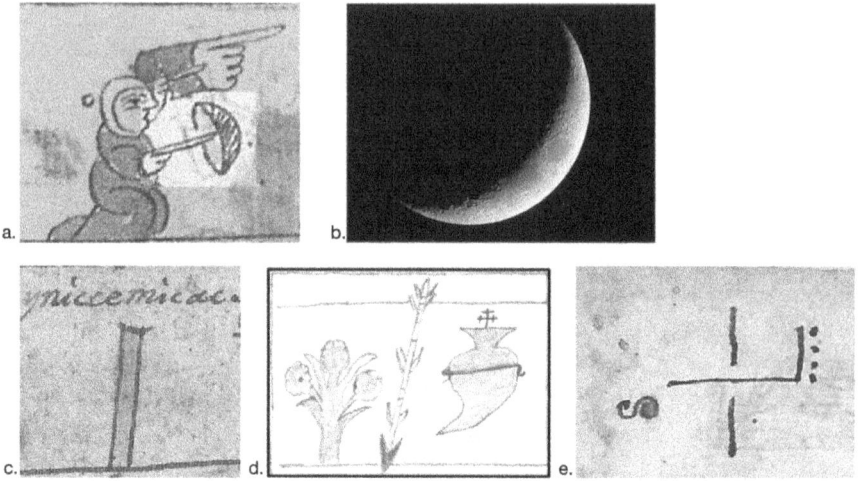

Figure 15.2. (a) The temporal relator "when" (no. 809, detail) and the moon; (b) "eternity" and verticality (details from no. 808[c], 813[d] and 810[e])

phenomena thus made it possible to allude to the passage of time (figures 15.2a and 15.2b).[5]

In the pictorial catechism reproduced in figure 15.1, the word denoted by the representation of this gesture is a "when" alluding to time in general, not to a precise moment. Like the temporal relator itself, this gesture appears to refer to distance in time and can signal either past or future. In this case, it is unnecessary to specify how the term is formulated in Spanish or in the different possible Indigenous languages that might be used to teach doctrine: the link between term and image is extralinguistic and pragmatic.

Verticality: "Eternity" and "Firsts"

"Eternity" was transcribed by the gesture of anchoring an object to the ground (e.g., a stick or arrow). Here, in contrast, Nahuatl is useful in order to understand its meaning. Missionaries translated the adjective "eternally, forever" into the Nahuatl term *cemihcac*—which is composed of *cem*—"one, entirely, wholly"—and *ihcac*— "to be standing."

In three pictorial catechisms where semiotic elements are strongly associated with Nahuatl semantics and phonetics (and in contrast to the manuscript presented in figure 15.1), this term is transcribed by three slightly different images. The first (figure 15.2c) consists of a long rectangular brown shape drawn on the horizontal line that delimits the bands, most often serving as a ground line. The second image is more precisely an arrow seemingly embedded in a similar ground line from which flowers bloom in the image immediately to the left (figure 15.2d). The third image is more abstract, composed by a footprint and two vertical lines; I think that the footprint denotes the ground where the vertical line "stands," communicating the same idea of "eternity" (figure 15.2e). All of these signs refer to what is "entirely standing"—that is, what is eternal. Again, we see how a gesture—the act of embedding a stick or an arrow into the ground or, rather, the result of this act, namely an upright or standing stick—has been used to refer to a temporal concept. This is a very concrete representation of temporal anchorage. The traditional conceptualization of time as an axis or timeline (i.e., sagittal, transversal, or vertical) is thus converted into something else by these dynamic diagrams; it is a gesture that marks time.

The image used to denote the *primicias* ("first fruits") is also of interest. The Spanish-language word for this tax comes from the Latin *primitiae*; it designates "the first fruits of the Earth or livestock," as a payment required by the Church Commandments. In the manuscript reproduced in figure 15.1, we can see that this word has been denoted by a figure index pointing in the direction of a representation of the earth (symbolized by the orb, a globe topped by a cross). This figure is positioned on a cloud-shaped staircase (see figure 15.1, image no. 45). Not only does the globe depict a European idea, the fruits "of the Earth," but also the figure's location at the top of this stairs is very much Western-influenced. Indeed, he is standing on what could be compared to a catwalk. Here, the "first" is "what stands at the highest point"—in the heavens, where God is. Although the gestural expression of temporal notions often involves a front/back (future/past for French speakers, see Calbris 1990) or left/right line (Cienki 1998), here the imaginary temporal line is vertical and begins in Heaven.

THE HUMAN BODY

The preceding image for the *primicias* contrasts sharply with that found in another manuscript where the painter indicates time through references to the body. Note that in Nahuatl, *primicias* was translated as *in tlein yancuican mochihua, in yacatiuh* ("what is done first, what comes like the nose"): both in the Nahuatl language and in the physical world, the nose is indeed what leads.[6] This explains why, in a catechism preserved in the British Museum[7]—dating from the beginning of the eighteenth century and whose images are very closely linked to Nahuatl semantics and phonetics—the representation of a nose has been used precisely to refer to *primicias* (figure 15.3a).

This idea recalls the theory of conceptual metaphor expressed by Lakoff and Johnson (1985), who suggests that the metaphorical mapping of time in space has an experimental and physical basis. The image is also reminiscent of the concrete etymological origin of the word; in a way, the representation of this head profile

Figure 15.3. (a) The sign for "*primicias*" or "that which comes like the nose" (detail from *The Commandments of the Church*, no. 813, folios 8v and 9r); (b) series of signs corresponding to the syntagma "now and on the lips of our death" (detail from *Hail Mary*, no. 810, folios 4v–5r arranged with 5v–6r); (c) series of signs corresponding to the syntagma "now [and at the time of death]" (detail from *Hail Mary*, no. 823, folios 2v–3r arranged with 3v–4r)

"attests the metaphor, and maintains the link between the passage of the proper to the figurative sense" (Calbris 1985, 75).

Another corporeal reference to time appears in a representation of an open mouth placed next to a skull. This image depicts the following phrase from the Hail Mary: "(Now and) at the moment of our death" (figure 15.3b).

As translated into Nahuatl, this phrase appears as "[now and] when [we will be] on the lips of our death" ([*in axcan ihuan*] *in yquac ye tomiquiliztempan*; Molina 1675). Through the word *tomiquiliztempan* (from *miquiliztli*, "death," and *tentli*, "lips"), lips are what makes it possible to give a shape to a precise moment.[8]

In the catechism mentioned earlier in relation to eternity (see figure 15.2e), the association between an open mouth and a skull depicts the moment just before death, when one is on the very edge or lips of time. Even if this association between body, space, and time is not specific to Nahuatl, the correspondence between its pictorial and operative transcription suggests that the painter is drawing on an established repertoire of Indigenous correlations between time and the body.

OBJECTS AND BUILDINGS

The authors of these catechisms also used objects to refer to time. When depicting a penitent's request of the Virgin to "pray for us, poor sinners, now and at the hour of our death," in a catechism conserved in New York,[9] the painter transcribed the word "now" with a depiction of a man pointing at a bell (figure 15.3c).

This image might seem surprising, yet its design is both judicious and pragmatic. With the coming of Catholicism, the local landscape changed not only visually but aurally. In fact, the sensorium was transformed entirely, and the introduction of bells shifted the time perception. Whether in towns or in villages, the bells of the church began to mark the day, replacing the sounds of shells and drums that had been used to gather people and to provide rhythm in pre-Hispanic rituals. Its sound became indicator of when one had to stop activities to pray, go to church to listen to doctrine, or attend mass (Corbin 1994; Domínguez Ruiz 2007).

The images shown in figures 15.2 and 15.3 represent different strategies used by painters to refer to time: a range of images are connected with Nahuatl (figures 15.2c–e; figure 15.3a), while others can be understood in any language but are related to the natural environment or the sensory landscape (figures 15.2a and 15.3c). The images taught Catholic prayers while underlining daily time references associated with certain objects (the bell) and certain sounds (its ringing).

Similarly, in the list of Church Commandments, the word "Sunday" (kept as a Spanish loan in Nahuatl texts) corresponds to the image of a church (see figure 15.1, no. 10). Note that the "week" of seven days was itself a new concept, quite distinct from the thirteen or twenty days that formed the subdivisions of the *xiuhpohualli* and *tonalpohualli* pre-Hispanic calendars. Moreover, rather than the traditional day signs (*Calli*, "House"; *Tochtli*, "Rabbit"; etc.), "Sunday" was more precisely associated with the image of a religious building, and by extension with a dictated activity: going to mass.

Comparison across manuscripts allows us to underscore that there is heterogeneity in the way these catechisms refer to time. Combining this analysis with other variations indicators, I observed that images closer to Nahuatl or to ideas that could be described as autochthonous correspond to transcriptions of texts from the Franciscan or Dominican orders, while images more influenced by Christian thought correspond to Jesuit texts (Gaillemin 2022). This semiotic distinction may serve as a clue to pinpoint the source used to create a given manuscript.[10]

CONDENSING RITUAL SEQUENCES THROUGH PICTORIAL SYNECDOCHE

While one corpus of images refers to adverbs of temporality or deictics that indicate a *before* and *after*, other images do not refer directly to time but more broadly to ritual itself. For this reason, they are of particular interest to a reflection on ritual temporality. As we will see, a first group of these images seems to work to *condense* time, a concept explained more precisely below.

Mass is commonly organized around initial rites (hymn, veneration of the altar, penitential rite, etc.), the liturgy of the Word (readings from the Bible, psalms,

Figure 15.4. (a) *Explanation of the Holy Sacrifice of Mass*, Francisco Ambrosio Nuñez, Templo de San Felipe Tlalmimilolpa, Mex., eighteenth century (reproduced by Franco Carrasco 1986, 123); (b) detail of one quadrant: "The covering of the chalice and the crowning of thorns"

hymns, the homily, profession of the faith, etc.), the liturgy of the Eucharist (various gestures made by the priest such as genuflections, use of incense, elevation of the Host, washing of hands or rite of the *lavabo*, etc.), and concluding rites such as the final blessing.

During colonial times, some attempts were made to provide—via painting on canvas—extremely detailed explanations of these ritual sequences.[11] For example, in the eighteenth century, a painting by Francisco Ambrosio Nuñez in San Felipe Tlalmimilolpa (Toluca Valley, Mexico) (figure 15.4a) provides a comprehensive explanation of the Holy Sacrifice of Mass, represented by a single painting divided into thirty-six quadrants. Liturgical time is here distributed to describe and interpret the sequential episodes of the Holy Sacrifice. In addition to this sequencing, two distinct stories are told simultaneously: that of the actual sequence of the celebration of mass and a symbolic reference to its actual meaning (Franco Carrasco 1984, 123). For this purpose, each quadrant was divided into two parts: lower and upper. For example, the main scene showing the covering of the chalice appears below Jesus's crowning with thorns (in the cloud) (figure 15.4b).[12] I call this process "conflation," given that the image crystallizes the correlation made between two distinct temporalities: in this case, liturgical and biblical.

This example serves to illustrate the complexity involved in representing all the actions of the ritual of mass in a very different kind of pictorial artifact: a pocket-sized catechism. Therein, instead, most ritual gestures' sequences were condensed, by which I mean shortened or summarized through the representation of a single action corresponding to its climax, thus reducing a complex sequence to just one of

Figure 15.5. (a) The elevation of the Host to express the word "mass," no. 809, folio 6r, detail (in context: see figure 15.1, image no. 9); (b) *Doctrina christiana en la lengua Guaxteca cõ la lengua castellana*, fray Juan de la Cruz, Mexico: Pedro Ocharte, 1571, folio 40v, courtesy of the John Carter Brown Library, Providence, detail; (c) images for the sacrament of Confession (no. 809, folio 9v, detail); (d) *Confesionario breve . . .* , fray Alonso de Molina, 1565, folio 2, courtesy of the John Carter Brown Library, Providence, detail

its elements. Of course, figuring all the sequences would be impossible in such a tiny manuscript. That said, the use of this procedure, which can be seen as a "temporal synecdoche" (understood as the mention of a part in order to refer to a whole; see Dehouve this volume for a more detailed analysis of this type of trope), may also be explained by pedagogical need.

For example, among all the rites of the mass, and thus in most of the catechisms, the Elevation of the Host was chosen to illustrate the word "mass" (figure 15.5a). The Elevation is a reenactment of Jesus's gesture during the Last Supper, since it is the moment in which the body and blood of Christ are raised during the celebration of the Eucharist. This precise moment was insisted upon elsewhere too, since we find it reproduced in the engravings of doctrines published during the sixteenth century (figure 15.5b).

Similarly, and as in the engravings used in the *confesionarios* (confessional manual) printed in colonial times (figure 15.5c), a condensed image of the sacrament of

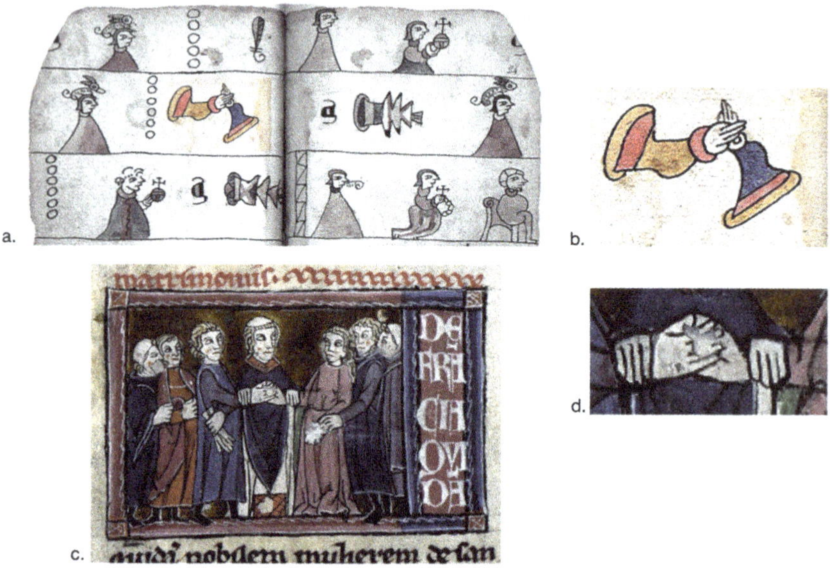

Figure 15.6. (a and b) *The Sacrament of the Matrimony* (no. 810, folios 23v–24r, detail); (c) and (d) *Mariage religieux*, circa 1250, Angers, BM, 0379 (0366), folio 153

Confession includes a combined "kneeling and joining hands to pray" associated with the figure of the priest "sitting and blessing with his hands" (figure 15.5d).[13]

In the same way, Communion was represented by a believer at the moment of receiving the Host from the priest, while Matrimony was reduced by the same synecdochic and temporal principles of selection to the gesture of two joined hands. Represented in various thirteenth-century illuminations (figure 15.6), the same gesture appears in engravings from Peter Canisius's catechism, published in Antwerp at the end of the sixteenth century.

Yet another example comes from the Five Church Commandments: it designates the rite of "Flowery Easter" (see figure 15.1, image no. 32). This rite was also reduced to just one of its elements: from the complex sequence of actions and rites interwoven during Easter, the painter chose to depict the gesture of offering flowers. This pictorial strategy emphasizes this act's importance as simultaneously metaphorical and concretized by a real gesture.

By visually highlighting what corresponds to the climax of each ritual, the artist adds a teaching that could not be provided by books containing only text written in alphabetical characters. Even though these catechisms are described as useful tools to convert or teach illiterate populations, they were not necessarily developed for this purpose alone. In fact, instead of reducing a text to abstract words that produce strange and impersonal combinations of letters and syllables that could have had very little relevance for newly converted populations, these catechisms provided an opportunity to show concretely how Christian rituals are to be interpreted and performed. The new Catholic, at least ideally, can thereby identify not only what *is done* (at mass for example) but also what he or she *must do*. Indeed, as noted above, these gestures are, in general, highly symbolic but are also actually carried out during a given ritual.

STRETCHING: THE STABILIZATION OF QUICK
GESTURES TOWARD LONG-TERM SYMBOLS

At a semiotic and temporal level, some images function differently than the ones just described. Indeed, some gestures seem to have been chosen to "stretch" time rather than narrow it. I propose that one missionary strategy was to stabilize certain short (or quickly executed) gestures by transforming them into symbols that referred to a long duration.

In this case, the chosen gestures or objects function not according to the procedure of synecdoche but to that of metaphor instead. An object or gesture is associated with a concrete action, and this serves to reference an abstract notion. This type of "transposition" is particularly useful for explaining a notion and for incorporating and anchoring it durably in memory.

New Objects, New Attitudes, and the Semantic Chain
("to Honor," "to Believe," and "to Commune")

With colonization, importance was given to the gesture of taking off a hat, which is a sign of humility and respect. It appears in a text explaining what must be done when entering the church. In the Decalogue, we observe that the meaning of this gesture was displaced and thereafter used metaphorically (figure 15.7a). From its physical embodiment as a concrete gesture, the image thus came to be used to express the act of honoring (in this case, "to honor your father and your mother").

Following the same procedure, a catechumen holds a (sacred) book in his hand, while another holds a rosary. Both objects are associated with a cross, and their representations served to transcribe the verb "to believe" (figure 15.7b and 15.7c).

Of course, in daily life, a believer does not have to hold a book or a rosary in his hands all day to show that he or she truly believes. I thus propose that these gestures became metaphors. If concrete postures are depicted, they serve to refer to an action whose duration is not condensed to a single moment. Showing the moment

Figure 15.7. Metaphoric gestures: (a) "to honor [your] father [and your] mother," *Ten Commandments*, no. 809, folio 5r, detail; (b and c) "to believe," no. 809 and no. 808, details

of grasping a book or a rosary, on the contrary, stretches this action into a longer temporality—after all, the idea is to never stop believing (Gaillemin 2018).

We saw above that certain painters condensed the stages of Communion, since the rite is summarized as the act of receiving the consecrated Host. In a surprising way, elsewhere it is the gesture of the embrace that other painters used to depict this sacrament: Jesus and another figure are linked, their necks wrapped with a single yellow scarf (see figure 15.1, images no. 23 and no. 27). Yet the etymology and profoundest meaning of the term "communion"[14] is indeed related to the idea of "union" (union with, community, sharing with, etc.). With this picture, then, the semantics of the sacrament were recorded visually, and the friendly gesture of embracing became a metaphor for the ritual act of Communion. This meaning must be kept in mind at the moment of opening one's mouth and receiving the Host: beyond eating it, the act symbolizes the communicant's union with all other Catholics, gathered together in the same faith, a union based on *communion* with God.[15]

This gesture is not only metaphorical but also "etymological": it provides a description of its first, concrete meaning. Moreover, for Calbris, "the initial gesture, more or less conscious over time, remains underground while the polysemic chain of the word is constituted, evolves and enriches itself with time" (Calbris 1985, 78).[16]

This again illustrates the complexity of the strategies put in place to develop this iconography. The significance of teaching and transmission would not here be summed up in the lesson and the learning of prayers. On the contrary, it would be enriched over time to yield much more fertile fruit—from the point of view of indoctrination and "making believe"—than could simple texts written in Latin characters.

Regarding the use of these gestures as metaphors, whose aim was to stretch action in time, it must be stressed that they are *new* gestures imported to New Spain. Indeed, we have presented transcriptions of verbs, such as the verb "to commune," that refer to unprecedented actions or notions among the Indigenous society. The act of "believing" was also new: Mesoamerican languages "lacked" such a verb, whose existence is, as Lenclud (1994) shows, entirely linked to a Western European conception of religion. Elsewhere "religion" and "belief" were not objectified, nor could they be essentialized. They were one aspect of a stance toward one's environment and could neither be affirmed nor denied, so it was not useful to name them.[17]

Like their associated verbs, this set of gestures and the concomitant attitudes to be adopted—within and according to the catechisms under consideration here—are comparable to a vade mecum of good religious behaviors to be practiced by *all* Christians. Note that such congregational representations are almost nonexistent in Mexican sources, given that pre-Columbian codices generally depict pious physical attitudes and gestures performed by deities, their incarnation (*ixiptlah*), and some specialized categories like dancers and priests, but the larger audience generally does not appear. Let us finally highlight that these time-stretching gestures are also associated with objects unknown in these lands before colonization. This is the case with the Holy Book, the hat, and the rosary—all objects whose uses were ineluctably linked with the new faith: Catholic postures and religious emotions that were now encouraged or, rather, imposed.

"To Create" and "to Wait": The Catholicization of Daily Actions
The Transfer of Sacredness

Older traditional gestures were submitted to a transfer of sacredness. Taken as an archetypal act of creation in Indigenous societies, spinning and weaving were used in some pictorial catechisms to designate the Christian God's primordial action, as for example in the sentence "when he created the world, Heaven and Earth" (figure 15.8).

As can be seen in the various images in figure 15.8, several types of symbols were used to transcribe the verb "to create." At first glance, the symbols seem different: a circle with a reverse-*C*-shaped line (810); a flower-like image with a yellow center and surrounded by pink and green "petals" (809); a teardrop-shaped element placed atop a disc on a pedestal (814); and a square with a yellow and blue surface separated by a stepped diagonal line and surmounted by vertical lines (830). I suggest that the common denominator of all these representations may well be

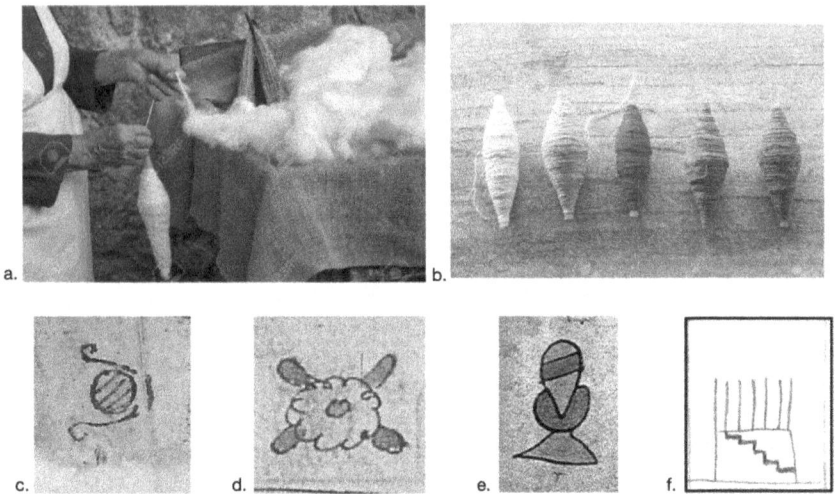

Figure 15.8. Spinning and weaving, or "to make" and "to create": (a) woman spinning wool with a spindle; (b) series of spindles with different shades of wool; details from nos. 810[c], 809[d], 814[e] and 830[f]

weaving: the first two images could refer to a ball of cotton or wool; the third refers more precisely to a spindle (*malacatl*); the last could be an image of the finished product—a piece of textile.

The relationship between textile art and creation is not surprising, particularly if we consider metaphors used in sixteenth-century alphabetical sources from Mexico associating the shape of the *malacatl* thickening during spinning with that of a woman's belly rounding out during pregnancy. Not only is the spindle one of the attributes par excellence of women, but its shape in action refers explicitly to fertility.[18]

The relationship between weaving and creation, in this case, is subject to a transfer of sacredness. While this gesture was already associated with deities such as Tlazolteotl[19] in Mesoamerica, its use in the context of the transmission of Catholic faith may indicate a semiotic strategy. It can be compared to the semantic integration of terms used during pre-Columbian times with Christian concepts, since a shift from the meaning formerly associated with textile creation and deities in the Mesoamerican pantheon leads to the creation of the Christian world as it appears in the Old Testament. The repetition of the motive of spindling, used as much for the verb "to create" as for the adjective "almighty" or the concluding expression of prayer "so be it,"[20] only emphasizes this new sacred meaning granted an otherwise everyday gesture.

The Christianization of Daily Gestures

In linguistic terms, following the work of William Hanks (2010) on Yucatec Maya, we know that several verbs, nouns, and adverbs taken from ancient and traditional Nahuatl have seen their semantics changed or "reduced" to strictly Catholic meanings.

The pictorial manuscripts analyzed here suggest that during the colonial period, everyday gestures—which were a priori not associated with the sacred—underwent a "reduction" to Catholicism. Beyond teaching the prayers and commandments, I think that one of the iconographic strategies employed through the elaboration of pictorial catechisms was to Christianize a series of formulations of more everyday use, such as the verbs "to wait" and "to come."

An example is found in the images used to transcribe the expression "when one expects *the coming* of a danger." Here, the meaning "to wait" is symbolized by an empty chair, while "the coming" corresponds to an image of the Savior descending from heaven on a ladder[21] (see figure 15.1, images no. 18 and no. 19). Now, it is interesting to note that the sentence does not mention the Savior or his coming; it only refers to the "coming" of a danger, not of God. Despite this, the painter has represented the Lord and thus associates, through an iconographic strategy, any coming, any event, even the most banal, with that of the descent of God to Earth. In line with this principle, not only gestures or behaviors were granted new meaning (if they were not entirely erased), but even daily verbs like "to come" were, through this process, thoroughly Christianized.

CONCLUSION

In conclusion, images and objects were as much "reduced" by colonization and Christianization as was language. The gestures and actions that the catechisms depict were translated into the new religion and its temporality, revealing a purposeful strategy aimed at inculcating religious belief in neophytes.

Over the course of this essay, we first observed various ways in which temporal adverbs were transposed into images, some referring to a colonial sound environment (the bell), nature (the moon), or the body. In the last case, we saw that bodily cues associated with time were also found in Nahuatl (the nose, the mouth).

Second, we saw that, for both pedagogical and pragmatic reasons, certain gestures belonging to long ritual sequences were chosen to refer to rites and their names. Following a synecdochic process, the elevation of the Host, genuflection before the blessing of the priest, and joined hands (respectively for mass, confession, and marriage) express, in a single image, complex rituals that are nevertheless composed of several gestures and stretched out in duration.

Finally, I proposed that other types of actions and gestures borrowed from the new daily life imposed by missionaries and involving the use of previously nonexistent objects (hat, devotional book, rosary) were intended to make tangible abstract notions such as honor and belief, the latter to be understood as "an intimate conviction externalized in a Creed and turned toward a personal God, in a spiritual relationship between the believer and the divinity" (Grellard 2017; my translation).

While this new form of belief is associated in these cases with newly inculcated behaviors, other gestures—such as those attached to weaving, for example, which had been executed daily since the pre-Columbian period yet had strong symbolic potential—underwent a transfer of sacredness. A final example demonstrated that, through certain images like that of a simple chair, a whole system of symbolic associations operates: the end of life, associated with the moment corresponding to the wait before death, is surreptitiously correlated to the wait for the coming of the Savior.

This essay focuses on the images used to account for terms and concepts evoking time, transposing actions occurring in ritual time, and on representations operating a transfer of domain (from the source domain to the target domain) via the use of conceptual metaphors. This allowed me to consider the multiple strategies employed by painters. I have highlighted that these artists used different iconographic and symbolic repertoires, both referring to gestures of the past or the present. All of these images, from my point of view, acted—in a holistic way—on the conversion of multiple domains such as the linguistic, iconographic, sensorial, material, postural, and kinesthetic ones.

NOTES

An earlier version of this work was written as a paper for a conference organized during my residency at the Institute for Advanced Studies in Nantes. I thank the Institute, the fellows of the 2018–2019 academic year, as well as my colleagues at the Getty Research Institute, where I made the final modifications. I am also grateful to Valentina Vapnarsky, Aurore Monod Becquelin, Danièle Dehouve, and Amyrose McCue Gill for editing and sharing their thoughts about several topics tackled by this study.

1. The manuscripts in this corpus are referred to herein by the numbers indicated by Glass in his 1975 census, beginning with no. 801. The total number of copies in the corpus depends on whether or not certain modern copies are also included. See Glass 1975, 281–96.

2. The "Testerian" writing (an outdated but useful epithet that is widespread among specialists) is an "attached" script, meaning that it was "created to stabilize a limited corpus of specific ritual discourses and linked to a ritual institution that defines the rules of transmission and enunciation of those same discourses" (Déléage 2013, 169). It never "detached"

itself from the genre of Christian catechisms and doctrines, which means that it did not evolve to encode other content. The "Testerian" writing is also "secondary," that is, it recodes a text previously encoded in Latin script. The images of the pictorial catechisms are therefore not autonomous but correspond to a pre-existing text. The images or signs of this script can combine several elements and denote a syllable, a word, or a compound expression. They are sequenced one after the other—generally from left to right, more rarely in a boustrophedon fashion. Depending on the manuscript, the number of morphemes or lexemes transcribed varies. Consequently, and considering the variation from one manuscript to another, one can speak of more or less "selective" or "partial" writings (plural). The study of these signs and the words they denote, associated with that of the syntax of each of the sentences transcribed, allows us to find the language of formulation of the source text that served as a starting point for the author's transcription into images. My research shows that certain manuscripts could be read in different languages, and that the syntax of the images could also sometimes be closer to that of the texts formulated in Latin or Spanish.

3. While some of the metaphors described here may be linked to Nahua language and culture, others typically come from Western Catholic culture and were imposed upon the neophytes and catechumens of New Spain. However, neither the dates of the manuscripts nor the links between word and picture are the topic of this study; on these themes, see Boone, Burkhart, and Tavárez 2017; Gaillemin 2014, 2022.

4. No. 809, *Ms. Mexicain 78*, folios 5v and 6r.

5. In fact, the image of the sun—a very common motif in several scriptural systems—served to depict the term "day"; the image of several suns was used to denote "every day" or "daily"; and so on. In Nahuatl, too, *moztla* refers to "tomorrow"—or, generally, "in the future"—while the reduplication *momoztlaeh* can be translated as "every day."

6. This expression in Nahuatl is also used to refer to the first soldiers who enter a battle or to a first row of prisoners. On the relationship between vocabulary relating to body parts and to space and its representations, Levinson (1994, 839) explains that "Zapotec, Nahuatl, Tzeltal, and no doubt many other Mesoamerican languages of unrelated stocks utilize a similar core set of body-part terms often with almost exactly the same shape applications." Body parts have extended spatial uses in Mesomerica, some of which may be linked to the temporal meaning.

7. No. 813, *Egerton Manuscript*, folio 9r.

8. "The term for 'mouth' is associated with cavity, edge, and lid in all three languages [Zapotec, Nahuatl, Tseltal]." This observation suggests that, rather than independent inventions, "these systems are semantic calques based on high-prestige languages during various periods of imperial extension" (Levinson 1994, 839).

9. No. 823, *Catecismo en geroglifico*.

10. However, it does not mean that the Franciscans or the Jesuits were their painters or that certain manuscripts are older than others.

11. The term "sequence" here is to be understood to indicate a succession of chronological events that are interconnected and thus form a coherence.

12. Only one reproduction appears in Franco Carrasco's article, and a complementary study of the upper interpretive scenes promises to be very informative. For a comparison with other "audiovisual" methods used in Europe during the modern era, see Trémolières and Celton 2018.

13. In both cases, it is possible that the representation of the heart (*yolotl*) placed between priest and penitent is related to the *teyolia* or "soul" (based on the same root *yol-*), from which the verbs *yolmelahua* "to straighten the heart" and *yolcuitia* "to have the heart taken" were composed in order to translate the verb "to confess." That said, the reference to the heart is found in other neologisms composed in other languages in order to translate the same action. In the case of "confession," therefore, the representation of a heart does not allow us to prove that there is a particular connection between these signs and the Nahuatl language.

14. Even in Nahuatl translations, the term *comunion* has generally been conserved in Spanish (*comunión*) or juxtaposed with the explanatory periphrasis: *in icelilocatzin inacayotzin in Totecuiyo Jesu Christo* ("the reception of the flesh of Our Lord Jesus Christ"). It is rare to find the neologism alone: *tlaceliliztli* ("the action of receiving").

15. Note that during mass, the congregation is also encouraged to greet their neighbors and potentially to embrace them in greeting, a gesture attributed to Pope Leo II during the second half of the seventh century (Bruzen de La Martinière, Banier, and Le Mascrier 1723–43, 58).

16. My translation.

17. The analysis here is based on the fact that the word "belief" is indeed a neologism, just as the image that transcribes this new vocabulary borrows typically Christian and Western references and objects. Nevertheless, on the specific question of belief, see also Grellard 2017.

18. The most famous quote about this association is mentioned in the Florentine Codex: *Zazan tleino, zan cemilhuitl otzti. Malacatl*: "What is it that in one day only becomes big with child? A spindle"; Sullivan 1963, 136–37; Sahagún, [1577] 1979, book VI, ch. 42, folio 199r.

19. About the connotations of spinning and weaving in relation to the concept of creation, see also Klein (1982), Sullivan (1982), Mikulska (2001). This correlation has also been observed by Boone and Burkhart, who read it as an ideography that "reflect[s] the prodigious amount of manual labor required to make woven fabric in early modern Europe and especially in Indigenous Mexico, where all thread was hand spun and all cloth hand woven" (Boone and Burkhart 2017, 57).

20. In Nahuatl, the expression "almighty" has been translated as *ixquich ihueli*, literally "who can do everything," or *cenhuelitini*, "who can entirely," expressions based on the verb *hueli*, "to can, to be able" ("poder" in Spanish). As for the expression "so be it," the verb

chihua, "to do" (also used as a synonym of "to create"), is used in the formula *ma iuh mochihua* (literally "may it be done").

21. In other places, this coming is indeed that of the Lord, for example in the phrase "he will *come* to judge the living and the dead."

REFERENCES

Boone, Elizabeth Hill, and Louise M. Burkhart. 2017. "The Pictographic Vocabulary: Ideography, Phonography, and Syntax." In *Painted Words. Nahua Catholicism, Politics, and Memory in the Atzaqualco Pictorial Catechism*, edited by Elizabeth Hill Boone, Louise M. Burkhart, and David Tavárez, 53–66. Washington, DC: Dumbarton Oaks Research Library and Collection.

Boone, Elizabeth, Louise Burkhart, and David Tavárez. 2017. *Painted Words: Nahua Catholicism, Politics, and Memory in the Atzaqualco Pictorial Catechism*. Washingon, DC: Dumbarton Oaks Research Library and Collection.

Bruzen de La Martinière, Antoine-Augustin, Antoine Banier, and Jean-Baptiste Le Mascrier. 1723–43. *Cérémonies et coutumes religieuses de tous les peoples du monde*. Amsterdam: J. F. Bernard.

Calbris, Geneviève. 1985. "Geste et parole." *Langue Française* 68: 66–84.

Calbris, Geneviève. 1990. *The Semiotics of French Gestures*. Bloomington: Indiana University Press.

Cienki, Alan. 1998. "Metaphoric Gestures and Some of Their Relations to Verbal Metaphoric Expressions." In *Discourse and Cognition: Bridging the Gap*, edited by Jean-Pierre Koenig, 189–204. Stanford: CSLI Publications.

Corbin, Alain. 1994. *Les cloches de la terre: Paysage sonore et culture sensible dans les campagnes au XIXe siècle*. Paris: Albin Michel.

De la Cruz, fray Juan. 1571. *Doctrina christiana en la lengua Guaxteca cō la lengua castellana*. Mexico City: Pedro Ocharte.

Déléage, Pierre. 2013. *Inventer l'écriture: Rituels prophétiques et chamaniques des Indiens d'Amérique du Nord, XVIIe–XIXe siècles*. Paris: Les Belles Lettres.

Domínguez Ruiz, Ana Lidia M. 2007. *La sonoridad de la cultura: Cholula; Una experiencia sonora de la ciudad*. Mexico City: Universidad de las Américas Puebla / Porrúa.

Franco Carrasco, Jesús. 1984. "La misa explicada de San Felipe Tlalmimilolpan, Méx. Una pintura didáctica del siglo XVIII." *Anales de Instituto de Investigaciones Estéticas* 54: 119–26.

Gaillemin, Bérénice. 2014. "Les catéchismes testériens: Un corpus homogène?" In *Nouveaux chrétiens, nouvelles chrétientés dans les Amériques*, edited by Pierre Ragon, 83–104. Nanterre: Presses Universitaires de Paris Ouest.

Gaillemin, Bérénice. 2018. "Outils pédagogiques ou armes politiques? Mettre en scène la conversion dans et avec les catéchismes mexicains." *Archives de sciences sociales des religions* 182: 49–74.

Gaillemin, Bérénice. 2022. "¿Imágenes universales? La relación entre el idioma y la imagen en los catecismos pictográficos coloniales de México." In *Vestigios manuscritos de una nueva cristiandad*, edited by Berenice Alcántara Rojas, Mario Alberto Sánchez Aguilera, and Tesiu Rosas Xelhuantzi, 133–59. Mexico City: UNAM.

Glass, John. 1975. "A Census of Middle American Testerian Manuscripts." In *Handbook of Middle American Indians*, vols. 14 and 15 of *Guide to Ethnohistorical Sources*, edited by Robert Wauchope, Howard F. Cline, Charles Gibson, and H. B. Nicholson, 281–96. Austin: University of Texas Press.

Grellard, Christophe. 2017. "Les ambiguïtés de la croyance." *Socio-anthropologie* 36: 75–89.

Hanks, William F. 2010. *Converting Words: Maya in the Age of the Cross*. Berkeley: University of California Press.

Klein, Cecelia F. 1982. "Woven Heaven, Tangled Earth: A Weaver's Paradigm of the Mesoamerican Cosmos." *Annals of the New York Academy of Sciences* 385 (1): 1–35.

Lakoff, George, and Mark Johnson. 1980. *Metaphors We Live By*. Chicago: University of Chicago Press.

Lenclud, Gérard. 1994. "Attribuer des croyances à autrui: L'anthropologie et la psychologie ordinaire." *Gradhiva* 15: 3–25.

Levinson, Stephen. 1994. "Vision, Shape, and Linguistic Description: Tzeltal Body-Part Terminology and Object Description." *Linguistics* 32: 791–855.

Mikulska, Katarzyna. 2001. "Tlazoltéotl, una diosa del maguey." *Anales de Antropología* 35: 91–123.

Molina, fray Alonso de. 1565. *Confesionario breve en lengua mexicana y castellana*. Mexico City: Casa de Antonio de Espinosa.

Molina, fray Alonso de. 1675. *Doctrina Christiana y Cathecismo en lengua Mexicana: Nuevamente emendada, dispuesta, y añadida para el vso, y enseñança de los naturales*. Mexico City: Por la Viuda de Bernardo Calderon.

Sahagún, Bernardino de. (1577) 1979. *Códice Florentino: Manuscrito 218–20 de la Colección Palatina de la Biblioteca Medicea Laurenziana*. 3 vols. Mexico City: Secretaría de Gobernación / Archivo General de la Nación.

Sherman, William H. 2008. "Toward a History of the Manicule." In *Used Books: Marking Readers in Renaissance England*, 25–52. Philadelphia: University of Pennsylvania Press.

Sullivan, Thelma D. 1963. "Nahuatl Proverbs, Conundrums, and Metaphors, Collected by Sahagun." *Estudios de Cultura Náhuatl* 4: 93–177.

Sullivan, Thelma D. 1982. "Tlazolteotl-Ixcuina: The Great Spinner and Weaver." In *The Art and Iconography of Late Post-Classic Mexico*, edited by Elizabeth Hill Boone, 7–37. Washington, DC: Dumbarton Oaks.

Trémolières, François, and Yann Celton. 2018. "Michel Le Nobletz précurseur des 'tableaux de mission.'" *Textimages*. http://revue-textimage.com/conferencier/08_christianismes _en_transfert/celton_tremolieres1.html.

PICTORIAL MANUSCRIPTS

No. 808, *Doctrina Cristiana en lengua mexicana, Ms. Mexicain 77*, fonds mexicain, Bibliothèque Nationale de France, Paris, 21/15 cm, 21 folios.

No. 809, *Catecismo, Ms. Mexicain 399*, fonds mexicain, Bibliothèque Nationale de France, Paris, 20.5/15 cm, 11 folios.

No. 810, *Catecismo de Atzaqualco, Ms. Mexicain 79*, fonds mexicain, Bibliothèque Nationale de France, Paris, 15/10.5 cm, 30 folios.

No. 813, *Doctrina Christiana, Egerton Manuscript 2898*, Farnborough Fund, British Museum, London, 22.5/16.5 cm, 30 folios.

No. 814, *Phillips Ms. (ex-Bullock Collection)*, Bodmer Fondation, Cologny (Geneva), Switzerland, 15.2/11.4 cm, 35 folios.

No. 823, *Catecismo en geroglifico*, Hispanic Society of America, New York, 21.3/15.7 cm, 8 fol.

No. 830, *Libro de oraciones, 35–53*, Museo Nacional de Antropología, Ciudad de México, México, 15.6/11 cm, 11 folios.

16

The Liturgical Challenge to Historical Temporality

From St. Dominic's Ways of Prayer to the Contemporary Ikoots Mipoch
Dios *(God's Words) of San Mateo del Mar (Oaxaca, Mexico)*

FLAVIA G. CUTURI

INTRODUCTION

In this chapter, I argue that the orations from the Ikoots (Huave) ceremonial genre *mipoch dios*, "God's words," performed in the Ombeayiüts (literally, "our mouth") language, in the religious and political rituals of San Mateo del Mar (Oaxaca, Mexico), share a particular "monosemic attitude," as they are prescriptive and detailed, especially as regards gestures and the sequence of acts that must be fulfilled. Each ritual therefore assumes an intrinsic position toward both a macro and a micro temporal context—respectively, history, and the ritual itself—since they must confront and control their temporalities.

According to Dominican liturgists, and Catholic liturgists generally, in theological terms, liturgy has a foundation that is basically monosemic (conveying one single meaning) rather than polyvalent (open to various interpretations): if the latter were the case, in the Church there would be no communicative unity, and it would not be possible to talk to God in the same way and with the same intentions in all possible spatial and temporal contexts. Rather, within their linguistic-cultural context, rituals bear monosemic intentions to a certain degree, which over time are revealed by repetition of Latin words and gestures (according to an inner micro temporal division), keeping the same meaning to as great an extent as possible, so that everyone may recognize each other, and continue to recognize each other, by communicating with deities as a single body and voice. The monosemic attitude is a way to resist and struggle against history, the temporality of everyday

https://doi.org/10.5876/9781646426829.c016

life, and the arbitrariness which puts at risk the specific conventions established by each ritual.

The semantic and morphological tools that we find in Huave religious and civil texts seem to fulfill (control) both temporal dimensions: at the micro level, the texts describe actions and gestures of the ritual in a very detailed way by using, for the most part, chains of positional verbal roots in dependent forms (without tense markings) to indicate the stages of the ritual acts that must be performed over the ritual time. At the macro level, meanwhile, the implementation of dependent verbal forms carries a prescriptive value that ensures that gestures and actions are replicated in the same way and with the same meaning over historical time, and places the ritual in a context that defies the passing of historical time as well as the risk of arbitrariness. From the above set of linguistic and rhetorical strategies, I derive parallel "monosemic intentions" in Dominican liturgy and Ikoots-Huave ritual texts. I wish to show too that the Dominican and Ikoots texts share the same attitude of challenge toward history and arbitrariness.

NOTES ON THE CATHOLIC LITURGY AND ITS MEANING

By Catholic "liturgy" we refer to *locus theologicus* (Sorci 2005), which is simultaneously comprehension and celebration of the "mystery" of the Church, as well as the action through which the Church is constructed as community and assembly, that is, the *ecclesia*. According to historian Jean-Claude Schmitt (1999), the Catholic Church is based on a set of distinctive gestures that repeat the Eucharistic Sacrifice to create a gestural community through disciplined, standardized, shared, and recognized movements. The process of codifying, standardizing, and unifying the liturgy has been a constant aim in the Church's history. An important step in this process took place at the Council of Trent as part of an effort to counteract the Protestant drift and thus unify the Catholic Church. This was the same period when the use of the missal started to become widespread and the word *liturgy* entered the terminology in use.

Liturgical unification was not just a matter of identity for the Catholic Church and its religious orders. Behind it also lay a theological reason: according to liturgist theologians, communication with God, the celebration of the "mystery of salvation" that Christ embodied, and the commemoration of Jesus Christ's life are all a source of Grace, the starting point of the action of Christ, and together are part of sacramental space, and as such cannot be left to arbitrary or unruly actions.

In his *Introduzione allo spirito della liturgia*, Cardinal Ratzinger, at the time Prefect of the Congregation for the Doctrine of the Faith, stated that universality is an essential feature of Christian worship. It is never simply an event in the life of a community that finds itself in a particular place, and it is never just an event organized by a particular local Church: "Creativity can never be an authentic category in liturgical matters [. . .]. In modern theories [. . .] artistic creativity is the free extension of man, which is unconnected to any measure or aim, and cannot be submitted to any requirement of meaning. This manner of creation has no place in liturgy. [Liturgy] does not exist on the basis of individual whim or of collective planning. It is, on the contrary, the descent of God to our world, His appearance here, and truly brings about liberation" (Ratzinger 2001, 164–65; my translation).

To emphasize the nonarbitrary origin of the liturgy, the Constitution of the Dominican Order declares that "each liturgical celebration, since this is the act of Christ, the priest, and His body, the Church, is the sacred action *par excellence*. No other action of the Church can equal its effectiveness to the same degree" (in Egüés Oroz 1997, 15; my translation).

On the basis of this theological principle, in the Christian liturgy there is a constant effort to unify the various ritual forms that existed in the medieval period, especially. The Dominican Order of Preachers has played a key role in this process (González Fuente 1981, 2004). It has been active in Mexico since right after the Conquista (Fernández Rodríguez 1994; Pita Moreda 1992). In the present study, I focus mostly on the Order's history, not just because it has been central to this process but also because it evangelized the Istmo of Tehuantepec (Medina 1992) and the Ikoots-Huave, the Zapotecs, the Mixes, and the Chontals. The Dominican presence has had a distinctive and enduring liturgical influence on Indigenous rituals, as have had conflicts for land and tribute with Indigenous groups (Arellanes 2006; Canterla y Martín de Tovar 1982).

In a recent essay on Dominican liturgy, Egüés Oroz notes another important aspect: "liturgy needs signs and symbols, where the symbolic dimension must be performed with clarity, and symbolically defined and concrete," meaning that "a symbol can rarely be polyvalent. In the event that it is polyvalent it ceases to be significant" (Egüés Oroz 1997, 41–42).

The liturgical coding process evidently goes back to this monosemic vision of symbols and production of a unified spread of liturgy. Since then, written instructions have been given in books called *ordines* (which were already known in the Renaissance), in "rituals" (*liber agendorum, ordinarium*, i.e., books about the local liturgy, since the fourteenth century), as well as in ceremonial books, the constitutions of religious orders, the "lectionary," "processionaries," and "missals."[1] Missals are the most recent, and were diffused widely by the Friars Minor starting with the *Editio Princeps* (1474), under the rite of the Roman Church (Nocent 1978).

It should be pointed out that the corpus of these books imposed by the Dominicans as part of their evangelization work has been assimilated into the metatextual references made within the religious texts, *mipoch dios* (God's words) repeated by an Ikoots *miteat poch* (father of the word), a sort of master of ceremonies and expert on ritual discourse. These texts constitute a large and heterogeneous corpus of orations in Ombeayiüts, which are recited from memory by the *miteat poch* on ceremonial occasions in the religious and political ritual calendar, as well as important events in people's lives. Although we lack documents from the colonial period clarifying how this corpus has come about, it should be kept in mind that the evangelization of the Ikoots was conducted in Ombeayiüts (Canterla y Martín de Tovar 1982, 62–63; Cuturi 2015, 11) as well as in Latin, which is used even today in texts employed by the Church. While the Dominican liturgical texts provided a temporal and ritual frame of reference, these were subjected by the Ikoots to interpretation and processes of radical incorporation and transformation (Hanks 2010). This may have happened to a heightened degree during the century in which the Ikoots managed their entire ritual calendar without the involvement of priests: that is, from the mid-nineteenth century, when all the missions within the Mexican Republic were secularized, until the establishment of an oblate parish in San Mateo in 1960 (Signorini 1979, 23). The following extract of *mipoch dios* demonstrates how liturgical texts have been incorporated into Ikoots orations, giving them sacred character; they are evoked, one by one, as the principal tools stabilizing the absolute time within which each ritual is placed and the ritual calendar is carried out ("camina").

From the Pentecost Prayer, verse 12:[2]

1.

al-ko-kiaj	*ma-xeang-iw*	*Nangaj*	*serial*		
3St.Ev.Deix	3Dep-3Pl	Sacred	lectionary		

this may be there to raise the sacred lectionary

2.

ma-linch-aw	*wüx*	*nangaj*	*firma-mento*	*okweaj*	*kompas*
3Dep-to line up-3Pl	Adp-on	sacred	basis	Poss	Support

he aligns it on the sacred basis of its sacred support

3.

nangaj misal nangaj manual nangaj librero nangaj calendario nangaj caticismo
sacred missal, sacred manual, sacred bookcase, sacred calendar, sacred catechism

4.

Para	kon	a-wün-ayé	a-jüy	nangaj	ongwiiüts
To	Ev	3S-to take out-Rec	3S.-to walk	sacred	night

perhaps to extract it (from the texts), the holy night walks (the dates of holy celebrations),

5.

aaga	kon	ayaj	a-rang-üw	tilüy	nüt	tilüy	ores
Det.	Ev.	Dx.	3Atp-to make-3Pl.	Adp.in-Int	Day	Adp.in-Int	hours

that's how they do it, on that same day, at that same hour

These sacred texts are the source of emulation for actions which, if they are to be effective in time and beyond historical contingency, must be completed in the same way and at the same points of the ritual calendar.

FROM ST. DOMINIC'S MANNER OF PRAYING, TO . . .

Since the very beginning of the Dominicans' history, which is related to us in the work of Humbert of Romans, heart, mouth, and body must participate together in divine worship (*ad cultum divinum digne paragendum tria concurrere debent, scilicet, cor, os et corpus*). This means that the body (i.e., inclinations and prostrations) corresponds to interior movements (*motus*): if the body leans, the heart inclines, and if the posture is upright, it means that the heart also rises toward God (González Fuente 1981, 223–27). Everything referring to "reverence in divine worship through corporeal activity" (*ad observantias corporales divini cultus*) has always been an essential subject in Dominican tradition, as well as the principal topic of medieval clerical tradition.

For the Dominicans, pastoral-liturgical identity is founded in part on the exemplary distinct body postures made by St. Dominic during the act of prayer, which correspond to the postures of the "soul." These forms of prayer, canonized by the Dominicans into nine standardized ways of prayer, became the object of an enduring and impressive exegesis (see Fueyo 2001). The nine ways of prayer were considered innovative to the point that they were illustrated in a 1280 manuscript by an anonymous friar from Bologna. The same work included (*De modo orandi corporaliter sancti Dominici*) "some verses of the Scripture that endorse the tenor of each manner and form of praying" (Fueyo 2001, 14). Even if this text had been preceded by a similar one, albeit different, attributed to Pietro Cantore, its innovation lies in "[its] pedagogical goal (which obliges the friars to imitate the gestures of prayer of the founder of their order), and in the extraordinary character of a saint's prayer, which a normal friar is incapable of achieving" (Schmitt 1999, 285).

It is important to stress that the *De modo orandi* suggests an innovative and strict decomposition of the physical movement of prayer, which imposes at the same time a rationalization of the gesture's ethics and a standardization of communication (Schmitt 1999, 189). Why was such care given to the codification of praying manners at that time, and why should we be interested in it today?[3] First, because each form of prayer corresponds to a specific body position, which becomes an essential signifier in the communication with God; second, because rather than being polyvalent, each position is an "icon" (Fueyo 2001, 43) that condenses a distinctive and totalizing spiritual experience, namely, "the soul's rejoicing with its God."

The anonymous friar who painted St. Dominic's ways of praying, shown in the image below (figure 16.1), was not satisfied with the written text, and thus provided pictures of the positions.[4] Indeed, images better describe the magnitude of St. Dominic's spiritual experiences. Pictures in this case speak louder than words. Indeed, images reflect the will to transmit "an individual identity and a collective [identity] within the Order through identification with the saint" (Aubin 2017, 21). The pedagogical and hagiographic purpose of encoding such experiences places liturgical actions on a universal scale, initiating a challenge to history and arbitrariness.

Since we currently lack sources and documents concerning evangelization practices among the Huave-Ikoots (such as catechisms), we will attempt to show the convergence between Ikoots texts and Catholic ceremonial books in which gestures, actions, and body positions are described. In Ikoots public ceremonial orations of *mipoch dios*, actions, gestures, movements, and body positions are described using Ombeayiüts verbal roots, which are mostly adjectival and positional roots, such as (*lemb-* "to stand"). In contrast, in the lexicon that describes the "bodily ways" of praying, the verbal roots used to define the body positions are not positional, with the exception of those that express standing in a respectful position. It is unclear whether these movements and positions were acquired following imposition by the Dominicans. I would not want to take a stand on this issue, especially after in-depth discussions about the Dominican liturgy with historians from the order,[5] who excluded any possible Ikoots emulation.

The terms that define the bodily ways of praying and communicating with Saints in Ombeayiüts are as follows:

lemb-em
he stands up straight, standing straight

a-kieel
he kneels

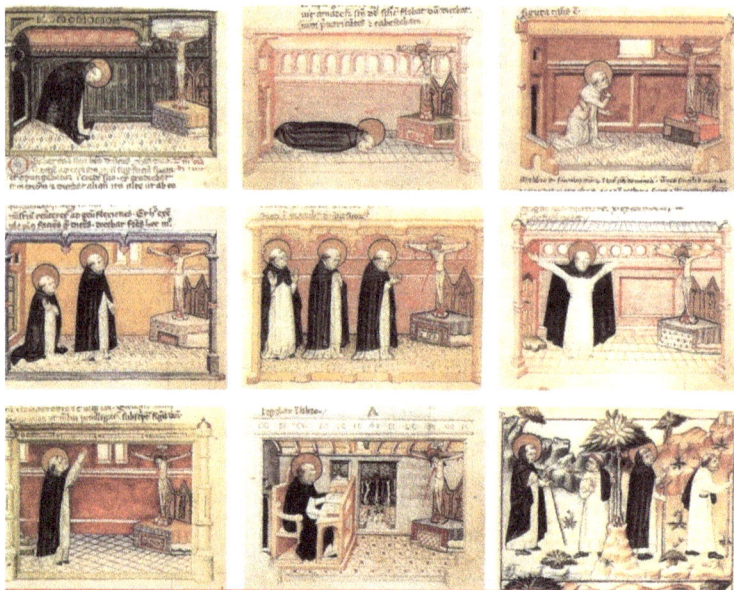

Figure 16.1. Picture from The Nine Ways of Prayer of Saint Dominic (Tugwell 1997). From De Modo Orandi, circa 1260–88, Vatican City, Biblioteca Apostolica Vaticana, Codex Rossianus 3

ajmiük wüx
  he falls upon, he kneels and inclines his head slightly [literally, "by one third"]

ajmiük tiül oleaj dios
  he falls before the Saint's foot, he kneels and inclines his head [literally, "by a half"]

axim oleaj dios
  he smells the Saint's foot, prostration

What I wish to stress in this chapter is the use of morphological tools in both Catholic and Ikoots liturgical texts, rather than lexical ones. This is especially true in the texts that aim to convey a prescriptive value. By virtue of this prescriptive value, liturgical texts and the actions to be completed place rituals on a temporal scale that is absolute and everlasting, in terms both of Catholics' canonical vision of time and the vision of time in which the Ikoots situate their collective and private life stages. The effectiveness of the rituals is guaranteed by the connection between the actions to follow and the prescriptive manner in which they are expressed.

By indicating the morphological tools that enable worshippers to embody the text's liturgical content as part of a "universal" framework, and assuming that they are nonpolyvalent, I intend to prove that no arbitrary value can be affected by the pass-ing of time. To this end, I would like to propose a comparison of four different texts: the first is a Latin missal printed in 1837 (the original on which it is based dates back to the mid-1600s); the second comes from a Spanish ceremonial book published in 1692. The missal and the ceremonial book, as explained previously, are tools for litur-gical unification and for the homogenization of gestures and Catholic ritual actions, which have been used historically by missionaries for evangelizing native peoples. Among the Ikoots of San Mateo they have been incorporated into ritual actions as a sacred reference point and are evoked in their orations as a source for the establish-ment of the absolute time ("out of history") in which these rituals are to be held. Accordingly, I propose a parallel analysis with two texts taken from the corpus of the *mipoch dios*: the first is the *miverso poj* (turtle's song), performed in 1963 by *miteat poch* Albino Cienega; the second is a wedding oration transcribed in Ombeayiüts from a dictation by the *miteat poch* Jorge Cepeda.[6] As will be seen, these *mipoch dios* contain no prayers or supplications directed at the saints; rather, they have prescrip-tive communicative aspects and meta-ritual descriptive elements, which I consider parallels to the ritual prescriptions or Catholic liturgical instructions.

The Latin text is the *Missale Romanum decreto Sacrosancti Concilii Tridentini restitutum S. Pii V Pontificis maximi jussu editum Clementis VIII et Urbani VIII, auctoritate recognitum in quo omnia accurate suis locis disposita sunt, et Missae novis-simae sanctorum adjectae* (1837, 157–58), which I reproduce here with its translation in English:

DOMINICA IN PALMIS

Completa Tertia, et facta aspersione aquae, more solito, Sacerdos indutus pluviali vio-laceo, vel sine casula, cum ministris similiter indutis, procedit ad benedicendum ramos palmarum, sive aliarum arborum in medio ante Altare, vel cornu Epistolae positos. Et primo cantatur a Choro Antiphona. [. . .]

Deinde Sacerdos stans in cornu Epistolae, non vertens se ad populum dicit in tono Orationis Missae Ferialis: (Dominus vobiscum; r. Et cum Spiritu tuo)
[. . .]

Postea Subdiaconus in loco solito cantat sequentem Lectionem in tono Epistolae, et in fine osculatur manum Sacerdotis [. . .] Deinde cantatur pro Graduali.

The third [canonical hour] completed, and water having been sprinkled in the usual way, the priest, dressed in a violet cloak, or without Mass dress, with the ministers dressed in the same manner, passes to bless the branches of palms or other trees in the center of the altar, or on the right side of the altar. At the beginning, the antiphon is sung by the choir [. . .]

At the end, the priest, standing at the right side of the altar, without showing his face to the people, speaks with the tone of prayer of Ferial Mass [. . .]

Afterward, the subdeacon, in the usual place, sings the following reading with the tone of Epistolae, and finally, the hand of the priest should be kissed [. . .] At the end the song of the Graduale is sung.

In the Latin text, the action of the priest and the subdeacon unfolds in the present tense (*procedit, dicit, cantat*), with the completive aspect. The action is placed in a chain of actions and positions are described in detail, each one determining the stages of the ritual but above all carrying with it a specific meaning. The actions are linked together by connectives with different anaphoric and temporal functions: *deinde* (by the end), *postea* (after), *in fine* (finally), without changing tense, and using the passive voice (*cantatur*, osculator). The use of the passive, with no mention of an active agent, provides a strong prescriptive and generalizing value to the set of actions that unfold to complete the ceremony.

The segments of the following Spanish text are taken from the *Ceremonial dominicano en el qual se trata de las cosas que conducen al modo uniforme y orden de celebrar los Oficios Divinos, con las ceremonias del Orden de Predicadores. A lo ultimo va el arte de canto llano con reglas especiales, y fáciles, para que con brevedad pueden aprovechar los principiantes*,[7] written by Joseph de San Joan in Madrid in 1694. From its very title, the text's purpose is explicit and obvious: to standardize and provide an order to the actions of which a religious celebration is composed.

Capítulo XIII

En la misma Bula manda el Santo Pontifice [Pio V], que quando el Sacerdote, en la Missa, levanta las manos estendidas, que las tenga de modo, que las palmas miren àzia el Altar, no que la palma de la una mire àzia la otra: Sacerdos quoque cum manus elevas extensas, ambas ad Altare versas, non autem ad invicem oppositas teneat. (folio 164)

Chapter XIII

In the same Bull, the Holy Pontiff [Pius V] orders that when the Priest, in the Mass, raises his outstretched hands, he should keep them in such a way that the palms face the Altar and one palm does not face toward the other: *Sacerdos quoque cum manus elevas extensas, ambas ad Altare versas, non autem ad invicem oppositas teneat.* (folio 164)

Since this chapter of the text regards a Papal Bull addressed to priests, the normative tools are very explicit and carry a strong performative value: the use of the verb "to order" in the present tense has a perlocutionary effect, which is expressed through the Spanish exhortative conjunctive: "que las tenga," "que las palmas miren," "que la palma de la una mire," and so forth. In my understanding, the Spanish text conveys an obligational meaning that is stronger than the Latin version found in the first text of our comparison. It is worth stressing that this communicative strategy is a feature present in all the Ceremoniales dominicanos.

This chapter, as well as the one discussed below, was written for the friars and nuns of the Dominican Order, and is part of 221 folios (approximately 442 pages) of detailed requirements for everything that takes place in daylight hours. Each requirement dictates in great detail how to perform prayers and rituals throughout the year, and how to follow the canonical time that regulates their entire lives, providing them with a universal, standard meaning.

As can be seen from the quoted excerpts, everything is regulated: the detailed minimal hand movements and positions, gestures, and sequences of actions as well as a multitude of other obligations that each churchgoing man or woman must know and perform perfectly according to his or her status. There is no space for "creativity" or for individual arbitrariness: it is clear that this is where the monosemic unity between gesture and meaning is accomplished and becomes explicit. Another example:

CAPITULO VII "EXPLICASE A LO QUE SE HA DE HAZER DESDE EL
DOMINGO DE RAMOS HASTA LA PASCUA"

[. . .] Despues de la Oracion, que se dize sobre Asperges [aspersiones], estando el Prior delante las gradas del Presbyterio, buelta la cara àzia el Altar, y el Diacono delante del Prior teniendole el Missal, bendizirà los Ramos, los quales les tendrà puesto el Sacristan sobre las gradas del Presbyterio; pero de modo que caygan à la mano derecha del Prior, el qual cantarà la Bendicion, que pone el Missal, de modo que se cantan las Oraciones de las Horas.

CHAPTER VII "EXPLAINING WHAT TO DO FROM PALM SUNDAY UNTIL
EASTER"

[. . .] After prayer, which is given upon Asperges, the Prior, standing before the steps of the Presbytery, *turns* his face toward the Altar, and the Deacon, standing in front of the Prior holding the Missal, *will bless* the palm leaves, which the Sacristan *will have laid* on the steps of the Presbytery; but *in such a way that* these *are dropped* from the right hand of the Prior, who *will sing* the Blessing, which is included in the Missal, *thus in such a way that* the Prayers of the Hours *are sung*. [italics added]

As in the previous excerpts, the present tense also prevails in this extract, followed by the future tense and the prescriptive subjunctive mood. In these verbal sequences, the details which regulate the elements necessary to compose the "scene" are framed together with its protagonists and their body postures. In this way, the ritual itself is situated in an intrinsic temporality, in an everlasting temporal framework, which is necessarily monosemic, immutable, and removed from secular time.

. . . TO THE WAYS OF PERFORMING THE IKOOTS *MIPOCH DIOS*

The Ikoots (Huave) of San Mateo del Mar feature an extended repertory of ceremonial orations, *mipoch dios*, performed mostly in Ombeayiüts ("our tongue," i.e., Huave) in their religious and civil rituals (Cuturi 2015). We do not know how the *mipoch dios* orations, possessed by the *miteat poch*—Ikoots masters of ceremonies who control all aspects of the ritual cycles—were constructed. The texts of the *mipoch dios* include many descriptions of actions, gestures, and movements that are part of the ritual itself. Only in some of these texts—which are mainly enunciated by the authorities of the Church and the municipality—do we find an intense and direct communication with the saints, made up of requests and promises. The majority of the ceremonial texts enunciated by the *miteat poch* have a descriptive character, and this encourages us to interpret them as meta-ritual expressions, parallel to the ritual prescriptions or Catholic liturgical instructions. However, the interpretive key of this parallelism between "liturgies" is not grounded in translation between the texts but rather, on an Ikoots theory. The interpretation I would propose is that the effectiveness of these ritual texts is based on pragmatic and rhetorical tools that the Ombeayiüts language offers to communicate both the monosemic and historical content of the rituals. The role of morphological, rhetorical, and poetic tools is enhanced to stress the different steps of ritual action, but above all, to make the whole ritual performance more effective.

These patterns are illustrated below with two excerpts of *mipoch dios*: the first comes from the *miverso poj* (turtle's song) performed by Albino Cienega (recorded in 1963), and the second from an oration devoted to preparations for a mass in celebration of a wedding, transcribed many years ago from a dictation by the *miteat poch* Jorge Cepeda.[8]

From Albino Cienega's oral performance of *miverso poj* (verse 7):

I.

Al-ko-kiaj	**ma-xeang-iw**	*teat Cruz de Plata,*	**ma-xek-iw**	*mi-xiül*
3St-Ev-Deix	3Dep-to lift-3Pl.	teat Silver Cross	3Dep-graft-3Pl	3Ps-stick

perhaps he's there to lift *Teat* [i.e., Señor, Father] Silver Cross, to insert his stick

2.

ma-xijind-eaw   *wüx*   *otüeng*   *nangaj sagrado   templo,*

3-Dep-lean-3Pl.   Adp-on belly [wall] holy   holy   temple

to lean it (carefully) against the wall of the holy church.

3.

al-ko-kiaj   **ma-xeang-iw**   *cruz bandera amb*

3St.Ev.Deix   3Dep-to.lift-3Pl. Cross flag   go-Dir.

ma-xek-iw   *mixiül,*

3Dep-to.graft-3Pl 3Ps-stick

perhaps he's there to lift the Cross to insert his stick

4.

ma-xijind-eaw   *Wüx*   *otüeng*   *nangaj*

3Dep-to.lean-Pl.   Adp-on wall   holy

Sagrado   *Kalüy*   *y*   *kawak*

Sacred   North   and   South

to lean it (carefully) against the holy wall [of the] holy sacred North and another [wall] of the South,

5.

Aag   *kon*   *Ayaj*   *a-rang-üw*   *xa-teat-iün*

Det   Ev   Deix   3Atp-to do-   1Pos-father-1Pl-excl
                              3PL

til-üy   *nüt*   *til-üy*   *ores.*

Adp.in   day   Adp.in   hours

(Tp)-Int   (Tp)-Int

perhaps this is what our ancestors do, on the same day, at the same hour.

From Jorge Cepeda's notes of *mipoch dios* texts to be performed at weddings:

1.

Atow   *kon*   *nej* *til-üy*   *wüx*   *santa*   *madrugada*

Cmp   Ev   3S   Adp.in(Tp)-Int Ado-on Holy   dawn

domingo *al-ko-ma-jüür* *a*   *noik*   *ijkiaw* *hores*

Sunday   3St-Ev-to have Det Num1   Num2   hours

Also perhaps in [this hour] of the holy morning of Sunday of that time, already perhaps has around two hours

2.

ma-ngia-iw	ma-tajk-üw	repicar	mi-manchiük
3Dep-to lissen-3Pl	3Dep-to.do-3Pl	to sing	3S.Pos-iron
nuestro	Bien	Jesus Cristo	
our	Good	Jesus Christ	

they are listening to the bells singing, of our good Jesus Christ

3.

para	kon	ma-j-paj	teat	ma-jpaj	müm
To	Ev.	3S.Dep-Atps-to call	father	3S.Dep-Atps-call	mather
que	ma-mb	chete-m			
to	3S.Dep-to	sit-3S.Dep			

so that perhaps he calls the father, calls the mother to go and sit

4.

ma-tün	perdon	ma-tün	misericordia	
3S.Dep-to ask	forgiveness	3S.Dep-ask	mercy	
ma-pea-iw	ma-jmel-iw su	santo	templo	bendito
3.Dep-arrive-3Pl	3.Dep-enter-3Pl	holy	temple	blessed

to ask forgivness, to ask for mercy, so that they manage to enter their holy blessed temple

5.

ma-to-iw	ma-jmel-iw	Su	santo	templo	bendito
3.Dep-same-3Pl	3.Dep-to enter-3Pl	his	holy	temple	blessed
ma-jo-iw	ma-mb	netam	mbaj	rosario	
3.Dep-bring-3Pl	3S.Dep-to.go.Dir	important	flower	rosary	

so that they get into his holy blessed temple all the same, so that they bring (Dir. centrifugal) the important Rosary

6.

ma-ngoch	kon	nej	müm del rosario	ma-jmiük	kon
3S.Dep-to find	Ev.	3S.	mather rosary	3S.Dep-to fall	Ev.
tiül ombas	nangaj iüt				
Adp.in body	holy land				

to pray perhaps to the mother of the rosary, to kneel (fall) perhaps toward the body (in front) of the holy land (total prostration?)

7.

Pinawan	*su*		*santo*	*templo*	*sagrado*	*Bendito*
Middle	his		holy	temple	sacred	Blessed
ma-jiüng-üw	*al-ko-kiaj*		*nangaj*	*padre*	*nuestro*	
3Dep-sing-3Pl	3S.Est-Ev-Deix		holy	father	our	

in the middle of the holy blessed sacred temple so that they sing [where] perhaps the sacred father of ours is

8.

Ya	***mü-j-ch-iw***		*kon*	*Nangaj*	*Ave*	*Maria*
Already	3Dep-Atps-dar-3Pl		Ev.	holy	Ave	Maria
ma-tajk-üw	*presentar*					
3Dep-the same as-3Pl	present					

so that already they give, perhaps, a sacred Ave Maria, so that they present themselves

9.

Wüx	*netam*	*oleaj*	*wüx*	*Netam*	*owix*	*mi-teat-iüts*
Adp.on	important	foot	Adp.on	important	hand	1Pos-father-1Pl.Incl
Santo	*Patron*	*San*	*Mateo*	*Apóstol*	*Evange-lista*	
Saint	Patron	Saint	Matthew	Apostolic	Evangelist	

(bowing or kneeling) in front of the important foot, in front of the important hand of our Patron Saint Matthew Apostolic Evangelist

The differences between these examples of *mipoch dios*, the Latin missal, and the Dominican ceremonial texts are very significant, starting from the aesthetics of the Ombeayiüts text. The *mipoch dios* segment belongs to oral practices, and because of that, its sonorities are obtained through repetitions and echo effects, which add intense rhythm to the prayer, as well as an emotional charge to the message.

But here I wish to focus on the pragmatic use of the dependent verbal form (highlighted in bold characters), which I identify as the main tool expressing a polite and respectful attitude, as well as a prescriptive dimension, in order to endow the message with obligational and enduring effect and to keep it out of historical temporality, even if rituals are anchored to this.

Part of such transcendence belongs to a forgotten history that dates back to an undefined past when these rituals began to be performed just as they had been handed down by ancestors, as made explicit at the beginning of the *mipoch dios*. In the first line, we find the temporal-locative adverb *tilüy* embedded in a formula purposely used in ritual speeches to justify ritual continuity. This is achieved through repetition, that is, by using the same expression since a time considered to be unknown, as expressed by the verbal form combined with an adverbial meaning *atow*, "to be the same."

The reference to the ancestors warrants the repetition of the ritual without any modification or change, so that the ritual through the same gestures implies the possibility of communicating with the saints, again with the same language and the same meanings. In this sameness resides the communicative efficacy and the success of the relationship with the saints, meaning that benefits and protection are received from them.

The *miteat poch* are the messengers of the ancestors' voice: the ancestors have left the words that express how movements, positions, and gestures should be performed to honor the saints, following the intrinsic temporality of the ritual stages and connected to the absolute temporality of the cycle of festivities. This set of balanced practices is opposed, as in the missals and ceremonials, either to the temporality of history and its possible effects, or to the arbitrariness of the means for communicating with the saints.

The dependent timeless verbal forms, which have the effect of being respectfully prescriptive, "similar" to the future participle and the exhortative conjunctive in Latin, are the most effective morphological instrument for obtaining, through words, this type of normativizing effect, which is a guarantor of communicative continuity with the saints. In the Ikoots orations, no direct or future imperative forms are used; nor would it be possible to use performative verbs such as *mandar* (to order), which does not exist in the Ombeayiüts lexicon, just as there is no modal verb like *deber* (must).

In fact, in contexts such as church, which is one of the sacred collective spaces where many of the rituals take place (another being the assembly space; see Cuturi 2000), the *miteat poch* is "obliged" to produce his ritual speech to describe the planned ritual actions using primarily two of the resources of indirect speech: the evidential affix of doubt, *kon*, and the dependent verbal forms (which I have underlined in bold). Even more so, dependent verbal forms are implemented when the performed texts describe actions that are seen as the legacy of ancestors, and not the creation of the *miteat poch* or any other living person.

To illustrate the broad pragmatic values of the dependent verbal forms in this textual genre and their communicative effects, I propose the following distinction in their implementation in *mipoch dios* texts: in the Turtle's song, the position of the *miteat poch* in relation to the use he makes of ritual language and its tools; in the wedding text, key elements indexing a local "theory" of ceremonial communicative practices, which I detail further, together with the temporal scale on which these are located.

The key device to complete the entire process of normativization of ritual actions is indirect speech carried out through dependent verbal forms. It places the actions on an absolute timescale beyond any historical commitment; in this process of normativization, the use of this verbal form makes explicit the agency (Cuturi 2007) of the *miteat poch* with regard to the contents of the text and its interpretation, making clear to the audience his position in the management of the ritual action, and the various temporalities in which that is located.

In short, the dependent verbal form

1. guarantees the respect with which the content of the sentence has to be stated;
2. indicates that the speaker (the *miteat poch*) is not exerting his authority as a temporarily positioned subject over the conveyed content. He is a messenger and at the same time the person who materially possesses the texts he has learned from another *miteat poch*; however he is not the "owner" of the content of the sentences, that is, of the actions that "have to be fulfilled." He is not a witness to the ancestors' ritual actions, and for this reason he has no responsibility over the contents of the prayer inherited from them and their indefinite past;
3. and is a form of indirect speech which places the content (i.e., the ritual acts)
   i. in a prescriptive, conscious, intentional, and teleological perspective;
   ii. on an absolute timescale (the calendar of the religious feasts and observances);
   iii. within a normative framework, with the purpose of repeating it through time, without changes;
   iv. and far away from the changes that history could imprint on it, and therefore beyond the possible changes that contingent history could produce on it, in formal and meaningful terms.

Moreover, from the perspective of a possible theoretical formulation of the ceremonial communicative practices of the Ikoots, the dependent form, since it is atemporal and final, is the tool that

1. connects in a teleological perspective one action with another in a sequence that constitutes and completes the ritual;
2. clarifies the aim of an action whose meaning is found in what it generates, that is, in the action that follows achievement of an explicit goal, namely, accomplishing the sequences of all the stages of the ritual;

3. determines the syntax of the ritual through the creation, determination, and prescription of the sequence of actions, that is, the order and manner in which gestures, positions, actions, and so forth, must be performed according to the codes of respect;

4. and establishes a relative temporality within the ritual itself, but in the frame of the absolute timescale, which is necessarily ahistorical.

As I have stressed, the rituals have been passed down from ancestors, and the people of San Mateo have lost the memory of the origin of this heritage: this is a real historical fact, although it belongs to an indefinite past. What the ancestors did was already fulfilled, and its fulfillment is an act that generated what has been performed ritually from that time until now. For this reason, when referring to those events performed by the ancestors, the (direct) atemporal *arangüw* (they do) form we mentioned in the Pentecost Prayer (verse 12:5) is properly used, expressing that the action has really been accomplished.

To conclude, the indirect speech of the Ikoots ritual, through the use of the dependent form—which reconnects to the past without witnesses and contributes to the oblivion of the facts that have determined it—prescribes that the ritual must be repeated in the same way, challenging the change that history might determine, and avoiding individual "creativity" as a potential source of polysemy, widely feared by the Catholic Church.

Indirect speech guarantees that the same words with the same respectful gestures and the same positions ordered in sequences that are repeated over time, albeit performed by different people, repeat (put into effect) the same meanings, thus achieving the same ritual efficacy experienced by ancestors. This efficacy is supposed to guarantee the same shared communication with the saints for everyone, conveying the same meanings linked to specific gestures, positions, and actions, agreed *by them*, or perhaps *with them*. This ensures that each established and normalized ritual occasion belongs to absolute time and generates positive effects in the daily life of all.

All of the above demonstrates the presence of a meta-ritual consciousness that handles at least two different macro temporalities and evaluates each according to its contradictory effects: on the one hand, it is in historical temporality that the ancestors passed down to the people of San Mateo the rituals and the words that describe exactly how to execute them; on the other hand, the absolute timescale is performed through the repetition of identical gestures and words, allowing everyone to communicate with the saints. This kind of consciousness seems parallel to those found in ritual prescriptions or Catholic liturgical instructions: both have the ambition of pursuing a monosemic dream that neutralizes the potential effects of history (change, arbitrariness, oblivion, individual creativity), ensuring imperishable communication with the saints.

NOTES

1. These texts are part of a corpus of reference books on which the Dominican liturgy, approved in 1267 by Pope Clement IV, is based. This corpus has been almost changelessly maintained throughout history even after the Council of Trent (González Fuente 1981, 272–74).

2. Glosses: Adp: adposition; Atp: atemporal; Atps: antipassive; Dx: deixis; Cmp: comparative; Dep: dependent; Det: determinative; Ev: evidential; Incl: inclusive; Int: intensifier; Num: numeral; Pl: plural; Ps: possessive; Rec: reciprocal; S: singular; St: stative; Tp: temporal.

3. Churchgoing Christians, or people who have lived in a Christian society, should be aware of the meaning of prayer. Referring to St. Dominic, Friar Luis de Granada says that prayer is "a healthy shelter from everyday flaws as well as a clean mirror in which both God and men are reflected" (Fray Luis de Granada circa 1500, quoted in Fueyo 2001, 39); it is also obvious that the apostolic mandate is at the basis of any prayerful attitude: "Inviting, calling and asking people to get closer to God and to love Him" (39).

4. As Aubin reports (2005, 19), Schmitt (1984) believed that this was the first time that prayers to a saint were represented in images; in this respect, the manuscript of the Nine Ways of Prayer is an unparalleled document in medieval literature.

5. I wish to thank Fray Antolín Gonzales Fuente and Fray Egenio Torres, from whom I learned a great deal, for the time they gave me in discussing possible links between the Ikoots texts and Dominican liturgical texts. It is entirely my responsibility to interpret their words.

6. I was lucky to meet *miteat poch* Jorge Cepeda (†) when he was already very old. His transcribed texts were given to me by his nephew, *teat* Francisco Cepeda (†), as well as the recording of the *miverso poj* (turtle song) performed by *miteat poch* Albino Cienega (†), which I transcribed and translated with the fundamental help of *teat* Juan Olivares (†). I owe them all a great debt.

7. Dominican Ceremonial, in which all the things that bring people to the uniform and ordered way of celebrating the Divine Services are presented, as well as the ceremony of the Dominican Order. In the end, the Plainchant is given, along with its special rules, so that even beginners can approach it.

8. Men who hope to become a *miteat poch* must learn the vast corpus of *mipoch dios* by listening to other *miteat poch* and following their ritual actions. Clearly this involves learning not only the orations but also everything beyond speech that is necessary to conduct a ritual correctly (flowers, food, candles, assistants, body positions, specific objects and spaces, and so on). Some *miteat poch* request family members to transcribe the texts they recite in public for rituals, because each of these may diverge from what they have learned. The performance

of orations is based on strength of memory, skill in using one's voice, and rhythm and breathing, never on reading.

REFERENCES

Arellanes Cancino, Nimcy. 2006. "Dominicos, conflictos por tierras en el Istmo de Tehuantepec. Siglos XVIII–XIX." *Anuario Dominicano, Oaxaca, 1529–2006*. Vol. 2, 401–90.

Aubin, Catherine. 2005. *Prier avec son corps à la manière de saint Dominique*. Paris: Cerf.

Aubin, Catherine. 2017. *Orar con el cuerpo a la manera de Santo Domingo*. Salamanca: Editorial San Esteban.

Canterla y Martin de Tovar, Francisco. 1982. *La Iglesia de Oaxaca en el Siglo XVIII*. Sevilla: Escuela de Estudios Hispano Americanos.

Cuturi, Flavia. 2000. " 'Tal vez estamos aquí': Autoridad, responsabilidad y 'antideíctico' en las interacciones dialógicas rituales huaves." In *Les Rituels du dialogue: Promenades ethnolinguistiques en terres amérindiennes*, edited by Aurore Monod and Philippe Erikson, 401–30. Nanterre: Société d'ethnologie.

Cuturi, Flavia. 2007. "Modalità dell'agentività nelle pratiche discorsive huave." In *Agency e linguaggio: Etnoteorie della soggettività e della responsabilità nell'azione sociale*, edited by Aurora Donzelli and Alessandra Fasulo, 61–83. Roma: Meltemi.

Cuturi, Flavia. 2015. "El 'canto de la tortuga': Entre poética y acción ceremonial en San Mateo del Mar (Oaxaca, México)." *L'Uomo* 1: 7–34.

Egüés Oroz, Inmaculada. 1997. *La celebración litúrgica en la Orden de Predicadores: Un espacio de "fronteras."* Salamanca: Editorial San Esteban.

Fernández Rodríguez, Pedro. 1994. *Los dominicos en la primera evangelización de México, 1526–1550*. Salamanca: Editorial San Esteban.

Fueyo Suárez, Bernardo. 2001. *Modos de orar de Santo Domingo*. Salamanca: Editorial San Esteban.

González Fuente, Antolín. 1981. *La vida litúrgica en la Orden de Predicadores: Estudio en su legislación 1216–1980*. Roma: Istituto Storico Domenicano.

González Fuente, Antolín. 2004. "Litúrgia dominicana: Orígenes y presents." *Archivo Domenicano* 25: 325–38.

Hanks, William F. 2010. *Converting Words: Maya in the Age of the Cross*. Berkeley: University of California Press.

Medina, Miguel Ángel. 1992. *Los dominicos en América: Presencia y actuación de los dominicos en la América colonial española de los siglos XVI–XIX*. Madrid: Editorial MAPFRE.

Missale Romanum decreto Sacrosancti Concilii Tridentini restitutum S. Pii V Pontificis maximi jussu editum Clementis VIII et Urbani VIII [. . .]. Roma. 1837.

Nocent, Adrien. 1978. "Storia dei libri liturgici romani." In *La liturgia, panorama storico generale*, vol. 2 of *Anàmnesis*, edited by S. Marsili, A. Nocent, M. Augé, and A. J. Chupungco, 165–68. Genova: Marietti 1820.

Pita Moreda, Maria Teresa. 1992. *Los Predicadores novohispanos del siglo XVI.* Salamanca: Editorial San Esteban.

Ratzinger, Joseph. 2001. *Introduzione allo spirito della liturgia.* Alba: San Pablo Edizioni.

San Joan, Joseph de. 1694. *Ceremonial dominicano en el qual se trata de las cosas que conducen al modo uniforme y orden de celebrar los Oficios Divinos* [. .]. Madrid.

Schmitt, Jean-Claude. 1984. "Between Text and Image: The Prayer Gestures of Saint Dominic." *History and Anthropology* 1 (1): 127–62.

Schmitt, Jean-Claude. 1999. *Il gesto nel Medioevo.* Roma: Laterza.

Signorini, Italo. 1979. *Los Huaves de San Mateo del Mar: Ideología e instituciones sociales.* Mexico City: Instituto Nacional Indígenista.

Sorci, Pietro. 2005. "Liturgia luogo teologico dell'ecclesiologia." In *La Chiesa tra teologia e scienze umane, una sola complessa realtà*, edited by R. La Delfa, 193–216. Roma: Città Nuova.

Tugwell, Simon. 1997. *The Nine Ways of Prayer of Saint Dominic.* London: Darton Longman and Todd.

17

Biblical Landscapes and Migration Histories

The "Ten Lost Tribes of Israel" in Colonial Highland Guatemala

SERGIO ROMERO

TIME, HISTORY, AND LEGITIMATION IN
POSTCLASSIC HIGHLAND GUATEMALA

During the Postclassic (950 to 1523 CE), the highland Maya sociopolitical unit was the *chinamit* ("fence," Nahuatl).[1] The chinamit encompassed a population of nobles (*ak'animaq*) and commoners (*al k'ajol*) and the territories they possessed. Chinamits incorporated new members (the formerly enslaved, for example) and increased their influence by means of alliances with other chinamits, forming larger units called confederations (*winäq*). Chinamits could, however, secede, as when the Kaqchikel separated from the K'iche' Confederation in 1470. Secessions (*yujuj*) were not always successful, however, and could have dire consequences for the parties involved. The Tuquche', for example, were annihilated when their separation from the Kaqchikel Confederation failed before the walls of Iximche' in 1493.[2] Chinamits and confederations competed for control of strategic resources, tribute, and labor. Led by the *ajawa'* (lords) and inspired by a militarist ideology in which battle prowess legitimized their rule, chinamits endured multiple wars during the Postclassic (Carmack 1981; Hill and Monaghan 1987; Orellana 1984; Romero 2024).

Elite self-representation in Postclassic highland Guatemala was dramatized in "migration histories," in which ancestral founders leave mythical places of origin and after numerous trials finally reach the territories they claim as their own. Myth and legitimation were inscribed in the same temporality in Postclassic and early colonial

https://doi.org/10.5876/9781646426829.c017

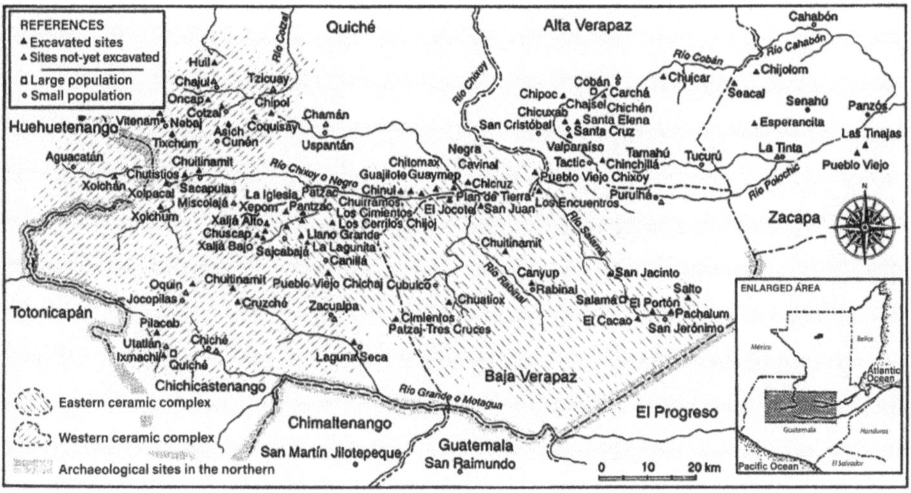

Figure 17.1. The Guatemalan Highlands in the Postclassic

ritual (Romero 2014).[3] Called by various Nahuatl and Maya names—Tulan ("Place of Reeds," Nahuatl); Chicomoztoc ("Seven Caves," Nahuatl); Wuqub' Pek, Wuqub' Siwan ("Seven Caves, Seven Ravines," K'iche')—these mythical places were sites in an ideological and ritual complex that spread through Mesoamerica from the Late Classic (750–950 CE), reaching its maximum expansion in the late Postclassic. Epic journeys not only were a hallmark of chinamit foundation stories but also legitimized their successors, the rulers of the highland Maya. According to Maya chronicles, rulers sometimes had to seek further validation of their authority and the symbols of power at mythical cities known as *suywa'*, where a powerful lord known as *Nakxit* or *Wemak* bestowed them with the accoutrements of office. The *ideología zuyuana* developed local variations, adapting to unique elite interests. It structured Maya politics, creating a pan-Mesoamerican system of political discourse, names, ritual practices, and political landscapes (Folan, Bolles, and Ek 2016; López-Austin and López Luján 1999). In the Memorial de Sololá,[4] for example, Q'aq'awitz, ancestral founder of the Xajil, leads the Kaqchikel from the mythical Tulan in the East to the Guatemalan highlands (see figure 17.1).[5] The narrative weaves together founders, local histories, and territories. Of course, this version of the story was contested by non-Kaqchikel elites. There is not one, but many versions of ancestral migration histories (Carmack 1981; Romero 2014, 2024).

MAYAN MIGRATION HISTORY UNDER SPANISH COLONIAL RULE

Migration history survived the transition from the Postclassic to the Spanish colonial period because it continued to legitimize the power and privileges of indigenous elites. Spanish law formally recognized the rights of *señores naturales* if they converted to Christianity and paid allegiance to the Spanish King.[6] Multiple examples of Mesoamerican migration histories survived in *lienzos* and codices and in alphabetic manuscripts. In Highland Guatemala, the latter include the Título de Totonicapán, the Título Tamub', the Título de los Indios de Santa Clara, el Título Jilotepeque, el Título Kaqkoj, and the Título de Santa María Ixhuatán (Carmack and Mondloch 1983; Contreras 2009; Romero 2014; Van Akkeren 2009).

This documentary corpus was transmitted for at least two hundred years after the Conquest. In migration histories, events occur in an epic space-time in which the mighty deeds of ancestral founders yield historical and even cosmic transformations with consequences reaching deep into the Spanish colonial period. The genre allows the incorporation of new event series, in which new episodes are added at the beginning or at the end of a narrative. The addition of preceding epic cycles (prequels) reframes the past to continue to validate the traditional authority of elites in a new present. Subsequent event cycles (sequels), in contrast, perform a complementary role, legitimizing new forms of authority provided power remains in the hands of Maya nobles. The incremental nature of migration history is grounded on Postclassic chronologies, which are divided into cycles bounded by historical milestones or calendrical events. The duration of cycles and their political implications are diverse: the Round of K'atuns in Yucatan (20-year cycles), the *juna'* (year) of the Kaqchikel Confederation after 1493 (400-day cycles), the *xiuhmolpilli* ("bundle of years," Nahuatl; 52-year cycles), and so forth (Edmonson 1988; Knowlton 2010; Smith 2002).[7] The Maya conceive history as a form of cosmic repetition that allows for innovation forwards or backwards. The system made possible a relatively smooth incorporation of European elements, reframing indigenous histories in European space-time without compromising ancestral legitimation practices and rituals. It had the added benefit of making biblical history, Western chronologies, and European calendars intelligible in Mesoamerican categories. The juxtaposition of pre-Hispanic and biblical history in Maya migration histories, and the simultaneous use of the Julian-Gregorian calendar and the *tonalpohualli-cholq'ij* dates in Mesoamerican annals, are examples of sequential repetitions in which each element reiterates, clarifies, and complements the other. Maya poetics, grounded on parallelism, works in the same fashion. Cycles are reiterations, reiterations are metric repetitions. Similarly, Maya poesis is also cyclic.

In the next section, I discuss this dialectic of incorporation and repetition with examples from the sixteenth-century documentary record in K'iche' and Kaqchikel, two Mayan languages spoken in the highlands of Guatemala. After their early con-version, K'iche' and Kaqchikel nobles began to portray themselves as descendants of the Ten Lost Tribes of Israel, while claiming also to be progeny of the warrior lords from the Mesoamerican Tulan. Traditional migration histories were juxta-posed as sequels of Old Testament history in which the ancestors of the Highland Maya were cast as protagonists of biblical events. Mesoamerican time frames were thus a temporal background for the incorporation of European religious narratives. Framing pre-Hispanic oral traditions in biblical history, even placing chinamit founders on biblical landscapes, "humanized" Maya ancestors as *señores naturales* and legitimized their hereditary rights under Spanish colonial rule. As we will see below, biblical history was an argument used by both sides as Maya elites and their Dominican allies sought to preserve as much of the traditional power structure as would be permissible under Spanish *policía*. The following section discusses one of the most popular and influential sixteenth-century biblical narratives: the myth of the Ten Lost Tribes of Israel.

THE TEN LOST TRIBES OF ISRAEL

The story of the Ten Lost Tribes of Israel was well known among Christians and Jews of all quarters of life in medieval Europe. It embodied fears, millenarian expec-tations, and the literal expansion of the world in European eyes after Columbus's travels, remaining current well into the seventeenth century (Popkin 1989; Volpato 2018, 2020). Based on canonical and apocryphal texts, the Ten Lost Tribes of Israel story was widely known in Europe by the time Columbus set out on his first voy-age in 1492.[8] According to 2 Esdras, an Apocrypha appended to the Vulgate until the Council of Trent explicitly excluded it from the biblical canon in 1548, some of the Jews exiled to Assyria by Sargon in 735 BC chose to leave their exile behind, moving to an unknown land called Azareth. They settled there, founding a sove-reign kingdom, and lived henceforth according to their ancient ways. They were never heard of again, however. The Ten Lost Tribes turned into a key narrative ele-ment of Christian and Jewish millenarian movements, including Spanish *conversos*, in the fifteenth and sixteenth centuries. The unknown land and the exotic popu-lations that Columbus encountered during his travels confirmed the millenarian prophecies that many Europeans believed in. The expulsion of the Jews from Spain, Columbus's "discoveries," and the expansion of the Ottoman Empire were seen in the light of eschatological biblical traditions and interpreted by millenarian pro-phets such as the Franciscan Joaquin de Fiore as signs of the imminence of the End of Time (Volpato 2018). The Ten Lost Tribes story also allowed a fleeting reconcili-ation of biblical history with the new humanism emerging in Europe in response to Columbus's travels. The peoples of the Americas, especially those living in sedentary societies with ritual practices recalling those of the ancient Hebrews, were seen by some as likely descendants of the Ten Lost Tribes. This universalization of biblical history was a requisite to defend the humanity of the "Indians" in the heated debates among Spanish theologians in the middle of the sixteenth century. The identification of a genealogical link between native Americans and the ancient Hebrews confirmed the views of those, such as the Dominican Francisco de Vitoria (1483–1546), who saw the native inhabitants of the "Indies" as fully human and therefore deserving of the same rights and protections as European subjects of the Spanish King.

Not surprisingly, the Ten Lost Tribes story crossed the Atlantic on the Spanish *naos*, reaching the western highlands of Guatemala in the 1530s. Several Highland Maya *títulos* (deeds) and pastoral texts in K'iche' and Kaqchikel bear variations of this story as prequels of pre-Hispanic migration histories, as outlined above. The appropriation by Highland Maya elites of the myth of the Ten Lost Tribes implied, first, the transfer of apocryphal texts as detachable, translatable wholes, and then, their subsequent discursive recontextualization. The cyclic and incremental structure of migration history enabled the smooth textual incorporation of the myth of the Ten Lost Tribes of Israel. The myth buttressed the genealogical claims of Maya elites and helped secure the support of powerful Spanish allies and, among the latter, uphold the case of those seeking to protect indigenous communities from *encomenderos* and Spanish officials. Maya nobles added it to their migration histories, thus inserting their own genealogy into the universalist, colonialist legitimation frame imposed by the Spanish. This reiterated migration histories in a Christian garb, making them relevant and intelligible in Spanish colonial society,

Several manuscripts identifying Maya ancestors as Israelites or Hebrews and describing epic migrations from biblical lands appeared in the 1550s. They include some of the oldest alphabetic texts in a Mayan language. Among them we find several *títulos* and one book of sermons, the Theologia Indorum in both Kaqchikel and K'iche' versions. The documents were authored by members of the chinamits Kaweq and Tamub' (K'iche'), and Xpantzay (Kaqchikel), covering a large swath of Highland Guatemala. The provenience and early composition dates of the manuscripts, and the fact that the Dominican-sponsored Theologia Indorum is the only pastoral text explicitly mentioning the "Ten Lost Tribes of Israel" suggest a connection between this narrative and the Order of Preachers. Dominicans taught alphabetic writing to Maya nobles, and the latter shared with the former their history, traditions, and language expertise. Maya nobles were key protagonists of the initial crystallization of Christian language in the highlands. Shared political interests and strategic decisions on both sides set the stage for the emergence of a Mayanized biblical history encompassing the Ten Lost Tribes. The next section examines the role that the Dominican Order played in the diffusion of the story.

THE DOMINICANS IN GUATEMALA AND
THE "TEN LOST TRIBES OF ISRAEL"

The Dominicans gained a foothold in Guatemala in 1529 when Domingo de Betanzos (1480–1549) founded the first convent in Santiago de Guatemala. Although Betanzos soon returned to Mexico City, Bartolomé de las Casas (1474 or 1484–1566) was active in Nicaragua as early as 1535. In 1537 he signed agreements with Pedro de Alvarado (1485–1541) and Bishop Francisco Marroquín (1499–1563) for the "peaceful conquest of the *Tierra de Guerra*," later renamed the Verapaz (Bierman 1960; Cabezas 2019; Fernández Rodríguez 1994; Saint-Lu 1968). To implement their strategy, Las Casas and his companions formed an alliance with surviving members of the K'iche' nobility to enter the Verapaz. Through the good offices of Don Juan de Sacapulas, last *ajpop k'amja*[9] of the defeated K'iche' Confederation, the Dominicans entered the Verapaz under the protection of the *ajpop* Jun B'atz, who was ruler of Chamelco at the time. In these early Verapaz contacts, the Dominicans implemented a strategy of cooperation with Maya nobles, turning the latter into active participants in the Christianization of their subjects (Bierman 1960, 1964; Saint-Lu 1968).[10] Las Casas's companions were active also in the western highlands, where they proceeded in a similar way. According to the Memorial de Sololá, Friar Pedro de Angulo (circa 1500–62) and Friar Juan de Torres arrived in Sololá in 1542 to begin the Christianization of the Kaqchikel.[11] In 1545 the first large Dominican "expedition" arrived in Guatemala, including among its members the now famous Friar Domingo de Vico. Domingo de Vico (circa 1485–1555) is perhaps the most renowned *lengua* in Guatemala. He wrote *artes* and dictionaries and edited a collection of sermons, the Theologia Indorum, written in K'iche' and Kaqchikel with summaries in at least four other highland Mayan languages. Vico was *guardián* of the Dominican convent in Santiago de Guatemala for two years, when he had daily contact with Kaqchikel and K'iche' nobles. The Theologia Indorum was probably written and edited there under his supervision (Acuña 1985, 2004; Sparks 2011; Van Akkeren 2010).

Recent scholarship on the Ten Lost Tribes suggests that the narrative was probably taken to the Guatemalan highlands by members of Las Casas's entourage. Las Casas lived in Santo Domingo between 1523 and 1529 at a time when the purported genealogical connection between the natives of the Indies and the ancient Israelites was being hotly debated. The *bachiller* Juan Roldán, author of a manuscript treatise on the Ten Lost Tribes, for example, lived in Santo Domingo at the time, where he probably met Las Casas. Interestingly, Roldán's manuscript wound up among the personal papers of Friar Miguel Orozco, provincial of the Andalusian Dominican province, who participated in the famous Sepúlveda–Las Casas debate in Valladolid between 1550 and 1551. Roldán presents five arguments supporting the claim that the natives of the Indies were descendants of the Ten Lost Tribes: First, according to his estimates, it took their ancestors a year and a half to trek from Nineveh to the Americas, the time span that the Israelites wandered after leaving their exile (2 Esdras); second, the number of inhabitants of the Indies was as large as the number of Israelites (Hosea 1); third, there were otherwise unexplainable similarities between indigenous languages and Hebrew, the language of the Israelites; fourth, there were also countless resemblances between the rites and customs of the Hebrews and those of the inhabitants of the Indies; finally, the indignities, abuse, violence, and death the latter suffered at the hands of the Spanish were the punishment that God had promised them for embracing idolatry during their exile (Arcos 1601, 672–73). The arguments are basically the same as those expostulated in a sermon in the Theologia Indorum devoted to the Lost Tribes, as we will see below. Although Las Casas argued against the identification of native Americans with descendants of the ancient Hebrews in his Apologetica Historia Sumaria, he and his companions were familiar with the arguments (Las Casas 1967, 387). Vico must have considered them important enough to merit a whole sermon in the Theologia Indorum. As far as I know, the Theologia Indorum is the only text in the vast homiletic literature in Mesoamerican languages directly engaging with the "Ten Lost Tribes." The Theologia Indorum is unique in the homiletic literature in Mayan languages in that it is addressed to the noble class. It is meant specifically to indoctrinate and provide the knowledge needed by converted Maya lords, a product of the Dominican policy of crafting alliances with the nobility, which lasted at least into the 1570s.[12] The Dominicans believed that a confirmation of a genealogical link between the Maya and the ancient Israelites would be beneficial to their Christianization project, enhancing the ability of the Maya to hold their ground against *encomenderos* and their sympathizers among the secular clergy and government officials. Encomenderos and Spanish merchants were virulent opponents to the Leyes Nuevas (1542) and saw them as a personal threat (Pereña et al. 1992, 25–101). The Mendicants, especially Las Casas's Dominicans, were blamed for these new laws and were harassed, vilified, and even forced to flee before encomendero mobs (Cunill 2011; Las Casas 1967; Percheron 1980; Remesal 1619).

As mentioned earlier, in addition to the Theologia Indorum, traces of the "Ten Lost Tribes" appear in several *títulos* (deeds). All are dated to the 1540s and 1550s, when the Lascasian project had not yet run its course. Biblical history entered the highlands in catechetical discourse, but Maya elites soon began to use it also in secular documents to buttress their authority as *señores naturales*.[13] In the following sections, I analyze fragments from three manuscripts (Theologia Indorum, Título de Totonicapán, and Título Tamub') to identify the textual strategies used to reconcile Maya and biblical history in the myth of the Ten Lost Tribes. The three documents represent three diachronically consecutive stages in the Mayanization of biblical narrative: introduction, repetition, and naturalization. The Theologia Indorum exemplifies the introduction stage, the earliest drafting of Christian language: fully developed in form but often tantalizingly close to unorthodoxy. The Título de Totonicapán in turn illustrates the repetition of existing Christian language, showing additions and modifications. Finally, the Título Tamub' epitomizes the naturalization stage, in which notarial texts bear only short, formulaic references to biblical events and Catholic rituals and signs. At that time, authors and readers—predominantly Maya nobles and Mendicants—were already familiar with Christian doctrine and ritual. Thus, the story of the Ten Lost Tribes spans three stages in the diachronic development of Christian language in the Maya highlands. It was an enduring narrative whose diffusion coincided with the earliest indoctrination of the highland Maya.

THE THEOLOGIA INDORUM: INTRODUCING THE "TEN LOST TRIBES" TO THE HIGHLAND MAYA

The Theologia Indorum is not only one of the most extensive books of sermons ever written in Mayan languages but also one of the earliest.[14] Drafted by a group of anonymous indigenous writers under the supervision of Friar Domingo de Vico, it is a wonderful example of the Christian appropriation of traditional Maya discourse. It adapted Maya poetic form to make doctrine and biblical history persuasive and intelligible for an audience of recent Maya converts. Several manuscript copies in K'iche' and Kaqchikel, as well as summarized versions in Tz'utujil and Q'eqchi', have survived. Although the Theologia Indorum was never published, it was hand-copied many times by Dominican and Franciscan scribes, making its way to the shelves of convent libraries in highland Guatemala. It was meant to be a template for the oral delivery of sermons, as attested by the vocative forms and entreaties opening and closing each sermon, and by a narrative structure characteristic of European homiletic literature: introduction, content delivery, conclusions, and recapitulation coda, known in the medieval catechetical tradition as *epilogo* (Dansey Smith 1978, 46–47). Whereas the authorial voice is that of a Spanish priest, the audience is constructed as plural, male, and indigenous. A few sermons were addressed specifically to the *ajawab'* (lords), a unique feature of the Theologia Indorum in the homiletic production in K'iche'an languages, which usually does not differentiate between noble and commoner audiences. The Theologia Indorum also avails itself of parallel repetition (couplets, triplets, etc.), the hallmark of Maya poetics, as well as of numerous metaphors found also in manuscripts with undisputable pre-Christian pedigree, such as the Popol Wuj and the Memorial de Sololá. It references God with the title Dios Nimajaw (God the Great Lord), which contributes to portraying the Christian deity as a powerful Lord, merciless with His enemies but generous with those who give Him their loyalty. In this regard, Yahweh was not different from Q'aq'awitz and B'alam Kitze', pre-Hispanic heroes who were also warriors, as attested in the K'iche' and Kaqchikel sources. The Memorial de Sololá, for example, uses Nimajaw (Great Lord) only in reference to the mythical lord Nakxit, to the Spanish King, and to the Christian God (*Memorial* 2024, 25, 96). It has been argued that the Theologia Indorum was drafted as a *theologia in extenso*, a systematic, detailed exposition of Christian doctrine along the lines of Thomas Aquinas's Summa Theologica (Sparks 2014). Nevertheless, the Theologia Indorum had very different goals and a very different discursive and rhetorical structure. Rather than expostulate about the intricacies of Catholic dogma, which it often glosses over, it seeks to make the Christian God, the Church, and biblical history intelligible for the Maya, in particular the nobles, who were the main interlocutors of Dominicans in the first decades after the Spanish invasion. It was the product of a unique set of historical circumstances, in which the Dominicans, inspired by Bartolomé de las Casas, were trying to implement a model of "Pacific Conquest" through persuasion and conversion of Maya elites. The Dominicans would guarantee Maya elites some of their hereditary privileges in exchange for conversion and submission to the King. The key role of noble conversions in the Dominican project explains the choice of discourse genres, address forms, and topics in the Theologia Indorum. For example, the Old Testament is elaborated in much more detail than the New Testament. Substantial space is given to the Book of Exodus, the Book of Ruth, and the Books of Maccabees, especially to chapters in which battles are fought or miracles performed by Yahweh, God of the Israelites. The Theologia Indorum makes biblical history intelligible by means of equivalences between biblical and Maya categories and discourse genres (see table 17.1). First, it equals the Postclassic sociopolitical unit, the chinamit, with the Israelite "tribe" (lines 1–5). It also incorporates metaphors and tropes distinctive of Postclassic historical discourse, as mentioned earlier. In line 17, it references the descendants of Maya-Israelite ancestors as *uq'ab' utux* (their branches, their buds), an arboreal trope found also in sixteenth-century K'iche' and Kaqchikel chronicles. Line 22 calls the Creator deity Tz'aqol B'itol (the Creator, the Shaper), a pre-Hispanic couplet resignified to reference the Christian God. Finally, line 23 uses the triplet *q'ij, ik', ch'umil* (sun, moon, stars), found also in the Memorial de Sololá, to reference celestial bodies.

TABLE 17.1. Sermon 101 of the Theologia Indorum (de Vico 1553–1615)

Fragment of Sermon 101 Theologia Indorum (K'iche')[a]	English translation (Sergio Romero)
23 ¶ Vnabepaſ̣ vuak4al	Chapter one hundred and one, (on the)
24 tçih coponic chic lahuſ̣ chic chinamit ahiſra(e)l. chi q(ui)huy[u]bal.	arrival of Israel's ten chinamits to their hills.
1 ¶ Are ri quitçalihic ahhier(usa)l(em). mixkabijh canok xepe	Here the return of the Jerusalemites that we mentioned before. They came from
2 chila Babilonia xulquilaɛabeſ̣. camaɛ xa e hu(n) chi china[-]	Babylon to resettle their homeland. They formed a single chinamit,
3 mit xa hu[n] 4hob vcahal qui4oheic q(ui) tuq(ue)l chic xq(ui)laɛabeſ̣. hie[-]	a single [. . .] group, settling alone
4 ru(sa)l(e)m. E are ri e lahuh chic chinamit xbe chila Asiria ru(ma)l.	in Jerusalem. Ten chinamits had been exiled to Assyria because of
5 Sarmanasar. Ma x4o ui xetçalih chic chila chila (x)çacſ̣	Sarmanasar, but none of them returned. Their story
6 ui quitçihoxic. mahabi ala xe4utu[n] chi ui kitçih nabe chi	was forgotten. No one taught it any more. In truth,
7 e 4iy chicoponic ma4uhabi chic xetçaliſ̣ chulok xa abaſ̣	many [of them] went, but none returned. Only stones,
8 xa che. xquiçi4ih xquiɛihila xebe ui chila xa quimac xa	only sticks did they worship and pray to over there. For their sins and
9 pu quitçelal x[e]oɛotax ui xecanax ui canok rumal. D(ios). n(imahau). Are	and evil (deeds), they were exiled and enslaved by God the Great Lord. This
10 4u ri hun nutçih chirah nubijſ̣ chiuech yx varalic vinak are	is the story that I am about to tell you, you people here! What
11 ri mixkabijh quiçachic 4hahcar ahiſrael vue chiri yx pe[-]	we have just told you is that a part of Israel was lost. Whether you all
12 tinak ui xa quicha chiuecſ̣. xa uçu4uliq(ui)l quehe canutiqui[-]	have come from there, I will tell you [now]. I begin thus
13 ba ubixic. chiuech ma nabe ritçelal ta nu4ux. chiuecſ̣ xa	to tell you the whole truth. It is not out of malice toward you, for
14 ynimaxic xa pu yloɛoxic vumal xa rumal mix4oxoma[-]	you all are respected and beloved by me. It is because your own
15 tah zcakin y4oheic kitçih ui 4ut cami chiquih ahiſrael yx	history is understood a little better now. It is a definitive truth today that you all
16 petinak ui yx camic umam v4ahol Abra(ha)m. yſaac. Jacob.	come from Israel. You all are grandchildren, sons of Abraham, Isaac, and Jacob.

continued on next page

TABLE 17.1—*continued*

	Fragment of Sermon 101 Theologia Indorum (K'iche')[a]	English translation (Sergio Romero)
17	yx camic vtux vɛab vtçilaɧ vinak xe4ohe oher chupa(m) vcha[-]	You all are buds, offshoots of good people who lived a long time ago,
18	bal Dios Ni[mahau]. maui xaloɛ q(ue)he canubijh. chiuech 4o retal ca[-]	[following] the Word of God, the Great Lord. I am not telling you [this] in vain. There is
19	nubijh co puch ri ki quitçihoxic. Are rumal. 4o 4hakap.	evidence of what I am telling you, of their story. Because there are still a few relics
20	v4hab v4habal. Dios. yvu4 xa yyuhu[n] chic chi tçakbal tçiɧ.	of the Word of God among you, though you have mixed them with lies.
21	Are ri hun v4habal Dios 4o yvu4 ri quixcha xa hu(n)	One is when you claim that there is only
22	tçakol. bitol. kachuch kakahau. xbano cah xbano	One Creator and Shaper, our grandmother and grandfather, who made heaven
23	vleu. xbano. ɛih. y4. 4humil xbano huyub taɛaɧ xba[-]	and earth, who make the sun, the moon, and the stars, who made hills and plains,
24	no. cho. palo xbano pu 4hutichicop. nimachicop xba[-]	who made lakes and seas, who made small and large animals, who
25	no echa 4uxu(n) ru4 naypuch xohubano. xohuvinaki.[-]	created sustenance and food, and who also made us, created us.
/168v/		
1	riçah. Oh uuinak tçak oh uvinak bit. xuban vbaɛ ka[-]	We are his creatures! He made our eyes, our chin. You also say that
2	uach. kixcacate xbano naipu kakan kaɛab quixcha	he made our legs and arms,
3	Are chiyao mialanic 4aholanic Are puch chiyao tçiynic	He gave us the ability to father daughters and sons, he gave us [...][b]
4	a4inic tçibani[c] 4otonic. Are puch chiyao çuanic bixanic q[ue][-]	[...], paintings and carvings. He gave us also flute music and songs,
5	monic batçinic are pucɧ cɧiyao vinakire(m) 4azle(m) quixcha a[-]	weaving and spinning, he gave us human form and life, as you say.
6	re 4u hun retal nutçih rij. xaui xere Dios. nimaɧau ri tça[-]	This is a sign of what I am telling you, as only God the Great Lord, the
7	kol bitol xbano ronohel ri chibijh. hutala 4u cha chiueta[-]	Creator, the Shaper made all that you say. How could you possibly learn
8	maɧ ui ri. Vue ta maui yx ri canubijɧ ata xita ui vtçihoxic	that? Are you all not those (who say it)? I will tell you where you heard the story.

continued on next page

TABLE 17.1—*continued*

Fragment of Sermon 101 Theologia Indorum (K'iche')[a]	English translation (Sergio Romero)
9	ri vue ta maui vtux vue ta maui ix vɛab abraham kitçifʃ	Aren't you Abraham's buds and offshoots? In truth,
10	tcih ui ri chiri ix petinak ui chiri petinak ui utçihoxic	you have come from there, and from there the story has come
11	chixiqui(n) chi4ux ix uaralic vinak. hutala 4u cha xiueta[-]	into your ears and hearts, you people here! How could you possibly have learned it otherwise?
12	ma[h] chire vue ta maui yuetaa(m) vtçihoxic. vue ta puch	Don't you know the story? Have you not
13	maui ytao(n). ma xa xiuachi4afʃ ta ua ubanic cafʃ vleufʃ	heard it? You have not just dreamed up the creation of heaven and earth.
14	Are chi naypuch hu[n] chic retal. xiueleçafʃ rih yvunum	Here is another clue: You used to cut off the foreskin of your penis in the days
15	oher. xaui q(ue)he q(ui)banofʃ ahiʃrael ri E vma(m) e u4ahol A[-]	of old. This is what the Israelites, Abraham's children, and grandchildren
16	braham. are chi naipuch. hu(n) retal. xutçahiçafʃ rib palo xofʃ[-]	used to do too. Another clue is that the sea dried up[c] when we
17	y4oui vlok ta xohpe chila 4haka ha. 4haka palo. xtoɛ pa[-]	crossed over, when we came from the other side of the water, of the sea. The sea
18	lo chi4hamiy ta xuhak rib ha. quixcha apax pe ui vtay[-]	was prodded with a staff and the water opened up, as you say. Where did that
19	quil ri mata xq(ui)ta ychuch ykahau. oher. Are cami ta xe[-]	news come from? Did your mothers and fathers not hear it in the days of old?
20	eleçax ulok chila Egipto. ychuch ykahau oher rumal	Were your mothers and fathers in the old days not freed from Egypt by
21	Moyʃen. xaui xere v4hamiy. moiʃen. Camirix quitçi[-]	Moses? It was Moses's staff that did it.
22	hoh yxiquin mam yxiqui(n) kahau 4iy chi nabek retal	Probably your great-grandfathers and great-great-grandfathers told you. There are
23	40 chupam y4oheic. x4ohe oher chi qui4oheic. Judios. xa[-]	many other clues in your traditions of what existed in the days of old, and in Jewish traditions.
24	et vɛalahobiçaxic. vumal chiuech. kitçih ui chi yx retal	It is unnecessary to explain it yet again to you. In truth, I am certain that you all are
25	yx pu vtçihel ahiʃrael Canunao xa xq(ui)çach ychuch y[-]	descendants, offspring of the Israelites, but your mothers

continued on next page

Table 17.1—*continued*

Fragment of Sermon 101 Theologia Indorum (K'iche')[a]	English translation (Sergio Romero)
/169R/	
1 kahau v4habal Dios. n(imahau). xa huhu(n) chic 4az4oh yvumal xo[-]	and fathers forgot the Word of God, the Great Lord. Only a few [relics] remained
2 loxoxinak chuxol tçakbal tçih yvumal.	alive, which you all mixed up with lies.

a. I use here the colonial orthography of the Theologia Indorum copy in the Manuscript Library, American Philosophical Society in Philadelphia.

b. Unreadable in the manuscript.

c. Like the crossing of the Red Sea in Exodus.

THE "TEN LOST TRIBES" IN SERMON 101 OF THE THEOLOGIA INDORUM

In the sixteenth century, Christians interpreted biblical history literally. It was regarded as a source of factual and universally valid historical knowledge. All human beings were believed to be descendants of Adam and Eve, sharing the same biblical genealogy (Popkin 1989, 63). Some Dominicans believed, as explained earlier, that an identification of a direct historical link between Maya ancestors and the ancient Israelites would vindicate the intrinsic humanity of the Highland Maya. It would immediately falsify claims that *indios* were not truly human and, in consequence, undeserving of the rights and protections afforded to subjects of the King. Sermon 101 of the Theologia Indorum argues for a genetic relationship between the ancient Israelites and the ancestors of the K'iche' and the Kaqchikel. It presents apparent similarities between Israelite and Postclassic K'iche' and Kaqchikel rituals and oral traditions as evidence. It calls these convergences -*etalil* (signs) of Israelite beliefs and practices, listing four and claiming they were sufficient proof of the relationship. The list includes the belief in a single Creator deity,[15] the story of the crossing of the Red Sea,[16] the opening of the sea by Moses's staff, and the practice of circumcision (see Fol. 168v, lines 6–22 in table 17.1).[17] The sermon posits that Maya ancestors did once have knowledge of *v4habal Dios* (the Word of God), which they forgot when they moved out of the Holy Land, "mixing truth with falsehood" (Folio 169r, line 1–2).[18] The likelihood of an independent emergence of genetically unconnected similarities was unthinkable, of course, in a medieval Christian mindset that considered Revelation absolute truth.[19] Interestingly, K'iche' and Kaqchikel pastoral discourse of the late 1540s and early 1550s was not doctrinal in a narrow sense but encompassed also traditions based on Apocrypha such as the one we discuss here. These texts were appropriated by the Maya, and knowledge of them diffused. In the meantime, short references to the "Ten Lost Tribes" began to appear in documents of notarial genres as well. Biblical history complemented rather than contradicted pre-Hispanic Maya history, providing a frame that made the latter useful for Maya lords to legitimize their rule under Spanish colonialism. The next section examines how the "Ten Tribes" story was integrated into the official history of the K'iche' of Totonicapán, and the role it played in advancing the interests of K'iche' elites.

TÍTULO DE TOTONICAPÁN: THE "TEN LOST TRIBES" STORY EXPANDS IN THE HIGHLANDS

The Título de Totonicapán was written after the Theologia Indorum but shows substantial thematic overlap with it. The purpose of *títulos* (deeds) was to defend and legitimize territorial claims of Maya elites with selective recapitulations of Postclassic and colonial Maya history. Written by K'iche' nobles from Chwi Miq'ina' ("Over the Hot Springs," K'iche')—known in Nahuatl and Spanish as "Totonicapán"—the Título de Totonicapán based its arguments on rights of conquest inherited from K'iq'ab', who led the K'iche' Confederation to its maximum territorial expansion in the middle of the fifteenth century (Carmack and Mondloch 1983). The manuscript consists of three historical sections, followed by a genealogy of the lords of Q'umarka'j, ancient seat of the K'iche' Confederation, and a list of K'iq'ab's conquests, including Totonicapán. It ends listing the milestones marking the territory claimed by the lords of Totonicapán (see table 17.2).

NARRATIVE AND HISTORY IN THE TÍTULO DE TOTONICAPÁN

The Título de Totonicapán integrates biblical and pre-Hispanic histories, locating Mesoamerican toponyms on a biblical landscape, and describing others as distorted names of biblical sites. Maya ancestors are portrayed as descendants of the ancient Israelites, recapitulating the myth of the Ten Lost Tribes of Israel. Whereas the tribes of Israel are identified as chinamits, as I mentioned earlier, Assyria, the place of their exile, is described as *ramaq' Salmanasar* (Salmanasar's amaq') (see folio 6v, lines 15–16 in table 17.2). *Amaq'* references a chinamit's rural settlements outside the urbanized citadels where elites had their seat. The Israelites are denounced as apostates who "worshipped trees and stones in their exile" (*Xa che abah xquiçiqih chila xepe ui*) (folio 6v, lines 19–20). God the Great Lord "expels the Israelites for their sins and evils" (*Xa quimac, xa pu quitzelal xcoɛotax ui rumal Dios nimaahau*) (folio 6v, lines 20–21), restating the central point of the Ten Lost Tribes narrative. The text continues, in the manner of pre-Hispanic migration histories, listing places—calling them *huyub* (hills)—that the Israelites-Maya crossed in their trajectory from Assyria: Mara, Xelimkutz, Sin, Rabiqin, Xiney, Caxerot, Chi Qates, Etoni, Hor, Chi Boch, Chi Abatin, Xaret, Arnon, Matan, Xchamel, Bemot, and Chi Moab (folio 7r., lines 1–7). Some of these toponyms nativize biblical names, others cannot be identified, as they probably underwent cumulative scribal errors distorting the original orthography. The Título identifies Israelites (ah Ysrael), Canaanites (ah Canaan) and Hebrews (ah ebreo) as K'iche' ancestors.[20] The authors describe themselves as "sons, grandchildren of Adan, Eva, Enoch, Abraham, Isaac, Jacob," though this knowledge was lost "in the war" (folio 7r, lines 15–17). At this point, the righteousness (*uçuquliquil*) that Maya ancestors had abandoned is reintroduced. As a sign of God's mercy toward the highland Maya, God returned this knowledge to them through the words of the Spanish Friars (*Xa qu rumal xquiçach quidiyos, xa qu cha xeyxouax rumal Dios nimaahau, ri qute uçuquliquil*) (folio 7r, line 17–19). Note that God's name *Dios* (God) is a Spanish loanword, chosen after much debate among Dominicans and Franciscans, lest native names direct Christian ritual to pre-Hispanic deities (García-Ruiz 1992).

TABLE 17.2. Fragment of the Título de Totonicapán (Carmack and Mondloch 2007, 66–70)

	Título de Totonicapán (K'iche')	English translation (Sergio Romero)
FOLIO 6v		
	. . .	
15	Є Are qu ri e lahuh chi chinamital xebe chila	Є These are the ten chinamits that went to Assyria, Salmanasar's homeland, but never came back. Nothing was heard from them again, and they never reappeared. In truth, many left but none returned. There they worshipped sticks and stones only. Because of their sins and evil, God the Great Lord exiled them. These are the names of the hills they crossed in their journey:
16	Asiria ramaε Salmanasar. Xmalo chi ui	
17	xetzalij chi ui uloε. Chila xsach ui quitzihoxic.	
18	Xmalo ui xequtun ui. Kitzih chi e qi chi copanic,	
19	machi qut xetzalih ui uloε. Xa che abah xqui-	
20	çiqih chila xepe ui. Xa quimac, xa pu qui-	
21	tzelal xcoεotax ui rumal Dios nimaahau.	
22	Vae ubi huyub mixcholotahic xeyqou ui. ___	

continued on next page

TABLE 17.2.—*continued*

Título de Totonicapán (K'iche')	English translation (Sergio Romero)

FOLIO 7R

	Título de Totonicapán (K'iche')	English translation (Sergio Romero)
1	Mixcholotajik: Mara ubi nabe huyu ta xuhɛax	Mara was the name of the first hill they crossed when they came across the other side of the sea, the second Xe Limkutz, the third Sin, the fourth Rab'ik'in, the fifth Xiney [Sinaí], the sixth Kaxerot, the seventh Chi K'ates, the eighth Etoni, the ninth Jor, the tenth Chi B'och, the eleventh Chi Ab'atin, the twelfth Xaret, the thirteenth Arnon, the fourteenth Matan, the fifteenth Xchamel, the sixteenth Chi Moab'.
2	uloɛ ghaka palo, ucab Xelimcutz, rox Sin,	
3	ucah Rabiqin, ro Xiney, uuaɛaɛ Caxerot,	
4	uuuk Chi Qates, uuakxaɛ Etoni, ubeleh Hor,	
5	ulahuh Chi B'och, u-	
6	hulah Chi Abatin, ucablah Xaret, roxlah	
7	Arnon, ucahlah Matan, rolah Xchamel, uuaɛlah Bemot, uuuɛlah Chi Moab	
8	Ri qute quicoheyc, quiqouibal rumal Diyos niña-	This was where Israelites, Canaanites, and Hebrews made their crossing thanks to God the Great Lord. The Israelites had three different groups: the Israelites [proper], the Canaanites, and the Hebrews. All of them were our grandfathers and fathers, the people from which we came: our origin and ancestry in the East. Listen! I will clarify it for you, I will explain the truth. Our grandfathers and fathers lost themselves in war, but we are still grandchildren and children of Adam, Eve, Enoch, Abraham, Isaac, and Jacob. Because they had lost their God, God the Great Lord.
9	ahau, quiyiɛ puch ah Canan, ah Ebreos	
10	puch, ah Ix-rael. Oxib chi bi chi conohel ah Ysrael, ac Cana-	
11	an, ah Ebreos, queuchaxic, e kamam, ɛaka-	
12	hau ri oh ri qut e kaxe, kaqoheyc puch, kelic pu	
13	uloɛ relebal ɛih. Xchita pu uloɛ, xchiuachin pu u-	
14	uach uumal. Xchinbih qut uçuquliquil chi-	
15	uech uloɛ. Xa pa labal xeçach ui kamam kaka-	
16	hau, oh umam uqahol Adan, Eva, Enoc, Abra-	
17	ham, Yssac, Jacob. Xa qu rumal xquiçach quidiyos,	
18	xa qu cha xeyxouax rumal Dios nimaahau,	
19	ri qute uçuquliquil	

continued on next page

TABLE 17.2.—*continued*

Título de Totonicapán (K'iche')	English translation (Sergio Romero)
20 Є Xa xquipoo, xa xquihalqatih quitzih Uuεub Pec,	They confused the correct way of saying the names, they distorted them into Wuqub' Pek, Wuqub' Siwan, Sewan Tulan, as they called them. Pan Parar,
21 Uu-εub Çiuan, Çeuan Tulan xecha chi rech Pan Pa-	
22 rar, Pam Paxil, Pan Qaela, xecha. = Are qu	

FOLIO 7v

1 ri Pan Paxil, Pan Qaela xequibih. Are ri chu-	Pan Paxil, Pan Kayala, they called them as well. The place they called Pan Paxil, Pan Kayala was inside Paradise. That's where we were created and shaped by God the Great Lord. His Name could not be [uttered] because of their sins. What they called Sewan Tulan was actually Sineyeton, what they called Wuqub' Pek, Wuqub' Siwan was actually Pa Pek, Pa Siwan. It was in the East where at once and in loneliness they disappeared in Assyria because of Salmanazar.
2 pam Parayso Terenal xohq, ak ui, xohbit ui	
3 rumal Dios nimaahau. Maui xutzin chi	
4 ubi cumal rumal qut quimac. Are qu ri	
5 Çeuan Tulan xquibih cha qut uçuquiliquil	
6 Sineyeton. Are qu ri Uukub Pec, Uukub Çiuan	
7 ri tzih ui, are ri Pa Pec, Pa Çiuan xeuar ui chila chi	
8 relibal εih. Xa quehunelic uloε, xa pu e huça-	
9 chic ta xeçach chila Asiria rumal Salmana-	
10 sar.	

continued on next page

HISTORY AND BIBLICAL LANDSCAPE

The Título reorganizes sacred landscapes to reconcile pre-Hispanic and biblical history. Pre-Hispanic migrations and biblical events are regarded as factually true, presupposing an identity between them that was distorted due to the "lies" that K'iche' ancestors believed in during their exile. Identifying onomastic correspondences between pre-Hispanic and biblical geographies and locating pre-Hispanic migrations on biblical landscapes are the two textual strategies used in the first sections of the Título. An implied distinction between events involving founders and events involving their descendants emerges in the text. After the crossing of the Four Founders (B'alam Kitze, B'alam Aq'ab', Majukotaj, and Iki B'alam) from the East, K'iche' history moves to Mesoamerica. K'iche' ancestors, according to the Título, skewed and replaced biblical names, replacing them with old pre-Hispanic toponyms (*Xa xquipoo, xa xquihalqatih quitzih Uuεub Pec, Uuεub Çiuan, Çeuan*

TABLE 17.2.—*continued*

Título de Totonicapán (K'iche')	English translation (Sergio Romero)
11 Uae hupah tzih xchinbih, uae uqoheyc aha-	In this story, I will tell you about the power of lords, about the beginning of the yellowest and greenest hills, Pa Siwan Pa Tulan, the writings on Siwan Tulan, as they say. It was believed in the time of lies that the sun was a girl and the moon was a boy. They called the sun Junajpu, the moon Xb'alamkej, and the constellations Centipede Blood. We are grandchildren and sons of the Israelites, of Moses. Our grandfathers and fathers hailed from Israel's chinamits when they came from the East. It was at Babylon that the lord Nacxit passed on the beginning of our genealogy.
12 varem, uxe puch tzij ri ubixic ri ɛanalah	
13 huyub, raxalah huyub ri. Pa Çiuan, Pa Tulan	
14 xquibih utzibal pec, utzibal çiuan	
15 Tulan, xecha. Ta xenimatah chupam ri tzaɛbal	
16 tzih, ta xecha chi rech ri ɛih, ic hun ɛapoh, hun	
17 qahol xecha. Hunahpu xecha chirech ri ɛih,	
18 Xbalanqueh chuchax ri iq cumal. Uquiq Qiɛab	
19 chuchax ri qhumil cumal. Oh umam oh uqa-	
20 hol ah Ysrael, Santu Moysen. Chupam quichina-	
21 mital ah Ysrael xel ui e kamam, e kakahau,	
22 ta xepe chi relibal ɛih. Chila pa B[ab]elonia couiçan	
23 oɛ ahau Naɛxit ri uxe kamamaxic.	

continued on next page

Tulan xecha chi rech Pan Parar, Pam Paxil, Pan Qaela, xecha) (folio 7r, lines 20–22). The text elaborates on this process, identifying two purported biblical names as the etymological source of pre-Hispanic toponyms in migration histories: Çeuan Tulan is identified as the biblical Sineyeton, probably a reference to the Sinai desert, while Uuɛub Pec, Uuɛub Çiuan is identified as a biblical site named with the couplet Pa Pec, Pa Çiuan. The latter seems to be a reference to Paradise, which the Título had previously named as the place where God created the K'iche' and other Highland peoples.[21] Other sites in pre-Hispanic migration histories are placed in Paradise (folio 7v, lines 1–3). In short, pre-Hispanic and biblical narratives interleave by means of mutual identifications between pre-Hispanic and biblical toponyms, on the one hand, and a relocation of K'iche' mythical landscapes to Paradise, on the other.

TABLE 17.2.—*continued*

Título de Totonicapán (K'iche')	English translation (Sergio Romero)

FOLIO 8R

	Título de Totonicapán	English translation
1	kaqaholaxic. Ta xquiquxlaah quipetic e na-	And then the *nawal* people planned their
2	ual uinaɛ, nah[t] xopan wi quimuɛubal chi cah,	migration here. Their eyesight reached far into the sky and onto earth. Nothing under the sky compared to their vision. They
3	chi uleu. Maui qo ta cuhunamah ruc xkimu-	were great wisemen, the leaders of the Wuq
4	ɛuh ronohel xe cah. E nimaq etamanel, e qamol	Amaq' of Tekpan. Thus was their journey from across the sea, from across the ocean at Pa Tulan, Pa Siwan.
5	ube ronohel Uuk Amaɛ Tlecpan. Quehe qut	These are the names of the first people; these are the names of the first K'iche'. The
6	quipetic vae qhaka cho, qhaka palo Pa Tulan, Pa	first lord was B'alam Kitze', grandfather and father of ours, the Kaweq.
7	Çewan ___ ___ ___ ___	The second lord was B'alam Aq'ab', grandfather and father of the Nijaib'.
8	Vae qut e quibi nabe uinaɛ, vae nabe Qiche	The third was Majukotaj, father and
9	e cahib chi uinaɛ. Are nabe ahau Balam	grandfather of the Ajaw K'iche'.
10	Qitze ri kamam, kakahau oh Cauekib, are qut	And the fourth was Ikib'alam. These were the first K'iche's.
11	ucab ahau ri Balam Aɛab, umam ukahau Ahau	B'alam Kitze was the first lord. Kaqapaluma was his wife.
12	Nihayib. = Rox qut ahau ri Mahucotah ri	B'alam Aq'ab' was the second lord. Sunija' was his wife.
13	quimam quikahau e Ahau Qiche. Ucah qut	Majukotaj was the third lord. Kaqixaja' was his wife.
14	ahau ri Iqui Balam. Are qut uae nabe Qiche	Iki B'alam came as a bachelor from the East.
15	Balam Qitze nabe ahau, Cakapaluma ubi rixokil.	
16	Balam Aɛab ucab ahau, Çuniha ubi rixokil,	
17	Mahucotaj rox ahau, Cakixaha ubi rixokil,	
18	Iqui Balam xa ki qahol xpe chi relibal ɛih.	

K'ICHE' MILITARISM AND BIBLICAL GEOGRAPHIES

The rule of highland Maya lords (*ajawarem*) was established and consolidated by the military prowess of founders and their descendants. The Título locates the beginning of the K'iche' at Pa Çiuan, Pa Tulan, probably a clipped form of Uuɛub Pec, Uuɛub Çiuan, and Tulan, mentioned before (folio 7v, lines 11–15). Uuɛub Pec, Uuɛub Siwan and Tulan are described as the "greenest hills, yellowest hills" (*ɛanalah huyub, raxalah huyub*), a couplet and a trope meaning "luscious and beautiful," found also in other colonial manuscripts and still used today in both K'iche' and Kaqchikel ceremonial discourse. Chronologically these events occurred before conversion to Christianity, when the K'iche' still "believed in lies" (*ta xenimatah chupam ri tzakbal tzih*), when the "sun was a girl, and the moon a boy" (*ta xecha chi rech ri εih, ik hun εapoh, hun qahol xecha*), the sun was called Junajpu, and the moon Ixb'alamkej (folio 7v, lines 17–18).[22] Nevertheless, the text also restates a genealogical connection with the Israelites and with Moses in particular. The ancestors, who were "grandchildren, sons of the Israelites and Moses," descend "from the chinamits of Israel in the East" (folio 7v, lines 19–22). Even the previously discussed legitimacy bestowed by the lord Nakxit hails from Babylon (*Chila pa B[ab]elonia couiçan oε ahau Naεxit ri uxe kamamaxic*) (folio 7v, line 22–23). Mythical history is thus anchored in biblical landscapes. The migration story of the K'iche', Kaqchikel, and Wuq Amaq' from Tulan in the East, led by the Four K'iche' Founders, turns into a migration from biblical lands. The Título articulates biblical and pre-Hispanic histories as consecutive narrative segments, interleaving also mythical landscapes. The historicity of protagonists and events is not questioned but simply reordered.

The legitimation work of pre-Hispanic migration history continued for hundreds of years after the Spanish invasion. The Ten Lost Tribes myth became a key element of migration histories. Whereas earlier sources such the Theologia Indorum and the Título de Totonicapán include detailed accounts or repetitions of the story, later documents bear only oblique references to it. This suggests that the narrative had been naturalized by then, becoming an active element of elite self-legitimation discourse, as in the Título Tamub', which we will examine next.

THE TÍTULO TAMUB': THE NATURALIZATION OF THE "TEN LOST TRIBES"

The Titulo Tamub, written by Don Juan de Torres (1547–99),[23] begins with a short recapitulation of Tamub' migration history and a ruler genealogy, in which Tamub' founders K'opichoch and K'ochijlan come from Babylon, in the East (see table 17.3, line 8). As we saw in the Título de Totonicapán, events following the arrival of the Founders occur entirely on Mesoamerican spaces, following henceforth pre-Hispanic migration histories. Later *títulos*, such as the Título de los Nimaqachi, not analyzed in this chapter, include short references to the "Ten Lost Tribes" as well. They presuppose audience knowledge of the story and mention it only cursorily. The substantial section of the manuscript, the ruler genealogy, is as detailed as the one in the Título de Totonicapán (see table 17.3, lines 19–23).

The cyclic nature of Highland Maya history allowed a reframing of ancient pre-Hispanic myths into a biblical narrative. But, far from denying their own history, Maya nobles were able to recast it in a way that would be useful in the new colonial situation. Genealogies continued to have the lion's share of document space, especially in later manuscripts. Azareth (Título de Totonicapán) or Babylon (Título Tamub') replaced Tulan as the origin of chinamit founders. Such differences in narrative detail suggest the simultaneous circulation of various versions of the story,

TABLE 17.3. Folio 1 of the Título Tamub' (Contreras 2009)

	Título Tamub' (K'iche') (Historia Quiché de Don Juan de Torres)[1]	English translation (Sergio Romero)
1	Wakamik chupam keb' rajilab'al ik' Septiembre ruk' junab'	Today, September the 2nd of 1812, we shall write about the daughters and sons who were the beginning of our genealogy, we the nine sons of women, as our fathers and grandfathers used to say.
2	mil ochocientos dose xchiqatz'ib'aj wi uj jule chik mi'al k'ajol,	
3	uxe' qamamaxik, qak'ajolaxik uj b'elejeb' chi al,	
4	xecha qamam, qaqajaw.	
5	E puch b'elej chi nim ja. Wa k'ute kib'i' xujpoqowik,	There were nine houses, and these are the names of those who begat us: K'opichoch was the first, and his wife was Jun Kur. K'ochojlan was the second, and his wife was Xb'it K'u. They came from the East, from the other side of the sea, of the ocean. They left from a place named Babylon.
6	xujkirow puch, Kopichoch ub'i', Jun Kur ub'i' rixoqil;	
7	K'ochojlan ub'i' jun chik Xb'it K'u ub'i' rixoqil.	
8	Chi la' k'ut xepe wi chi releb'al q'ij, ch'aqa cho, ch'aqa palo	
9	ta xe xelik chi la' naypuch B'ab'ilonia ub'i'.	
10	Wakamik ri xepax wi, xejachow wi chi nima konojel ri lajuj	At this point, they divided and separated themselves into eighteen groups and eighteen languages. They were split in power and glory. They walked away and came here. They were chased away, abandoning their hills and valleys. They were powerful people who had bows of fire, who had fire and flint. They included the Puma, and the Jaguar, the Tekum B'alam as it was called when they came, when they [...]
11	uwajxaq k'al chi molaj, chi ch'ab'al puch. Xepaxik chi pusil chi	
12	nawalil puch, xeb'in wi ta xepetik, ta xkoqataj, ta xkikanaj puch	
13	kijuyub'al, kitaq'ajal. E pus nawal winaq k'o chab'i, q'aq', k'o	
14	uq'aq', tijax; k'o ri koj, b'alam k'o ri Tekum B'alam ub'i' nawal	
15	chi ke ta xepetik, ta kulik chi ri'tab' qala mam.	
16	Nab'e xe'ul wi, xeyaluj wi, xeb'ayataj wi, xepe chi k'ut, xe'ul	First, they arrived but delayed and dithered in Chi Xuchiy. Then they came here with their loads and tumplines, with their shields.
17	chi ri' chi xuchiy, xepe chi kuw chi xuchiy, xe'ul chi ri' ik,	
18	patan, xpe chi ik, patan, xe'ul chi k'ut chi' pokob'.	

continued on next page

TABLE 17.3.—*continued*

Título Tamub' (K'iche') *(Historia Quiché de Don Juan de Torres)*[a]	*English translation* *(Sergio Romero)*
19 [Chi ri'] k'ut xk'ajolax wi. Xuk'ajolaj Kopichoch Sipak k'ut, xu-	There they begat [children]. K'opichoch begat Sipak, and K'ochojlan begat the second generation. There they met Majkinal and K'oq'anawil, the eight chinamits, and the four chinamits of grandfathers and fathers, the twelve houses, the twelve lordly lines.
20 k'ajolaj Kochojlan uka le winaq. K'a chi ri' k'ut xeriq, ko wi	
21 kib' ruk' ri Majkinal, ruk' puch Kokanawil, ri wajxaqib'	
22 chinamit ruk' kajib' kajib' chinamit kimam, kiqajaw, kab'lajuj	
23 chi nim ja, kab'lajuj puch chi ajawarem.	

a. I use the transcription of the manuscript published by Contreras (2009). Contreras's publication used the Unified Alphabet and did not, unfortunately, include a facsimile of the original.

some mentioning Babylon, others Assyria. The Theologia Indorum was not the unique source of, but only an example of, the kind of Christian doctrinal and historical traditions circulating in the Maya highlands. Biblical and pre-Hispanic historical narratives were inscribed in the same temporality, forging a hybrid ideological background for effective elite legitimation rituals into the nineteenth century.

EPILOGUE

The Ten Lost Tribes myth expanded through the western highlands of Guatemala in the sixteenth and seventeenth centuries. Unfortunately, few manuscripts have survived from this time, as the number of notarial documents in highland Mayan languages decreased substantially after the sixteenth century. The power of the nobles continued into the nineteenth century, however. Nobles predominantly held cabildo offices, and pre-Hispanic titles continued to be inherited into the nineteenth century. The "Ten Lost Tribes" left an enduring imprint on Highland Maya migration histories until the demise of the genre after Independence from Spain in 1821. Independence led to a rapid decline of the Maya noble class, who were incapable of responding to the challenges presented by the new Guatemalan state, which was intent upon dismantling a legal framework based on the Leyes de Indias to deliver indigenous lands and labor to the plantation economy (González 2014; Woodward 1993). Oral traditions legitimizing the rule of nobles disappeared in the nineteenth century. Some founders became cultural heroes, icons of emerging postchinamit identities, however. New founders emerged as well, such as Manuel Tzo'k in the township of Nahualá in western Guatemala, which seceded from Santa

Catarina Ixtahuacán in 1863 starting a violent boundary conflict that continues to this day (Romero 2017). Biblical narratives continue to be told with the renewed fervor of rapidly expanding Pentecostal denominations in Highland Maya communities. Old Testament landscapes and biblical narratives keep playing a role in the moral economy, religion, politics, and self-understanding of the highland Maya.

NOTES

1. I write Maya words with the official Unified Alphabet used in Guatemala, except for fragments from colonial documents, which appear in the original colonial orthography. Nahuatl words are written with the colonial orthography as well.

2. The Tuquche' were the third chinamit in rank in the Kaqchikel Confederation after the Sotz'il and the Xajil.

3. Migration histories were foundational charts of chinamit elites. Maya nobles considered themselves direct descendants of ancestral founders. Pilgrimages and migration histories played the same role in the Classic (250–950 CE), as attested in hieroglyphic inscriptions in sites such as Copán (Tokovinine 2008).

4. The Memorial de Sololá is a compilation of chronicles and other documents written in Kaqchikel by Xajil nobles from the 1550s to the 1650s in Santa María de la Asunción Sololá, known today as Sololá. The Xajil were the second chinamit in rank in the Kaqchikel Confederation after the Sotz'il (Romero 2024).

5. Q'aq'awitz's party included the Kaqchikel, the K'iche', and the Wuq Amaq' (Seven Amaq'), a collective name given to highland chinamits dominated by the former in the late Postclassic.

6. *Señores naturales* were indigenous rulers sanctioned by their own laws and traditions. Spanish laws demanded respect of their dignity, rights, and sovereignty, although in practice this was often not the case.

7. Cyclicity does not necessarily entail the use of calendars, however. When event cycles follow one another, they do not need to be bounded by dates, as can be seen in oldest annals in the Memorial de Sololá, for example (Romero 2024).

8. Apocrypha are texts outside the accepted canon of Scripture, forming a complex, diverse body of works. The Second Book of Esdras (2 Esdras), one of the main sources for the story of the Ten Lost Tribes, had a long history in the Catholic biblical tradition. St. Jerome included it in the Vulgate, but the Council of Trent decided to exclude it from the canon in 1546, together with 1 Esdras; 3–4 Maccabees; the Prayer of Manasseh; and Psalm 151.

9. The *ajpop* (He-of-the-Mat) was the highest office in the chinamit; the *ajpop k'amja* (He-of-the-Rope-House-Mat) was the second office in rank.

10. When the Order of Preachers started to implement their Christianization project, the Highland Maya still inhabited their dispersed ancestral settlements, and some of the

elite continued to inhabit their ancient citadels. The *congregación*, the forced resettlement of rural populations in Spanish-style towns, did not begin in Solola', for example, until 1547 (Romero 2024).

11. De Angulo and de Torres were also famous *lenguas*. Juan de Torres wrote the first *arte* of the Kaqchikel language and was also coauthor of the *Doctrina en lengua guatemalteca*, published in 1556 in Mexico City.

12. The alliances between Maya lords and Spanish officials brokered by the Mendicants in the 1550s were crucial to secure Spanish rule in the Maya highlands. Maya lords provided foot soldiers for Spanish entradas to unconquered territories and were also firm supporters of Dominican efforts to penetrate into areas not yet under Spanish control. In return, Maya nobles kept some of their ancestral privileges, traditional chinamit offices, and control of the *cabildo* (Cunill 2011; Luján Muñoz 1986; Percheron 1980; Romero 2024).

13. There are no documents in other Mayan languages bearing the story. It is likely, however, that now-lost Q'eqchi' and Poqom manuscripts mentioned the Ten Lost Tribes, as Las Casas companions were very active in the Verapaz.

14. It was probably drafted a few years before the first published catechism in a highland Maya language, Bishop Francisco Marroquín's Doctrina Cristiana en Lengua Guatimalteca, which saw the light of day in 1556.

15. This claim is controversial, as K'iche' and Kaqchikel sources are ambivalent on the issue. Whereas the Popol Wuj, for example, clearly describes a plurality of Creator deities, the Memorial de Sololá could be interpreted as describing only one.

16. According to the Memorial de Sololá, Q'aq'awitz, ancestral founder of the Kaqchikel, opened a path across the sea using his staff of office after leaving Tulan.

17. The text describes it as *xiueleçaɦ rih yvunum* (You used to remove the skin from your penises). The Postclassic Maya practiced blood sacrifice, in which blood would be drawn from perforations in soft tissue such as earlobes and the penis. I am not aware, however, of any evidence of actual foreskin extirpation/mutilation.

18. *Xa huhu[n] chic 4az4oh yvumal xoloxoxinak chuxol tçakbal tçih yvumal* (Just a few of them were left alive by you but mixed in with lies of yours). The lies are, of course, any ritual practices and beliefs that the Spanish saw as heathen.

19. In relation to the origins of these apparent convergences, the sermon asks: *hutala 4u cha chiuetamaɦ ui ri. Vue ta maui yx ri canubiɦ ata xita ui vtçihoxic ri* (How did you learn about them? Are you not who I say you are? Where did you hear those stories?). The Speaker takes for himself the privilege of identifying the Other. There is no dialogic language here.

20. The Título divides the Israelites into three groups: Israelites (ah Ysrael), Canaanites (ah Canaan), and Hebrews (ah Ebreo).

21. Sixteenth-century manuscripts in Highland Mayan languages are recent copies of lost originals, showing errors and orthographic inconsistencies that probably were not in the original text.

22. This is the only Highland Maya source claiming that the sun was believed to be female and the moon male.

23. Don Juan de Torres held the office of Atzij Winaq Ekoamaq, highest office of the Tamub', and was a former member of the K'iche' Confederation.

REFERENCES

Acuña, Rene. 1985. "La Theologia Indorum de Domingo de Vico." *Tlalocan* 10: 281–307.

Acuña, Rene. 2004. "La Theologia Indorum de Vico en Lengua Quiché." *Estudios de cultura maya* 24: 17–45.

Arcos, Miguel de. 1601. "Papeles varios reunidos por Miguel de Arcos." In *Fondo Antiguo, Libros del Siglo XVII, Manuscritos*. Sevilla: Biblioteca de la Universidad de Sevilla.

Bierman, Benno. 1960. "Fray Bartolome de las Casas und die Grundung der Mission in der Verapaz." *Neue Zeitschrift für Missionswissenschaft* 16: 110–23, 161–77.

Bierman, Benno. 1964. "Missionsgeschichte der Verapaz." *Jahrbuch für Geschichte der Stadt, Wirtschaft und Gesellschaft Lateinamerika* 1 (54): 117–56.

Cabezas, Horacio. 2019. *Pedro de Alvarado: Gobernador y Adelantado de Guatemala*. Guatemala City.

Carmack, Robert. 1981. *The Quiche Maya of Utatlan: The Evolution of a Highland Maya Kingdom*. Norman: University of Oklahoma Press.

Carmack, Robert, and James Mondloch. 1983. *Título de Totonicapán: Texto, traducción y comentario*. Mexico City: Universidad Nacional Autonoma de Mexico.

Carmack, Robert, and James Mondloch. 2007. *Título de Totonicapán: Edición facsimilar, transcripción y traducción*. Guatemala City: Cholsamaj.

Contreras, J. Daniel. 2009. "Historia Quiché de Don Juan de Torres." In *Crónicas Mesoamericanas*, edited by H. Cabezas, 107–27. Guatemala City: Universidad Mesoamericana.

Cunill, Caroline. 2011. "Tomás López Medel y sus instrucciones para defensores de Indios: Una propuesta innovadora." *Anuario de Estudios Americanos* 68: 539–63.

Dansey Smith, Hilary. 1978. *Preaching in the Spanish Golden Age*. Oxford: Oxford University Press.

Edmonson, Munroe. 1988. *The Book of the Year: Middle American Calendrical Systems*. Salt Lake City: University of Utah Press.

Fernández Rodríguez, Pedro. 1994. *Los dominicos en la primera evangelización de México, 1526–1550*. Salamanca: Editorial San Esteban.

Folan, William J., David D. Bolles, and Jerald D. Ek. 2016. "On the Trail of Quetzalcoatl/ Kukulcan: Tracing Mythic Interaction Routes and Networks in the Maya Lowlands." *Ancient Mesoamerica* 27: 293–318.

García-Ruiz, Jesús. 1992. "El misionero, las lenguas mayas y la traducción." *Archives de sciences sociales des religions* 77: 83–110.

González, Matilde. 2014. *Modernización capitalista, y violencia: Guatemala (1750–1930)*. Mexico City: El Colegio de México.

Hill, Robert, and John Monaghan. 1987. *Continuities in Highland Maya Social Organization: Ethnohistory in Sacapulas, Guatemala*. Philadelphia: University of Pennsylvania.

Knowlton, Timothy. 2010. *Maya Creation Myths*. Boulder: University Press of Colorado.

Las Casas, Bartolomé de. 1967. *Apologética Historia Sumaria*. Vol. 1. Mexico City: UNAM.

López-Austin, Alfredo, and Leonardo López Luján. 1999. *Mito y realidad de Zuyuá, Fideicomiso Historia de las Américas*. Mexico City: Fondo de Cultura Económica.

Luján Muñoz, Jorge. 1986. "El Reino Pokomam de Petapa, Guatemala hacia 1524." *Anales de la Academia de Geografía e Historia de Guatemala* 60: 159–74.

Marroquín, Francisco. 1905. *Doctrina Cristiana en Lengua Guatemalteca ordenada por el reverendísimo señor Francisco Marroquín*. Santiago de Chile: Imprenta Elzeveriana.

Memorial de Sololá: Nueva Traducción del Kaqchikel y Comentarios (Memorial of Sololá: New Translation from the Original Kaqchikel and Commentary). 2024. Guatemala City: Universidad Mesoamericana.

Orellana, Sandra. 1984. *The Tzutujil Mayas: Continuity and Change, 1250–1630*. Norman: University of Oklahoma Press.

Percheron, N. 1980. "Christianisation et resistance indigene dans le pays quiche a l'epoque coloniale." In *Rabinal et la vallée moyenne du Rio Chicoy. Baja Verapaz-Guatemala*, edited by M. F. Fauvet-Berthelot, A. Ichon, N. Percheron, and A. Breton, 77–169. Guatemala City: Editorial Piedrasanta.

Pereña, Luciano, J. M. Pérez Prendes, E. Baciero, A. García, L. Resines, P. Borges, and M. Cuesta. 1992. *Utopía y Realidad Indiana*. Salamanca: Universidad Pontifica de Salamanca.

Popkin, Richard H. 1989. "The Rise and Fall of the Jewish Indian Theory." In *Menasseh Ben Israel and His World*, edited by Yosef Kaplan, Henry Méchoulan, and Richard H. Popkin, 63–82. Leiden: E. J. Brill.

Remesal, Antonio de. 1619. *Historia de la Provincia de San Vicente de Chiapa y Guatemala de la orden de nuestro glorioso padre Sancto Domingo*. Madrid: Francisco de Angulo.

Romero, Sergio. 2014. "Mito y lengua en las crónicas indígenas de Guatemala." *Anales de la Academia de Geografía e Historia de Guatemala* 89: 125–48.

Romero, Sergio. 2017. " 'Brujos,' mitos y modernidad en la historia oral k'iche'." *Estudios de cultura maya* 50: 249–70.

Romero, Sergio. 2024. *Memorial de Sololá: Traducción y Anotaciones Críticas*. Edited by H. Cabezas. Guatemala City: Universidad Mesoamericana.

Saint-Lu, Andre. 1968. *La Vera Paz: Esprit evangelique et colonisation*. Paris: Centre de Recherches Hispaniques, Institut d'Etudes Hispaniques.

Smith, Timothy. 2002. "Skipping Years and Scribal Errors: Kaqchikel Maya Timekeeping in the Fifteenth, Sixteenth, and Seventeenth Centuries." *Ancient Mesoamerica* 13: 65–76.

Sparks, Garry. 2011. "Xalqat B'e and the Theologia Indorum: Crossroads between Maya Spirituality and the Americas' First Theology." PhD diss., University of Chicago, Chicago.

Sparks, Garry. 2014. "The Use of Mayan Scripture in the Americas' First Christian Theology." *Numen* 61 (4): 396–429.

Tokovinine, Alexander. 2008. "The Power of Place: Political Landscape and Identity in Classic Maya Inscriptions, Imagery, and Architecture." PhD diss., Department of Anthropology, Harvard University, Cambridge, MA.

Van Akkeren, Ruud. 2009. *Título de los indios de Santa Clara La Laguna*. Vol. 2 of *Crónicas Mesoamericanas* 2. Guatemala City: Universidad Mesoamericana.

Van Akkeren, Ruud. 2010. "Fray Domingo de Vico: Maestro de Autores Indígenas." *Revista de Estudios Mayas* 2 (7): 1–61.

Vico, Domingo de. 1553–1615. "Theologia Indorum." William Gates Collection. American Philosophical Society: Manuscript Collection. Philadelphia.

Volpato, Marco. 2018. "El mito de las tribus perdidas entre España, Europa y el Nuevo Mundo." In *Visiones imperiales y profecía: Roma, España, Nuevo Mundo*, edited by S. Pastore and M. García-Arenal, 267–93. Madrid: Abada Editores.

Volpato, Marco. 2020. "Il Doctor Roldán e la teoria dell'origine ebraica degli amerindi nel primo Cinquecento." *Rivista di Storia e Letteratura Religiosa* 1: 21–62.

Woodward, Ralph L. 1993. *Rafael Carrera and the Emergence of the Republic of Guatemala, 1821–1871*. Athens: University of Georgia Press.

Index

About the Authors

Chloé Andrieu, Researcher, CNRS and Université Paris 1 Panthéon Sorbonne, Archéologie des Amériques (chloe.andrieu@cnrs.fr)

M. Charlotte Arnauld, Honorary Research Director, CNRS and Université de Paris 1 Panthéon-Sorbonne (charlotte.arnauld@orange.fr)

Cédric Becquey, Researcher, Centro de Estudios Mayas, Instituto de Investigaciones Filológicas, Universidad Nacional Autónoma de México (cedric.becquey@gmail.com)

Johann Begel, Beneficiary of the UNAM postdoctoral fellowship program (Centro de Estudios Mayas, Instituto de Investigaciones Filológicas), tutored by F. Zalaquett Rock (johann.sinan.begel@gmail.com)

Alain Breton, Honorary Research Director, CNRS and Université Paris Nanterre, Laboratoire d'Ethnologie et de Sociologie Comparative (alain.breton78200@orange.fr)

Marie Chosson, Associate Professor, Institut National des Langues et des Civilisations Orientales (marie.chosson@inalco.fr)

Flavia G. Cuturi, Full Professor of Cultural Anthropology, Department of Human and Social Sciences, University of Naples "L'Orientale." (flaviagcuturi@gmail.com)

Danièle Dehouve, Honorary Research Director, CNRS and Université Paris Nanterre, Laboratoire d'ethnologie et de Sociologie Comparative (daniele.dehouve@gmail.com)

Bérénice Gaillemin, University of Warsaw, Poland (b.gaillemin@uw.edu.pl)

Alexander Geurds, Associate Professor, Faculty of Archaeology, Leiden University; Associate Professor, School of Archaeology, University of Oxford; Research Fellow, Wolfson College, University of Oxford (a.geurds@arch.leidenuniv.nl)

Rosemary A. Joyce, Distinguished Professor Emerita of Anthropology, University of California, Berkeley (rajoyce@berkeley.edu)

Leonardo López Luján, Director Proyecto Templo Mayor-INAH, National Institute of Anthropology and History, México

Alessandro Lupo, Full Professor of Ethnology, Dept. of History, Anthropology, Religions, Art History, Media, and Performing Arts, Sapienza University of Rome (alessandro.lupo @uniroma1.it)

Dominique Michelet, Honorary Research Director, CNRS and Université de Paris 1 Panthéon-Sorbonne, Archéologie des Amériques (d.m.a.michelet@gmail.com)

Aurore Monod Becquelin, Honorary Research Director, CNRS and Université Paris Nanterre, Laboratoire d'ethnologie et de Sociologie Comparative (aurore.monod.b@gmail .com)

Philippe Nondédéo, Researcher, CNRS and Université Paris 1 Panthéon Sorbonne, Archéologie des Amériques (philippe_nondedeo@yahoo.com)

Tsubasa Okoshi, Professor, Department of Hispanic Studies and director of the Research Center for Latin American Studies of Kyoto University of Foreign Studies, Japan (okoshi56 @gmail.com)

Divina Perla-Barrera, Postdoctoral Fellow, Labex DynamiTe (CNRS and Université Paris 1 Panthéon Sorbonne, Archéologie des Amériques) (divinaperlabarrera@gmail.com)

Perig Pitrou, Research Director, CNRS, Maison Française d'Oxford, Laboratoire d'anthropologie sociale, Collège de France, Université PSL (perig.pitrou@college-de -france.fr)

Sergio Romero, Associate Professor, University of Texas at Austin (sergio.romero@austin .utexas.edu)

Julien Sion, CEMCA, Archéologie des Amériques (julien.sion@hotmail.fr)

Carlos Efraín Tox, Universidad San Carlos de Guatemala, Escuela de Historia (careftt@gmail.com)

Fidel Tuyuc Nij, Universidad San Carlos de Guatemala, Escuela de Historia (cftn363 @gmail.com)

Valentina Vapnarsky, Research Director, CNRS and Université Paris Nanterre, Laboratoire d'Ethnologie et de Sociologie Comparative; Director of Studies, École Pratique des Hautes Études, Laboratoire d'anthropologie sociale, Université PSL (valentina.vapnarsky @cnrs.fr)